CONTEMPORARY TOURISM: AN INTERNATIONAL APPROACH

Contemporary Tourism: An International Approach

Chris Cooper and C Michael Hall

Routledge
Taylor & Francis Group

LONDON AND NEW YORK

First published by Butterworth-Heinemann

First edition 2008

This edition published 2011 by Routledge
2 Park Square, Milton Park, Abingdon, Oxon OX14 4RN
711 Third Avenue, New York, NY 10017, USA

Routledge is an imprint of the Taylor & Francis Group, an informa business

Notice
No responsibility is assumed by the publisher for any injury and/or damage to persons or property
as a matter of products liability, negligence or otherwise, or from any use or operation of any
methods, products, instructions or ideas contained in the material herein.

British Library Cataloguing-in-Publication Data
A catalogue record for this book is available from the British Library

Library of Congress Cataloging-in-Publication Data
A catalog record for this book is available from the Library of Congress

ISBN: 978-0-7506-6350-2

Transferred to Digital Printing in 2012

Contents

List of figures

List of tables

Acknowledgements

We have a number of people to thank for their witting – or unwitting – help in our ideas and writing for this book. As commissioning editor, Sally North at Elsevier Butterworth Heinemann has, as always, been a constant source of encouragement, and when necessary, gentle pressure.

Colleagues at The University of Queensland's School of Tourism have been generous with their ideas and knowledge – in particular David Solnet, Noel Scott and Giuseppe Marzano. We are particularly grateful to David for contributing Chapter 12 on service management. Others who have helped include Jenny Douglas and Rose Willett at UQ, as well as the Cooper household who have tirelessly helped a technically less-than-competent author with formatting issues and diagram layouts.

Although Michael did not need the assistance of the Cooper household he would still like to thank them for their continued assistance of Chris. In addition he would like to thank Dick Butler, Tim Coles, Dave Crag, David Duval, Stefan Gössling, Michael James, John Jenkins, Alan Lew, Dieter Müller, Stephen Page, Nicola van Tiel, Jarrko Saarinen, Daniel Scott, Sarah Wall and Allan Williams, as well as colleagues and students in marketing at the University of Canterbury's Department of Management, who have all contributed in various ways, to helping develop some of the ideas within. Fiona Apple, Nick Cave, Bruce Cockburn, Stephen Cummings, Ray Davies, Ed Kuepper, Rufus Wainwright and Rachel Yamagata also helped ensure that the book was completed. Finally, he would like to thank Jody for her moral support while working on this book.

Chris Cooper, Brisbane, Australia and Michael Hall, Christchurch, New Zealand.

Section 1
Contemporary Tourism Systems

Chapter **1**
Contemporary tourism systems

Chapter objectives

After reading this chapter you will

- Understand the core elements in the service dimension of tourism
- Understand that the tourism experience does not exist independently of the interaction of tourism consumers and producers
- Recognize the different stages in the tourism system and their implication for the tourist experience
- Appreciate the importance of scale of analysis in studying tourism
- Identify some of the key constraints on tourism-related travel
- Understand the characteristics that are used to define concepts of tourism, tourist and mobility

Introduction

Contemporary tourism is at the same time one of the most significant yet misunderstood phenomenon in the world today. It is something that is engaged in by many people in the developed world and is regarded as an important mechanism for economic development not only in the industrialized countries but also in many developing countries. The extent of tourism activities across the globe and the sheer number of people who travel means that tourism is often described as one of the world's largest industries. Yet tourism is simultaneously an agent of cultural and change and a substantial contributor to environmental change, including at the level of global environmental change. Given the popular image of tourism as being connected to leisure and fun, the scope of the study of tourism is serious indeed.

This chapter examines some of the key concepts by which we analyse and describe contemporary tourism. These concepts lie at the core of the field of tourism studies and set out the domain of tourism research. Because tourism is essentially an experiential industry, that is people are consciously seeking to purchase particular experiences that are primarily ephemeral or intangible, tourism is regarded as a service industry. Therefore, the chapter first discusses the service dimension of tourism, a theme that pervades this book. This chapter then goes on to outline the concept of the tourism system and its implications with respect to understanding how tourism is consumed and produced, and approaches to defining tourism, tourist and mobility including some of the constraints on mobility.

The service dimension of tourism

The essential characteristics of services are that they cannot be produced without the agreement and cooperation of the consumer and that the outputs produced are not separate entities that exist independently of the producers or consumers (Hill 1999). One of the key service characteristics of tourism is that the main location at which the consumption of experiences occurs is outside of the home environment of the purchaser. Although tourism is a service industry this does not mean that it is completely intangible – far from it. Tourism is based on a complex set of infrastructure and physical resources that have a significant impact on the places in which they are situated. However, what is being purchased by the tourist is the experiences provided by this infrastructure and set of resources, and not the infrastructure itself. Because tourism is an experience-based product it means that in order to be able to understand tourism phenomenon we need to be able to understand both its consumption and production. This is an almost deceptively simple statement but its implications are enormous: tourism cannot be understood by looking at one aspect in isolation, consumption cannot occur without production and vice versa. The inseparability of production and consumption is therefore one of the hallmarks of tourism with the value of the tourism experience therefore being determined by both the consumer and the producer of the experience and the tourism product (Figure 1.1). The inseparability of consumption and production also means that the factors that make up consumption and production are constantly feeding back on one another, thereby influencing the development of tourism products and their appeal to consumers.

In seeking to understand contemporary tourism we are therefore seeking to understand the interrelationships between consumers and producers and the variety of experiences that are created. Yet one of the distinguishing aspects of tourism from other service- and experience-based products is that it refers to the experience of people voluntarily travelling outside of their place of permanent residence. This therefore means that the primary focus of much of tourism is the places or destinations that people travel too in order to satisfy their motivations for particular experiences. The mobile nature of tourism provides another really important dimension in its understanding in that because the service and tourist experience does not exist independently of the direct interaction between consumers and

Figure 1.1   Locating the tourism experience and tourism product

producers, it therefore cannot be stocked or have its ownership transferred. In order to understand the tourist experience we therefore have to be able to chart how it changes over time in order to see how the different elements of consumption and production come together to produce different experiences and therefore different outcomes for the consumer and the producer.

The tourism system

In order to be able to understand the complex and dynamic nature of the contemporary tourism experience many tourism researchers utilize the concept of a tourism system. A system is an assemblage or interrelated combination of things or elements forming a unitary whole (Hall 2000). At its most basic, the tourism system consists of consumption and production and the experiences that are generated. In order to increase our understanding of tourism we are therefore also interested in identifying those elements and factors that contribute to tourism consumption and production.

Given that movement is integral to tourism one way in which the tourism system can be understood is through the travel paths taken by individual consumers. This approach is usually termed a geographical system of tourism and consists of four basic elements as follows:

1 A *generating* or *source region* – which is the permanent residence of the tourist and the place where the journey begins and ends.
2 A *transit route* – which is the path through the region across which the tourist must travel to reach his or her destination.
3 A *destination region* – the region which the tourist chooses to visit and which is a core element of tourism.
4 The *environment* – that surrounds the other three regions.

The geographical tourism system model is useful for identifying the flow of tourists from one location to another and the importance of connectivity between the generating region and the destination (Figure 1.2). Of course, there might be more than one destination and therefore a whole system of destination regions and transit route regions can exist for some tourists. Nevertheless, the basic form

Figure 1.2 The geographical tourism system

of the geographical tourism system is sufficient to illustrate a range of important dimensions of tourism:

1 While the destination is the focal point of tourism activity, tourism will have affects over all elements of the tourism system. For example, while assessment of the economic and environmental affects of tourism can clearly be undertaken at the destination, a full assessment of impacts as a result of a tourist trip will need to include not only what happens at the destination but also in getting too and from that destination.

2 Destinations are accessible to tourism source regions. Such a statement may seem to be obvious yet its implications are profound. Different destinations will be variably accessible to source regions and vice versa. This means that some destinations will have natural advantages over others in relation to their accessibility and therefore potential market area. This is a factor that destinations will seek to exploit in competition with other destinations.

3 In relation to travel to the destination, different elements of the system will have different productive components even though they are used by the same consumer. The different elements that enable the production of tourism are identified in Table 1.1. In examining Table 1.1 it is important to realize that it does not suggest that the elements that have been identified only occur in specific regions, rather it highlights the relative importance of various aspects of the tourism industry from the perspective of the consumer as they go from one stage of their trip to another, and hence from one part of the tourism system to another.

Table 1.1 Main elements of tourism production at different components of the tourism geographical system

Generating region	Transit region	Destination
Distribution and promotion channels for the destination in the source region • travel agents • tour operators • online retailers and distributors Transport infrastructure	Transport links between the source region and the destination • aviation services • bus and train services • cruise and ferry services • private and hire cars Transit facilities, i.e. food, accommodation, toilets where tourists have to stop prior to final destination	Facilities and attractions • accommodation • meetings and exhibitions • theme parks • casinos • retail • visitor centres • national parks • restaurants • activities • amenity resources Transport infrastructure • local transport

CASE STUDY
The environmental impact of tourism in the Seychelles

The Seychelles is a republic of just over one hundred islands in the south-west Indian Ocean. Tourism is the second most important source of foreign exchange for the islands which has made the country one of the wealthiest in Africa. Because the environment is an extremely significant component of the attractiveness of the islands for tourism, particularly with respect to scuba diving, snorkeling and other water-based activities, the country has made extensive efforts with respect to land and marine conservation. Simultaneously, the Seychelles has also sought to expand its tourism market, particularly at the wealthier end of the visitor spectrum.

In order to ascertain the environmental impacts of tourism on the islands Gössling et al. (2002) undertook an ecological footprint analysis of the approximate 1 18 000 international leisure tourists who visited the country in 2000. Ecological footprint analysis estimates how much of the biophysical output of the earth is required to meet the resource consumption and waste absorption needs of an individual or a given community, region, state or continent (Rees 1992). Unlike other impact studies which occur just at the destination, studies of the ecological footprint of tourism incorporates the travel of consumers to and from the destination thereby including all elements of the tourism system.

Gössling et al. (2002) reported that long-distance travel was the biggest contributor to the ecological footprint of tourism on the island with more than 97 per cent of the energy footprint being a result of air travel to and from the destination. Just as tellingly the authors extrapolated the footprint of a typical journey to the Seychelles (10.4 days) to 1 year and found that a single journey to the Seychelles required almost the same area as available per human being on a global scale.

Gössling et al.'s study of the ecological footprint of tourism in the Seychelles also found that although 'high-value tourists might generate the largest foreign exchange earnings per capita ..., they also seem to be characterized by the highest resource use per capita'. The authors' concluded, 'environmental conservation based on funds derived from long-distance tourism remains problematic and can at best be seen as a short-term solution to safeguard threatened ecosystems' (2002: 209). Such a conclusion therefore presents a significant challenge to not only our understanding of how to evaluate the environmental impacts of tourism but also how to manage such impacts. Although the suggestion by Gössling et al. (2002) that in order to reduce the environmental impacts of tourism there is a need to attract visitors from closer generating areas, the reality is that for many destinations, including the Seychelles, only a small market is locally accessible.

Key sources

Gössling, S., Hansson, C.B., Hörstmeier, O. and Saggel, S. (2002). Ecological footprint analysis as a tool to assess tourism sustainability. *Ecological Economics* 43, 199–211.

Gössling, S. and Hall, C.M. (2006). *Tourism and Global Environmental Change*. London: Routledge.

Rees, W.E. (1992). Ecological footprints and appropriated carrying capacity: what urban economics leaves out. *Environment and Urbanisation* 4(2), 121–130.

Discussion questions

1 If the greatest environmental impacts of tourism occur in travelling to and from destinations how might the overall environmental impact best be reduced?

2 As a tourism manager, what initiatives could you undertake at the destination to reduce the environmental impact of tourism?

3 What affect might the imposition of a 'green tax' have on travel to destinations such as the Seychelles?

Because contemporary tourism experiences are simultaneously produced between the consumer and the producer another interesting dimension of the geographical tourism system model is that at each stage of the system the consumer will therefore be encountering different elements of the tourism industry. This therefore means that the tourist experience will be different not only from one region to another but also even within regions as different service encounters occur and different environments, sites and people are encountered. Importantly, each new experience of the tourist will be added to the previous sum of experiences therefore leading to new sets of understandings and expectations. The traveller is therefore constantly gaining new information as they travel through the tourism system which will not only influence the nature of the experience and decision-making processes in this trip, but significantly, in later trips as well. Tourist travel within the basic geographical tourist system can therefore be regarded as consisting of five stages in which different psychological elements regarding the consumption of tourism exist (Table 1.2):

1 Decision to travel
2 Travel to destination
3 Activities at destination
4 Travel from destination
5 Recollection of the trip and destination upon return to permanent residence.

Table 1.2 Key elements of consumer psychology at different components of the tourism geographical system

Generating region	Transit region	Destination
1 Travel decision-making and anticipation		
	2 Travel to the destination	
		3 Experiences at the destination
	4 Travel from the destination	
5 Recollection of the trip and destination experiences and influence on future tourism decision-making		

The different stages of the travel experience create a major issue for studying the behaviour and motivations of tourism consumers. This is because where a consumer is at different stages of their trip may lead to different responses with respect to the nature and quality of the tourism experience. Just as significantly, it highlights the importance of understanding the prior tourism experiences of a consumer when seeking to explain or predict future preferences, decisions and activities. An important concept here is to think of consumers having tourism careers in the same way that we think of personal careers in terms of employment and education. Our prior employment experiences and what we have learned in those positions influences future choice of employment. Similarly, our previous travel experiences when combined with new information sources assist us in determining where we may chose to travel to next. In fact, in some cases such as working holidays, our travel and employment careers may even be closely entwined, especially as international experiences come to be valued in an increasingly globalized economy and labour market. This perspective therefore means that in some cases when studying the consumption of tourism within the tourism system we may increase the scale of analysis from one that just focuses on a very specific part of one trip to one that may utilize a lifecourse or life-stage perspective and looks at several years or even decades of tourism consumption in order to understand tourism phenomenon. Of course, while such studies are possible they are actually very difficult to do. Nevertheless, the concept that prior tourism experiences influences future ones over the course of a lifetime is a very important element in seeking to understand tourism consumer behaviour.

If the nature of the tourism experience changes at different stages of the tourism system what does this mean for how we understand the tourism product. Can there even be such a thing? The answer is yes, but the complexity of the tourism experience given its constant co-creation means that it is extremely difficult for producers to be able to control the experiences that the consumer has with absolute certainty that it will meet the consumer's expectations including perceptions of value. A tourism product is a particular set of commodified tourism experiences. However, it is important to recognize that there is more than one form of tourism product and that these different forms of product are often consumed simultaneously as we discuss in Chapter 4. The different forms of product include:

- *The trip product*: This is the overall trip that a tourism consumer experiences including all firms, organizations and service moments from the initial decision to purchase to the return home. In some cases, such products are the result of packages put together by travel agents. One way of reducing uncertainty for consumers and producers with respect to the quality of such trip products is to provide all-inclusive packages in which many elements of the trip are included. Where consumers have assembled their own itineraries, the trip product is one they have produced rather than one packaged by a retailer or agency. Such products and consequent arrangements of the tourism system are therefore more individualized than those provided by agencies and consequently more open to chance and surprise.

- *The destination product*: This is the sum of all experiences the tourist has at the destination as a result of encounters with firms, people, communities and the destination environment. The destination product is usually best identified through the marketing and promotion campaigns of destination marketing organizations (DMOs) which seek to commodify what the DMO identifies as being the key experiences that a destination can provide the consumer. A characteristic of the destination product that distinguishes it from the products of many other industries is that the DMO does not actually own the product that it is promoting. To a limited extent this also occurs with the offerings of some tourism firms, such as those that provide sightseeing opportunities, e.g. nevertheless, it is most pronounced at the destination level. We discuss the destination product in detail in Chapter 9.

- *The tourism business product*: This is the set of experiences provided by an individual firm or agency over different stages of the trip. In some cases, e.g. with respect to all-inclusive package holidays where the same firm owns or controls the core elements of the tourism system at each stage, the tourism business product may be virtually synonymous with the trip product. However, in the majority of cases the consumer is actually encountering a series of different business products one after the other. In order to provide quality assurance to consumers within destinations, many tourism firms will cooperate with each other so as to provide a more consistent standard of service and visitor experience.

- *The service product*: This is the individual sets of service encounters that the tourism consumer experiences through their trip and at the destination. The service product can be formal or informal in nature. The service product is formal when it is related to the experience production of tourism businesses. Each tourism business product actually consists of a series of service products, each of which is a service 'moment of truth' for the consumer and the producer. Informal service products exist through the interaction of the consumer with people, communities and the environment at the destination outside of those provided by tourism businesses. Although such experiences are not the result of a formal tourism business they are nevertheless experiential products that exist within the product that is marketed and promoted by DMOs. We discuss the service product in more detail in Chapters 4 and 12.

The consumption of the various combinations of the different types of tourism product helps create the wide variety of tourist experiences that characterize destination, travel and operation offerings. The potential range of product combinations can help ensure that consumers find a variety of experiences that match their expectations and motivations. The challenge for the tourism industry of course is to find the right series of combinations for different sets of consumers, and this provides the foundation for much of what is contained in this book.

Another implication of our understanding of the tourism system is that it is constantly subject to change. Changes in one element in the either the production or consumption of tourism will affect other elements in the system. For example, changes in transport in the transit component will affect the relative connectivity between destinations and generating areas. Changes at a destination, such as the imposition of new visa requirements, may affect the relative attractiveness of a destination with respect to other potential destinations. Similarly, alterations in the perception of the relative safety of destinations for travellers will also affect tourist flows. In the case of an example of change at the generating area, the introduction of a new set of foreign exchange rates, may affect the flow of tourists to destinations on the basis of the relative favourability of exchange rates. Such a situation reinforces Mill and Morrison's observation that the tourism system 'is like a spider's web – touch one part of it and reverberations will be felt throughout' (1985: xix).

Who are the tourists?

Given the potential extent for change in the tourism system it becomes important that we can chart the patterns of consumption of tourism consumers. In order to do this we need a clear set of terminology. The term 'tourist' is the concept we use to describe those consumers who are engaged in voluntary temporary mobility in relation to their home environment. Key concepts here are 'voluntary', 'temporary' and 'mobility'. If an individual is temporarily away from their home environment on an involuntary basis, e.g. as the result of a war, natural disaster or other crisis, they are usually termed 'refugees' or if, at worse they have been forced into cross-border labour or sexual slavery, then they may be referred to as 'trafficked persons'. If someone has moved from one location to another on a permanent basis then they are usually referred to as a migrant.

The concept of mobility in the context of tourism studies refers to the capacity of individuals to move from one location to another. In order to be able to do this individuals need to be able to overcome various factors that act as constraints on tourism-related mobility including:

- *Income*: People need sufficient disposable income to be able to engage in tourism once they have satisfied other basic needs.
- *Time*: There needs to be time available for travel, just as importantly the amount of time available will be a major determinant on how far people can travel and therefore influence their destination choice.
- *Political rights*: In order to be able to travel, particularly internationally, people need to have the political right to travel to particular destinations. Such rights are given by the nation state of both the generating region and the destination and are enabled through international law as well as systems of passports, visas and travel regulations.
- *Health*: Poor health, frailty or disability may constrain travel options.
- *Information and education*: Potential travellers need to have information in order to be able to access the tourism system and reach destinations.
- *Safety and security*: Concerns over the perceived level of safety and security will affect the selection of destinations and transport medium and may even influence the decision as to whether to travel at all. Safety factors include perceived threat of crime, political instability and health risks.
- *Family*: The requirement of looking after family members will influence travel decision-making, particularly for care-givers.
- *Legislated holidays*: The availability of officially legislated holidays will affect travel patterns. In the US, Thanksgiving and Christmas holidays are the two most significant in terms of the number of people who travel away from their home. Nevertheless, there are substantial variations between countries with respect to statutory leave requirements and public holidays. For example, Australia,

Netherlands and the UK have 20 days statutory leave days per year whereas France has 25 and China 10 (World Tourism Organization 1999; Hall 2005).

- *Work*: Even if there are legislated holidays individuals still need to feel that they are able to take holidays. Richards (1999), e.g. reported that two-thirds of respondents to a survey reported that reducing their working hours in order to engage in leisure and tourism was perceived to have a negative or very negative effect on their careers. In Japan there is even a term, *karashi*, that refers to death from overwork (Hall and Brown 2006).
- *Location*: The relative location of where someone lives on a permanent basis in relation to transport will be a constraining factor on his or her travel behaviour.
- *Gender*: Gender may act as a constraint on travel because of fears over personal security or cultural issues regarding the appropriateness of travel for members of certain genders.
- *Culture*: The situation of individuals in different cultures creates variations with respects to attitudes towards tourism, particularly when temporary movement away from home is associated with what are regarded as non-essential behaviours. The development of a consumer culture is therefore arguably one of the essential factors in influencing the growth of tourism.

Given the range of such constraints it should therefore come as little surprise that the majority of the world's population do not go on international or even long-distance holidays that are typically associated with tourism in the developed world. Yet even in developed countries there are significant proportions of the population that do not engage in long-distance holiday travel. In the UK this is estimated at around 20 to 30 per cent of the population (Hall and Brown 2006). In the case of the US, Hall (2005) used US national transportation survey data to illustrate the increase in long-distance trip generation associated with a rise in income. In the US, the trip generation rate almost triples when one transitions from the very low income group to a very high income group. Whereas 46 per cent of the lowest income group households made zero long-distance trips, just 17 per cent of the highest income group did so. Furthermore, income also influences the mode of travel. Lower income groups were much more likely to travel by road (either by car or bus) when compared to other income groups. The share of air travel also steadily increased in relation to rising income levels as does the distance of the average one-way trip, although no substantial differences were noticeable with respect to overall trip duration.

Despite the fact that many people do not travel there are also many who do. These are the people we usually refer to as tourists. However, there are substantial challenges with respect to the statistical analysis of tourists. Most importantly the need to define 'tourist' and 'tourism'. Principle features that need to be defined in a statistical or 'technical' approach to tourism include:

- *The purpose of travel*, e.g. the type of travel such as visiting friends and relations (VFR).
- *The time dimension* involved in the tourism visit, which may set minimum and maximum periods of time spent away from permanent residence and time spent at the destination.
- *Situations in which travellers may not be defined as tourists*, e.g. the voluntary nature of their travel, whether they are military or whether people are in transit from one location to another.

At the World Tourism Organization's (WTO) conference on tourism statistics held in 1991 tourism was defined as comprising 'the activities of a person travelling outside his or her usual environment for less than a specified period of time and whose main purpose of travel is other than exercise of an activity remunerated from the place visited', where 'usual environment' is intended to exclude trips within the areas of usual residence and also frequent and regular trips between the domicile and the workplace and other community trips of a routine character, where 'less than a specified period of time' is intended to exclude long-term migration, and 'exercise of an activity remunerated from the place visited' is intended to exclude only migration for temporary work (cited in Chadwick 1994: 66).

With respect to the definition of a tourist the WTO recommended that an international tourist be defined as: 'a visitor who travels to a country other than that in which he/she has his/her usual residence for at least one night but not more than 1 year, and whose main purpose of visit is other than the exercise of an activity remunerated from within the country visited'; and that an international excursionist (e.g. a cruise-ship visitor) or day-tripper should be defined as '[a] visitor residing in a country who travels the same day to a country other than which he/she has his/her usual environment for less than 24 hours without spending the night in the country visited and whose main purpose of visit is other than the exercise of an activity remunerated from within the country visited' (1991). In the case of a domestic tourist the travel time limit away from the home environment should be 'not more than 6 months' (WTO 1991; United Nations 1994).

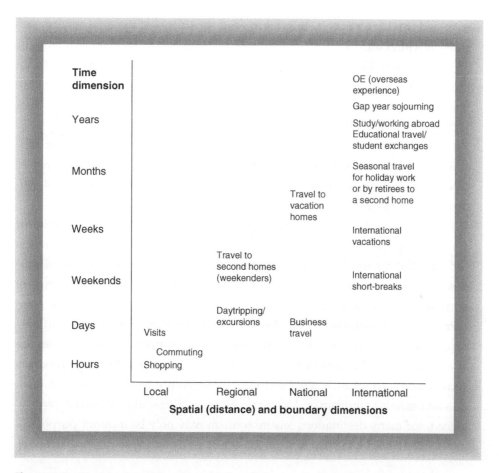

Figure 1.3   The characteristics of tourism in relation to time, distance, boundaries and description of purpose of travel (after Hall 2003)

Although the above guidelines are useful in thinking about tourism and measuring it statistically, there are significant variations between countries with respect to defining tourist activity as well as in collecting tourism data. Nevertheless, approaches to defining tourist and tourism rely on four different characteristics to define and hence measure activity (Figure 1.3):

1 *Time*, i.e. as discussed above how long someone is away from their place of permanent residence will affect their statistical and general description. For example, if undertaking a trip that does not require an overnight stay before returning the person would be classified as a day-tripper or excursionist. If undertaking an

extended trip, e.g. of over 12 months in some jurisdictions, a person may be classified as a migrant.

2 *Space* (distance), i.e. how far does a person travel before being classified as a tourist? In some jurisdictions a minimum travel distance is required before being classified as a tourist. Such an approach can differentiate tourism from localized leisure or other travel behaviour such as commuting.

3 *Boundary crossing*, i.e. crossing a national border can enable a person to be classified as an international tourist arrival and/or departure depending on where a person is in the tourism system. Boundaries are also significant for the development of domestic and regional tourism figures.

4 *Purpose of travel*, i.e. as noted above some purposes are deemed suitable for definition of a person while others are not, e.g. military and diplomatic travel is not classified for tourism purposes, although a wide range of other travel purposes, such as health and education can be. The identification of the range of purposes for travel and application to tourism is extremely important for the management of international travel flows through the provision of different visa requirements within national jurisdictions. However, the range of purposes are also significant as they reflect the development of new forms of tourism products such as medical tourism, health tourism, sport tourism, educational tourism, business and meetings tourism and VFR as well as more 'traditional' leisure tourism. Indeed, for many destinations leisure tourism may only be a minor purpose of travel. In addition, some trips will be characterized by multiple purposes of travel.

Contemporary perspectives

Although important for determining tourism and tourists from a technical perspective the elements identified in Figure 1.3 have also been argued as providing the basis for rethinking tourism as a form of temporary mobility. Coles et al. (2004, 2005) have argued that in order to understand voluntary temporary human movement or mobility, what we might refer to as a theoretically oriented concept of tourism, i.e. one that seeks to incorporate all dimensions of tourism phenomenon, an appropriate framework for tourism needs to be developed. This framework involves the relationships between tourism, leisure and other social practices and behaviours related to human mobility, e.g. retirement and amenity migration, second homes, sojourning, gap years and working holidays. Many of these forms

of mobility beyond a more traditional divide between tourism (temporary movement) and migration (permanent movement) have only recently become apparent
yet they are an increasingly important part of what is studied in tourism and, just
as importantly, what destinations and firms try and achieve with respect to
promoting tourism.

One of the reasons why old barriers between different forms of human mobility, such as tourism and migration, have been severely eroded is that improvements in transport technology has made it easier for those with sufficient time and
money to travel further and quicker than ever before. Travel which once took
2 or 3 days to accomplish may now be completed as a daytrip. In addition,
advances in travel technology have also been matched by developments in communications and information technology allowing people to have greater access to
the world as actual or potential destinations than ever before. Importantly, for
many people in the developed world this means that tourism is now an everyday
part of life and travel is something that they readily engage in and indeed, expect
to engage in (Hall 2005). Simultaneously, and as one would expect from our knowledge that tourism consumption and production are inseparable, we have also witnessed an explosion in the number of places and firms that are seeking to attract
the mobile, and an absolute expansion in the number of people who are mobile
and the different types of tourism product they consume.

Approach of this book

A contemporary understanding of tourism requires the utilization of contemporary approaches. We have therefore drawn heavily upon other subject areas and
disciplines to inform our chapters and understanding of contemporary tourism. In
particular, we encourage readers to explore the literature on marketing, services
and we point to the key references in our annotated reading lists. As a result of this
wider perspective, this book utilizes an approach to managing, marketing and
developing tourism that goes well beyond the 'popular' conception of tourism as
holiday travel, as important as this form of tourism activity is, and instead
embraces a broader understanding that sees such leisure-oriented holiday travel
as part of a realm of voluntary temporary mobility (Figure 1.4) (Hall 2005, 2007).
Such temporary movements of people for the consumption of tourism products
and experiences are the focal point of this book. Importantly, this book takes a

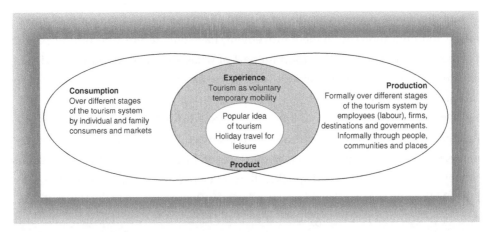

Figure 1.4 Understanding the nature of contemporary tourism

product-oriented approach that seeks to convey how products and experiences of tourists should be understood from the perspective of tourism firms and organizations in order that they can be best managed in order to reach satisfying outcomes for consumers, firms and destinations.

This book is divided into five key sections so as to reflect a contemporary approach to understanding the tourism system. This first section of this book outlines our approach to a contemporary tourism system and in Chapter 2 goes onto examine tourism products and markets. Chapter 2 shows how contemporary tourism products and markets are inextricably linked and draws upon marketing theory to help understand tourism products and market evolution.

The second section examines the contemporary tourist with respect to tourist behaviours and flows (Chapter 3) and contemporary tourism marketing (Chapter 4) where we draw heavily upon contemporary marketing theory to help understand contemporary tourism marketing.

The third section examines some of the key dimensions for understanding tourism destinations. Chapter 5 describes the various ways in which destinations are perceived by consumers and the consequences this has for tourism destinations. Most significantly, this chapter emphasizes that the destination is the sum of its component parts: attractions, resources, people and individual businesses. The majority of which are not under the direct control of any DMO. Chapter 6 discusses the key role of government in tourism destinations and the emerging role of governance strategies and tourism policy. Chapter 7 examines the consequences of visitation to destinations while Chapter 8 looks at some of the responses to the implications of visitation via planning and management mechanisms that seek to achieve sustainable development objectives. Chapter 9 discusses the marketing of the contemporary tourism destination and identifies a range of contemporary issues facing destination marketers.

The fourth section on the contemporary tourism industry deals with various scales of analysis. It takes a contemporary approach that examines firstly, how we measure and assess the size of the industry and debates surrounding its component parts (Chapter 10). We then go on to identify a range of key issues facing the industry (Chapter 11). These issues include human resources, technology, globalization, networking, knowledge management and entrepreneurship. Chapter 12 looks at the importance of taking a service management approach to delivering and managing the tourist experience and draws heavily upon the services management literature as it applies to tourism.

The final section discusses key emerging issues in tourism and how these are affecting tourism futures. Such concerns include not only security issues but also the role of pro-poor tourism, environmental change and virtual tourism.

Chapter overview

This chapter has provided an account of some of the key conceptual issues by which we come to understand contemporary tourism. The chapter first identified tourism as a form of service industry. This was very important as it not only highlighted several of the characteristics of services but it also emphasized the key point that the consumption and production of tourism experiences and hence tourism product are inseparable. The one affects and informs the other. Some of the implications of this are then played out through the concept of the tourism system. The tourism system approach initially starts as a geographical approach but, as we have seen, then starts to have affects on how we understand the psychology of tourism and mobility, the different dimensions of tourism product and how they are simultaneously consumed by the tourist, as well as how the interaction of consumption and production are different over different stages of the system. This chapter then went on to consider how we define key concepts in tourism and how these then tie back in to our understandings of consumption and production and the importance of the product and the experience. Most significantly, the chapter emphasized that a contemporary approach to tourism must look at all aspects of voluntary temporary mobility in order to be able to identify the potential full range of products and experiences that exist in contemporary tourism. We argue that such an approach will not only help us better understand contemporary tourism but also, by using the concepts, findings and strategies in this book, help increase returns to firms, destinations and the tourist.

Self-review questions

1 What are the distinguishing features of *services* as they apply to tourism?
2 Why is it difficult to discuss tourism *consumption* in isolation from *production*?
3 What are the five stages of a trip in relation to the *tourism system*? Discuss how the different stages of a trip might lead to different psychological dimensions of tourism.
4 What are the *constraints* that affect tourism? Discuss how such constraints affect your own travel decision-making and behaviours.
5 In seeking to understand tourism should more attention be given to the *immobility* of people?
6 Recall the four different *characteristics* that help define and hence study tourism activity.
7 Why have the concepts that describe *human mobility*, such as tourism and migration, become more closely connected in recent years?
8 How important are *time* and *space* in understanding tourism?
9 Are there differences in *popular* or public understandings of tourism and those of tourism researchers and managers?
10 Identify a particular environmental impact of tourism and review its relative importance in each component of the tourism system.

Recommended reading

1 Lew, A., Hall, C.M. and Williams, A.M. (eds) (2004). *A Companion to Tourism*. Oxford: Blackwell.
Provides a detailed collection of review chapters on key aspects of tourism, including issues associated with its definition.
2 Lennon, J. (ed.) (2003). *Tourism Statistics: International Perspectives and Current Issues.* London: Continuum.
An excellent overview of various issues associated with tourism statistics in a range of different national jurisdictions.

3 Hall, C.M. and Page, S. (2006). *The Geography of Tourism and Recreation: Space, Place and Environment*, 3rd edn. London: Routledge.

   Chapter 2 provides a detailed account of issues associated with defining tourism demand and research on international and domestic tourism statistics.

4 Lovelock, C. and Gummesson, E. (2004). In search of a new paradigm and fresh perspectives. *Journal of Service Research* 7(1), 20–41.

   Details some of the contemporary thinking with respect to understanding services and service marketing.

5 Coles, T., Hall, C.M. and Duval, D. (2005). Mobilising tourism: a post-disciplinary critique. *Tourism Recreation Research* 30(2), 31–41.

   Discusses the significance of a mobilities based approach to tourism and its implications for key concepts.

6 Hall, C.M. (2005). *Tourism: Rethinking the Social Science of Mobility.* Harlow: Prentice-Hall.

   Provides a more detailed extension of the mobilities approach and provides links into contemporary sociology, geography and regional development thinking in relation to tourism in both quantitative and qualitative terms.

7 Shaw, G. and Williams, A.M. (2004). *Tourism and Tourism Spaces.* London: Sage.

   Discusses the connections between the consumption and production of tourism at an aggregate level.

8 Hall, D. and Brown, F. (2006). *Tourism and Welfare: Ethics, Responsibility and Sustained Well-Being.* Wallingford: CABI.

   Provides an excellent account of the issues of participation and non-participation in tourism and how this relates to ethical and quality of life concerns.

9 Hall, C.M. and Williams, A.M. (eds) (2002). *Tourism and Migration: New Relationships Between Consumption and Production.* Dortrecht: Kluwer.

   The various chapters in this book provide various examples of the connections between tourism and migration and how this may affect our understanding of what constitutes tourism.

10 Gössling, S. and Hall, C.M. (2006). *Tourism and Global Environmental Change.* London: Routledge.

   Provides a challenging account of the implications of thinking about the impacts of tourism over all the stages of the tourism system and beyond.

Recommended web sites

Pacific Asia Travel Association (PATA): www.pata.org
United Nations World Tourism Organization: www.world-tourism.org
World Travel and Tourism Council: www.wttc.org

References cited

Chadwick, R. (1994). Concepts, definitions and measures used in travel and tourism research. In J.R. Brent Ritchie and C. Goeldner (eds), *Travel, Tourism and Hospitality Research: A Handbook for Managers and Researchers*, 2nd edn., pp. 65–80. New York: Wiley.

Coles, T., Duval, D. and Hall, C.M. (2004). Tourism, mobility and global communities: new approaches to theorising tourism and tourist spaces. In W. Theobold (ed.), *Global Tourism*, 3rd edn., pp. 463–481. Oxford: Heinemann.

Coles, T., Hall, C.M. and Duval, D. (2005). Mobilising tourism: a post-disciplinary critique. *Tourism Recreation Research* 30(2), 31–41.

Gössling, S., Hansson, C.B., Hörstmeier, O. and Saggel, S. (2002). Ecological footprint analysis as a tool to assess tourism sustainability. *Ecological Economics* 43, 199–211.

Gössling, S. and Hall, C.M. (2006). *Tourism and Global Environmental Change*. London: Routledge.

Hall, C.M. (2000). *Tourism Planning*. Harlow: Prentice-Hall.

Hall, C.M. (2003). Tourism and temporary mobility: circulation, diaspora, migration, nomadism, sojourning, travel, transport and home. *International Academy for the Study of Tourism (IAST) Conference*, 30 June to 5 July 2003. Finland: Savonlinna.

Hall, C.M. (2005). *Tourism: Rethinking the Social Science of Mobility*. Harlow: Prentice-Hall.

Hall, C.M. (2007). *Introduction to Tourism in Australia*. Melbourne: Pearson Australia.

Hall, C.M. and Page, S. (2006). *The Geography of Tourism and Recreation: Space, Place and Environment*, 3rd edn. London: Routledge.

Hall, C.M. and Williams, A.M. (eds) (2002). *Tourism and Migration: New Relationships Between Consumption and Production*. Dortrecht: Kluwer.

Hall, D. and Brown, F. (2006). *Tourism and Welfare: Ethics, Responsibility and Sustained Well-Being*. Wallingford: CABI.

Hill, P. (1999). Tangibles, intangibles and services: a new taxonomy for the classification of output. *Canadian Journal of Economics* 32(2), 426–446.

Lennon, J. (ed.) (2003). *Tourism Statistics: International Perspectives and Current Issues*. London: Continuum.

Lew, A., Hall, C.M. and Williams, A.M. (eds) (2004). *A Companion to Tourism*. Oxford: Blackwell.

Lovelock, C. and Gummesson, E. (2004). In search of a new paradigm and fresh perspectives. *Journal of Service Research* 7(1), 20–41.

Mill, R.C. and Morrison, A.M. (1985). *The Tourism System: An Introductory Text*. Englewood Cliffs: Prentice-Hall International.

Richards, G. (1999). Vacations and the quality of life: patterns and structures. *Journal of Business Research* 44, 189–198.

Shaw, G. and Williams, A.M. (2004). *Tourism and Tourism Spaces*. London: Sage.

United Nations (1994). *Recommendations on Tourism Statistics*. New York: United Nations.

World Tourism Organization (WTO) (1991). *Resolutions of International Conference on Travel and Tourism, Ottawa, Canada*. Madrid: World Tourism Organization.

World Tourism Organization (1999). *Changes in Leisure Time*. Madrid: World Tourism Organization.

Chapter 2
Contemporary tourism product markets

Chapter objectives

After reading this chapter you will

- Understand the various approaches to tourism products
- Appreciate the concept of experiences as tourism products
- Recognize the various approaches to tourism markets
- Be aware of the changing nature of tourism markets and the 'post-tourist'
- Understand the significance of tourism market segmentation
- Recognize the importance of the tourism product market
- Recognize the importance of market stories in market shaping
- Understand the nature of exchanges and interactions in tourism product markets

Introduction

This chapter introduces the pivotal concept of tourism product markets as a key to understanding contemporary tourism marketing. This chapter begins with a discussion of tourism products, stressing that a contemporary approach to tourism products recognizes that the tourism consumer is a co-producer of products, delivering a marketing approach that allows interaction with the tourist in a continuous process. A contemporary approach is to engineer experiences as tourism products, appealing to the 'post-tourist' market and delivering memorable engaging tourism experiences that 'transform the visitor. This chapter then considers tourism markets and how consumer behaviour is changing. It is clear that to reach and understand these new markets demands deep and meaningful research and contemporary approaches to market segmentation. The main message of this chapter is that tourism products and markets are inextricably linked. The chapter introduces the concept of tourism product markets to provide a framework for the interaction of buyers and sellers in tourism. Tourism product markets allow the clear definition of tourism products and the boundaries between them. Finally, this chapter examines the nature of the continuous exchanges and interactions in tourism product markets and the response of marketers to the challenges that these present.

Tourism products

As we noted in Chapter 1, tourism products are complex and multi-facetted. As a result they have generated a considerable debate as to their nature and definition, including whether they are sufficiently different to merit a separate approach to marketing. All products package together utilities and benefits for the consumer. The traditional view of a tourism product has been inherited from economics and is based on the framework of exchange. In tourism, this exchange takes place at a destination and within a particular socio-political, environmental, technological and economic setting. There are two elements to this approach:

1 The nature of the social exchange as a purchase takes place.
2 The functional nature of the tourism product included in the transaction.

More recently, new perspectives have been introduced including those based on relationships, the co-creation of value and the recognition of intangible products. These new perspectives are based on the concept of services marketing rather than physical goods. They allow consideration of all market actors and recognize that they will have a continuous relationship with each other. This provides a more realistic approach to the tourism product as it integrates both goods and services and recognizes that tourists will purchase both as they construct a trip. This approach recognizes the tourism consumer as a co-producer of goods and delivers a marketing approach that allows interaction with the customer in a continuous process. This can then be taken a step further by viewing the tourism product as a bundle of tangible and intangible product attributes, with all products lying on a continuum between these types of attributes. The tourism product can also be viewed along a second continuum: from a single component; through a composite of components that are packaged or bundled together; to the total destination product itself. Gilbert (1990) extends these ideas arguing that the tourism product is in fact the total experience. He defines the tourism product as:

> an amalgam of different goods and services offered as an activity experience to the tourist (Gilbert 1990: 20).

Clearly then, there are a number of approaches to the tourism product. For example, building on Gilbert's notion of the tourism product as the total experience, the tourism product can be disaggregated into stages of the vacation from anticipation and planning, to booking, travel and evaluation. The merit of this approach is that it takes into account the important pre- and post-product purchase stages that influence future buying behaviour as noted in Chapter 1. A second approach is to view the product as synonymous with the destination, such that the tourism product is an 'amalgam' of destination elements including attractions; supporting services such as accommodation and food and beverage; and transportation (Figure 2.1). There are significant implications of this 'amalgam' for tourism marketing, particularly the challenge of managing quality across the various elements, each of which is often supplied by a different organization. This approach is perhaps mirrored in the more traditional approach to understanding tourism products that is drawn from the physical goods marketing

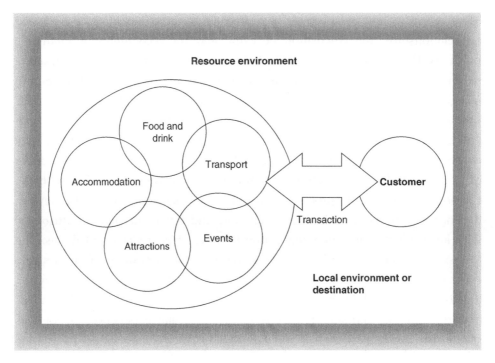

Figure 2.1   The tourism market

(*Source*: Cooper et al. 2005)

literature (Kotler et al. 2004). This approach argues that products have three key dimensions:

1 The core product delivers the product's benefits and features and provides a reason for purchase. An example here would be the offer of a vacation in Hawaii.
2 The facilitating product must be present for the tourists to use the services. For a vacation these include transportation and accommodation. It is interesting that it is this part of the product that is cut to a bare minimum in the business model of low cost carriers. They replace paper tickets with e-tickets and bookings are made on the Internet to avoid interaction with an expensive sales person. The low-cost carrier business model delivers the facilitating elements of the product in a different way.
3 The augmented product delivers added extras that allow the product to compete. For a vacation in Hawaii it may include a free night, free transfer or

complimentary drinks on arrival. For low-cost carriers, in the early days of their operation, free seating was common, but some carriers now augment their service by providing allocated seating.

Finally, products can be viewed as evolutionary, beginning with the development and formulation of new products, and then building sales along a cycle of evolution. Development of new products is the main form of innovation in tourism and is essential for sector growth. New products are important to diversification, increasing sales and profits and competitive advantage. As the product becomes established it may then move through the various stages of the product life cycle, an approach adapted by Butler (1980) for destinations in the 'tourism area life cycle'.

Experiences as tourism products

An example of the development of a new product in tourism, and a core concept of this book, is the idea of the product as an experience. This is different to Gilbert's (1990) idea of the tourism product as the total vacation experience; rather in this case we are looking at specific tourism products developed and engineered as experiences.

As tourism markets mature they seek authentic tourism products. Suppliers and destinations are responding to this challenge by delivering experience-based products. Pine and Gilmore (1999) have termed this trend the 'experience economy'. In the experience economy, changing values from older to younger generations mean that consumers are seeking new meaning and self-actualization in their tourism consumption patterns as they move beyond material possessions and services to experiences. Tourism products are increasingly being formulated to serve this demand by engineering experiences to match the expectations of the market place, not only in tourism but also across the services sector. Here, Pine and Gilmore (1999) see experiences along two dimensions: (1) passive to active and (2) absorption to immersion, with the ability of a good experience to 'transform' the visitor. Experiences are therefore personal, memorable, evoking an emotional response as the tourist enters into a multi-facetted relationship with both the actors and destination setting of the experience.

At the destination, 'experience providers' sequence and stage carefully choreographed activities, personal encounters and authentic experiences, designed to create long-lasting memories, engaging travel and increased customer loyalty. O'Sullivan and Spangler (1998: 5) classify experience providers into three types:

1 *Infusers*: manufacturers who 'infuse' their products with experiences
2 *Enhancers*: service providers who use experiences to heighten satisfaction or differentiate from competitors
3 *Makers*: service providers who create experiences as the core of their service

For the destination, delivering and engineering the experience involves infrastructure, narrative content and a context, each of which are heightened by technology. Effectively, engineering these experiences demands that destinations and operators migrate to experience-oriented tourism strategies, where the common thread is authenticity, delivering experiences that are perceived to be real, unsullied and rooted in the destination. Here, the notion of 'endemic resources' such as food and culture deepen the experience and link to sustainability strategies at the destination by building on the core appeal and adding value at each stage of the experience. It is the delivery and dimensions of authenticity that will be central to the maturing of the experience economy at the destination level and will begin to influence the buying decision. Each of these elements has been factored into Tourism Tasmania's 'experience product strategy' which is detailed here as a case study.

CASE STUDY
Tourism Tasmania's 'experience product' strategy

Introduction

Engineering tourism experiences is at the cutting edge of contemporary tourism product development, recognizing the expectations of a marketplace that is used to high-quality entertainment, visual images and sound in their own homes. The overarching tourism strategy for the Australian island state of Tasmania (Tourism 21) aims to increase jobs and tourism expenditure through a number of strategies, one of which is linked closely to the experience economy (Pine and Gilmore 1999). The Tasmanian experience strategy contributes to this overarching goal by greater engagement with the visitor through the development of holiday experiences on the island (Tourism Tasmania 2002). The strategy builds-in the key elements of narrative and engagement (in this case through the local community and interpretation), high-quality memorable experiences and endemic tourism through food and wine – all designed to 'transform' the visitor.

Understanding the market

The strategy recognizes that tourists' needs and desires are changing and that the island may not have kept up with these developments. Tourism Tasmania has therefore under-pinned the strategy with research designed to understand the triggers that lead con-sumers to purchase a Tasmanian vacation. The research identified five key tourism market segments for the island:

1 International visitors
2 Touring visitors
3 Short break visitors
4 Special interest tourists
5 Niche visitors

Understanding the product

Tasmania has identified three core attributes of its product and which form the basis of the experiences:

- Nature
- Cultural heritage
- Fine wine and food

However, the strategy recognizes that on their own, these attributes are not a sufficient reason to visit, after all many other destinations have similar attributes. In addition, Tourism Tasmania has recognized that it has placed too much emphasis on the 'supporting elements' of the product (infrastructure, accommodation, transport and service) and not enough on the holiday experience. Whilst visitors do expect high-quality support for their visit in terms of service and accommodation, this is expected in all destinations and does not give Tasmania a competitive edge.

As a result of this thinking, the strategy develops a new approach to combining these elements of the Tasmanian product by 'augmenting' it with experiences tailored to market needs. The mission of the strategy is to create:

> extraordinary and unforgettable holiday experiences by focusing on presentation, interpretation and customer engagement (Tourism Tasmania 2002: 1).

Engineering the experience

Tourism Tasmania defines an experience as:

> Memorable events or interactions that engage people in a personal way and connect them within a place – Tasmania, its people and their ideas' (Tourism Tasmania 2002: 4).

The key here is the notion of the experience-based product as 'memorable and personalized', in other words, augmenting experiences are wrapped around the core elements of the island's product (Pine and Gilmore 1999). The strategy is based on engineering experiences through developing means of connecting visitors to place, delivering quality infrastructure and personalized service underpinned by interpretation and engagement (Figure 2.2).

The context of the experience is a visit to the island. Engineering the experience builds upon combining the island's three core attributes of nature, cultural heritage wine and food with 'community enthusiasm and involvement, highly developed interpretative skills, local knowledge and a passion for place' (p. 7). The strategy views communities as critical stakeholders and as such the strategy is dependent on community support. Communities are viewed as keepers of the stories of their areas and the strategy is therefore seeking community engagement and looking to them for interpretation of local places. The strategy also has the notion of 'endemic tourism' as a core element by encouraging interaction with communities and the island's food and wine.

The strategy envisages that experiences will be designed in clusters focused on key precincts around the island and linked by tourism routes. These distinctive combinations of experiences allow spatial differentiation across the island and for each cluster, brand appeals are developed and tied back to the overall Tasmanian brand. For each cluster the strategy engages the tourism industry to package vacation experiences to attract key market categories. For some clusters there are gaps in provision and Tourism Tasmania has developed a portfolio of development opportunities to fill these gaps.

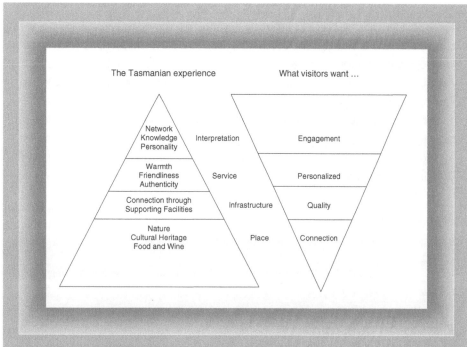

Figure 2.2   The Tasmanian experience concept

(*Source*: Tourism Tasmania 2002)

Linking the Tasmanian brand to experiences

It is important that the experiences are linked to the Tasmanian brand, which communicates the island as an experience-rich destination. Effectively the experiences become the delivery of the brand on the ground for the visitor. The brand and the experience support each other so that the Tasmanian brand promise is that of a host of unforgettable experiences based on the three core attributes of the island. To support this approach, a brand management system has been developed to communicate and integrate the delivery of the experience. For intermediaries, sales tools have been developed to help them package products for targeted consumers based on the experience clusters.

Benefits of the approach

The goals of the Tasmanian experience strategy will deliver the following benefits:

- Boost the island's economy through tourism spending and job creation.
- Boost yield for tourism businesses.
- Enhance the sustainability of Tasmania's natural and cultural assets.

These benefits will be achieved by deepening visitor and community appreciation of the cultural and natural environment. In addition, heightened awareness and appreciation of local food and wine will sustain and enhance the profitability of local suppliers and businesses. In terms of boosting the tourism economy, the strategy will encourage new markets, repeat visits and facilitate memories and market stories.

The strategy represents a significant shift in thinking for the Tasmanian tourism sector. It will therefore require the sector to share research and knowledge, and will involve a major education and communication exercise to achieve the change in focus and branding of the island.

Key sources

Pine, J.B. and Gilmore, J.H. (1999). *The Experience Economy*. Harvard: Harvard Business School Press.
Tourism Tasmania (2002). The Tasmanian Experience. Creating Unforgettable Natural Experiences Tourism Tasmania Hobart.

Discussion questions

1 Discuss the pros and cons of engagement with the experience strategy from the Tasmanian community's point of view.
2 The strategy is very dependent on the technique of interpretation to transform the visitor experience. What are some of the problems that accompany this technique?
3 What should be the shape of the education and communication exercise undertaken to make the Tasmanian tourism sector aware of their role in the experience strategy?

Tourism markets

Tourism markets are comprised of actual and potential consumers. White (1981) defines markets as:

> self-reproducing social structures among cliques of firms and other actors who evolve roles from observations of each other's behaviour (White 1981: 518).

This definition works well for tourism and supports the approaches to products and markets outlined in this chapter. These approaches can be summarized as:

1 Products and markets evolve together with the tourist as a co-producer of goods.
2 They deliver a marketing approach that allows interaction with the customer in a continuous process.

This approach recognizes that the environment is volatile and that markets and emerging product structures are dynamic. For example, the tourism market has changed as a result of increased travel, shifting values and perceptions and demographics. Feifer (1985) has termed these new consumers 'post-tourists'. They are experienced, discerning and caring of the places that they visit, demonstrating ethical consumption and behaviour at the destination. Post-tourists demonstrate changing values and preferences, increasingly seeking authenticity and well-managed, tailored individual experiences that allow them to both get closer to and also participate in the intimacy of the destination, in other words, they seek the type of experience products that are being developed in Tasmania.

This new consumer behaviour is resistant to traditional forms of marketing and for marketers, is more difficult to understand and analyse as market segments are less stable, constantly fragmenting and reforming. Addressing this challenge of the 'post-tourist' demands a contemporary approach to segmenting and analysing tourism markets. This approach must be based on deep and meaningful research that delivers specialized and tailored solutions to destinations and operators. Traditionally tourism market research has been locked in the 1960s – with large-scale omnibus and national-level holiday taking surveys – and has been unable to deliver support to contemporary market segmentation approaches.

Contemporary approaches to research, particularly using qualitative and multi-variate analysis approaches are needed to understand the 'post-tourist' market and to support the development of new segmentation techniques. Deep and meaningful research underpins new approaches to segmentation that can deliver detailed customer profiles and identify elements of consumer behaviour. Market segmentation is central to understanding the relationship between tourism products and markets. It involves dividing a tourism market into distinctive sub-sets each with common characteristics such that the formulation and positioning of tourism products and experiences are designed to attract pre-identified segments. This approach can deliver a full understanding of the needs of the segment, which itself becomes the focus for the marketing effort. To be effective, market segments must be:

- *Measurable*: Marketers must be able to 'calibrate' the segment in order to access it.
- *Accessible*: The segment must be 'reachable' through promotion.
- *Substantial*: The segment must be large enough to support the design of particular tourism products.
- *Sustainable*: The segment must be durable in time if it is to justify the design of products.
- *Actionable*: An organization must be able to develop products that will compete effectively for the segment's purchases.

Traditionally, tourism marketing has not utilized sophisticated segmentation techniques, preferring instead to use single variable segments based on say, demographics (the youth market), geography (the German market) or buyer behaviour (the business market). However, as the tourism market has matured it has also fragmented and the old techniques of segmentation are no longer adequate. Increasingly, tourism is seen as a way to express lifestyle by purchasing products such as adventure tourism, eco-tourism or cultural tourism. Examples of new segmentation approaches include psychographics, where the underlying psychology of the tourist is analysed; attitudinal and ethical segmentation where travel behaviour is the basis for segmentation; and technographics which analyses the ability to use technology for searching and purchasing tourism products.

Tourism product markets

It is clear from this chapter so far that tourism products and tourism markets are inextricably linked. The 'product market' concept recognizes this interdependence and treats 'product markets' within a framework of the interaction of buyers and sellers in a marketplace (Figure 2.3). The concept of product markets is intuitively appealing and fundamental to marketing theory. This is because they help explain how markets function and evolve, how new products are accepted and whether market boundaries are distinct or shifting. In other words, because product markets are formed by the interaction of tourists and suppliers, their boundaries are flexible as they represent the aggregate of many exchanges. This is outlined in

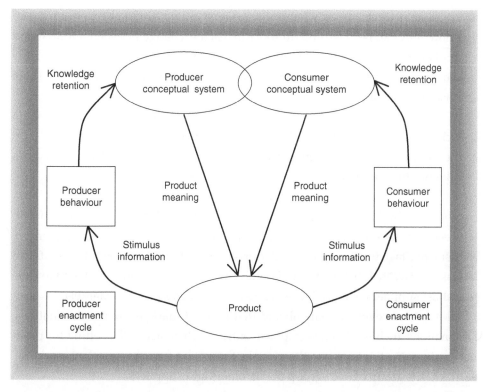

Figure 2.3 A sociocognitive market system
(*Source*: Rosa et al. 1999)

Rosa et al.'s pioneering paper on the subject (Rosa et al. 1999). They see product markets as 'meeting grounds for buyers and sellers' (Rosa et al. 1999: 64). Two further definitions of 'product markets' are helpful in describing the concept:

> [the] set of products, judged to be substitutes within those usage situations in which similar patterns of benefits are sought and the customers for whom such usages are relevant … they are bounded arenas in which prices and quantities for substitutable goods and services are negotiated by consumers and producers and are separated from other bounded arenas by gaps in demand between the product groupings (Day et al. 1979: 10).

> The area of actual and potential exchanges, between consumers and producers, involving the offerings of producers and the wants of customers, and with respect to a particular situation (Bourgeois et al. 1987: 370).

Product markets are very helpful in understanding different types of tourism and how they can be classified. In tourism, each exchange between a tourist and a supplier is unique, simply because of the nature of tourism supply as highly heterogenous, and the many different levels of involvement by the tourist. There are two processes at work here:

1 Exchanges can be grouped and aggregated into a product market.
2 The product market concept shows that both the supplier and the tourist can influence these exchanges.

In other words, different tourism product markets are defined by the interaction between suppliers and tourists and include eco-tourism, dark tourism, adventure tourism, heritage tourism or cultural tourism. In each product market, tourists can be classified by their behaviour and involvement, as their 'wants' will tend to cluster, whilst suppliers will tend to specialize in particular product markets.

It must, however, be remembered that product markets are not destinations. Destinations are bounded geographical entities, which act as the setting for product markets. Destinations can therefore be the setting for many product markets – each with its group of own group of customers and suppliers.

The concept of product markets is useful for tourism because it allows:

- The definition of tourism product markets based on particular groups of attributes.
- Identification of differences and delimitation of boundaries between tourism product markets.

Creating product markets: market stories

One way that product markets are created is through market stories. Here, both consumers and producers achieve shared understanding of a product market – and its boundaries – through conversations built around product offerings. In this way, the various actors that create a product market make sense of the environment from market-shaping knowledge. This knowledge comes from, and is observable in, the narratives surrounding both the physical products and the tourism experiences of market actors. In a tourism product market, these actors will include

Table 2.1 The changing nature of market stories with product maturity

Characteristics of stories about emerging product markets	Characteristics of stories about mature product markets
Highly complex	Less complex
Less accurate	More accurate
Judgements disagree	Judgements agree
Disagree on product image	Agree on product image

Source: Rosa and Spanjol (2005)

consumers, producers, operators, media, retailers, intermediaries, government agencies and destination marketing organizations.

For the consumer, these stories are important, particularly when they are not familiar with the product. Travel blogs and product review Internet sites such as mytripadvisor.com now play a growing role in consumer decision-making. As product markets evolve, so these market stories change. In newly emerging product markets, consumers face new product ideas that do not readily fit into existing categories and the stories are highly variable. As tourism products mature, the stories align more closely with each other as agreement over the product market is reached (Table 2.1). Skydiving is a classic product market and the following case study demonstrates how both the activity of the skydiving and its participants interact to shape and bound the skydiving product market.

CASE STUDY
Market-shaping behaviour in adventure tourism product markets: skydiving

Introduction

At first glance skydiving does not appear to be an activity that human beings were designed to perform – to step out of an aircraft at thousands of feet above sea level is nonsensical. Celsi et al.'s pioneering 1993 paper examines how this product market is structured and provides insights into how market stories and activities have developed both the structure of the skydiving product market and the experience itself.

Skydiving is part of the growing adventure tourism product movement that includes activities such as bungee jumping and white water rafting. Whilst there is no agreed definition of adventure tourism, Swarbrooke et al. (2003) characterize adventure tourism as a niche area with descriptors such as uncertainty, risk, danger, challenge, stimulation, excitement and focus. Indeed, adventure tourism involves considerable risk to participants as Bentley et al.'s (2001) analysis of injuries and fatalities in New Zealand hospitals shows. They found that 22 per cent of visitor fatalities were due to participating in adventure tourism.

As this case study shows, adventure tourism is characterized as much by the process of engagement and the tourists' state of mind as the activity itself. A common distinction is between hard and soft adventure, and in this case study, skydiving is definitely in the 'hard' category defined as 'activities with high levels of risk, requiring intense commitment and advanced skills (Swarbrooke et al. 2003: 33).

The skydiving market

Adventure tourism shows how tourism products have differentiated and specialized to cater for a small part of the tourism market with special needs. For the 'post-tourist', consumption of tourism represents a lifestyle choice – a search for fulfilment and happiness, and for transforming and individual experiences. Here, adventure tourism delivers a high involvement and extraordinary experience that is intense, positive and intrinsically enjoyable. However, until the 1980s, the 'experience' of consumption was not recognized in consumer behaviour models. Yet, feelings, fun and leisure all play a part in understanding the use and consumption of products and are closely linked to the consumer's level of involvement with the product.

Skydiving, along with underwater diving, hang gliding or mountain climbing is a dangerous and potentially lethal activity. Yet, skydivers are drawn from a population who have mortgages, insurance, wear car seat belts and recycle. Despite this they engage in an activity with high physical risk, and indeed some do die. In Figure 2.4, Celsi et al. (1993) suggest that three factors conspire to make people want to skydive:

1 The external environment which increasingly encourages risky, dramatic behaviour.
2 The availability of outlets for skydiving and through technology, the theatrical 'props and equipment for play'.
3 The individual's own psychological makeup and their pre-disposition to risk and thrill-seeking behaviour. Often they seek to live their lives through leisure experiences as a foil to their working life.

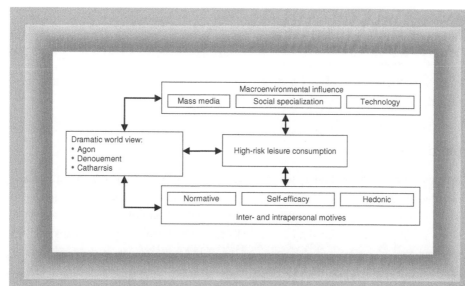

Figure 2.4 An extended model of high-risk leisure consumption
(*Source*: Celsi et al. 1993)

Given these factors, skydiving exemplifies the phenomena of the 'post-tourist' as it is very difficult to identify measurable characteristics of the group and to reach them for marketing purposes.

The skydiving product

Celsi et al. (1993) describe skydiving as:

A dramatic, self-fulfilling behaviour that occurs on a specific stage with carefully cast actors and co actors. The act is clearly defined, with the skydive planned and rehearsed (Celsi et al. 1993: 21).

Although the pre- and post-dive activities are important, the actual activity itself is of relatively short duration; e.g. Celsi et al. (1993) suggest that active skydivers will only be exposed to risk for around 8 hours in any year.

The growth of skydiving has created its own clubs, suppliers and folklore. Like many adventure pursuits, in the early years of amateur skydiving, professional equipment was not available and the participants relied on army surplus materials. This has changed however with the growth of the activity, and specialist suppliers produce parachute equipment for the sport.

Market stories and theatre

There are two strong characteristics that shape the product market of skydiving. The first is the very strong sense of group identity that characterizes the skydivers, whilst the second is the choreographed nature of the skydiving activity.

Skydivers

There is no doubt that extreme activities such as skydiving create a very strong bond between participants. For example in Celsi et al.'s (1993) research on skydiving, based on a club in the USA, skydivers view themselves as a family. As part of the experience, skydivers see themselves as creating a new self-identity and camaraderie, perhaps transcending that of normal group belonging. This is because not only is the activity so extreme, but also because the experience is a shared one with its own technical language. In skydiving, the market actors play various roles based either upon:

- their level of experience – students, novices, intermediates and experts (here progression though the various stages of initiation (e.g. the first jump) is seen as a rite of passage); and
- their part in the overall drama – owners, instructors, dive organizers and pilots.

Skydiving

The theatrical experience of skydiving is supported by its own technical language and props including parachutes, jumpsuits, helmets, goggles, logbooks, wrist altimeters, cameras, airplanes and landing markers. It is interesting that the equipment and language of adventure sports has permeated everyday life; clothing styles, fabrics and colours, as well as phrases such as 'just do it' owe their origins to extreme adventure sports.

The activity of skydiving is highly structured with an identifiable beginning, middle and end. This is very much along theatrical lines equating to an opening, performance and finale, rather as described by Pine and Gilmore (1999) as the basis for the experience economy. O'Sullivan and Spangler (1998) break experiences into three key stages and these are clear in Celsi et al.'s (1993) description of the choreographed nature of skydiving:

1 *Pre-experience*
   - On the ground – coordinating and rehearsal.
   - The ascent – anticipation as the airplane ascends to the dive point.

2 *The experience*
  - The exit – total commitment to the activity by stepping out of the aircraft.
  - Free fall – the main reason for skydiving, bringing a sense of freedom.
  - Under canopy – once the parachute has opened bringing a sense of relief, but also disappointment.
3 *Post-experience*
  - Post-performance rituals – feedback and congratulations to participants.

Each stage has its own rituals and stories, as do the interruptions to this highly choreographed activity when accidents occur. Indeed, as well as physical risk, stories surround the fact that if participants fail to deal with the failures in the activity then there is also an element of psychological risk. Above all, the activity is characterized by the intensity of emotion and the rituals surrounding it.

It is this combination of a close-knit group of participants, with a highly choreographed activity that interacts to create market-shaping activity and so defines the skydiving product market.

Key sources

Bentley, T., Page, S., Meyer, D., Chalmers, D. and Laird, I. (2001). How safe is adventure tourism in New Zealand? An exploratory analysis. *Applied Ergonomics* 32(4), 327–338.

Celsi, R.L., Rose, R.L. and Leigh, T.W. (1993). An exploration of high-risk leisure consumption through skydiving. *Journal of Consumer Research* 20, 1–23.

O'Sullivan, E.L. and Spangler, K.J. (1998). *Experience Marketing: Strategies for the New Millennium*. Pennsylvania: Venture.

Pine, J.B. and Gilmore, J.H. (1999). *The Experience Economy*. Harvard: Harvard Business School Press.

Swarbrooke, J., Beard, C., Leckie, S. and Pomfret, G. (2003). *Adventure Tourism: The New Frontier*. Oxford: Butterworth Heinemann.

Discussion questions

1 List as many adventure tourism activities as you can. Place these in a continuum from 'hard' to 'soft' adventure noting the criteria that you use to classify each activity.
2 What characteristics of tourists might be used to produce a market segmentation based on 'adventureness'?
3 As a market researcher, how might you begin to research and measure market stories?

Interactions and exchanges in product markets

The concept of exchange and interaction permeates the discussion on tourism product markets. The continuous interaction between market actors takes place within the context of a tourism destination. Each exchange or interaction has all the classic features of a service encounter. As such it is possible to benchmark the exchanges and interactions against a quality level. The challenges of the interactions that take place in tourism product markets are found in Figure 2.5. It is clear from Figure 2.5 that whilst these interactions display the classic characteristics of services, they are exacerbated by the nature of tourism not only as an activity, but also as a product.

Both tourists and suppliers are now designing strategies to deal with these challenges. Tourists are seasoned travellers and fully understand the tourism market place – they will purchase late, travel flexibly and understand their rights if the product or service is not as described. For the supplier these strategies include relationship marketing and service quality management:

1 Relationship marketing is designed to secure a loyal customer base, creating, maintaining and enhancing strong relationships with consumers.
2 Service quality management is designed to 'industrialize' service delivery by guaranteeing standardized and consistent services.

These two strategies combined will help retain customers, avoid price competition, retain employees and reduce costs. The strategies are augmented by other techniques such as yield management to adjust pricing to demand and so smooth out the demand curve; strong branding to communicate product attributes and reduce any perceived risk of purchase; managing the evidence of the interaction through investment in the physical environment or 'servicescape'; and staff training as the tourist's short exposure to the product means that staff are part of the interaction.

Chapter overview

This chapter has outlined the concept of contemporary tourism product markets as a key to understanding tourism marketing. Product markets assist in the understanding of tourism products, particularly in tourism where there is much debate

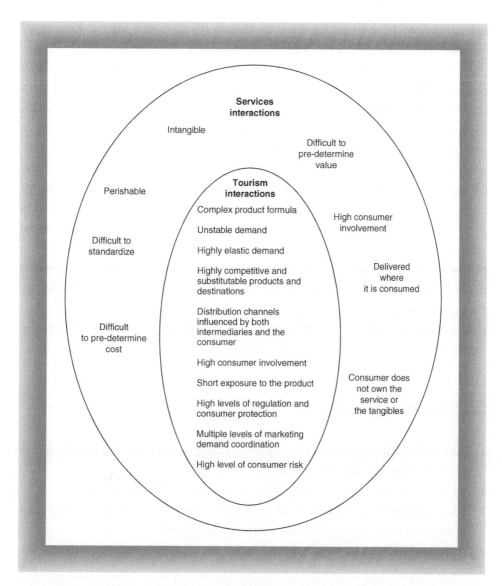

Figure 2.5 The environment of product market interactions

as to the nature of the product. An important point here is to recognize that the tourism consumer is a co-producer of products. This allows for the development of a marketing approach that emphasizes the importance of continuous interaction with the tourist. Here this chapter introduced the contemporary approach of experiences as tourism products and outlined as a case study, Tasmania's tourism experience product strategy. The experience product appeals directly to the 'post-tourist' market; a market that is used to high-quality visual and experiential products from entertainment and the media and also looks for authenticity. This chapter considered the changing nature of the tourism market and in particular the need for tourism to engage in deep and meaningful market research and innovative marker segmentation. The message from this chapter is that tourism products and markets are inextricably linked, hence the strong endorsement of the concept of tourism product markets. They provide a framework for understanding the interaction of buyers and sellers in tourism and allow the clear definition of tourism products and the boundaries between them. The pivotal position of the various actors in a market have led to the study of 'market-shaping' stories where consensus emerges amongst market actors as to what constitutes a particular product market. This is clearly demonstrated by the case study on skydiving. Finally, this chapter examined the nature of the continuous exchanges and interactions in tourism product markets and the response of marketers using relationship marketing and service quality management.

Self-review questions

1 Outline the main approaches to conceptualizing tourism products and devise your definition of a tourism product.
2 Why is the tourism experience product well-suited to the 'post-tourist'?
3 What might be the key elements of a market research project to underpin a market segmentation approach based on 'technographics'?
4 How does the behaviour of the post-tourist differ from that of a typical inclusive tour client?
5 What do you understand by the term 'tourism product market'?
6 Choose a tourist product market (e.g. adventure tourism or eco-tourism) and define the market and product characteristics of that market. How distinct are the product market boundaries?
7 Using the media and the Internet, find examples of market stories shaping tourism product markets?
8 How do the interactions and exchanges in a tourism product market differ from those in a product market based on physical goods?

9 What strategies can a tourism organization devise to overcome the nature of product market exchanges and interactions in tourism?

10 What are the key advantages of taking a product market approach to tourism marketing?

Recommended reading

1 Celsi, R.L., Rose, R.L. and Leigh, T.W. (1993). An exploration of high-risk leisure consumption through skydiving. *Journal of Consumer Research* 20, 1–23.
An innovative paper exploring the product market dynamics of the skydiving product market.

2 Cooper, C., Scott, N. and Kester, J. (2005). New and emerging markets. In D. Buhalis and C. Costa (eds), *Tourism Business Frontiers*, pp. 19–29. Oxford: Elsevier Butterworth Heinemann.
Chapter exploring the nature of product markets and in particular how new markets emerge.

3 Kandampully, J. (2002). *Services Management*. The New Paradigm in Hospitality. Melbourne: Hospitality Press.
A clear exposition of services theory and its application to tourism and hospitality.

4 Kotler, P., Bowen, J. and Makens, J. (2004). *Marketing for Hospitality and Tourism*, 4th edn. New Jersey: Prentice Hall.
Thorough text covering all the mainstream approaches to both products and markets.

5 Kotler, P., Brown, L., Adam, S. and Armstrong, G. (2004). *Marketing*, 6th edn. New Jersey: Prentice Hall.
A classic text covering the generic marketing theory of products and markets.

6 Pine, J.B. and Gilmore, J.H. (1999). *The Experience Economy*. Harvard: Harvard Business School Press.
A groundbreaking book reconceptualizing the way we think about experiences as products.

7 Rosa, J.A. and Spanjol, J.R. (2005). Micro-level product market dynamics: shared knowledge and its relationship to market development. *Journal of the Academy of Marketing Science* 33(2), 197–216.
A thorough discussion of the approaches to, and the literature of, product markets including the role of market stories.

Recommended web sites

Discover Tasmania (promotional web site): http://www.discovertasmania.com/
Marketing Your Business – Tourism Western Australia: www.westernaustralia.com/.../Growing+your+business/How+to+Grow+Your+Business/Marketing+Your+Business.htm
Specialty Travel Index: http://specialtytravel.com/
Tasmania online (government web site): http://www.tas.gov.au/
Tourism Australia: http://www.tourism.australia.com
Tourism Tasmania corporate web site: http://www.tourismtasmania.com.au/

References cited

Bourgeois, J.C., Haines, G.H. and Sommers, M.S. (1987). Product market structure: problem, definition and issues. In M. Houston (ed.), *Review of Marketing*, pp. 327–384. Chicago: American Marketing Association.

Butler, R. (1980). The concept of a tourist area cycle of evolution: implications for management of resources. *Canadian Geographer* 24(1), 5–12.

Day, G.S., Shocker, A.D. and Srivastava, R.K. (1979). Customer-oriented approaches to identifying product markets. *Journal of Marketing* 43, 8–19.

Gilbert, D.C. (1990). Conceptual issues in the meaning of tourism. In C.P. Cooper (ed.), *Progress in Tourism, Recreation and Hospitality Management*, Vol. 2, pp. 4–27. London: Belhaven.

Feifer, M. (1985). *Going Places*. London: Macmillan.

Kotler, P., Bowen, J. and Makens, J. (2005) *Marketing for Hospitality and Tourism*, 4th edn. New Jersey: Prentice Hall.

Kotler, P., Brown, L., Adam, S. and Armstrong, G. (2004). *Marketing*, 6th edn. New Jersey: Prentice Hall.

Pine, J.B. and Gilmore, J.H. (1999). *The Experience Economy*. Harvard: Harvard Business School Press.

O'Sullivan, E.L. and Spangler, K.J. (1998). *Experience Marketing: Strategies for the New Millennium*. Pennsylvania: Venture.

Rosa, J.A., Porac, J.F., Spanjol, J.R. and Saxon, M.S. (1999). Sociocognitive dynamics in a product market. *Journal of Marketing* 63(4), 64–77.

Rosa, J.A. and Spanjol, J.R. (2005). Micro-level product market dynamics: shared knowledge and its relationship to market development. *Journal of the Academy of Marketing Science* 33(2), 197–216.

White, H. (1981). Where do markets come from? *The American Journal of Sociology* 87(3), 517–547.

Section 2
The Contemporary Tourist

Chapter 3
Contemporary tourists, tourist behaviour and flows

Chapter objectives

After reading this chapter you will

- Understand different approaches to categorizing types of tourism
- Appreciate the factors that have contributed to the growth of international tourism
- Understand the significance of wildcard events that may slow or reduce tourism growth
- Identify factors that may explain the short-term stability of tourist flows and patterns
- Understand the roles of distance and accessibility as key factors in determining tourism flows
- Understand the characteristics of mass and alternative tourism
- Understand the nature of special interest tourism
- Appreciate psychographic and motivational approaches to explaining tourist behaviour
- Appreciate the significance of life-course approaches to explaining changes in tourism behaviour over the life of an individual

51

Introduction

The movement of tourists with respect to both the number of people travelling and the geographic spread of where people travel has continued almost unabated since the end of World War II. Multiple reasons exist for the growth in international and domestic travel. However, critical are increasing disposal incomes and available time for travel. Yet there are also a number of other factors that determine both the generation of tourists from countries and their reception at destinations. This chapter will therefore examine a range of factors that determine the patterns, flows and behaviours of contemporary tourists. These will be examined at various scales of analysis and detail.

Macro-level analyses of tourism examine the movement of people in aggregate form (Table 3.1). Therefore, descriptions of tourism at this level focus on the spatial aspects of tourism (i.e. tourist patterns and flows), and on different forms of tourism (i.e. broad accounts of tourism) that have been defined on the basis of activity or motivation. Micro-level analyses of tourism seek to explain individual tourist behaviours on the basis of theories of tourist psychology and motivation. There is clearly a link between individual and aggregate accounts of tourism as aggregate descriptions of tourism are the sum of behaviours of large number of individuals. There is therefore a third group of analyses of tourism that may be described as mid- or meso-level accounts of tourism that seek to integrate aggregate and individual accounts of tourist behaviour, examples here include the use of time-geography techniques (Hall 2005b; Coles et al. 2006).

Table 3.1   Scales of analysis of tourism

Scale of analysis and description of tourism	Focus	Key concepts
Macro	Aggregate	• Distribution, patterns, flows • Activity
Meso	Combines aggregate and individual analysis	• Mobility, trip stage, life course, travel career
Micro	Individual	• Personality, psychographics/lifestyle • Motivation, expectation, satisfaction

The first section of this chapter describes international travel movements. The second section then explains changes in tourism at a macro-level with reference to structural factors that influence tourism as well as other descriptions of different types of tourism. The third section examines contemporary tourist behaviours and demands at a micro-level by examining how individual travel preferences may be explained in terms of psychographics or personal motivations. The final section outlines a meso approach that examines how travel motivations and constraints change over an individual's life.

International travel movement

The movement of tourists is not evenly spread around the globe. Tourism is subject to a range of influences and factors that determine its relative distribution. Flows are not random but are patterned. Tables 3.2 and 3.3 provide figures on the number of international visitor arrivals for different regions of the world and the

Table 3.2 International tourism arrivals and forecasts 1950–2020 (millions)

Year	World	Africa	Americas	Asia and Pacific	Europe	Middle East
1950	25.3	0.5	7.5	0.2	16.8	0.2
1960	69.3	0.8	16.7	0.9	50.4	0.6
1965	112.9	1.4	23.2	2.1	83.7	2.4
1970	165.8	2.4	42.3	6.2	113.0	1.9
1975	222.3	4.7	50.0	10.2	153.9	3.5
1980	278.1	7.2	62.3	23.0	178.5	7.1
1985	320.1	9.7	65.1	32.9	204.3	8.1
1990	439.5	15.2	92.8	56.2	265.8	9.6
1995	540.6	20.4	109.0	82.4	315.0	13.7
2000	687.0	28.3	128.1	110.5	395.9	24.2
2005	806.8	37.3	133.5	155.4	441.5	39.0
Forecast						
2010	1006	47	190	195	527	36
2020	1561	77	282	397	717	69

Source: WTO (1997, 2006).

Table 3.3 Average annual growth in international tourism arrivals and forecasts 1950–2020 (%)

Year	World	Africa	Americas	Asia and Pacific	Europe	Middle East
1950–2000	6.8	8.3	5.8	13.1	6.5	10.1
1950–2005	6.5	8.1	5.4	12.5	6.1	10.1
1950–1960	10.6	3.7	8.4	14.1	11.6	12.3
1960–1970	9.1	12.4	9.7	21.6	8.4	11.5
1970–1980	5.3	11.6	4.0	13.9	4.7	14.3
1980–1990	4.7	7.8	4.1	9.3	4.1	3.1
1980–1985	2.9	6.1	0.9	7.4	2.7	2.7
1985–1990	6.5	9.5	7.3	11.3	5.4	3.5
1990–2000	4.6	6.4	3.3	7.0	4.1	9.6
1990–1995	4.2	6.1	3.3	8.0	3.5	7.3
1995–2000	4.9	6.7	3.3	6.0	4.7	12.0
2000–2005	3.3	5.7	0.8	7.1	2.2	10.0
Forecast						
2010	4.2	5.6	3.9	7.3	3.0	7.0
2020	4.5	5.1	4.0	7.4	3.1	6.7

Source: WTO (2006).

relative growth in tourism for those regions since 1950. One of the immediate results of an analysis of international tourism in terms of patterns of movement is that international tourism has historically been concentrated in North America and Europe. However, there is change over time as the Asia-Pacific region is experiencing significant growth relative to Europe and the Americas.

The WTO's (1997, 2001) forecasts predict that by 2020 international arrivals are expected to reach nearly 1.6 billion. Of these worldwide arrivals in 2020, 1.2 billion will be intraregional and 378 million will be long-haul travellers. By 2020, the top three receiving regions will be Europe (717 million tourists), East Asia and the Pacific (397 million), and the Americas (282 million), followed by Africa, the Middle East and South Asia.

East Asia and the Pacific, Asia, the Middle East and Africa are forecast to record growth at rates of over 5 per cent a year, compared to the world average of 4.1 per cent. However, these regions started at a significantly lower base rate of international travel than Europe and the Americas. Europe and Americas are anticipated to show lower than average growth rates given that they represent more mature markets in terms of uptake of international travel. Europe is expected to maintain the highest share of world arrivals, although there will be a decline from 60 per cent in 1995 to 46 per cent in 2020 (WTO 2001). Of course, it is important to bear in mind that these are global aggregate figures. The more localized that an examination of tourism patterns and flows is, the more likely it is to find variation in tourism numbers, particularly in terms of the impact of 'wildcard' – high magnitude, low frequency – events such as hallmark events which may increase arrivals or political conflicts, or natural disasters which may reduce arrivals at a destination or even reduce the overall amount of travel within, to and from the affected region (Hall 2005a). In fact, the only events which have had affects on the entire global tourism system since modern tourism began in the 1850s are:

- World wars or major international conflicts.
- Serious economic depression or periods of severe recession over a large number of countries.
- Rapid increase in the price of a major energy source that is used for transportation, particularly oil.
- Outbreaks of contagious disease.

The following case study traces the impact of wildcard events on tourism in Thailand since December 2004.

CASE STUDY
Thai tourism post-tsunami

The Boxing Day (26 December 2004) Tsunami had a substantial impact on tourism around the Indian Ocean, but its greatest impact in tourism terms was on Thailand. In 2004, there were 11.68 million visitors to Thailand, just missing the 12 million target because of the tsunami in the last week of the year. Tourism accounted for 6.4 per cent of the country's US $164 billion economy in 2004. The tsunami killed more than 5400 people in Thailand, half of them tourists. Although the direct impacts in terms of destruction of coastal infrastructure were substantial, the greatest effects were with respect to the image of the destination in terms of safety in area affected by the tsunami. In mid-2005, the Tourism

Authority of Thailand (TAT) announced that the losses of the Thai tourism industry may be as much as 50 billion baht (US $1.2 billion), 52 per cent higher than the government had originally forecast. Tourists did not return as quickly as expected to Thailand's south-west resorts including Phuket, Krabi, Khao Lak and Phi Phi, substantially affecting earnings of hotels, airlines, restaurants, tour operators and souvenir vendors. In addition, even though tourism numbers for the whole country had recovered, the money earned from them was less than anticipated because many of the most expensive resorts, such as the Anantara Coco Palm Resort & Spa in Khao Lak, were destroyed in the tsunami and had not yet been rebuilt. Since the disaster, hotel and airline bookings for the affected areas were down 70 per cent as at mid-2005, despite cleanup efforts, the development of a tsunami-warning system, and a US $750 million government rebuilding budget.

Thailand-wide, foreign visitor arrivals were up about 2 per cent by mid-2005, as people visited other parts of the country including the northern city of Chiang Mai. Indeed, William Heinecke, Chief Executive of Minor International, Thailand's biggest resort and fast-food restaurant operator, said in an interview. 'Thailand as a destination has never really faltered, in spite of all these crises. The number for tourists haven't declined for Thailand and won't decline this year, they just went to different places.'

Thailand's government gave the tourism authority an additional 2.5 billion baht in July 2005 to help revive the tourism industry after it had spent most of its annual 4.6 billion baht budget trying to restore tourist confidence post-tsunami, including hosting the Miss Universe pageant. The extra money was used to market the country as a destination for Asian tourists. In commenting on the extra income Juthamas Siriwan, Governor of the TAT Juthamas said that the tourism authority was hoping to reach the pre-tsunami target of 13.3 million visitors. 'Realistically, if we don't do anything it will be less than 12 million, maybe 11.9 million, but if we can inject marketing to particular markets I hope it will increase, I'm more aggressively looking into marketing to Japan, China, Southeast Asia, Singapore, Hong Kong, Malaysia, to offer them a beautiful holiday weekend.'

The Phuket region usually accounts for almost a third of Thailand's international tourist arrivals. Six months after the tsunami struck, tourism in Phuket had still not recovered. A slight upturn in arrivals in February and March was followed by a slump in arrivals. According to Phuket province's social welfare office 460 tourism businesses employing 2800 people had closed since the tsunami. According to Chan Wongsatyanon, a regional executive of the Thai Tourism Service Association, in April and May hotels had an occupancy rate of 15–20 per cent: 'the tsunami on December 26, the Indonesian earthquake on March 28 and the explosions at Hat Yai airport had a huge impact. In June we forecast an occupancy rate of below 10 per cent ... The most important issue now is how we can restore tourist confidence' (in Ghosh 2005: 25). In the same period in 2004 the occupancy rate of Phuket hotels was 70 per cent. According to Mr. Chan the task for Phuket tourism was to bring back tourists who had switched to Vietnam and the Philippines as destinations even though Phuket hotels were offering discounts of between 40 and 60 per cent to customers. In response, Thai Airways, the national carrier, and 30 hotels in Phuket, Phang Nga and Krabi were pooling funds for an advertising campaign to restore tourist confidence. Future bookings for Phuket looked promising with expectations of a gradual return of European tourists to the region. However, there were ongoing concerns about the affect that future negative publicity on Thailand may have not only with respect to the post-tsunami situation, but also more so in relation to political instability in Thailand. The democratically elected government was deposed in a military coup in 2006 and there is ongoing political violence in the country's southern provinces as a result of the actions of separatist groups seeking independence for the Muslim-majority area and government forces.

Although TAT has sought to ensure that tourism companies are aware that the provinces affected by the separatist movement are more than 1000 km (620 miles) south of Bangkok, and well away from popular areas for international tourists, potential visitors who see images of political violence in Thailand are not necessarily that knowledgeable of the country's geography. Furthermore, political violence is not necessarily isolated to the southern region. On 3 April 2005, there were bombings of Hat Yai airport, a Carrefour hypermarket and a hotel in Songkhla province, 800 km south of Bangkok, killing 2 people and injuring about 60. Bombings also occurred in Bangkok in 2006 most notable of which was the series of bombings on New Years Eve which killed 3 people and wounded 34, with 9 of those being foreign tourists (Mydans 2006). In response to the New Years Eve explosions Thailand's tourism minister said that the series of bomb blasts in Bangkok on New Years Eve would have a significant impact on the tourism industry through the remainder of 2007. The seriousness of the bombings for tourism was also evidenced by the issuing of travel warnings to Thailand by the governments of Australia, the United States and the UK, all significant non-Asian markets for Thai tourism. However, the damage that such events potentially play on Thailand's image as 'the land of smiles' was also to be seen in comments by Thai Travel Agents Association (TTAA) President Anek Srichivachart who said that tourism would be affected by news and perceptions of violence in Bangkok, but unless such violence continued, it would not be major. Instead, he observed that if the incidents did not linger in the headlines and did not continue to take place, then the impact could be minimal (BizAsia 2007).

Key sources

BizAsia (2007). Bangkok bombings to impact Thailand's foreign tourism from 2007. *BizAsia* 2 January.

Bloomberg (2005). Tsunami may cost Thailand 50 billion baht in tourism. *Bloomberg* July 19.

Ghosh, N. (2005). Where are the tourists? *The Straits Times* 11 June, 25.

Mydans, S. (2006). Bombs in Bangkok kill 3 and wound more than 30. *International Herald Tribune* 31 December.

Tourism Authority of Thailand news and press releases: www.tatnews.org

Tourism Authority of Thailand web site: www.tourismthailand.org

Discussion questions

1 How much information with respect to tourist security and risks should tourism organizations provide to tourists?

2 To what extent is it true to say that travellers react more to perceived risk as opposed to real risk in undertaking travel and decision-making?

3 What information does the TAT provide to (a) tourists and (b) the media with respect to the effects of political instability in Thailand or other types of risks that tourist may perceive.

The stability of tourism: tourism inertia

One of the most significant observations of flows of international tourists is that there is a great deal of year-to-year stability in aggregate travel patterns. This situation has long been recognized, as Williams and Zelinsky (1970: 563) in one of the seminal works on international tourism observed, 'Evidently, once established, a stream of tourists has its own inertia, and one can predict future flows with considerable confidence without being able to explain the causes of past or present patterns'. Nevertheless, identifying causal factors remains useful. For example, the hypothesis of reciprocity, that is a flow of tourist in one direction should generate a counterflow in the other direction, is not generally supported when examining international tourism data. Nevertheless, Williams and Zelinsky (1970) suggested several reasons as to the factors that may explain the short-term stability of tourist flow patterns and which remain relevant to contemporary travel patterns:

- Information fed back to people in the generating country from tourists who have made previous visits to the destination country.
- Distance as a factor influencing travel patterns (including route, time and cost distance rather than just absolute distance).

- The presence or absence of other types of international connectivity, past or present, will tend to stimulate or inhibit international tourist patterns. Examples of connectivity include international trade, labour migration, political allegiances and shared culture. It was also noted that political–cultural barriers would inhibit tourist flows.

- Some factors of attractiveness, such as climate, have a strong influence on travel flows. For example, the existence of a heliotropic or sun-seeking factor in international tourism is borne out in the north–south flows that can be identified in terms of the substantial northern European international travel to the Mediterranean and similar flows from Canada and the northern United States to the southern United States, Mexico and the Caribbean.

- The relative cost of different potential destinations.

- The existence of intervening opportunities, i.e. the potential for a stopover while undertaking long-haul travel between other countries, some of the best known examples here include Hong Kong and Singapore with other countries such as Malaysia, Thailand and Vietnam also competing for hub status and therefore a potential stopover location for travel flows between Europe and Australasia.

- Events have only a short-term effect on travel flows.

- The stability of destination image in generating areas.

- National cultural traits in generating areas with respect to factors such as risk.

Distance as a determinant of the flows and patterns of contemporary tourism

Many of the factors identified by Williams and Zelinsky have been picked up in contemporary tourism literature (e.g. Lew et al. 2004; Shaw and Williams 2004). For example, Hall (2005a) focused on the importance of distance as an explanatory variable for the distribution of tourists and tourism production. He argues that the distribution of travel behaviour in space and time reflects an ordered adjustment to the factor of distance, whether it be in the form of space–time, economic, network, cognitive, social or cultural distance. According to Tobler (1970, 2004), the first law of geography is that everything is related to everything else, but near things are more related than distant things. This statement provides an accurate assessment of observed regularity in human behaviour and the role of distance as a fundamental concept with respect to notions of the relations between places, such as tourism destinations and generating regions. For example, travel and locational decisions are generally taken in order to minimize the frictional effects of distance, with some destinations being more accessible than others. Hall (2005a) has even gone so far as to suggest that there are six laws of tourism although they are related to mobility overall:

1 *The distribution of travel behaviour in space and time reflects an ordered adjustment to the factor of distance.* Types of distance that influence tourism include:
   - *Euclidean distance* which is the direct physical distance between locations.
   - *Time distance* which is the time taken to travel between locations.
   - *Economic distance (cost distance)* which is the monetary cost incurred in overcoming physical distance between two locations.
   - *Gravity distance* a subset of time/economic distance but reinforces notion that closer means less effort and is important for a range of behaviours including estimated size of markets for locations and attractions.
   - *Network distance* which is the distance between locations via intermediate points, as in a transport network or telecommunication network. This can also sometimes be referred to as *route* or 'Manhattan' distance.
   - *Cognitive distance (perceived distance)* which are judgements regarding the spatial separation of locations. Cognitive distance is particularly important for example to the ways that actual or potential travellers to collect, structure and recall information with respect to locations in physical space and establish mental maps.
   - *Social distance* which is a distance component associated with differences between social classes (which possess different socioeconomic characteristics) which may be expressed in terms of the locational characteristics of class or status.
   - *Cultural distance* related to the above but refers more specifically to differences between cultures and how that is expressed in perceptions of distance.
2 *Travel and locational decisions are generally taken in order to minimize the frictional effects of distance.* This concept is also often referred to as the 'law of minimum effort or least effort'. In tourism exceptions to this rule arguably apply when the trip itself is part of the attraction or is the 'destination', e.g. travel on a cruiseship.
3 *Destinations and locations are variably accessible with some destinations more accessible than others.* Accessibility is a variable quality of any location, but basically refers to

the ease of getting to a place and is closely related to the concept of movement minimization, especially when this is measured by the costs involved in overcoming distance.

4 *There is a tendency for human activities to agglomerate to take advantage of scale economies.* Scale economies refers to how activities, such as firm operations, may be concentrated in certain locations in order to make savings with respect to economic and time-distance costs. However, it can also apply to social relationships as well, for example, with respect to meetings and conventions.

5 *The organization of spatial and non-spatial aspects of human activity is essentially hierarchical in nature.* In part this occurs as a result of interrelationships between agglomeration tendencies and accessibility. More accessible locations appear to be the sites of larger agglomerations and vice versa. One of the implications from this is that for a given geographical area (e.g. country), there is a hierarchy of locations in terms of accessibility. For example, this is something that becomes readily apparent when considering relationships between airport traffic or that of other transport nodes and the areas they serve.

6 *Human activities and occupance are focal in character.* The nodes about which human activity is organized are agglomerations of varying size. Since these are hierarchically arranged it follows that there is a hierarchy of different sized focal regions. Again, this becomes evident when considering the order ranking of airports in any given country and the relative size of the regions that they service.

Of these six 'laws' Hall (2005a) argues that the first four are the most significant for describing contemporary tourism patterns, especially at a local level. Especially important is the concept of distance decay, which refers to the notion that the degree of spatial interaction (flows between regions, e.g. travellers) is inversely related to distance. The empirical regularity of this relationship is such that it is open to mathematical analysis through what are described as gravity models in a wide variety of fields such as transport and retailing. It is a deceptively simple but critical idea which in layperson's terms can be crudely restated as a tourist attraction or destination tends to attract more people from near locations than far ones. The concept is very important as it highlights the way in which the changed accessibility of a destination or attraction relative to that of other potential destinations and attractions available to the consumer, becomes a critical variable in the success of the destination in the market.

Describing tourism

Although mathematical modeling of human mobility, including leisure travel, is one way of analysing and describing tourism patterns and flows, a more common descriptive approach in tourism studies is to describe tourism according to the motivations, behaviours and activities of tourists or by other characteristics. For example, an extremely widely used term that combines aspects of both the characteristics of the tourist as well as the production of tourism experiences which is used by both academics and in the media is 'mass tourism' but what exactly is it?

Mass and alternative tourism

At its simplest, mass tourism refers to the production of industrially organized tourism that supports the movement of large numbers of people. The primary quantitative element of mass tourism is the large numbers of people undertaking long-distance travel that requires overnight stays away from home (e.g. Bramwell 2004). A secondary quantitative element of mass tourism is the relatively high proportion of visitors to a destination who have purchased a package tour (e.g. Burns 1999). However, many of the elements of mass tourism are more qualitative in scope with mass tourists often being stereotyped in terms of 'herd-like, lacking internal social distinctions, doggedly seeking amusement, and guided by mass produced tour books' (Furlough 1998: 248).

The beginning of mass tourism is usually identified with the development of the first packaged tours utilizing railway and/or steamship-based travel in the mid-nineteenth century. However, its contemporary form is usually associated with jet-based package tours. The expression mass tourism also arguably has an elitist connotation to it as it often implies travel by poorer, less well-educated people to destinations that the wealthier and 'more discerning' do not travel to, or have ceased travelling to. For example, Burns (1999: 46) described mass tourists as 'a continuous flux of visitors of middle class income and values expecting trained multilingual hotel and tourists' staff to fulfill their needs as wanted. They obviously expect western amenities'. As such the mass tourist is sometimes described as being dependent on their 'environmental bubble'. This bubble serves 'both to preserve some familiarity within a strange environment and to familiarise the traveller with strangers' (Mittleberg 1998: 28). A number of elements of mass tourism have been described (Buswell 1996; Burns 1999; Bramwell 2004; Duval 2004):

- Highly seasonal tourism demand.
- Middle and low class tourists from urban-industry areas.
- Large numbers of tourists in ratio with locals.
- Spatial focus on a few areas within the destination, associated with spatial concentration of facilities.
- Exploitation of local values, behaviours and languages.
- Organization by international tourism operators.
- Exploitation of natural resources.
- Undifferentiated products.
- Origin-packaged holidays.
- Reliance upon developed generating markets.

Because of these characteristics mass tourism is also usually regarded as being harmful to the destination. For example, Bramwell (2004: 19) stated that 'concentrated mass tourism resorts have been criticised as they can overwhelm local environmental systems'. Bramwell argues that in many cases, numbers of tourists may surpass the capacity that the host community can adequately handle and can discourage local economic and employment linkages. Stamboulis and Skayannis (2003) comment on the environmental degradation associated with mass tourism, and also the stress on the existing infrastructure and services within the destination. Similarly, Conway (2004: 190) notes that 'a very important *direct* environmental impact of mass tourism concerns the industry's increasing demand for receptor services that will take care of unwanted by-products'. However, the negative impacts of mass tourism are seen as extending beyond the physical environment. For example, Khan (1997: 989) states 'mass tourism development also creates an economic demand for the trappings of local culture' which indicates the possible commoditization of local cultures within the destination where mass tourism is occurring. Mowforth and Munt (1998) also argue that mass tourism, aided by large corporations, results in the mass displacement of communities.

Because of the negative impacts of mass tourism and changes in tourism consumption some people now argue that there is a move away from mass tourism towards 'alternative' or more 'special interest' forms of tourism. Eadington and Smith (1992: 3) defined alternative tourism as 'forms of tourism that are consistent with natural, social and community values and which allow both hosts and guests to enjoy a positive and worthwhile interaction and shared experiences'. Pearce (1992) developed the notion of *polar opposites* whereby alternative tourism and mass tourism were complete opposites, moving in different directions. Hunter (2002) described the differences between these two forms of tourism. Mass tourism involves large-scale businesses, large amounts of tourists being transported *en masse*, and experiences for the tourists which are much like their own home lifestyle (Hunter 2002). Alternative tourism, on the other hand, is described by Hunter (2002) as being small in scale, has minimal impacts on local culture and the environment, and the tourists wish to have a genuine experience of the local lifestyle with 'ecotourism', 'soft tourism' and 'sustainable tourism' being identified as some of these forms of alternative tourism. However, this dualistic approach to mass and alternative tourism has come to be substantially criticized.

Clarke (1997) argued that constructing sustainable tourism and mass tourism as polar opposites that represented the 'good' and the 'bad', respectively, was a conceptual barrier between both types of tourism (Clarke 1997). Instead, mass and sustainable tourism formed more of a continuum (Hall 1998, 2008) (Figure 3.1). Indeed, Bramwell in his review of mass coastal tourism in the Mediterranean noted that the 'appropriateness of mass tourism depends on the precise context of each destination' (Bramwell 2004: 18). Similarly, Butcher (2003: 26) argued that 'mass tourism can be sustainable' and that when researchers focus only on the new aspects of tourism (such as alternative tourism) they are being very narrow minded. These issues will be examined in more detail in Chapter 8 on tourism planning.

A further complicating element in discussions of mass and alternative tourism is that the attributes of the tourist are usually interwoven with attributes of the destination and the supporting infrastructure for the trip along all its stages. However, such a combination of elements is highly problematic in at least two ways. First, tourism is co-created meaning that destinations should not be seen as passive elements in the development of tourism and are as much contributors to particular forms of tourism as well as the patterns and flows of visitors associated with them. Second, and even more significant, it is quite likely that in the same trip a consumer can move between different forms of tourism, so that they are engaging in mass tourism at one point in time and alternative tourism at another. How would such a situation lead to an effective description of the tourist or might it actually reflect a characteristic of modern tourism?

Perceived attributes of mass tourism	Dimension	Perceived attributes of alternative tourism
High numbers	Tourist numbers (absolute and relative to population)	Low numbers
High numbers	Numbers of package tourists (relative to total number of visitors and absolute)	Low numbers
High concentration	Spatial distribution of tourists and infrastructure	Dispersed
Focus on price	Price/quality trade offs	Focus on quality
High levels	Level of dependency on external financing and investment	Low levels
Low	Economic return to destination community	High
High pressure	Pressures on physical and socio-cultural environment	Low pressure
Low	Levels of authenticity	High
High	Seasonality	Low
Low	Differentiation of product	High
High	Reliance on developed or mature generating markets	Low
High	Market power of international tourism operators	Low
Low	Degree of destination control of supply chain and distribution channels	High
Low-middle	Income levels of market (at generating area)	Middle-high
Low-middle	Education levels of market	Middle-high
Low	Interest in SIT	High

Figure 3.1 Continuum of idealized attributes of mass and alternative tourism
(*Source*: After Hall 1998, 2008)

Special interest tourism

The confusion between the description of the tourist and descriptions of types of tourist is also to be found in discussions of special interest tourism (SIT), a concept often closely associated with that of alternative tourism (e.g. Poon 1997). SIT occurs when travel motivation and decision-making is primarily determined by a particular special interest, that is often associated with 'serious leisure' (Hall and Weiler 1992; Stebbins 1992; Hall 2005a). Derrett (2001: 3) defined SIT as 'the provision of customised leisure and recreational experiences driven by the specific expressed interests of individuals and groups'. However, in a link to 'alternative tourism' she also related the concept to the development of 'new tourism', defined by Poon (1997: 47) as the 'phenomenon of large scale packaging of non-standardised leisure services at competitive prices to suit demands of tourists as well as the economic and socio-environmental needs of destinations'. The 'new' and 'experiential' dimensions of SIT were also picked up on in Novelli's (2005) collection of studies on 'niche tourism' which arguably also has links to ideas concerning the experience economy (see Chapters 1 and 4).

Despite empirical and theoretical difficulties in categorizing special interest travellers, SIT is often characterized, at least in part, by the tourists' search for novel, authentic and quality tourist experiences (e.g. Derrett 2001). However, it is important to recognize that SIT needs to be related to the primary motivations of the tourist to participate in a particular trip or activity rather than just the provision of activities which meet such motivations (McKercher and Chan 2005). Otherwise, in the course of the same trip, even on the same day, and using categories to be found in the tourism literature, a visitor to a city such as London could be categorized as an urban tourist, a heritage tourist (when they visit an historic site such as the Tower of London), a cultural tourist (when they go to an art gallery such as the National Portrait Gallery), a sports tourist (when they go to a stadium such as Stamford Bridge to watch a game of football), a food tourist (when they go to a Gordon Ramsay restaurant and eat some local food) and a shopping tourist (when they go to Fortnum and Masons to purchase some tea). And potentially each time they undertake one of these activities they may be added to the numbers of tourists that fit into that category.

Hall (1998) therefore distinguished between SIT which refers to cases in which the traveller's motivation and decision-making are primarily determined by a particular special interest (the demand or consumption characteristics) and specialty tourism which refers to the supply characteristics of producing more specialized tourism experiences within the context of the setting (e.g. rural tourism) and/or the activities (e.g. adventure tourism). Although there is an overlap between the two concepts, it is important to distinguish between the two because the size of the

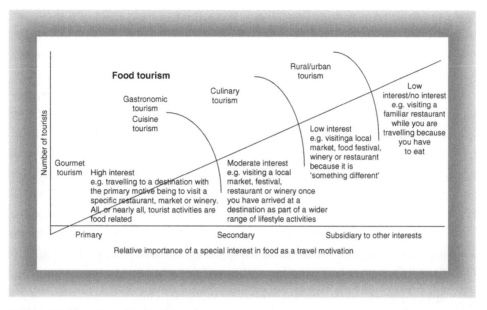

Figure 3.2 Food tourism as SIT

(*Source*: Hall and Sharples 2003: 11)

market that could be described under the rubric of SIT is substantially smaller than that which participates in specialty tourism activities. For example, during the course of a trip a tourist could participate in a number of specialty tourism activities with none of them constituting either the primary or even a secondary motivation to undertake the trip or choose a particular destination. In the case of the tourist visiting London as described in the previous paragraph the actual main reason to travel to London was to visit friends. Figure 3.2 illustrates the relationship between strength of motivation and number of tourists engaging in an activity with respect to different categories of what may be described as food tourism.

Micro-scale approaches

Identifying and amalgamating the various motivations of travellers is a useful exercise in market segmentation, but it is an exercise that is fraught with difficulties because it rests on assumptions of not only being able to adequately identify elements of another person's psychology but also, in many cases, being able to rely on other people being willing and able to explain their motivations to someone else. Macro-level constraints (as outlined in Chapter 1) such as money, time, culture, gender and health are obvious influences on individual travel decision-making but this section focuses more on some of the psychological variables that are utilized to explain tourism flows and patterns.

Several typologies of tourists have been developed that focus on psychological types or personality traits. Gray (1970) identified pleasure travel as being grounded in two basic motivations, sunlust or wanderlust. Wanderlust is a 'basic trait in human nature which causes some individuals to want to leave things with which they are familiar and to go and see at first hand different exciting cultures and places … a desire to exchange temporarily the known workaday things of home for something which is exotic' (1970: 57). In contrast, sunlust depends on the existence elsewhere of different or better amenities for a specific purpose than are available locally. In 1972, Cohen created a typology of tourists which had four different categories: organized mass tourist, individual mass tourist, the explorer and the drifter. Although perhaps more widely recognized in marketing terms is Plog's typology of psychocentric, midcentric and allocentric tourists (Plog 1974). Allocentrics are in line with Cohen's (1972) explorers and drifters, and do not partake in mass tourism. Allocentrics tend to seek new and exciting destinations and are prepared to take risks (Ryan 2003). Psychocentrics however are akin with the organized mass tourist and the individual mass tourist. Psychocentrics include tourists who are self-inhibited and have anxious or risk-averse personalities. These tourists will seek the familiar and are happier in an urban environment. They are very conservative about their travel arrangements and select to stay close to home or if they do travel abroad will travel to destinations favoured by tourists similar to themselves (Ryan 2003). Plog (2001, 2002) reintroduced the psychographic scales but with changed descriptors: allocentric became 'venturer' and psychocentric became 'dependable'. Plog also asserts that the tourist population, like any population, is normally distributed with the true venturer segment representing about 4 per cent of the population and the true dependable about 2.5 per cent. Such personality and psychographic type models, which are highly influential in tourism studies, raise interesting questions about co-creation of tourism experiences particularly with respect to how destinations and their products adapt to leisure tourists over time. Plog, for example, in the original formulation of his work on psychocentrics and allocentrics believed that the capacity to adapt, along with how tourists both perceived and experienced destinations, is an important element in determining destination success.

Another way in which tourism patterns and flows are often described at the individual level is with respect to tourist motivations. Motivation refers to the process by which an individual will be driven to act or behave in a certain way (Decrop 2006). An example of a very common way of using travel motivations to identify tourism patterns and flows is the use of international and domestic visitor surveys and international visitor information from entry controls (Hall and Page 2006). Such surveys often ask visitors for the primary reason for travel and typically offer options such as leisure/holiday, convention, business, education, and visiting friends and relations (VFR). An analysis of the results of such surveys will often reveal significant patterns in the seasonality of certain types of travellers. For example, in many western countries the peak period for VFR travel is Christmas with Easter also being significant, while in the United States the Thanksgiving holiday is peak period for VFR often exceeding Christmas. Leisure-holiday-related travel flows tend to be strongly influenced by factors such as school holidays, and climate conditions in the destination as well as the generating region. In contrast business travel tends to demonstrate relatively little seasonality with the exception being that Christmas and New Year tends to be a low point in business-related travel. Importantly, the patterns and flows of such motivationally categorized markets tend to demonstrate substantial inertia and significant rapid change only tends to occur at a time of external shocks.

More detailed analyses of travel motivations often focus on the concept of push and pull factors (Decrop 2006). These factors, that were originally derived from migration studies, seek to answer the question of why do people move? Dann (1977) argued that push factors reflect the desire to travel while pull factors are concerned with destination choice. Push factors are 'internally generated drives causing the tourist to search for signs in objects, situations and events that contain the promise of reducing prevalent drives'. In contrast pull factors are 'generated by the knowledge about goal attributes the tourist holds' (Gnoth 1997: 290–291). According to Dann (1976: 22), 'holidays are essentially experiences in fantasy … A certain picture is built up of a world that marks an escape from present reality, an environment for acting out psychic needs, and the playing of certain roles that cannot be fulfilled at home, and it is this which forms part and parcel of tourist motivation'. However, much of the research on tourism motivations does not account for change in motivation over time through the accumulation of experience and/or different stages in life. For example, Pearce and Lee (2005) observed that a core of travel motivation factors including escape, relaxation, relationship enhancement and self-development seemed to comprise the core of motivation for all travellers that they surveyed in their research. However, they also noted that different motivational factors appeared related to different levels of travel experience with factors such as experiencing different cultures or being close to nature being more important for experienced travellers. For less experienced travellers, motivations such as nostalgia, personal development, romance, recognition, security and stimulation were more significant.

Meso-level accounts of tourism

A key question in understanding and predicting individual travel behaviour is how do motivations and opportunities for travel and mobility change over time? It has long been recognized that past travel and life experiences influence future travel destination choices (Pearce 2005). However, such changes are not easily captured without the use of longitudinal data. A key point of interest for tourism researchers is the increased routinization of longer-distance leisure and tourism mobilities (Hall 2005a). Both transport and tourism researchers have identified the implications of the changing nature of social networks – larger and/or more dispersed set of social relationships – as being a critical factor in influencing travel behaviours that are undertaken in order to maintain such networks (Coles and Timothy 2004). The expansion of social and economic networks in terms of both activity and knowledge spaces has been referred to as the development of 'global generations' (Edmunds and Turner 2005) and is an important distinguishing factor of contemporary tourism from that of previous generations. Indeed, an important research question with respect to describing tourism patterns is the extent to which travel behaviours remain consistent over a generation.

One way in which generational change as well as individual changes in travel behaviour can be charted is through a life-course approach. The life-course paradigm emphasizes that changes in one dimension of the household-aging process, for example, are necessarily linked to changes in other dimensions, in seeking to explain behaviours. A life-course approach suggests that the timing and order of major life events (e.g. partnership, separation, birth of children, retirement) be considered with respect to the relationships between the individual, age cohorts and changing social structures. A life-course approach also aims not to impose the idea of a normal life path as articulated in traditional life-cycle models, instead what is central to the concept of the life-course is not the concept of stage but that of transition. Early transitions have implications for later ones with transitions occur in 'personal time', 'historical time' and 'family time'. Warnes (1992) identified several transitions that affect travel careers:

- Leaving the parental home
- Sexual union
- Career
- Family
- Children (income high/low)
- Career promotion
- Divorce or separation
- Cohabitation and second marriage
- Retirement
- Bereavement or income collapse
- Frailty or chronic ill health

Membership of a cohort is a central factor in life-course opportunities such as partnership, employment or the capacity to raise a family. However, the temporal category of birth cohort (or generation), which is a tool used by many researchers in examining consumer behaviour, may also be a factor related to value shifts, including with respect to travel (Mills 2000). As Mills (2000: 101) noted, 'Although one's spatial or physical location, for instance, may change as a consequence of migration, persons are born into not only a particular historical, but also a unique cultural and social context'.

A model for understanding the implications of a life-course approach for understanding travel behaviour is illustrated in Figure 3.3 in which the life-course domain is shown to be related to the accessibility domain and the mobility domain (Salomon 1983; Lanzendorf 2003; Hall 2005a). This has been done because lifestyle change is connected with changes in accessibility and mobility over the life-course, and the economic and time budgets that result, leading to different constraints on travel and changing motivations over time. In addition to indicating the factors that affect individual mobility, including with respect to tourism, life-course approaches also highlight generation patterns in travel behaviour (Pennington-Gray and Spreng 2002; Pennington-Gray et al. 2003). For example, the present generation of students (born late 1980s and later) are arguably the most mobile in

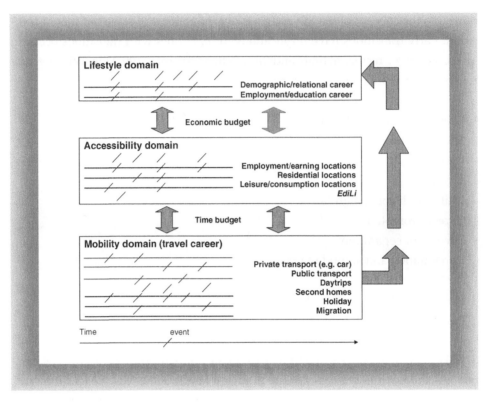

Figure 3.3 The construction of mobility biographies and life-courses
(*Source:* After Hall 2003)

terms of discretionary long-distance travel than any previous generation in terms of amount and distance of travel.

Chapter overview

This chapter has described a range of different approaches to explaining contemporary tourism behaviour and flows. The chapter started with an overview of growth in international tourism since 1950 with the remarkable factor in international tourism being the inertia in the tourism system. Several macro-level or structural, economic, spatial and social explanations for international patterns and flows were provided with wildcard events being identified as key factors in affecting tourism growth.

The chapter then examined mass and alternative categories of tourism with particular attention being paid to the way in which such descriptions conflate consumption and production dimensions of tourism. In addition, the notions of mass and alternative tourism were also identified as having moral elements associated with them that may detract from their empirical dimension. Similarly, the categorization of various types of SIT is also frequently confused.

Micro-level approaches that focus on describing individual travel behaviour were divided into psychographic and motivational approaches. Valuable as these approaches are it was noted that they often do not sufficiently account for changes over the life-course of an individual. Finally, it was noted that life-course approaches may give an appreciation of cohort dimensions of tourism behaviour that highlight the fact that younger contemporary tourists may well be the most mobile of any generation in terms of long-distance travel.

Self-review questions

1 What have been the major trends in international tourism since the 1950s?
2 Why has international tourism been characterized as having considerable inertia?
3 To what extent does distance affect tourism flows and patterns?
4 What are the key characteristics of mass and alternative tourism?
5 Does the term 'mass tourism' have an elitist connotation?
6 What are the implications of categorizing different types of tourism by activity rather than motivation?
7 How might psychographic approaches to describing tourism be related to the success of destination in attracting tourists?
8 What are push and pull factors with respect to tourism behaviour?
9 What are some of the key transitions that affect travel careers?
10 What advantages may a life-course approach have in explaining individual travel behaviour?

Recommended reading

1 Butcher, J. (2003). *The Moralisation of Tourism*. London: Routledge.
   A thought-provoking book on how various forms of tourism may be categorized and stereotyped.
2 Ryan, C. (2003). *Recreational Tourism*. Clevedon: Channel View Publications.
   A good introduction to leisure tourism.

3 Plog, S.C. (2001). Why destination areas rise and fall in popularity: an update of a cornell quarterly classic. *Cornell Hotel and Restaurant Administration Quarterly* 42(3), 13–24.
   This update of a highly cited work on tourism psychographics outlines the interrelationships between market and destination.

4 Pearce, P.L. (2005). *Tourist Behaviour: Themes and Conceptual Issues*. Clevedon: Channelview Press.
   Provides a good overview of contemporary understandings of tourism behaviour including the concept of travel careers.

5 Coles, T. and Timothy, D. (eds) (2004). *Tourism and Diaspora*. London: Routledge.
   A book focusing on the role of transnational networks as a factor in influencing tourism flows.

6 Hall, C.M. and Williams, A.M. (eds) (2002). *Tourism and Migration: New Relationships Between Production and Consumption*. Dordrecht: Kluwer Academic Publishers.
   A collection that examines the influence of migration on tourism flows.

7 Decrop. A. (2006). *Vacation Decision Making*. Wallingford: CABI Publishing.
   This book provides a useful overview of decision-making processes with respect to leisure travel.

8 Hall, C.M. and Page, S. (2006). *The Geography of Tourism and Recreation: Space, Place and Environment*, 3rd edn. London: Routledge.
   Chapter 2 provides a detailed account of issues associated with defining tourism demand and research on international and domestic tourism statistics.

9 Duval, D.T. (ed.) (2004). *Tourism in the Caribbean*. London: Routledge.
   This book has a number of chapters that examine the social, economic and environmental dimensions of mass and alternative tourism within the Caribbean context.

10 Williams, A.V. and Zelinsky, W. (1970). On some patterns in international tourist flows. *Economic Geography* 46(4), 549–567.
   Seminal article with respect to issues of inertia and change in international tourism flows.

Recommended web sites

Pacific Asia Travel Association (PATA): www.pata.org
The Virtual Tourist: http://www.virtualtourist.com/
United Nations World Tourism Organization: www.world-tourism.org
World Travel and Tourism Council: www.wttc.org

References cited

Bramwell, B. (2004). Mass tourism, diversification and sustainability in southern Europe's coastal regions. In B. Bramwell (ed.), *Coastal Mass Tourism: Diversification and Sustainable Development in Southern Europe*, pp. 1–32. Clevedon: Channel View Publications.

Burns, P. (1999). *An Introduction to Tourism and Anthropology*. London: Routledge.

Buswell, R. (1996). Tourism in the Balearic Islands. In M. Barke, J. Towner and M. Newton (eds), *Tourism in Spain: Critical Issues*. Wallingford: CABI Publishing.

Butcher, J. (2003). *The Moralisation of Tourism*. London: Routledge.

Clarke, J. (1997). A framework of approaches to sustainable tourism. *Journal of Sustainable Tourism* 5(3), 224–233.

Cohen, E. (1972). Towards a sociology of international tourism. *Social Research* 39, 164–182.

Coles, T. and Timothy, D. (eds) (2004). *Tourism and Diaspora*. London: Routledge.

Coles, T., Hall, C.M. and Duval, D. (2006). Tourism and post-disciplinary inquiry. *Current Issues in Tourism* 9(4–5), 293–319.

Conway, D. (2004). Tourism, environmental conservation and management and local agriculture in the Eastern Caribbean – Is there an appropriate, sustainable future for them? In D.T. Duval (ed.), *Tourism in the Caribbean*, pp. 187–204. London: Routledge.

Dann, G. (1976). The holiday was simply fantastic. *Tourist Review* 31(3), 19–23.

Dann, G. (1977). Anomie, ego-enhancement and tourism. *Annals of Tourism Research* 4, 184–194.

Decrop, A. (2006). *Vacation Decision Making*. Wallingford: CABI Publishing.

Derrett, R. (2001). Special interest tourism: starting with the individual. In N. Douglas, N. Douglas and R. Derrett (eds), *Special Interest Tourism*, pp. 1–24. Brisbane: Wiley.

Duval, D.T. (2004). Trends and circumstances in Caribbean tourism. In D.T. Duval (ed.), *Tourism in the Caribbean*, pp. 3–22. London: Routledge.

Eadington, W.R. and Smith, V.S. (1992). Introduction: the emergence of alternative forms of tourism. In V.L. Smith and W.R. Eadington (eds), *Tourism Alternatives: Potentials and Problems in the Development of Tourism*, pp. 1–12. Philadelphia, PA: University of Pennsylvania Press.

Edmunds, J. and Turner, B.S. (2005). Global generations: social change in the twentieth century. *British Journal of Sociology* 56(4), 559–577.

Furlough, E. (1998). Making mass vacations: tourism and consumer culture in France, 1930s to 1970s. *Comparative Studies in Society and History* 40, 247–286.

Gnoth, J. (1997). Tourism motivation and expectation formation. *Annals of Tourism Research* 24, 283–304.

Gray, H.P. (1970). *International Travel–International Trade*. Lexington, MA: Heath Lexington.

Hall, C.M. (1998). *Introduction to Tourism*. South Melbourne: Longman.

Hall, C.M. (2003). Tourism and Temporary Mobility: Circulation, Diaspora, Migration, Nomadism, Sojourning, Travel, Transport and Home. Paper presented at the *International Academy for the Study of Tourism (IAST) Conference*, 30 June–5 July, Savonlinna, Finland.

Hall, C.M. (2005a). *Tourism: Rethinking the Social Science of Mobility*. Harlow: Prentice-Hall.

Hall, C.M. (2005b). Time, space, tourism and social physics. *Tourism Recreation Research* 30(1), 93–98.

Hall, C.M. (2008). *Tourism Planning*, 2nd edn. Harlow: Prentice-Hall/Pearson Education.

Hall, C.M. and Page, S. (2006). *The Geography of Tourism and Recreation: Environment, Place and Space*, 3rd edn. London: Routledge.

Hall, C.M. and Sharples, E. (2003). The consumption of experiences or the experience of consumption? An introduction to the tourism of taste. In C.M. Hall, E. Sharples, R. Mitchell, B. Cambourne and N. Macionis (eds), *Food Tourism Around the World: Development, Management and Markets*, pp. 1–24. Oxford: Butterworth-Heinemann.

Hall, C.M. and Weiler, B. (1992). What's so special about special interest tourism? In B. Weiler and C.M. Hall (eds), *Special Interest Tourism*. London: Belhaven Press.

Hunter, C. (2002). Sustainable tourism and the touristic ecological footprint. *Environment, Development and Sustainability* 4, 7–20.

Khan, M.M. (1997). Tourism development and dependency theory: mass tourism vs. ecotourism. *Annals of Tourism Research* 24(4), 988–991.

Lanzendorf, M. (2003). Mobility biographies. A new perspective for understanding travel behaviour. Conference paper in *Moving Through the Nets: The Physical and Social Dimensions of Travel*, 10th *International Conference on Travel Behaviour Research*, 10–15 August, Lucerne.

Lew, A., Hall, C.M. and Williams, A.M. (eds) (2004). *A Companion to Tourism*. Oxford: Blackwell.

McKercher, B. and Chan, A. (2005). How special is special interest tourism? *Journal of Travel Research* 44(1), 21–31.

Mills, M. (2000). Providing space for time: the impact of temporality on life course research. *Time and Society* 9(1), 91–127.

Mittleberg, D. (1998). *Strangers in Paradise: The Israeli Kibbutz Experience*. New Brunswick: Transaction Publishers.

Mowforth, M. and Munt, I. (1998). *Tourism and Sustainability: New Tourism in the Third World*. London: Routledge.

Novelli, M. (ed.) (2005). *Niche Tourism: Contemporary Issues, Trends and Cases*. Oxford: Butterworth Heinemann.

Pearce, D.G. (1992). Alternative tourism: concepts, classifications, and questions. In V.L. Smith and W.R. Eadington (eds), *Tourism Alternatives: Potentials and Problems in the Development of Tourism*, pp. 15–30. Philadelphia, PA: University of Pennsylvania Press.

Pearce, P.L. (2005). *Tourist Behaviour: Themes and Conceptual Issues*. Clevedon: Channelview Press.

Pearce, P.L. and Lee, U. (2005). Developing the travel career approach to tourist motivation. *Journal of Travel Research* 43(3), 226–237.

Pennington-Gray, L. and Spreng, R. (2002). Analyzing changing preferences for pleasure travel with cohort analysis. *Tourism Analysis* 6(1), 1–13.

Pennington-Gray, L., Fridgen, J.D. and Stynes, D. (2003). Cohort segmentation: an application to tourism. *Leisure Sciences* 25, 341–361.

Plog, S.C. (1974). Why destination areas rise and fall in popularity. *The Cornell Hotel and Restaurant Administration Quarterly* 15(November), 13–16.

Plog, S.C. (2001). Why destination areas rise and fall in popularity: an update of a Cornell Quarterly classic. *Cornell Hotel and Restaurant Administration Quarterly* 42(3), 13–24.

Plog, S.C. (2002). The power of psychographics and the concept of venturesomeness. *Journal of Travel Research* 40(3), 244–251.

Poon, A. (1997). Global transformation: new tourism defined. In L. France (ed.), *The Earthscan Reader in Sustainable Tourism*, pp. 47–53. London: Earthscan Publications.

Ryan, C. (2003). *Recreational Tourism*. Clevedon: Channel View Publications.

Salomon, I. (1983). Life styles – a broader perspective on travel behaviour. In S. Carpenter and P. Jones (eds), *Recent Advances in Travel Demand Analysis*, pp. 290–310. Aldershot: Gower.

Shaw, G. and Williams, A.M. (2004). *Tourism and Tourism Spaces*. London: Sage.

Stamboulis, Y. and Skyannis, P. (2003). Innovation strategies and technology for experience-based tourism. *Tourism Management* 24, 35–43.

Stebbins, R.A. (1992). *Amateurs, Professionals and Serious Leisure*. Montreal: McGill-Queens University Press.

Tobler, W.R. (1970). A computer movie. *Economic Geography* 46, 234–240.

Tobler, W.R. (2004). On the first law of geography: a reply. *Annals of the Association of American Geographers* 94(2), 304–310.

Warnes, A. (1992). Migration and the life course. In A. Champion and A. Fielding (eds), *Migration Processes and Patterns, Vol. 1. Research Progress and Prospects*, pp. 175–187. London: Belhaven.

Williams, A.V. and Zelinsky, W. (1970). On some patterns in international tourist flows. *Economic Geography* 46(4), 549–567.

World Tourism Organization (WTO) (1997). *Tourism 2020 Vision*. Madrid: World Tourism Organization.

World Tourism Organization (WTO) (2001). *Tourism 2020 Vision – Global Forecasts and Profiles of Market Segments*. Madrid: World Tourism Organization.

World Tourism Organization (WTO) (2006). *International Tourist Arrivals, Tourism Market Trends, 2006 Edition – Annex*. Madrid: World Tourism Organization.

Chapter 4

Contemporary tourism marketing

Chapter objectives

After reading this chapter you will

- Be aware of the scope and definition of contemporary tourism marketing
- Be familiar with the evolution of marketing focus from goods to services
- Understand the nature and dimensions of the contemporary tourism marketing environment
- Appreciate the need for tourism market information and the role of research
- Recognize the central role of relationship marketing in contemporary tourism marketing
- Understand that technology is transforming the practice of contemporary tourism marketing
- Realize the importance of innovation and new product development (NPD) in tourism
- Be aware that corporate social responsibility (CSR) and ethics will play a growing role in contemporary tourism marketing

Introduction

This chapter introduces the dimensions of contemporary tourism marketing. The chapter outlines current thinking in terms of the scope and definition of marketing and in particular charts the shift in focus from goods to services. Driving this shift has been the recognition that tourism marketing must focus on both the tangible and intangible nature of the service. But above all it must focus on consumer needs and their involvement in the co-creation of the contemporary tourism experience and its products as we have noted in previous chapters. The chapter then outlines the dimensions of the increasingly turbulent and complex marketing environment for tourism, and concludes that particular types of organization will be best suited to success in this environment. This is a globalizing environment with demanding consumers interacting with connected knowledge-driven organizations. Finally, the chapter focuses on the contemporary tourism marketing practices that will be essential for success in this environment. These practices are research-driven market information delivering a deep knowledge of the consumer; relationship marketing focusing on the 'lifetime value (LTV)' of a continuous relationship with market actors; the imperative for innovation through new product development (NPD); the smart use of technology to build relationships with customers; and finally the evolution of tourism towards societal marketing. This involves the contemporary tourism marketer in recognition of the broader needs of society in their operations through ethical and socially responsible behaviour.

Definitions and contemporary tourism marketing approaches

Marketing as a concept is evolving quickly and interestingly for tourism, there is a growing trend to conceptualize marketing based on services rather than physical goods. There are many definitions of marketing and they all focus around the need to identify and supply customer needs. Inevitably, definitions tend to reflect the prevailing thinking of the time, with early definitions, for example, tending to stress the management of the marketing function. More recently, the focus is upon the many actors in the marketplace. Kotler et al.'s (2003) definitions are the most commonly used:

A market is

A set of actual and potential buyers who might transact with a seller. This market can be a physical or virtual space (Kotler et al. 2003: 20).

Marketing is

A social and managerial process by which individuals and groups obtain what they need and want through creating and exchanging products and value with others (Kotler et al. 2003: 12).

These definitions work well for tourism as they include the non-profit sector (such as destination marketing organizations (DMOs), but do not lose sight of the two central concepts of marketing – the concept of exchange and the imperative to supply consumer needs:

1 The concept of exchange states that exchange takes place when parties agree about a transaction and will be worse off without the exchange – it therefore creates value. Transactions are the way that tourism marketing managers calibrate exchange. Relationships in the tourism marketplace lead to exchanges and naturally have led to the concept of relationship marketing where the nurturing of the relationship is more important than single exchanges. Given the nature of tourism as a high involvement product, relationship marketing plays an important role.
2 The process of identifying and supplying consumer needs lies at the heart of tourism marketing. The marketing concept is tightly focused on delivering value to the consumer, where value is viewed as the difference in the benefits that consumer receives from the product and the costs of obtaining the product. There is an important difference here between tourism marketing and that of physical goods.

For tourism, a marketing orientation implies that an organization displays four characteristics which are as follows:

1 A dominant marketing philosophy which demonstrates an unwavering focus on the consumer and which is underpinned by research.

Table 4.1 Translating the marketing orientation into action

Task	Marketing function
Identifying consumer needs	Marketing research
Analysing marketing opportunities	Market segmentation and understanding relationships
Translating needs into products	Product planning and formulation
Determining product value in different seasons	Pricing policy and creation of value delivery
Making the product available	Distribution policy
Informing and motivating the customer	Promotion strategy and tactics

Source: Cooper et al. (2005: 583).

2 It encourages exchange and strengthens both its networks and loyalty through recognizing the importance of developing long-term relationships with customers.
3 A thought process accepting that strategic and tactical planning goes hand-in-hand and includes a tolerance of innovative thinking.
4 It demonstrates an integrated organizational structure geared to the organization's goals of delivering value to the consumer through business-to-customer and business-to-business activities.

The road to achieving these characteristics is shown in Table 4.1.

Evolution towards a services marketing approach

There are opposing views of the evolution of marketing.

Evolution by production orientation

Some authors have identified key stages of the evolution of marketing in terms of the orientation of production (see e.g. Kotler et al. 2003; Cooper et al. 2005). These stages are:

- *Production orientation*: The industrialization of tourism in the 1960s and 1970s saw a focus on making products available (beds and airline seats). This bred an inward-looking producer approach that did not need to consider the consumer.

- *Sales orientation*: Once more product was available, the emphasis switched to securing sales. The focus was on exchange rather than building a longer-term relationship, simply persuading consumers to buy rather than understanding their decision-making process.
- *Marketing orientation*: The marketing approach is driven by research to understand the consumer in a competitive marketplace. Many tourism organizations have yet to move to this stage, particularly small businesses (SMEs).
- *Societal marketing*: Here marketing is done in a way that 'maintains or improves the consumer's and society's well-being' (Kotler et al. 2003: 25). It takes into account the broader needs of society rather than just the consumer, and is exemplified by the movement towards corporate social responsibility (CSR), which is dealt with at the end of this chapter.

Evolution by marketing thought

The second approach to evolution has been pioneered by Vargo and Lusch (2004). They chart the evolution of marketing thought and show how it has swung from one extreme to the other:

1 Nineteenth century thinking viewed marketing as based on the exchange principle inherited from economics. This focuses on the unit of output and places the 'good' in the centre of the stage. When marketing is based on goods, it focuses on tangibility, embedded value and transactions.
2 A new paradigm emerged in the 1970s and 1980s that viewed services as different from goods. This contemporary thinking shifted marketing thought to a service-oriented view where the key drivers are intangibility, co-creation of value and relationship marketing.

Vargo and Lusch (2004) have articulated this second approach as the contemporary logic of marketing, and it is very helpful for contemporary tourism marketing. They state that whilst the four 'P's are a handy framework, they are in fact meaningless in an age where marketing is seen as an innovating and adaptive force and where the focus is on the continuous nature of relationships between all market actors. Their view is shared by Lovelock and Gummesson (2004) who agree that the dominant logic of marketing is reflected in an emphasis on provision of service, a theme that we stress throughout this book.

However, it is dangerous to take this trend too far. In fact, a maturing view recognizes that goods and services are both part of the marketing offering and in fact what has occurred is more of a paradigm shift away from manufacturing to a customer-centred approach. Here tourism organizations are beginning to collaborate, adapt to and learn about customer needs. As Vargo and Lusch (2004) see it, value is then defined by and co-created with the consumer rather than embedded in output. This approach to the product as the sum of services and goods has been termed 'the molecular approach' by Shostack (1977). He views products as made up of many parts, some tangible, some intangible, in other words an amalgam that is exemplified by the fragmented nature of the tourism product. This 'molecular' approach allows managers to manage the total product and to realize the synergies between parts of the amalgam.

However, we question whether contemporary tourism marketing has fully taken these ideas on board. In tourism, the very strong traditions of custom and practice, reflected in the conservative nature of the industry, mean that organizations are often a number of years behind other economic sectors in terms of their place in these evolutionary schemes. We suggest that tourism marketing remains rooted in the twentieth century and traditional approaches. In part this is due to the tradition of promoting managers up through the ranks rather than educating them, the view that tourism products somehow need a different approach, and the later adoption of technology in the sector. However, as the tourism market matures, there will be less of a place for the entrepreneur and professional marketing managers will be more in demand. The question is then whether the tourism sector has the professional and technical capacity to cope with the contemporary marketing environment.

The contemporary marketing environment for tourism

In the twenty-first century, the tourism sector operates within a turbulent environment of rapid and unpredictable change. In addition, advances in technology have led to both time compression where products are instantly available, and fundamental shifts in the way that tourism products are promoted and distributed. Overlying this is the heightened security concerns following '911', the inherent lack of loyalty in price-led tourism markets and the challenges of a knowledge-rich environment. Tourism markets are maturing and fragmenting as growth slows and competition increases. This is compounded by the paradox that much of the product in tourism is in fixed plant such as hotels or theme parks, whilst demand is fickle and unstable. This section of the chapter is structured using Day and Montgomery's (1999) four characteristics of the contemporary marketing environment:

1 demanding empowered consumers,
2 the connected knowledge economy,
3 globalizing markets,
4 adaptive organizations.

Demanding empowered customers

The contemporary tourism market is defined by the 'post-tourist' as noted in Chapter 2. They are demanding, empowered and knowledgeable travellers who understand the industry and how to take advantage of ticketing and pricing flexibility. As a result of the fragmentation of supply, technology and NPD, consumers have more choice, and more ways to purchase tourism. This group are time poor and demand on-time delivery of tourism products and services to a quality standard. As a group, they want more control, are less passive in the marketing process and effectively are the ideal group to work with in the co-creation of products.

However, their characteristics mean that traditional models of consumer behaviour and segmentation may not apply. Tourism marketers therefore must devise new ways of understanding these consumers through research, as outlined later in this chapter. The imperative of understanding the new consumer, and to working with them in the co-creation of products is clearly illustrated in the following case study.

CASE STUDY
Consumer behaviour and generation Y

Introduction

Much is written about generation Y and the fact that their attitudes, values and behaviour in the marketplace are different from preceding generations. Yet they represent the future of tourism consumption and the realities of their behaviour must be taken into account and researched. Yet there is little in-depth research on the tourism behaviour of generation Y – what for example will be the tourism behaviour of China's generation Y as they begin to travel the world? This case study outlines the consumer behaviour characteristics of generation Y and poses questions as to how this will impact on tourism marketing.

Generational marketing?

We outlined the life-course approach in Chapter 3 and a continuation of this theme is the robust debate over the usefulness of using generations as market segments:

- Supporters of 'generational marketing' recognize that each generation has distinctive values and beliefs, and these influence tourism demand. Generations also experience common environmental variables such as culture, politics, media and world events in a sense socially describing a generation rather than biologically. As a result each generation has specific consumer behaviours which allow targeting in terms of products, promotion and services.
- On the other hand, Kotler et al. (2005) raise the question as to whether specific marketing approaches and campaigns need to be devised for different generations – such as baby boomers or generations X and Y (or Z). They suggest that those generations themselves represent large groups in the population, and that it is perhaps difficult to devise marketing specifically for such a large group. This is supported when we consider the definition of a generation as the years between the birth of parents and the birth of their children, tending to average around 20 years. Add to this the fact that the pace of change in technology and society will change social values immensely in 20 years, and a single marketing approach may be inadequate. To make this worse, social trends are seeing couples having children later and the generational span in some countries is approaching 30 years.

Despite this argument against generational marketing, we believe that it has an important role to play in tourism marketing. Indeed, companies that have used the same marketing messages to different generations soon found that their approach was not working. Examples here include using the same marketing messages to generation Y that they used to their parents, or simply approaching generation Y as a linear extension of generation X.

Generation Y

There is a range of definitions of generation Y. Most definitions state that generation Y are those born from 1980 to 1994 (although some definitions state that generation

Y began in the late 1970s). They have been variously labelled as the 'millennial generation', 'connexivity kids', or the 'dot-com generation', but generation Y is now the accepted label for this demographic cohort.

The consumer behaviour of generation Y

Generation Y have been born into a period dominated by technology, the ability to be permanently connected to friends and peers through mobile phones and to the Internet using wireless, voice over Internet Protocol (VOIP) and mobile technology. The media, particularly broadband Internet and television, are important to this group in terms of reality TV and the spontaneous availability of programming. Digital convergence will heighten generation Y's abilities to treat new technologies as their own. This allows them to be consistently in touch, communicate and to join global networks – whether with friends on mobile phone networks, or in community web sites such as Myspace.com. They are also the most formally educated generation in history, aware of opportunities, world geography and tourism destinations.

Generation Y intuitively understand the importance of networks and how to leverage from them. They tire of well-known brands quickly and they enjoy finding adverts in other media, such as the Internet, rather than in the usual press and television placement. In terms of promotion, they respond more to humour, irony and honesty rather than the messages of their parent's generation where tourism brands pushed lifestyle and image.

For tourism, this means that successful tourism products and destinations must 'connect' with these consumers. It is less important to build products *for* them, but to build products *with* them in the classic model of co-creation. Generation Y recognize that knowledge is power and have a new language rooted in the digital age. This implies that marketing must use this language and provide truthful and comprehensive information. To summarize, generation Y are

- interested in experiences;
- opportunity focused;
- strongly influenced by their friends and peers;
- influenced by viral marketing and word of mouth;
- technologically literate;
- short-term-focused;
- not only brand loyal, but also respond to campaigns focused on local values;
- supportive of consensus and collaboration;
- concerned to achieve a work/life balance;
- concerned to be connected;

- strongly opinionated on social and ethical marketing issues and supportive of causes such as fair trade and volunteering;
- loyal to parents, friends and peers (indeed co-purchasing with parents is common);
- practical in their worldview.

As a target market for tourism, generation Y are racially more diverse than previous target markets such as the baby boomers. For example, Demoor and Zhang (2006) have done a groundbreaking study of generation Y in China. They see this generation as more aggressive and rebellious than previous generations, looking to enjoy life and to spend money. They are creative, and follow fashionable products, displaying the generational characteristic of low brand loyalty. This has important implications for countries marketing into China for the outbound market that is predicted to dominate world tourism flows in the first 20 years of this century.

Key sources

Demoor, P. and Zhang, W. (2006). China's Y generation. *Orion Journal of International Hotel Management* 2(1), 13–17.
Kotler, P., Bowen, J. and Makens, J. (2003). *Marketing for Hospitality and Tourism*. New Jersey: Prentice Hall.

Discussion questions

1 Taking the characteristics of generation Y outlined in this case study, what strategies would you use to market a destination to this group?
2 List the pros and cons of taking a generational approach to tourism marketing.
3 Generation Y are characterized by their use of connections and technology – how can this be used to attract them to tourism products?

Globalizing markets

Whilst tourism has always been an *international industry*, it has not necessarily demonstrated the characteristics of a *global industry*. These include the growth of large multinational firms, the movement of resources across borders and the increasing permeability of borders as we enter a 'borderless world'. Globalization is seeing distinct national tourism markets blurring to become globally linked markets, fuelled by homogenization of customer needs and low transport costs.

The tourism market in Asia is a good example here. Globalization imparts two opposing forces on the contemporary tourism market environment:

1 Homogenization of consumer preferences with communication convergence and the mass marketing of brands and lifestyles.
2 Fragmentation as mass markets break into molecular markets with smaller and smaller segments.

The connected knowledge economy

The contemporary tourism marketing environment is characterized by inter-organizational networks in both tourism value chains and destinations. This emphasizes the importance of collaboration between marketing organizations and the need to form alliances and partnerships. More than most economic sectors, delivering the tourism product involves the development of formal and informal collaboration, partnerships and networks. In both the value chain, and destinations, loosely articulated groups of independent suppliers link together to deliver the overall product. These networks of cooperative and competitive linkages are used to exchange knowledge and resources for competitive advantage. However, the growth of alliances, particularly cross-border alliances, does mean that markets are blurring within tourism and across other industries (such as technology) and as a result competitors in the tourism marketplace are emerging from unlikely sources – technology-driven companies such as Travelocity are a good example here. Finally, these organizations are becoming learning organizations. Using technology, they can remember consumers and their responses, learning more and more with each interaction. They make decisions based more upon facts than conjecture and are developing databases capturing market structure, market responses and market economics.

Adaptive organizations

A particular type of organization is required to succeed in this contemporary tourism marketing environment. Here Achrol (1991) foresaw success in this environment based on organizations that act on the basis of coalitions and exchange, and are ambidextrous and highly flexible to cope with complex and dynamic task environments. He sees these organizations as hubs of complex networks with boundary-spanning management, in many respects these organizations have strong analogies with destinations. Achrol's (1991) organizations are of two types:

1 *Market exchange companies*: These are organized around consumers and markets – effectively a grand marketing information system, brokering and clearing information, consumer needs, products and marketing services. Environmental scanning and adaptive mechanisms are driven by both the consumers and the market. The quality of its market information network will be the primary source of coordinating power. Many DMOs operate in this way.
2 *Marketing coalition companies*: These adapt to the turbulent environment by developing many different forms of functionally specialized organizations, working within alliances. Each organization is adapted to particular circumstances and is exemplified by specialist tour operators who can draw upon different elements of supply at different times to customize their product.

Both these types of organization will need to be directly wired into the pulse of their markets, and they will be flexible to react to market signals with customization and speed. This will require flat organizations that are dependent on the skills and competencies of their employees. Whilst this is still an unusual format for many tourism organizations, it will become the model for the future, based on networks, knowledge and flexibility.

The practice of contemporary tourism marketing

Given the characteristics of the contemporary tourism marketing environment, what are the key techniques and approaches that tourism marketers need to utilize in the twenty-first century? The final section of this chapter examines five of these approaches:

1 Research-driven tourism market information.
2 Relationship marketing.
3 The use of technology.
4 New tourism product development.
5 CSR and marketing ethics.

Research-driven tourism market information

Developing a tourism marketing information system – or knowledge management (KM) approach – is vital, yet unusual, for most tourism organizations. Such a system involves assessing information needs, and then developing and seeking that information to both underpin decisions and to meet strategic priorities. There is a variety of sources of market information available to the tourism marketer including:

- Internal records such as guest histories, comment cards or staff debriefs.
- External sources of market intelligence such as competitor information. In tourism much information on competitors and the composition of their products is readily and easily available through brochures and Internet sites. Increasingly, because of the explosion of information, tourism organizations are placing more emphasis on market intelligence, often from secondary sources, rather than engaging in the expensive exercise of primary data collection.
- Deep and meaningful research is the key to understanding the contemporary tourism consumer and their needs in tourism. This informs the marketer when and how to intervene in the purchasing decision process. Marketing research is therefore a key element in the total field of market information. It links the consumer with the marketer through information that is used to
  - identify and define marketing opportunities and problems;
  - generate, refine and evaluate marketing actions;
  - improve understanding of marketing as a process;
  - show how specific marketing activities can be made more effective (ESOMAR 1995: 4).

Marketing research rather than market research is relatively new in tourism compared to other economic sectors. In tourism, research on consumer behaviour is not well developed and research is not testing models. There are two reasons for this:

1 Tourism itself is a difficult activity to research. Not only is the purchase highly involving and with an emotional element, but also tourism is an ephemeral activity demanding sampling of a highly mobile population. This means that tourists may be interviewed about their holiday many weeks or months after the event. In addition, the location of tourism research is often noisy – in crowded airports or

other tourism venues. The travel decision-making process is also complex and difficult to isolate for research purposes and of course, domestic tourism is more difficult to measure than international travel as no national border is crossed. To compound these problems, there remains debate about definitions of tourism, the scope of the sector itself and the categories that should be used in research questions (such as for age) as we noted in Chapter 1.

2 Another reason for the research-averse nature of the tourism sector is due to the fact that the tourism sector has not felt the need for deep and meaningful tourism marketing research until recently. We must remember that most tourism organizations are SMEs with a lack of resources and formal training to engage in research. Not only is good marketing research expensive, it is often poorly managed in tourism organizations. The key here is the reporting process and the legibility of the information delivered to managers. In tourism this remains a huge problem, as often the reports of researchers have not been tailored for their audience, or the research is reported to an inappropriate part of the organization. This is often due to a lack of understanding of the research needs of differing areas of management activity (Ritchie 1994).

Nonetheless, continuous research is integral to the marketing information system of contemporary tourism organizations. It delivers competitiveness and profitability and is used for two main purposes.

Firstly, it is used to understand the following aspects of consumer behaviour:

- Market analysis and forecasting – market volumes, shares and revenues.
- Consumer research for segmentation and positioning – the quantitative measurement of customer profiles, awareness and purchasing habits; and the qualitative measurement of attitudes and perceptions of the tourism organization and its products.
- Service quality research to monitor service standards and satisfaction.

Secondly, it is used to underpin decisions on new products and new product opportunities:

- Product and price studies: product formulation, pricing, consumer testing and price sensitivity analysis.
- Investment analysis for new products.

- Promotions and sales research: efficiency of communication and consumer reaction to sales and advertising.
- Distribution research: distributor awareness of products.
- Evaluation and performance monitoring: for marketing control.

The future of research-driven market information

There are a variety of future trends evident in the world of tourism research. Firstly, is the need for a deeper understanding of the contemporary tourist. Here, Swarbrooke and Horner (2004) recommend a 10-point research agenda to understand tourism consumer behaviour. They say that research should

1 focus on tourism purchase decisions;
2 focus on perceptions of destinations and products;
3 improve the use of qualitative research;
4 understand tourists' perception of quality and their satisfaction with tourism experiences;
5 develop longitudinal research to allow temporal comparisons;
6 ensure that market segmentation techniques are research-led;
7 research tourists' evaluation of competing products;
8 research reasons for non-purchase;
9 research cultural and geographical differences in tourism behaviour;
10 explore the linkages between tourism consumer behaviour models and those in other sectors of the economy.

Secondly, tourism marketing would benefit from an effective KM approach to tourism research. This will ensure that academic, private sector and government research is used to assemble a knowledge bank of complementary sources and research projects focusing on understanding Swarbrooke and Horner's 10 priority areas.

Thirdly, tourism marketing research is drawing more upon qualitative techniques such as focus groups, critical incident research and Delphi surveys. These techniques are used to develop, screen and position products; and to understand the consumer and their use of products. There is also a greater use of secondary sources as the public sector is increasingly called upon to provide data from large tourism surveys in a form that allows re-analysis.

Fourthly, technology is radically changing tourism research through the ability of computers to cope with complex data analysis and complex consumer-behaviour choice sets. Also, the Internet and email offer a dramatic new channel for collecting and disseminating market information. This does, however, raise ethical and technical issues and has led to the development of new codes of conduct and concern for the ethical responsibilities of researchers (see e.g. ESOMAR 1995). Web-based surveys can be combined with easy-to-use survey analysis packages to allow tourism organizations to bypass commercial research companies. This delivers cost savings as well as more tailored research and reporting.

Relationship marketing

A key strategy in the marketing approach of Vargo and Lusch (2004) is to build relationships across the marketing networks of an organization. For tourism marketers, relationship marketing plays an increasingly important role both with other organizations and with businesses. Kotler et al. (2003) define relationship marketing as 'creating, maintaining and enhancing strong relationships with customers' (p. 390).

Relationship marketing differs from transactional marketing because it

- takes a longer-term view;
- emphasizes the relationship not the transaction;
- focuses on trust, partnership and research into the characteristics of the customers.

Relationship marketing is ideally suited to the new marketing paradigm and to tourism. It is suited to tourism as the customer controls the selection of the supplier, brand switching is common and word of mouth is a powerful promotional medium. It also recognizes that tourism organizations should work towards building the LTV of a relationship. This allows organizations to build 'customer equity', representing the sum of the LTVs of the organization's customers. As a result, one of the keys to success is the judicious identification of customer groups. Other keys to success are that tourism organizations must recognize that regular customers are not always profitable, instead relationship building will engender true loyalty. In turn this will deliver organizational growth and profitability for the organization because customer acquisition costs are reduced. As Kotler et al. (2003) state, customer satisfaction is a pre-requisite for loyalty, which can be built through relationship marketing. Classic 'customer binding' approaches that are used in tourism include:

1 Financial incentives such as frequent flier programmes, frequent guest schemes and car rental preferred customers.

2 Social benefits such as providing a personal shopper or a key executive who is applied to the customer.
3 Building structural ties such as reservation systems locked into particular suppliers or customers.

The success of relationship marketing can be measured through customer retention rates, or satisfaction surveys and recommendation rates – indeed customer relationship research is a growth sector in the research industry.

Fyall et al. (2003) note that relationship marketing for destinations can be viewed as given below:

1 A tactical promotional activity often tied to databases.
2 A strategic tool used to retain customers and lock them into particular products and brands.
3 A fundamental business philosophy leading to genuine customer involvement and co-creation. The philosophy is to establish, build and maintain successful life-long relationships with customers.

However, they also note that it is more difficult to apply relationship marketing to destinations, due partly to the nature of the destination product, but also the fact that to be successful it requires destination-level cooperation.

The use of technology

The Internet influences every aspect of the contemporary tourism business and has changed the culture and behaviour of how people purchase, search and communicate. It connects companies, customers and governments at low cost and without constraints of time or space and as such is a paradigm-breaking marketing tool. This is because it has significant advantages over traditional communication media; advantages such as reach, low cost, richness, speed of communication and interactivity.

As technology develops, it is having a profound impact upon how marketing is practiced. Indeed, technology facilitates many of the processes that are needed in the new marketing paradigm of relationship building and co-creation. These include communication with customers, interactivity, tools for research, massive data storage and the ability to build, track and maintain relationships.

Technology has created a whole new marketing industry – e-marketing, which can be defined as the promotion of a tourism product, company service or web site on-line and can include a variety of activities from on-line advertising to search engine optimization. It is also provides a medium and delivery mechanism for consumers to gather information and to make purchasing decisions.

E-marketing is ideally suited to tourism. It allows the development of on-line brochures that can deliver rich multimedia content, blending text, images, sound and video into multimedia documents to overcome the intangible nature of the product. Through video and interactivity it delivers the ability to 'test drive' the product. It also gives tourism organizations the ability to instantly change dates, prices and availability on-line so saving expensive brochure reprints. Technology also allows organizations to individually target customers through 'narrow casting' to customize messages, utilize email and web links to engage in 'viral marketing' and of course, the Internet gives SMEs and destinations a degree of global market reach previously unheard of.

E-marketing in tourism aims to generate traffic to an organization's web site, to engage the customer and to convert that traffic into sales. There is a range of mechanisms for closely engaging with the consumer through e-marketing and for tracking use of the web site. This includes how often they visit, for how long and which pages are browsed.

E-marketing involves three key principles (Nova Scotia Tourism Partnership Council 2003):

1 Generate traffic to the web site.
2 Engage the customer on the site.
3 Convert the visit to a booking or sale.

Generating traffic

Both new and returning customers will visit a tourism organization's web site. They may be attracted through traditional media or directed by other on-line marketing activities.

Engaging the customer

Good e-marketing provides content and links to add value to customers and so begins the process of interacting with them. It ensures that the customer uses the site and therefore the site must be as intuitive and useful as possible. This can be measured by the time they spend on the site, on-line feedback and viral marketing through the links they follow.

Conversion

Conversion is the measurable output of on-line marketing and can be measured by the number of links followed, a boost in awareness of a destination or actual bookings/sales. This can be tracked using research.

A major impact of technology has been upon the tourism distribution channel. Liu (2000) notes that electronic distribution has a number of advantages:

- Drastic cost reduction achieved through the electronic processing of bookings (such as e-tickets and electronic confirmations) and other transactions.
- Automation reducing labour costs and office space.
- Direct and personal links to the customer.
- It encourages customer-driven distribution through blogs and web sites (such as Mytripadvisor.com).

Of course, electronic distribution has decimated traditional intermediaries such as 'bricks and mortar travel agents'. Tour operators on the other hand, are reinventing themselves with the ability to flexibly package the product and to deal directly with their customers. This shows that electronic distribution works well for tourism where the product is fragmented and web portals allow companies to provide and deliver a dynamic assembly of all of the elements of the product (Travelocity and Expedia are good examples here). Buhalis (2003) suggests that in the future tour operators will fall into two distinct groups:

1 Multinational, large and vertically integrated operators with economies of scale, wide distribution and a global network, taking a high volume, low profit approach.
2 Small, niche differentiated operators focusing on particular destinations or products, taking a low volume, high profit approach.

Despite the obvious advantages of its use, technology does bring with it certain constraints when used in marketing. For example, there are concerns over the security of financial information and personal identity. Most web sites are in English so creating a barrier to access, and in some countries access to the Internet comes at a high cost. In the future the limits to this technology will be economic, in terms of investment; human, in terms of attitude and habits; and technological, in terms of computing power, storage and bandwidth.

In the future, digital convergence will provide overlapping and ubiquitous use of computer systems with other devices such as entertainment systems, phones, PDAs, MP3 players and other devices. For tourism, one of the most exciting marketing potential is the use of mobile devices to deliver marketing messages and information.

New tourism product development

An imperative for contemporary tourism marketing is innovation through NPD. Changing tastes, technology and heightened competition mean that NPD in tourism is vital. As products and destinations progress through the life cycle, they need to be continuously refreshed and revitalized. Moutinho (1994) states that new products are the lifeblood of tourism organizations, delivering increased revenue, competitiveness and facilitating market positioning, diversification and growth. Failure to innovate risks failing to meet consumer demands, engage with new technology and keep up with the competition. In the contemporary tourism marketing environment there are two key competitive pressures driving innovation:

1 Increased competition, market complexity and differentiation.
2 Decreased lead times and shorter life cycles.

Hodgson (1990) states that tourism has a number of distinctive characteristics that need to be considered when developing new products. As a result, the classic processes and stages of NPD are not always appropriate. The distinctive characteristics of tourism are given below:

1 Government regulation of products such as air routes and fares. This takes marketing decisions away from the tourism organization.
2 Public ownership and control of tourism resources means that many destinations and organizations are not purely commercially focused.
3 The inward-looking nature of many companies and organization acts as a constraint upon NPD.

4 The intangible nature of the tourism product means it is difficult to test and communicate, but easy to copy.

5 Many tourism organizations are research averse and do not have sufficient knowledge for NPD, nor the ability to monitor the success of the NPD process.

This means that for many tourism products the classic step-wise model of NPD is better replaced with the stage-gate process. The stage-gate process places a stronger element of risk control at each development stage and is increasingly preferred by practitioners (Figure 4.1). The advantages of the stage-gate process are that it allows a decision to be taken at each stage, it has a smaller number of stages than the classic step-wise model, and it is more suitable for the contemporary marketing approach because it can easily cross organizational boundaries of say finance and marketing.

An important consideration for NPD in tourism is the organization's ability to integrate the NPD process and outcome with the organization's existing products and marketing strategy. NPD also must consider the new product and its market placement. This will depend on:

1 *Product newness*: There is a range from completely new to supplements of existing products – the newer the product, the greater the unfamiliarity with the consumer and so the greater the risk of development (Table 4.2). In tourism there are few truly new products that demand a completely new marketing campaign. Indeed, because many tourism organizations follow a risk-averse path, real product innovation often comes from outside the tourism sector itself.

2 *Product complexity*: Complexity is measured by technology, number of product elements, functions and interfaces with customers and suppliers.

3 *Commercial constraints*: These include investment available for NPD, consumer pressure for 'green' products and legislation. In tourism, new products often have greater capacity. The new generation of Boeing and Airbus aircraft will require high levels of demand for viability.

As a result of these pressures, Moutinho (1994) notes that many new products in tourism fail due to

● poor assessment of consumer demand,
● poor assessment of the competition,

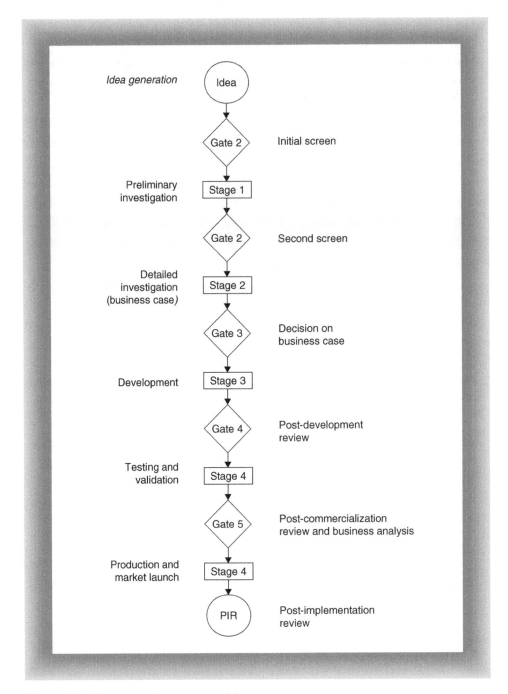

Figure 4.1 The stage-gate process model

Table 4.2   Degrees of product 'newness'

Definition of new product	Degree of 'newness'
New to the world	Entirely new
New product lines	New market entry
Additional lines	Supplements
Product improvements	Additional 'value'
Product re-positioning	Into new markets
Product cost reductions	For same performance

- poor planning and integration of the product into the organization,
- poor positioning of the new product,
- lack of resources to implement to NPD.

Up until this point we have discussed new 'products' rather than new 'services'. Here the question is whether 'new services development' is the same as 'new product development' or whether the processes are different. Of course there are similarities. For example, just as with products there are degrees of 'newness' of services. It is often more efficient to redesign services to freshen and more efficiently serve customers than to jettison and start again (see Berry and Lampo 2000). Nonetheless, we suggest that the two processes are different because new service development tends not to need large amounts of capital, but imitation and competition are more intense, demanding a speedier development process (Table 4.3). Finally, new service development suffers from the inherent conservatism of the sector and the fact that there is no tradition of new service design. For example when designing new tourism services, organizations:

1 tend not to use customers or customer information;
2 view the brand as less important;
3 are more likely to involve senior personnel;
4 develop a more formal process that requires greater organizational integration.

Corporate social responsibility and marketing ethics

Corporate social responsibility

At the beginning of this chapter we identified an evolution of marketing towards 'societal marketing' which takes into account the broader needs of society rather

Table 4.3 A framework for service redesign

Service redesign concept	Potential customer benefits	Potential company benefits	Challenges/limitations
Self-service: Customer assumes role of producer	Increases perception of control and speed of service; improves access; saves money	Lowers cost; increases productivity; enhances technology reputation; differentiates company	Requires customer preparation for the role; limits face-to-face interaction between customer and company; creates difficulty in obtaining customer feedback and establishing customer loyalty/ relationships
Direct service: Service delivered to customer's location	Increases convenience; improves access	Eliminates store location limitations; expands customer base; differentiates company	Creates additional logistical burdens; may require costly investment; requires credibility/trust
Pre-service: Streamlines activation of service	Increases speed of service; improves efficiency; shifts task from customer to service provider; separates service activation from delivery; customizes service	Increases ability to customize service; improves efficiency; increases productivity; differentiates company	Requires extra customer education and employee training to implement smoothly and effectively
Bundled service: Combines multiple services into a package	Increases convenience; customizes service	Creates opportunity to charge higher prices; differentiates company; aids customer retention; increases per-capita service use	Requires extensive knowledge of targeted customers; may be perceived as wasteful
Physical service: Manipulates the tangibles associated with the service	Increases convenience; enhances function; cultivates interest	Differentiates company; improves employee satisfaction; increases productivity	Can be easily imitated; requires expense to effect and maintain; raises customer expectation for the industry

Source: Berry and Lampo (2000: 267).

than just the consumer. This is exemplified by the movement towards CSR. CSR is growing in profile in the tourism sector and has tended to be driven by consumers and group pressure, rather than by tourism marketers. It represents a shift of marketing focus from an over-emphasis on profitable products and the consumer towards conducting business in the interests of the society in which an organization is based. The following case study demonstrates an international initiative making considerable progress towards CSR in the supply chain.

CASE STUDY
The tour operators' initiative

Introduction

CSR adds a new layer to the bottom line of tourism companies. Companies recognize that they must be accountable for their impacts upon the society, the environment and the economy. CSR is about customer satisfaction, looking after the workforce and environmental protection. For most tourism organizations, CSR is not yet part of their core business but there are efforts to integrate CSR throughout the supply chain.

Until recently, the tourism supply chain was a combat zone with members vying for dominance. Not only was this an issue between companies, such as say accommodation providers and tour operators, but it was also an issue between tour operators and destinations themselves, with operators often seeing destinations as an asset to strip. A number of new initiatives have been taken to change these practices, and in the tour operator sector in particular there are a range of approaches to secure ethical behaviour along the supply chain. In addition there are moves to instil a sense of corporate responsibility for partners and destinations in the supply chain, particularly in terms of sustainability. Indeed, it can be argued that the supply chain is the perfect medium to communicate these messages to suppliers and integrate them into contracting practices. This case study outlines one such initiative.

The tour operators' initiative

The tour operators' initiative (TOI) was established in 2000 to catalyse action in the tour operation sector. The TOI aims to integrate sustainability into business practices and work to promote and disseminate methods and practices compatible with sustainable development. The TOI is a voluntary, non-profit organization open to all tour operators regardless of size. The initiative has the support of the United Nations Environment Programme (UNEP), United Nations Educational Scientific and Cultural Organization (UNESCO) and the United Nations World Tourism Organization (UNWTO). Their mission is:

> We are tour operators concerned about the impact of our tours and activities. We recognise our responsibility to develop and operate in a manner that makes a positive contribution to the natural, social and cultural environment. We also recognise and accept our responsibility to operate in ways that reduce environmental impacts, benefit host communities, safeguard the livelihood of local people, and ensure the protection of destinations for future generations (TOI 2003: 11).

The initiative recognizes that suppliers and destinations are the core of a tour operator's product and that if those elements of the product are sustainable, with clean and pristine environments, then consumers will respond positively to their product. The approach has led to a range of benefits:

- Cost savings through efficient and reduced consumption of water and power.
- Increased revenues and shareholder value.
- Repeat custom and new business from clients who value a responsible tourism approach.
- Closer community relationships.
- A better image and reputation for tour operators.
- Enhanced brand values.
- Reduced risk of conflict with destination, governments and pressure groups.

As intermediaries, tour operators are unusual because unlike many other economic sectors, they directly influence the consumer's purchasing decision. They also have a major impact in the supply chain through supplier contracting (of say airline seats or hotel beds). It is this unique nature of the tourism supply chain that allows it to be such an important medium for the dissemination of good practice. The TOI has four key values:

1 Recognition of the importance of collaboration over competition in the supply chain.
2 A sustainable supply chain policy and management system.
3 Support for suppliers in reaching sustainability goals.
4 Integration of sustainability into supplier contracts.

The TOI approach

The TOI utilizes six elements in its approach:

1 *Product management and development*: selecting services and destinations taking into account their effects on the environment and society. This involves planning tours and itineraries that minimize negative impacts.
2 *Supply chain management*: selecting and contracting suppliers on the basis of their environmental and social performance and writing this into service agreements.
3 *Customer relationships*: raising client's awareness of responsible travel.
4 *Cooperation with destinations*: establishing long-term partnerships with destinations in terms of conservation.
5 *Sustainability reporting*: forty-seven indicators have been developed to measure tour operators' performance in the environmental, economic and social impacts of the total life cycle of their business operations. For example, in terms of product management, a measure would be the use of the train over the plane for transportation.
6 *Internal operations*: focusing on staff training, workforce conditions, office supplies and production of printed materials.

Response to these initiatives varies across the sector and are summarized in a published set of case studies (TOI 2003).

Key sources

The Tour Operators Initiative (TOI) (2003). *Sustainable Tourism: The Tour Operators' Contribution*. Paris: TOI.

Discussion questions

1 Why has this change in thinking amongst tour operators taken so long to emerge?
2 Draft the elements of sustainable practices that you might expect to see in a contract between a tour operator and a hotel supplier.
3 There are clear benefits for the tour operator in marketing their CSR to clients – what messages would form the basis of this promotion?

Marketing ethics

For a tourism organization, ethical values are the core beliefs and standards of that organization. Perhaps the best-known set of values is the global code of ethics for tourism developed by the UNWTO (WTO 2001). Ethics can relate to a variety of tourism issues such as the impact of tourism on the environment, cultures and communities; the marketing of fast food; the invasion of privacy through telemarketing or viral marketing; or the social impact of marketing alcohol.

An ethical approach to the tourism marketplace may be cynically used to pre-empt the development of legislation applying to say, responsible gambling. However, there is no doubt that the ethical tourism marketplace also attracts particular groups of consumers. Goodwin (2003) notes the growth of the ethical purchasing of tourism with an ethical purchasing index which calibrates the ethical marketplace.

Fennell (2006) questions how easy it is for tourism organizations to market to the ethical tourist. He asks whether ethical holidays are just a ploy to increase the margins for certain target market groups and to exploit a trend in society. Often, the host community is closely involved in these ethically acceptable tours, but may in fact be exploited or, as in the case of the Tasmanian experience strategy case in Chapter 2, they are simply treated as the cast on the destination stage set. In other words, the ethical tourism marketplace can be used cynically to gain competitive advantage.

Chapter overview

This chapter began by conceptualizing tourism marketing as involving exchange and a focus on the consumer. In terms of exchange, the contemporary approach demands a continuous relationship with marketing actors and has led to the development of relationship marketing and the notion of co-creation of products and experiences with the consumer. This leads to the consumer focus. Over time, marketing theory has changed from a focus on output in the form of physical goods, to the idea of services where the drivers are the co-creation of value and the building of relationships with market actors through relationship marketing. For tourism marketers these new approaches are performed in a turbulent and complex global environment. This environment is characterized by empowered, demanding consumers, who are showing generational shifts in need and wants, as outlined by the case study on generation Y. Suppliers in this environment are increasingly networked and knowledge driven, leading to a particular type of flexible, loosely structured organization that is emerging as a way to compete in this contemporary tourism marketing environment.

The chapter closed by considering five key contemporary marketing practices. In the knowledge economy, no organization can afford to ignore market information and not have a deep and meaningful understanding of their consumers. Tourism does not have a glowing record in this regard. In turn this market information fuels the practice of relationship marketing where the LTV of the relationship is viewed as more important than individual transactions. Of course, technology, both computing power and the Internet, has facilitated both of these practices and will continue to pervade contemporary tourism marketing as e-marketing matures into its own science. The chapter outlined the imperative of innovation and NPD and the need to carefully structure and integrate that process into the organization. Finally, we illustrated the growth of ethical marketing and the role of CSR, demonstrating this through a case study of CSR in the tourism supply chain.

Self-review questions

1 List the actors in the tourism marketplace and classify their roles in the market.
2 How might companies engineer 'co-creation' of tourism products and experiences?
3 Debate the notion that tourism lags behind other economic sectors in its marketing thinking and approach.
4 Identify the factors that have changed the contemporary marketing environment since 1980.
5 Why is the knowledge economy so significant for contemporary tourism marketing?
6 Draft an approach for a museum to collect market information about their customers without resorting to primary data collection.
7 What do you understand by the term 'LTV'?
8 Why is the Internet so well suited to contemporary tourism marketing?
9 Is there a difference between new product development and new service development?
10 What do you understand by the term 'CSR' in respect of contemporary tourism marketing?

Recommended reading

1 Buhalis, D. (2003). *eTourism: Information Technology for Strategic Tourism Management*. London: Prentice Hall. A wide ranging and through review of the use and impact of technology on tourism marketing.

2 Cooper, C.P. (2006). Tourism and knowledge management. *Annals of Tourism Research* 33(1), 47–64. A review of the new science of knowledge management and its application to tourism, including marketing.

3 Fennell, D. (2006). *Tourism Ethics*. Clevedon: Channelview. Excellent overview of tourism ethics.

4 Fyall, A. and Garrod, B. (2005). *Tourism Marketing. A Collaborative Approach*. Clevedon: Channelview. Edited volume thoroughly reviewing the use and role of collaboration and partnership in tourism marketing.

5 Kotler, P., Bowen, J. and Makens, J. (2005). *Marketing for Hospitality and Tourism*, 4th edn. New Jersey: Prentice Hall. Classic marketing text re-oriented with a tourism flavour.

6 Moutinho, L. (1994). New product development. In S.F. Witt and L. Moutinho (eds), *Tourism Marketing and Management Handbook*, pp. 350–353. Hemel Hempstead: Prentice Hall. A clear and thorough review of NPD in tourism.

7 Swarbrooke, J. and Horner, S. (2004). *Consumer Behaviour in Tourism*. Oxford: Elsevier Butterworth Heinemann. Excellent review of consumer behaviour for tourism.

8 The Tour Operators Initiative (2003). *Sustainable Tourism: The Tour Operators' Contribution*. Paris: TOI. A thorough set of case studies and the principles of CSR in the supply chain.

9 Vargo, S.L. and Lusch, R.F. (2004). Evolving to a new dominant logic for marketing. *Journal of Marketing* 68(January), 1–17. Classic paper on the evolution of marketing thought towards services.

10 Zeithmal, V., Bitner, M.J. and Gremler, D. (2006). *Services Marketing. Integrating Customer Focus Across the Firm*. New York: Irwin McGraw Hill. Excellent text on services marketing.

Recommended web sites

Aboriginal Tourism & Marketing Association: www.seeaboriginaltourism.com/
Marketing Your Business – Tourism Western Australia: www.westernaustralia.com/.../Growing+your+business/How+to+Grow+Your+Business/Marketing+Your+Business.htm.
New Orleans Online: www.neworleansonline.com/
Ontario Tourism Marketing Partnership Corporation: www.tourismpartners.com/
There's more to discover in Ontario: www.ontariotravel.net/

References cited

Achrol, R.S. (1991). Evolution of the marketing organization: new forms for turbulent environments. *Journal of Marketing* 55(4), 77–94.

Berry, L.L. and Lampo, S.K. (2000). Teaching an old service new tricks. The promise of service redesign. *Journal of Service Research* 2(3), 265–275.

Buhalis, D. (2003). *eTourism: Information Technology for Strategic Tourism Management*. London: Prentice Hall.

Cooper, C., Fletcher, J., Fyall, A., Gilbert, D. and Wanhill, S. (2005). *Tourism Principles and Practice*. Harlow: Pearson.

Day, G.S. and Montgomery, D.B. (1999). Charting new directions for marketing. *Journal of Marketing* 63(Special Issue), 3–13.

Demoor, P. and Zhang, W. (2006). China's Y generation. *Orion Journal of International Hotel Management* 2(1), 13–17.

ESOMAR (1995). *ICC / ESOMAR International Code of Marketing and Social Research Practice*. Amsterdam: ESOMAR.

Fennell, D. (2006). *Tourism Ethics*. Clevedon: Channelview.

Fyall, A., Callod, C. and Edwards, B. (2003). Relationship marketing: the challenge for destinations. *Annals of Tourism Research* 30(3), 644–659.

Goodwin, H. (2003). Ethical and responsible tourism: consumer trends in the UK. *Journal of Vacation Marketing* 9(3), 271–283.

Hodgson, P. (1990). New tourism product development. Market research's role. *Tourism Management* 11(1), 2–5.

Kotler, P., Bowen, J. and Makens, J. (2003). *Marketing for Hospitality and Tourism*, 3rd edn. New Jersey: Prentice Hall.

Liu, Z. (2000). Internet tourism marketing: potential and constraints. *Paper presented at the Fourth International Conference, Tourism in South East Asia and Indo China: Development, Marketing and Sustainability*. Thailand: Chiang Mai.

Lovelock, C. and Gummesson E. (2004). Whither services marketing? In search of new paradigm and fresh perspectives. *Journal of Service Research* 7(1), 20–41.

Moutinho, L. (1994). New product development. In S.F. Witt and L. Moutinho (eds), *Tourism Marketing and Management Handbook*, pp. 350–353. Hemel Hempstead: Prentice Hall.

Nova Scotia Tourism Partnership Council (2003). *E-Marketing Strategy for Tourism*. Nova Scotia: Nova Scotia Tourism Partnership Council.

Ritchie, J.R.B. (1994). Roles of research in tourism management. In J.R.B. Ritchie and C.R. Goeldner (eds), *Travel, Tourism and Hospitality Research. A Handbook for Managers and Researchers*, pp. 13–21. New York: John Wiley.

Shostack, G.L. (1977). Breaking free from product marketing. *Journal of Marketing* 41, 73–80.

Swarbrooke, J. and Horner, S. (2004). *Consumer Behaviour in Tourism*. Oxford: Elsevier Butterworth Heinemann.

The Tour Operators Initiative (TOI) (2003). *Sustainable Tourism: The Tour Operators' Contribution*. Paris: TOI.

Vargo, S.L. and Lusch, R.F. (2004). Evolving to a new dominant logic for marketing. *Journal of Marketing* 68(January), 1–17.

World Tourism Organization (WTO) (2001). *Global Code of Ethics for Tourism*. Madrid: WTO.

Section 3
The Contemporary Tourism Destination

Chapter **5**

Delivering the contemporary tourism product: the destination

Chapter objectives

After reading this chapter you will

- Understand the core elements in the destination concept
- Be able to identify the key elements that make up 'place'
- Understand the concepts of landscape, servicescape and experiencescape
- Understand the concept of a tourism resource and its dynamic nature
- Recognize the cultural basis for tourism resources and attractions
- Identify tourism attractions as a specific type of tourism resource
- Appreciate the specific challenges facing destination management and marketing organizations with respect to controlling the destination product

Introduction: the destination concept

The notion of a destination lies at the heart of tourism. The concept that people travel from home to a destination, stay there for a limited period of time, and then return is how the phenomena of tourism is generally understood. The destination concept is one of the most important, yet also most complex, aspects of tourism. It is complex because people, including marketers and researchers, refer to destinations of different scale. For example, Metelka (1990: 46) defined a destination as the 'geographic location to which a person is traveling'; Vukonic (1997) equated the term to that of a 'resort', while Gunn (1994: 107) saw a destination as being a 'travel market area' and referred to destination zones that are geographic areas 'containing a critical mass of development that satisfies traveller objectives' (Gunn 1994: 27). Tourism destinations are therefore described at different scales ranging from the country level to regions, towns or resorts, specific sites and even specific attractions that are visited by tourists. A destination is a spatial or geographical concept that is primarily defined by visitors from outside the location although many places seek to make themselves destinations for visitors in order to be able to benefit economically from tourism. A destination therefore, by definition, comes to exist by virtue of the people that visit it. If people from outside a location do not visit a place it is not a destination. That may seem like stating the obvious, but it is actually an extremely important point because it forces us to ask: How do places become destinations? And, as a follow-up to that, what are the implications of becoming a destination?

The above two questions therefore serve as the focal point for this and the following chapters. This chapter examines how places become destinations and the elements which then make up a destination. The following chapters examine how contemporary destinations are then government, managed, planned and marketed.

From places to destinations

Three principle meanings of the idea of place can be distinguished, all of which are important to understanding the nature of contemporary destinations:

1 Location
2 Locale
3 Sense of place

Place as location

In locational terms a place is a specific point on the earth's surface. This not only means that such a location has fixed geographical coordinates so that we can find them on maps but that it helps us to place locations in relation to each other – New York is 'there', London is 'here'. Obviously, mapping locations is important for tourism but more significantly the location of where somewhere is in relation to other places will determine how relatively accessible it is and therefore its potential market for visitors.

Place as locale

This refers to place as a material or physical setting for people's daily social relations, actions and interactions. The physical aspects of places are obviously important in terms of their capacity to manage visitors as well as providing resources and attractions for tourists. Place in this sense not only refers to urban settings, such as ethnic neighbourhoods and arts and heritage precincts, but also to landscapes, servicescapes and experiencescapes (Figure 5.1).

Landscapes

Landscapes are a visual idea and refer to how a portion of the Earth's surface is seen. Importantly, in most ideas of landscape it is something the viewer is outside of, whereas place tends to be something that one is inside of. Nevertheless, landscapes are clearly an important element for the image of place to outsiders – such as tourists – which they may then want to experience or gaze upon. The experience of landscape is determined not only by the cultural background of the consumer, but also by the environmental, political and cultural processes that lead to the creation of particular landscapes.

Servicescapes

Servicescapes refer to the physical facility in which a service is delivered and in which the service provider (firm or other organization) and the customer interact, and to any material or tangible commodities that facilitate the service (Bitner 1992). The idea of servicescapes was originally primarily applied to the immediate physical environment provided by firms in which they sought to use design principles to reinforce brand as well as provide positive service encounters. However,

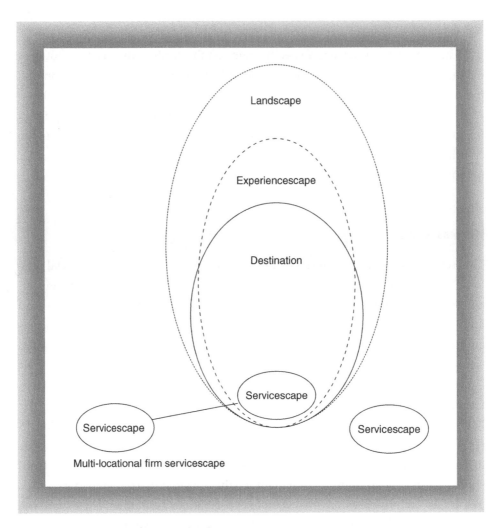

Figure 5.1 Elements of place as locale

for some businesses, particularly in the tourism industry, the servicescape of a firm is multi-locational. For example, the servicescape for an airline includes not only the aircraft, but also the gate and ticketing area for arrival and departure. In addition, for those booking direct with airlines the airline company's Internet portal represents a virtual servicescape while uniforms, food and tickets are also tangible elements of the service experience. Some firms, such as hotel and fast-food chains for example, present their servicescapes in virtually the same format no matter what the location so as to reinforce their presentation as a global brand. However, in order to appeal to local markets marginal changes may be made in design and presentation so as to appeal to local consumers. For example, the design of McDonald's restaurants has undergone significant changes around the world in recent years so that while there is still great consistency in menus and operating procedures there is greater variation in design. Nonetheless, local variation does also exist with respect to menu. For example, in Israel, several outlets serve Big Macs without cheese so as to permit the separation of meat and dairy products required of kosher restaurants, while in India McDonald's serve vegetable McNuggets and a mutton-based Maharaja Mac so as to meet the religious require-ments of Hindus (who do not eat beef), Muslims (who do not eat pork) and Jains (who do not eat any meat) (Watson 1997).

The servicescapes of many firms are also extremely complex environments. Resort complexes or theme parks, for example, have many design elements that ideally need to be brought together to establish a coherent servicescape for the consumer. A tourism destination is typically an amalgam of the many servicescapes of different firms and their facilities. In some cases, the landscapes within which the servicescapes of firms are embedded are also subject to the control and regulation of destination authorities in order to satisfy the perceptions of the consumer. For example, land-use regulation is used in many parts of the world to maintain rural landscapes in a particular fashion, similarly in many heritage precincts there are often restrictions on building and development, so that new structures will be architecturally sympathetic to the old. This deliberate shaping of place environ-ments to make places more appealing as destinations has become an integral com-ponent of place promotion and marketing and the development of a destination servicescape that transcends the boundaries of individual firms.

Experiencescapes

Experiencescapes are landscapes of produced experience. They are physical spaces of market production and consumption in which experiences are staged and con-sumed and are, in effect, stylized landscapes that are strategically planned and designed with market imperatives as the key design goal. According to O'Dell (2005: 16), experiencescapes 'are not only organized by producers (from place mar-keters and city planners to local private enterprises) but are also actively sought after by consumers. They are spaces of pleasure, enjoyment and entertainment . . .'. Experiencescapes serve to connect the servicescapes of different firms within a specific location. They are one of the means by which place is transformed into a destination product by virtue that experiencescapes have been consciously packaged through public-private partnerships. In one sense, the design and packaging of a place in order to produce a desired set of experiences is a logical expression of what Pine and Gilmore (1999) referred to as 'the experience economy' in which 'experiences drive the economy and therefore generate much of the base demand for goods and services' (Pine and Gilmore 1999: 65). Examples of experiencescapes include themed waterfronts and former industrial precincts, although many previously existing distinct communities may become transformed into packaged experiencescapes as a result of destination development and promotion processes. The thematic development of parts of a city for tourism and leisure purposes is an extremely common urban tourism strategy. Many cities, for example, have Chinatowns or other ethnic districts such as a 'Little Italy' or 'Little India' even though the social, political and economic processes that originally led to the creation of such ethnically distinct locations has long since past. Indeed, a major challenge in packaging destinations is not to then damage the characteristics that differentiated it from surrounding places. For example, Chang's (2000) study of Singapore's Little India Historic District suggested that its redevelopment had led to the taming of at least three dimensions of what had made the area distinctive:

1 A decline in traditional Indian-owned retail outlets and services (change in activities).
2 The transformation from a place of permanent residence into a retail attraction (change in community).
3 A dimming of its Indian cultural identity (changes in identity).

Such issues raise questions about how people experience place and this leads us to our third meaning of place.

Sense of place

This is the term that is used to refer to the subjective, personal and emotional attachments and relationships people have to a place. The notion of sense of place is usually applied in the context of people who live in a location on a permanent basis and reflects how they feel about the physical and social dimensions of their community. People might only consciously notice the unique qualities of their place when they are away from it, when it is being rapidly altered, or when it is being represented or marketed and promoted in a way they do not relate to. From this perspective, senses of place are extremely important when examining the affects of tourism development on a location as tourism-related changes may lead to changes in sense of place, possibly then leading to resentment towards tourism and even visitors. However, people can have multiple senses of places which have derived from the various places they have lived in or visited. Therefore, tourists may also develop a sense of places with respect to destinations. Perhaps the most obvious situation in which this occurs is when tourists have a second home in a location or they visit the same location on a regular basis as return visitors. In such a situation, the second home, which is often a place of relaxation, fun and social togetherness, can be regarded as more of a home than the place of 'permanent' residence, particularly when the second home has been passed down several generations of family (Hall and Müller 2004). Nevertheless, many visitors feel that they gain a sense of place when visiting tourism destinations as they experience the landscape and the people. Furthermore, some visitors may feel that they have a sense of place of a destination even before they have visited as a result of meetings with people from the location, other personal conversations, and what they have seen or heard in the media. Of course, the sense of place of a visitor to a destination may be substantially different from someone who lives there.

The resource base of tourism

From the above discussion we can see that various elements of place, some of which are purposively defined for visitor consumption, therefore act as resources for tourism. A tourist resource is that component of the environment (physical or social) which either attracts the tourist and/or provides the infrastructure necessary for the tourist experience (Hall 2007: 34). Tourism resources can be categorized as scarce (e.g. capital, labour, land) or free (e.g. climate, culture). Yet resources are an entirely subjective, relative and functional concept. What actually constitutes a tourism resource depends on the motivations, desires and interests of the consumer, and the cultural, social, economic and technological context within which those motivations occur. To repeat the frequently quoted words of Zimmermann's seminal work on resources, 'Resources are not, they become; they are not static but expand and contract in response to human wants and human actions'

(Zimmermann 1951: 15). A tourism resource therefore becomes a resource only if it is seen as having utility value, and different cultures and nationalities can have different perceptions of the tourism value of the same object. What may be a resource in one culture may be 'neutral stuff' in another. Or in other words, what may be a tourist attraction in one culture or location may not be recognized as an attraction in another. Tourism resources can therefore encompass a wide range of settings associated with different physical, topographical and climatic characteristics. For example, people from a farming area in rural New Zealand see sheep as an agricultural resource whereas for visitors from urban China or Japan they constitute a tourism resource as they see sheep as an attractive element of the landscape. Similarly, for people living in London the underground railway or 'tube' is primarily a means to commute to work although for many people from outside London taking a ride on the tube is an attraction in its own right. In other words, for those people from outside London the underground represents a tourism resource as well as a means of transport. Indeed, a challenge for many destinations is how to commodify tourism resources so that an economic return can be gained for their use. In the case of sheep in New Zealand noted above, one means has been to establish businesses that allow Chinese and Japanese tours to experience sheep directly by seeing sheep being shorn and rounded up by dogs, touch animals directly, and purchase sheep products, such as wool and lanolin, or even eat sheep.

A tourist attraction is a specific type of tourism resource. An attraction is a resource that tourists are prepared to experience for a purpose other than to support their travel, e.g. provision of accommodation, transport or other hospitality services. From this perspective a hotel in which tourists stay the night because it is convenient within the context of their overall trip is not an attraction but if the same tourists choose to stay the night in a specific hotel because of, for example, its historic associations then it is an attraction. Because attractions are a tourism resource this also means that what is attractive to one tourist may not be to another. However, some locations come to be widely regarded as attractions by virtue of the large numbers of people who visit them and have reached an 'iconic' status or because they are commercial operations. Classification of attractions is sometimes determined along the lines of:

- *Cultural or human-made*, e.g. townscapes, museums and national monuments.
- *Natural*, e.g. wilderness areas and national parks.

Yet, such a division between natural and cultural attractions is extremely problematic given that all tourism resources are inherently cultural. Indeed, a decision to set aside an area as national park is as much of a reflection of culture as it would be to farm the same area of land.

Resources are therefore inherently dynamic. New technologies or cultural appraisals can lead to the recognition of new tourism resources. For example, the development of new recreational technologies such as mountain bikes or sailboards meant that the tourism capacities of existing natural resources was considerably expanded and allowed some resort locations to overcome seasonal limitations. Indeed, natural tourism resources are often seasonal in nature. Some destinations (e.g. beach, mountain, skiing, hunting or fishing destinations) are especially seasonal because of either the nature of the main resource used by visitors or the environment in which the resource is located. Furthermore, as consumer preferences change, so does the perceived utility of particular tourism resources. For example, although the beach is seen as a primary tourism resource in many destinations, in Western societies it only became an attractive place to go swimming at the turn of the twentieth century. Few countries have sought to promote beach tourism as much as Australia, yet it only became legal to swim during the day at Manly Beach, arguably one of Sydney's main tourist attractions, in 1903. Furthermore, such sea bathing needed to be undertaken with substantial clothing on and not in mixed (i.e. male and female) company. As Archbishop Kelly commented in 1911 (*The Sun*, Sydney, 14 August 1911 in Hall 2007: 74–75):

> I think promiscuous surf-bathing is offensive in general to propriety, and a particular feature of that offensiveness is the attraction it has for idle onlookers … There is no border-line between vice and virtue. Our worst passions are but the abuse of our good ones. And I believe that the promiscuous intermingling of sexes in surf-bathing makes for the deterioration of our standard of morality … Woe betide Australia if she is going to encourage immodesty in her women.

Not only has what people wear when they go swimming changed, but also other aspects of tourism fashion. For example, until the late 1920s having a suntan was not seen as fashionable. However, in 1929 a great shift occurred in popular taste with suntans starting to be seen by many westerners as being desirable. The growth in popular media had much to do with this shift. In the northern summer of 1929 the fashion magazine Vogue featured models with a suntan for the first time as the models and the film stars of the then new Hollywood film industry had been holidaying in the South of France. At the same time as fashion setters in the film and entertainment industry started to wear a tan so was there a wider social and design movement, referred to as Art Deco, which featured houses and hotels with large windows that allowed light into rooms. In addition, the overall health benefits of sun and light came to be advocated as increasingly numbers of people worked inside factories and offices. For the first time having a tan was seen as an indication of being wealthy and having leisure time as opposed to earlier perceptions of a tan being associated with manual labouring in the outdoors. All these elements came together to make the tan desirable and those destinations and attractions where a tan could be gained also became desirable. Such a shift in fashion and cultural taste clearly had enormous implications for many locations. For example, it is hard to imagine destinations on the Mediterranean or island resorts in the Caribbean or the Pacific being as attractive as they are unless exposure to the sun is seen as relatively desirable. Indeed, the phrase 'sun, sand and surf' is often equated as a description of mass tourism destinations.

The massive shift in Western consumer tastes in the late 1920s and early 1930s with respect to the sun and the human body is one example of the implications of changes in culture affecting perceptions of what constitutes a tourism resource and therefore potential leisure attractions and destinations. Another example, which arguably had equally dramatic affects of leisure travel, was the shift that occurred in the late eighteenth and early nineteenth centuries in relation to landscape. Up until this time, mountains or wild rural landscapes were seen in Western culture as being not worthy of places to visit. Instead, the ideal landscape was regarded as being urban areas or well managed and highly designed gardens. However, with the arrival of the Romantic movement in art, literature and design in the late eighteenth century and the consequent reaction to the rapidly industrializing towns all began to change. Painting started to feature wild seas and mountain ranges often shrouded in mist. Poets, such as Wordsworth and Coleridge, also started to write of waterfalls, lakes and hill country. Such artistic reactions were highly significant as they had considerable influence on the popular taste of the upper class and the emerging and increasingly literate middle classes. Again, the implications for leisure travel in the early nineteenth century were staggering. Destinations such as Scotland, the Lake District of England, Wales, and the alpine areas of Switzerland and Austria suddenly became desirable landscapes to visit and experience whereas for most of the preceding history of European civilization they had been cast in a negative light.

The Romantic movement laid the groundwork upon which a popular appreciation of the value of wild land and nature would come to be based. For example, artistic, literary and political perceptions of the importance of contact with wild nature provided the stimulus for the creation of positive cultural attitudes towards wilderness in the United States and elsewhere and arguably laid the foundations for the creation of national parks and the development of ecotourism. In the United States, artist George Catlin called for the establishment of 'a nation's park' in 1832 to preserve the wilderness and its human and non-human inhabitants (Catlin 1968). Thoreau, in 1858, repeated these demands for preservation of wilderness 'for modesty and reverence's sake, or if only to suggest that earth has higher uses than we put her to' (cited in Nash 1982: 103). Once positive attitudes towards primitive, unordered nature had developed, the emergence of individuals and societies dedicated to the preservation of wilderness values as well as the development of a tourism industry to take people to see wild land was only a short step away. This transformation in landscape taste, as with the change in fashion with respect to having a suntan, was incredibly dramatic with enormous implications for what was perceived as a resource. Changes in taste meant that some locations that were previously avoided now became highly fashionable, and still are to the present day. Niagara Falls in the United States, the Swiss Alps and the highlands of Scotland are all locations that are now seen as significant tourist attractions and destinations to the stage where most people do not even realize that their value as a tourism resource was contingent on changed in landscape preferences. These examples are important as they highlight the cultural base of resources for tourism. Different cultures will have different understandings of what is a tourism resource and therefore what constitutes a tourist attraction. Just as significantly we must recognize that even within cultures changes occur and therefore perceptions of resources will also change.

Perceptions of resources change as a result in shifts in cultural taste. However, the attractiveness of locations will also be affected by more short-term factors such as perceptions of how safe a destination is or the extent to which resources exist following a natural disaster. Because perceptions determine understanding of resources so it becomes important to understand that there are often significant differences between reality and how potential tourists understand a destination or attraction. Therefore, the media play a critical role in influencing tourist understandings of place not only through formal travel programmes and documentaries, but also through general news stories and coverage as well as film and television entertainment.

Some destinations deliberately seek to utilize film and media as a way of positioning their destination through certain images (see Chapter 9 for a more detailed account of destination marketing). For example, Tourism New Zealand extensively assisted in the promotion of the film trilogy *Lord of the Rings* and promoted itself as 'Middle Earth' in much of its publicity in an effort to reinforce New Zealand's natural images. Jay Carr of the Boston Globe was quoted on the front page of the New Zealand Film Commission web site (www.filmnz.com/middleearth/index.html, accessed April 2006) as saying: 'Jackson is also cognizant that New Zealand's landscapes are wilder and more craggily mythic than most. They, too, become a presence in the film, quite apart from the inevitable computer-generated fantasyscapes and battle scenes'. The New Zealand government spent more than NZ$3 million in promoting the tourism and high-technology aspects of *Lord of the Rings* after the first film in the trilogy was released late in 2001. The importance of the media in changing perceptions of destinations is reflected in the comments of the then responsible minister, Peter Hodgson, who noted that the movie had the potential to rebrand New Zealand: 'This [film] has come out of a country which a lot of viewers might associate with sheep' (Campbell 2001: 24).

Although many destinations seek to proactively influence their image and perception of their attractions and resources, in many cases destinations have to be reactive, particularly at times of natural disaster or political insecurity. The growth of global media such as the Internet as well as satellite television has meant that events in a location can be seen almost instantaneously in other parts of the world. Therefore, as well as a focus on ensuring that desired physical and cultural resources are in place for visitors so information also becomes an important resource that destinations will seek to influence. This situation is analysed in more detail with respect to the case study of crisis management and the impact of Hurricane Katrina on New Orleans below.

From this understanding of tourism resources we can see that if a destination seeks to attract tourists, at least four things need to be available from the destination:

(i) Resources in the form of physical and cultural attractions to induce people to visit.

(ii) Resources in the form of facilities and services, including human resources, that enable them to stay at the destination.

(iii) Resources in the form of infrastructure and services that makes the destination accessible as well as the various attractions, facilities and services within the destinations accessible.

(iv) Information provision so that the consumer actually knows about the destination and its resources. From this perspective information itself is also a tourism resource and a gateway resource in that it creates awareness of the other types of resources that a destination has.

Given that consumption and production are simultaneous in tourism as a service industry, in addition to destination resources, consumer resources are also essential for tourism to occur. As Chapter 1 highlighted, in order to be able to engage in leisure travel some of the resources that people need to travel include time, money, the political rights to travel and health. The accessibility of a destination, and therefore its relative potential to attract visitors, is going to be dramatically impacted by the resources in its market area. The capacity of a destination to attract visitors is therefore a function of the resources that exist within the destination, the resources in the transit region and the resources of the generating region, including the personal resources of potential travellers.

CASE STUDY
Hurricane Katrina and New Orleans tourism

On 29 August 2005, the Gulf Coast region of the United States was hit by what is considered as one of the United States most destructive ever hurricanes. Hurricane Katrina, a Category 4 storm, made landfall on the Louisiana coast and travelled northeast through Mississippi and Alabama before being downgraded to a tropical storm in Tennessee the following day. A Category 4 storm implies:

- Winds 210–249 kilometre/hour (131–155 miles/hour).
- Storm surge generally 4–5.5 metres above normal.
- Extensive curtain wall failures with some complete roof structure failures on small residences.

- Shrubs, trees and all signs are blown down. Complete destruction of mobile homes. Extensive damage to doors and windows.
- Low-lying escape routes may be cut by rising water 3–5 hours before arrival of the centre of the hurricane.
- Major damage to lower floors of structures near the shore.
- Terrain lower than 3 metres above sea level may be flooded requiring massive evacuation of residential areas as far inland as 10 kilometres.

The final characteristic greatly increased the severity of the impact of the hurricane in New Orleans, Louisiana, as the city sits between 3 metres below sea level and 4 metres above sea level. Unfortunately, many residents ignored or were unable to fulfil the evacuation order and remained in New Orleans, while the major flood-control levees were breached covering approximately 80 per cent of the city in water. Hurricane Katrina triggered the city's ultimate 'worst-case-scenario' and the chain of events that followed indicated a general lack of preparedness even though the likelihood of such a disaster occurring had been predicted by many scientists and had also been the subject of several television documentaries.

The impact of Hurricane Katrina on tourism in Louisiana and New Orleans was dramatic. In 2005, US resident visitors to Louisiana numbered 17.3 million, a decline of 23 per cent from 2004. In the fourth quarter alone, visitors declined by 76 per cent. Total inquiries to the Louisiana Office of Tourism via the Internet, telephone and mail also plummeted immediately after Hurricane Katrina and the subsequent Hurricane Rita which affected southwest Louisiana (from over 3 million in the fiscal year 2004–2005 to just under 2 million in the fiscal year 2005–2006). Not surprisingly visitor spending in Louisiana dropped US $1.9 million in 2005 to $8 billion (Department of Culture, Recreation and Tourism 2006b). However, New Orleans is the focal point for the state's tourism industry. In 2004, more than 10 million visitors to New Orleans spent US $5 billion, with 40 per cent of revenues being generated by business conventions and meetings which made New Orleans the eighth largest US market for business conventions. The New Orleans Convention & Visitors Bureau (NOCVB) estimated lost tourism revenues of approximately US $500 million for each month that the city could not open for visitors (Yee 2005). Nevertheless, even with the cancellation of all city-wide conventions (using the convention centre and three or more hotels) scheduled for the city between September 2005 and April 2006 the NOCVB maintained its business operations by setting up a temporary office in Baton Rouge and with 90 staff working remotely across the USA. Indeed, a scaled down version of Mardi Gras, New Orleans' icon event was still scheduled for February as a means of reviving the city's tourism industry, with Donna Karl, vice president of NOCVB proclaiming, 'Mardi Gras is on … We're thinking that the city will be up rocking and rolling in the first quarter'. In addition, it was reported that where possible meetings were being swapped with New Orleans with the city being promised events for 2008 and beyond (Yee 2005: 8).

As damaging as the impact of Hurricane Katrina was on the physical and human resources of New Orleans, the media reporting on the Hurricane had substantial affects on the perception of New Orleans as a destination. A study conducted by Cunningham Research (2005) indicated that travellers were most concerned over their personal safety and their finances related to a trip to New Orleans. Fifty per cent of travellers who stated they were interested in visiting New Orleans were somewhat or extremely concerned over a hurricane being predicted before they left home, and an equal number were just as concerned over losing money from prepaid travel expenses and additional costs from delays. An overall negative impact on confidence with leadership at all levels of government was also regarded as influencing the attractiveness of New Orleans as a destination (CBS 2005). Indeed, a year after Hurricane Katrina hit, many problems still remained that not only affected the people of New Orleans but also the city's image. For example, an Australian newspaper article read: 'From the ghostly streets of New Orleans' abandoned neighbourhoods to Mississippi's downtrodden coastline, the first anniversary of Katrina's onslaught arrives with emerging signs of federal money at work: rented caravans parked in driveways of flood-ravaged homesteads, teams of army engineers overseeing levee repairs, beaches swept clean of debris' (Simmons and Fausset 2006). Despite four emergency spending bills approved by Congress to provide more than US $110 billion (A $145 billion) in aid, federal agencies had spent only US $44 billion with many displaced homeowners still waiting for temporary caravan accommodation (Simmons and Fausset 2006).

By mid-2006, the Louisiana Department of Culture, Recreation and Tourism (2006a: 1) reported that 'negative images of affected areas portrayed by the media … had resulted in a significant loss of interest in tourism'. Louisiana was expected to have lost 20 per cent of its visitor spending in one year (approximately US $2.2 billion), and New Orleans an average of $15.2 million/day, with a consequent loss of state tax dollars of approximately US $125 million/annum. Indeed, the state acknowledged that not only were tourist's image of the state and city affected, but also 'The State's image after the hurricanes has weakened investor confidence with regards to spending money in Louisiana' (Department of Culture, Recreation and Tourism 2006a: 3).

Nevertheless, even though negative aspects of the impact of Katrina were affecting the city's and the state's image and economy, the media was also seen as part of the solution with respect to redeveloping tourism. According to Louisiana State Senator Ann Davis Duplessis:

> I am afraid when the lights go off, when something will no longer be there and our people are no longer being talked about in the media constantly, others will feel less and less sympathetic. The world will become less sympathetic of our condition. If in the next catastrophe, damage reaches this stage or worst, hundreds of thousands people who are still trying to recover will not be ready. It is imperative therefore, the media continues the coverage at a level that it is 'in our face' and 'in the face' of the world. We need that sympathetic heart to be able to repair the level of this damage, so that we can rebuild. If news goes away in 2–3 months, I don't know how long it will take for us to go back to any semblance of normality (in Heyer 2005).

In response to the damage wrought by Hurricane Katrina on the physical and image dimensions of New Orleans and Louisiana tourism, the State of Louisiana launched a 'Rebirth Plan' (Department of Culture, Recreation and Tourism 2005; State of Louisiana, Office of the Lieutenant Governor 2005). Employment, housing, and the rebuilding of physical and social infrastructure were seen as important but so to was the provision of information and the development of a public relations campaign. According to the plan, 'People need new images of Louisiana, to replace the weeks of negative images on television' (Department of Culture, Recreation and Tourism 2005: 3). With respect to tourism five strategies were identified:

1 *Public relations campaign*: 'Immediately and aggressively promote those areas of the state currently open for business. An aggressive public relations campaign will be implemented'.
2 *Business assistance*: 'Rapidly develop and implement a statewide tourism small business assistance program, utilizing any and all available federal, private and state funds'.
3 *Infrastructure*: 'Facilitate the rapid rebuilding and improvement of the state's infrastructure'.
4 *Image*: 'rebuild and enhance Louisiana's national and international image as an attractive, compelling, unique tourism destination …'.
5 *Lead agency*: The Office of Lieutenant Governor to serve as the lead agency with respect to policy setting, intergovernmental relations, and as an information clearing house (Department of Culture, Recreation and Tourism 2005: 7).

In 2006, the state amended its tourism marketing plan so as to increase the number of visitors in the areas impacted by Katrina. The state proposed that US $28.5 million be invested in a national campaign and other initiatives designed to bring out-of-state travellers back to the New Orleans region, and Southeast and Southwest Louisiana with the primary targets being leisure travellers as well as convention and business travellers. The initiative included:

1 Convention and interactive marketing, promotions to travel agents and related activities.
2 An awareness campaign focusing on New Orleans, Southeast Louisiana and Southwest Louisiana. This campaign will target drive-in and national travellers as well as international travellers.
3 Niche marketing programmes designed to promote family activities and festivals and cultural attractions unique to the areas most affected by the storms.
4 Coordinated marketing efforts between the Department of Culture, Recreation, and Tourism and the Louisiana Department of Economic Development to regain investor confidence for spending money and creating jobs in Louisiana (Department of Culture, Recreation and Tourism 2006a: 4).

By September 2006, significant progress had been made with respect to restoring the tourism resources of New Orleans and Louisiana. Prior to Hurricanes Katrina and Rita, 21 per cent of the nation's travellers and 53 per cent of Louisiana's regional market expressed an intent to travel to Louisiana in the next 24 months. Immediately after the hurricanes, the national number dropped to 13 per cent and the regional market dropped to 37 per cent. As of May 2006, the regional number had increased to 47 per cent (Department of Culture, Recreation and Tourism 2006b: 4). Other changes in infrastructure are noted in Table 5.1. A year after Katrina almost two-thirds the number of flights pre-Katrina were flying out of Louis Armstrong International Airport to 77 per cent the number of destinations. However, substantial growth was expected into the future as attractions were being reopened and convention and business travel started to return to the city. Nevertheless, the long-term future of tourism in New Orleans will likely be affected by the redevelopment of the city, including the development of new flood protection practices and infrastructure, as well as the impact of any future hurricane on the city.

Key sources

Louis Armstrong Airport: www.flymsy.com/
Louisiana Office of Tourism: www.crt.state.la.us/tourism

Table 5.1   Key tourism resource indicators for New Orleans and Louisiana pre- and post-Hurricane Katrina

Indicator	Pre-Katrina	September 2005	September 2006
Daily commercial flights from Louis Armstrong New Orleans	162	19	112[a]
Statewide hotel availability (rooms)	80 000	42 000[b]	70 000
New Orleans hotel availability	38 000	20 000[b]	28 000
New Orleans metropolitan area hotels (number)	140		103
New Orleans, number of restaurants	34 000		1562
New Orleans Parish Police Force, number of officers	1680		1469
New Orleans Parish Police Force, ratio of police/citizens	1/289		1/157
New Orleans Parish, number of citizens	485 000		220–235 000
Metropolitan New Orleans, number of citizens	1.3 million		1.1 million

[a]This figure represents 13 185 seats or 59% of pre-Katrina level of seats per day.
[b]January 2006 figures.
Source: Derived from Department of Culture, Recreation and Tourism (2006b); New Orleans Metropolitan Convention & Visitors Bureau (2006).

Louisiana Rebirth Plan, Louisiana Department of Culture, Recreation and Tourism: www.crt.state.la.us
New Orleans Convention & Visitors Bureau: www.neworleanscvb.com
New Orleans Convention Center: www.mccno.com
New Orleans Superdome: www.superdome.com

References

CBS (2005). Poll: Katrina response inadequate: http://www.cbsnews.com/stories/2005/09/08/opinion/polls/main824591.shtml (accessed 23 August 2006)

Cunningham Research (2005). Study of 2005 Hurricane impacts on tourism: http://www.cunninghamresearch.com/release.html (accessed 17 July 2006)

Department of Culture, Recreation and Tourism (2005). *Louisiana Rebirth: Restoring the Soul of America*. Baton Rouge: Department of Culture, Recreation and Tourism.

Department of Culture, Recreation and Tourism (2006a). *Tourism Action Plan Amendment: Louisiana Tourism Marketing Program*. Baton Rouge: Department of Culture, Recreation and Tourism.

Department of Culture, Recreation and Tourism (2006b). *Louisiana Rebirth Scorecard*. Baton Rouge: Department of Culture, Recreation and Tourism.

Heyer, H. (2005). New Orleans Needs 10 Years Minimum. *Travel Wire News* November 22, New Orleans Metropolitan Convention & Visitors Bureau (2006). *New Orleans Metropolitan Convention and Visitors Bureau Issues 'State of the City' Report*. New Orleans: New Orleans Metropolitan Convention & Visitors Bureau. http://www.travelwirenews.com/cgi-script/csArticles/articles/000066/006625.htm

Simmons, A. and Fausset, R. (2006). New Orleans Disaster Still Overwhelms. *The Age*, 29 August.

State of Louisiana, Office of the Lieutenant Governor (2005). *Lt. Gov. Landrieu Unveils Plan to Rebuild Tourism and Cultural Industries. Press Release*, September 20, Baton Rouge: State of Louisiana, Office of the Lieutenant Governor.

Yee, A. (2005). New Orleans vows to let the carnival go on – but will anybody come? *Financial Times (Europe)* 21 September, 8.

Discussion questions

1 How might marketing best contribute to disaster management for tourism destinations?
2 With reference to the web sites discuss the further progress the city has made with respect to regaining tourism numbers?
3 How does the New Orleans example highlight the extent to which image and perception, as well as infrastructure and attractions, constitute a tourism resource?

Chapter overview: Developing destinations

The different dimensions of place are a critical element in understanding the contemporary destination. Places become destinations by virtue of being visited. Places seek to become destinations so as to reap the economic benefits of attracting visitors, as well as to promote a destination for purposes of investment and migration. Yet as the destination product is the sum of all experiences the tourist has at the destination as a result of encounters with a variety of tourism resources including firms, people, communities and the destination environment (see Chapter 1), this is an extremely difficult product to manage. As the service dimensions outlined in Chapters 1 and 12 indicate, as a service, tourism is a very difficult product to control in the same manner that the quality of a physical product would be controlled. Indeed, the destination product that is promoted by destination marketing organizations (DMOs) is quite different from many other commercial products in that the DMO does not 'own' the product it is promoting while the development of the product is itself the result of an amalgam of different public and private firms and organizations, many of which may not even be aware of each other's existence.

The concepts of servicescape and experiencescape therefore highlight the extent to which firms and destinations will seek to produce experiences that consumers desire through design and regulation of the physical environment that visitors experience. Yet the service encounters that are experienced through social interactions between producer and consumer are far harder to control. To an extent these can be managed within the firm via training programmes, although outside of the commercial environment social interactions between visitors and members of the destination community are impossible to control except in the most totalitarian states. This situation illustrates the difficulties associated with the notion of destination management. Quite simply, destination management or marketing organizations in liberal democracies have only a limited degree of control over the encounter between consumers and producers of the tourist experience, with perhaps the exception of those visitors who have purchased an all inclusive package tour at a destination where they do not speak the local language. Nevertheless, for all visitors, social interactions are also defined partially by the configuration of the servicescapes encountered in destinations.

The issue of control of all elements of the tourist destination product, or rather the relative lack of control, clearly lies at the heart of understanding the contemporary destination. Unlike many other business products or services destination management or marketing organizations do not own the product that they are managing or marketing. This constitutes a significant point of difference in the business and organizational dimensions of tourism from that of many other commercial and public sectors. Destination management is therefore focused on the gaining of control, or at least seeking to increase the levels of certainty of appropriate provision, in relation to the delivery of the key elements of the tourism product to the consumer. Ideally, destination management is concerned not just with the consumption of the tourism product but also with how the tourist gains value over each element of the value chain and how producers also add value, and therefore increase returns to the destination, over the supply chain. This broader perspective on what destination management is seeking to achieve cannot be stressed enough as it influences how destinations are governed with respect to tourism (Chapter 6), the affects of tourism on destinations (Chapter 7) and the planning of tourism in destinations (Chapter 8). Nevertheless, it also highlights the importance of understanding the wide array of factors that affect the viability of tourism destinations.

Self-review questions

1 Why is the question of what constitutes a *destination* determined by the visitor?
2 How does *scale* affect the ways in which destinations are usually described?
3 What are the three main approaches to describing *place*?
4 Why might it be difficult to manage visitor experiences in a *servicescape* or *experiencescape*?
5 Why are all tourism resources *cultural* in origin?
6 Why is *information* a tourism resource?
7 What is the term that is used to refer to the subjective, personal and emotional *attachments* and *relationships* people have to a place? Is it possible for people to have multiple place attachments?
8 For some people a *second home* or holiday destination might feel more like a home than their place of permanent residence. Why might this be the case?
9 Why is the issue of *control* such an important element in understanding contemporary destination management?

Recommended reading

1 Framke, W. (2002). The destination as a concept: a discussion of the business-related perspective versus the socio-cultural approach in tourism theory. *Scandinavian Journal of Hospitality and Tourism* 2, 93–108.
   This article describes two idealized approaches in describing the destination concept.
2 Leiper, N. (2000). Are destinations 'the heart of tourism'? The advantages of an alternative description. *Current Issues in Tourism* 3, 364–368.
   A critical perspective of the destination concept and its utility in tourism studies.

3 Cresswell, T. (2004). *Place: A Short Introduction*. Oxford: Blackwell.
   Provides a good introduction to the main themes in the study of place including current debates over supposed non-places, such as airport terminals.

4 Davidson, R. and Maitland, R. (1997). *Tourism Destinations*. London: Hodder and Stroughton.
   This book provides a good introduction to the issues involved in destination management and marketing, particularly within a European context.

5 Bitner, M.J. (1992). Servicescapes: the impact of physical surroundings on customers and employees. *Journal of Marketing* 56, 57–71.
   A seminal article with respect to the notion of servicescapes which has had a substantial impact in the marketing literature.

6 Singh, S., Timothy, D. and Dowling, R. (eds) (2003). *Tourism in Destination Communities*. Wallingford, CT: CAB International.
   An edited collection that provides a range of perspectives with respect to destination communities and the issues that tourism raises within them.

7 Ringer, G. (ed.) (1998). *Destinations: Cultural Landscapes of Tourism*. New York: Routledge.
   An edited book that provides a useful collection of readings on the cultural construction of destinations.

8 Hall, C.M. (2005). *Tourism: Rethinking the Social Science of Mobility*. Harlow: Prentice-Hall.
   Chapter 6 provides a detailed discussion of the production of tourism destinations.

9 Smith, S.L.J. (1996). *Tourism Analysis: A Handbook*, 2nd edn. Harlow: Longman.
   Provides one of the best discussions of the various analytical methods that may be brought to bear in the analysis and identification of tourism destinations.

10 Lew, A., Hall, C.M. and Williams, A.M. (eds) (2004). *A Companion to Tourism*. Oxford: Blackwell.
   Provides a detailed collection of review chapters on key aspects of tourism destinations, including specific destination types and attractions such as the tourist-historic city.

Recommended web sites

European Travel Commission: www.etc-corporate.org/
Scottish Destination Management Association: http://www.scotland-sdma.org.uk/
UNEP Government and policy support: http://www.uneptie.org/pc/tourism/policy/home.htm
UNESCO World Heritage site: http://whc.unesco.org/
Visit Britain: www.visitbritain.com/

References cited

Bitner, M.J. (1992). Servicescapes: the impact of physical surroundings on customers and employees. *Journal of Marketing* 56, 57–71.

Campbell, G. (2001). Planet Middle Earth. *Listener* 15 December, 16–24.

Catlin, G. (1968). An artist proposes a national park. In R. Nash (ed.), *The American Environment: Readings in the History of Conservation*, pp. 5–9. Reading, MA: Addison-Wesley Publishing.

Chang, T.C. (2000). Theming cities, taming places: insights from Singapore. *Geografiska Annaler* 82B, 35–54.

Gunn, C.A. (1994). *Tourism Planning*, 3rd edn. London: Taylor and Francis.

Hall, C.M. (2007). *Introduction to Tourism in Australia: Development, Issues and Change*, 5th edn. South Melbourne: Pearson Education Australia.

Hall, C.M. and Müller, D. (eds) (2004). *Tourism, Mobility and Second Homes: Between Elite Landscape and Common Ground*. Clevedon: Channelview Publications.

Metelka, C.J. (1990). *The Dictionary of Hospitality, Travel and Tourism*, 3rd edn. Albany: Delmar Publishers.

Nash, R. (1982). *Wilderness and the American Mind*, 3rd edn. New Haven and London: Yale University Press.

O'Dell, T. (2005). Experiencescapes: blurring borders and testing connections. In T. O'Dell and P. Billing (eds), *Experiencescapes: Tourism, Culture and Economy*, pp. 11–33. Copenhagen: Copenhagen Business School Press.

Pine, J. and Gilmore, J. (1999). *The Experience Economy: Work is Theatre and Every Business a Stage*. Boston, MA: Harvard Business School Press.

Vukonic, B. (1997). Selective tourism growth: targeted tourism destinations. In S. Wahab and J. Pigrim (eds), *Tourism, Development and Growth: The Challenge of Sustainability*, pp. 95–108. London: Routledge.

Watson, J.L. (ed.) (1997). *Golden Arches East: McDonald's in East Asia*. Stanford, CA: Stanford University Press.

Zimmermann, E.W. (1951). *World Resources and Industries*, Revised edition. New York: Harper and Brothers.

Chapter **6**
Governing the contemporary tourism product

Chapter objectives

After reading this chapter you will

- Understand the development of the concept of governance
- Identify the key characteristics of governance
- Understand the reorganization of the state along new functional and territorial lines
- Recognize the importance of multi-level governance, particularly in policy areas that have become highly globalized
- Appreciate the complexity of governance in contemporary tourism
- Understand the major roles of government in contemporary tourism
- Identify different types of tourism policy

Introduction

The focus of this chapter is the government and governance of tourism, an issue that has become a major concern to stakeholders in tourism in recent times. That is, the design, implementation and monitoring of public policies and strategies with respect to contemporary tourism. This involves the horizontal and vertical coordination of government at various levels, the private sector, and non-government organizations as well as the wider population. This occurs over scales ranging from the global through to the local. The chapter also discusses the various roles of the public sector and the changing nature of government intervention in tourism, which may be described as a shift from *government* to *governance*. Nevertheless, the nation state and its national government are still regarded as extremely important sovereign actors in tourism policy. Different roles of government in tourism are described which may then be analysed via a policy typology that enables the reader to understand the various means by which governments approach tourism policy in order to achieve certain policy objectives. The chapter will then examine the importance of cooperative strategies as a means of gaining producer support in the overall marketing, planning and development of a destination.

From government to governance

In public policy terms there has been a substantial transformation of the perceived role of government in general, and in tourism in particular, in recent years. This shift is sometimes referred to as a move from government to governance. Central to this shift has been a change in the relative role of state institutions, i.e. government agencies, in securing state-sponsored economic, environmental and social projects. For example, in developed countries many of the activities of the welfare state approach that existed until the beginning of the 1980s, including management of leisure and cultural facilities, are now operated and implemented by private sector providers or non-government organizations. Therefore, rather than the implementation of government policies being undertaken by a sole government agency, there is now a greater emphasis on partnerships. These partnerships may be between government departments and state-owned or part-owned organizations that operate on a commercial basis (para-governmental organizations), the private sector and non-governmental organizations in which the role of government agencies and departments are to steer organizational networks and partnerships in a required direction (Hall 2005).

Rhodes (1996, 1997) identified a number of characteristics of governance:

- Interdependence between organizations.
- The concept of governance is broader than that of government and includes a role for non-state actors (i.e. private sector, non-government organizations and interest groups, including organizations in the voluntary sector).
- The boundaries between the public and other sectors is now far more opaque.
- The need to exchange resources and negotiate shared purposes between organization members of networks leads to ongoing interaction between members of networks.
- The rules of interaction within a network is set by its members with trust being critical for the maintenance of network relationships.
- Many networks have a significant degree of autonomy from government and are self-organizing.
- Although the state does not necessarily occupy a privileged position it can imperfectly and indirectly steer networks.

The latter characteristic of governance identified by Rhodes and the significance of partnership relations between state agencies and other organizations has meant that both the development as well as the implementation of government policies has become extremely complex. Jessop (1997) referred to this situation as one of 'meta-governance' as it requires the steering of multiple agencies and organizations, which although operating autonomously of one another, remain linked together through their involvement in common policy issues and associated funding and benefits. This situation is extremely relevant to tourism as it well describes the problem of many destination marketing organizations (DMOs), which are often part or fully funded by government or even a part of the formal structure of the state, i.e. a government agency, and their role in trying to bring together other public agencies, tourism producers and even destination communities in common causes with respect to destination marketing and/or development. As noted frequently in this book, one of the key management characteristics of DMOs is that they do not own the products they are selling or promoting. Therefore, it is perhaps not surprising that ideas of partnership and collaboration are extremely important to understanding the relationships between individuals and organizations that exist in tourism networks.

Another important element in the development of the concept of governance is the changing nature of the nation state with state roles being reorganized functionally and territorially along sub-national, supranational and even trans-territorial lines.

Sub-national state refers to the role of the local state (city, local or regional government) as a political actor at both domestic and international levels. For example, there is the development of a new regionalism in many parts of Europe and North America by which regional governments have acquired new rights and responsibilities as well as being more aggressive in seeking to acquire economic benefits. A good example of sub-national state activity in tourism is international destination marketing and promotion even when national tourism organizations may already be involved in such activities.

Supranational states and organizations refer to organizations such as the European Union (EU) in which there are considerable regulatory capacities while in many policy areas the EU also seeks to steer member government policies in certain directions. In tourism there are many supranational organizations that influence tourism at global or international levels. At a global level, organizations such as the UNWTO (United Nations World Tourism Organization), IATA (International Aviation Transport Association) and the WTTC (World Travel and Tourism Council) affect various dimensions of nation-state tourism policies as well as the sub-national state. The WTTC, a private sector-based organization with membership by invitation only, has been extremely influential in achieving goals including adoption of tourism satellite accounts and liberalization of the tourism sector (Hall 2005). 'WTTC's mission is to raise awareness of the full economic impact of the world's largest generator of wealth and jobs – Travel and Tourism. Governments are encouraged to unlock the industry's potential by adopting the Council's policy framework for sustainable tourism development' (http://www.wttc.org/framesetaboutus.htm).

Trans-territorial states and organizations refer to organizations that have territorial boundaries that include the territories of constituent members. For instance a number of trans-border regional agencies have been established within Europe with the support of the EU and national and regional governments. One of the best examples of such a development in both general and tourism terms is the Øresund region of Denmark and Sweden.

Øresund: 'one destination, two countries'

The Øresund region links the region of Skåne in south-western Sweden with Zealand in Denmark. The most concrete as well as symbolic example of the Øresund region was the construction of the cross-border Øresund bridge, across the Øresund Strait, between Denmark and Sweden and which links the cities of Malmö (Sweden) and Copenhagen (Denmark) by road and train. Although a physical connection between Denmark and Sweden had been mooted since the nineteenth century a new governance structure of an integrated region did not appear until the 1950s. Various economic and political factors delayed both the physical and political connectivity of the cross-border region until the convergence of a number of economic, political and intellectual interests in the late 1980s. These interests found organizational manifestation in a number of institutions that promoted the Øresund concept. Foremost among these are the region's governing body the Øresund Committee (Øresundskomiteen) which is a forum for local and regional politicians and authorities from both side of the Øresund Strait. The Committee has been described as a 'classic example' of governance without government (Pike et al. 2006: 139). According to the OECD (2003):

> The committee is composed of local and regional bodies from both sides of the sound and – which is quire exceptional for transnational regionalism – by the two national ministeries ... The process of integration in Øresund is therefore achieved not through the set up of an additional government layer but through the voluntary coordination of policies of its members (OECD 2003: 160).

The key institutions of the Committee are the Copenhagen Regional Authority and the region of Skåne. However, also of great importance are a number of other organizations that contributed to the institutionalization of the Øresund region concept. These include:

- Scandinavian Academy of Management (a business and economics think tank).
- Medicon Valley Academy (a network organization that facilitates the collaboration of educational institutions and biomedical, biotechnological and pharmaceutical firms).
- Copenhagen capacity (a marketing organization aimed at attracting and retain firms and industries).
- Wonderful Copenhagen (a tourism marketing organization, Copenhagen has the region's international airport hub).
- Øresund University (a network composed of universities in the region).
- Øresund Science Park (a network of the various science parks in the region).

According to Tangkjær (2000; Berg et al. 2000) the establishment of different institutions and organizations followed an 'open house' strategy in which every organization interested in contributing to cross-border integration was welcomed into the broader network so long as they followed some basic rules such as not questioning the actual vision of regional integration. The development of such networks was regarded as important part of the regional strategy as it was seen as a way to not only mobilize support but also manifest the idea of an integrated region (Berg et al. 2000; Ek 2005). The development of such networks has practical implications for tourism as they encourage greater mobility within the region both directly through requirements for business travel and meetings but also as a justification for further transport provision. In addition, running parallel to the institutionalization of the Øresund regional concept was the development of place marketing and promotional strategies that sought to reinforce an Øresund place identity both internally and externally.

In business and industrial terms the region was marketed as a European 'hub of excellence' with the region being branded a 'human capital' so as to reinforce the positive social, economic and natural environment of the region, including a well-educated workforce and the geographic concentration of certain industries. In addition, other programmes, some of which were funded by the EU were also created to reinforce regional identity. These included language and cultural programmes, including 'Cultural Bridge 2000' to parallel the opening of the Øresund Bridge. According to Ek (2005: 79):

> Through the use of maps and regional statistics, the Øresund region was represented as a fact rather than a vision or dream, and the 'Øresund citizen' was characterized as a well-off, mobile, postmodern cosmopolitan with a high degree of cultural capital and a larger curiosity about the world inherited from the Vikings and their interest in trade and travel (the common image of the Vikings as ravagers and warriors is quite misleading).

Nevertheless, even though the notion of a human capital is used in external advertising and promotion, Ek (2005) argues that this brand/identity has never successfully been adopted by the citizens of the region.

Key sources

Berg, P., Linde-Laursen, A. and Lofgren, O. (2000). *Invoking a Transnational Metropolis: The Making of the Øresund Region*. Lund: Studentlitteratur AB.

Ek, R. (2005). Regional experiencescapes as geo-economic ammunition. In T. O'Dell (ed.), *Experiencescapes: Tourism, Culture and Economy*, pp. 69–89. Copenhagen: Copenhagen Business School Press.

Maskell, P. and Törnqvist, G. (1999). *Building a Cross-border Learning Region: Emergence of the North European Øresund Region.* Copenhagen: Handelshøjskolens Forlag.

Øresund region: www.oresund.com

Øresund tourism: www.visitoresund.info

Skåne region: www.skane.com

Wonderful Copenhagen: www.visitcopenhagen.com

References

OECD (2003). *OECD Territorial Reviews: Øresund, Denmark/Sweden.* Paris: OECD.

Tangkjær, C. (2000). *Åbent Hus: Organiseringen Omkring Øresundsregionen.* Copenhagen: Handelshøjskolens Forlag.

Discussion questions

1 What are the advantages and disadvantages of a cross-border approach to destination promotion and management?
2 On what basis is Øresund an example of trans-territorial and supranational governance?
3 Why might the Øresund integrated region serve to increase human mobility, including tourism, within the region?

Multi-level governance

Although the regional scale has clearly emerged as an important one with respect to governance, 'determining the actual impact of the new regional governance is fraught with difficulty because it requires us to isolate the effects of one actor or set of actors among others' (Pike et al. 2006: 141). For example, the nation state is still the key element in international policy making and regulation and national governments remain central to the formulation of public policy. Yet there is little doubt that the processes of globalization have created a situation in which some policy areas that were at one time the sole realm of national governments in the developed countries have become internationalized, while other policy concerns have been translated down to the regional level.

Examples of policy fields that have become increasingly internationalized include the aviation, environment, human rights, international trade and migration. These represent areas that by their nature are policy problems that cross international boundaries. Therefore, one of the best ways in which they can be dealt with is the development of international institutions such as international law and regulation as well as the development of formal management agencies. Environmental issues, e.g., such as climate change, marine pollution and the loss of biodiversity, are policy matters that cross national boundaries because what happens in one country with respect to pollution or greenhouse gas emissions can have effects in other countries. Although tourism is limited as an international policy field there are numerous policy areas that are subject to international convention that directly or indirectly affect the flows of tourists or tourism development. Tourism has therefore become subject to what is described as multi-level governance in which destinations, as well as individual tourism products, are now subject to multi-level governance structures in which local, regional, national and supranational institutions and agencies all have a role. The complex nature of emergent levels of institutions and relations is illustrated in Figure 6.1. According to Marks and Hooghe (2004: 16):

The dispersion of governance across jurisdictions is both more efficient than, and normatively superior to, central state monopoly. The claim that governance

Figure 6.1 Elements of multi-level governance institutions and relations affecting tourism

must operate at multiple scales in order to capture variations in the territorial reach of policy externalities. Because externalities arising from the provision of public goods vary immensely – from planet-wide in the case of global warming to local in the case of many city services – so should the scale of governance. To internalize externalities, governance must be multilevel.

However, the growth of new supranational and regional institutions is not without its critics given that in many cases such institutions are often not democratically accountable to wider populations even though their decisions may have tremendous economic, social and environmental impacts on such populations. Furthermore, the complexity of multi-level governance is further complicated by the existence of private representative organizations, transnational businesses and non-governmental organizations that also act at domestic and international scales. For example, in tourism campaigns have been organized to encourage people not to visit particular countries because of their human rights or environmental record by non-government organizations.

The development of supranational institutions, such as international conventions, may also have significant long-term implications for tourism. For example, when international commercial aviation agreements were first being negotiated there was a divergence between the United States who advocated a free market and Britain and many other countries, particularly from Europe who argued for tight political restrictions, in part because of concerns that the market would become too dominated by American airlines. Governments secured the right to control all aspects of air travel to their country, including airline ownership, by allowing the country to set rules saying that only nationals of a given country could own and control an airline based in that country. However, the economic globalization of the aviation sector via improvements in transport technology and changes in constraints on trade and human mobility has meant that in many cases national airlines may be uneconomic to operate without there being direct government support. As Giovanni Bisignani, Director General of the International Air Transport Association stated 'Airline ownership restrictions became national rights … Now the flags on our aircraft are so heavy they are sinking the industry' (quoted in Phillips 2005: 13).

Regional changes in aviation regulation have occurred. American aviation has been relatively deregulated since the early 1980s although considerable direct and indirect federal government exists for major carriers. Aviation in Europe was opened to limited competition in the mid-1990s when the EU ended restrictions on cross-border operations with the EU. Australia and New Zealand also have a deregulated internal aviation market although international aviation rights beyond their borders remain regulated. Nevertheless, despite a degree of deregulation of the aviation regime that was developed in the post-Second World War era and the increasing financial pressures on airlines particularly since 2001, the preeminence of national governments in determining international aviation flows remains. For example, Alitalia and Olympic airlines are struggling to stay afloat and have only done so with large amounts of state aid. Sabena the national airline of Belgium went bankrupt in 2001. However, the privately owned regional airline DAT, renamed SN Brussels, purchased the name rights and the Sabena brand has continued. Air France controls KLM (Netherlands) and Lufthansa (Germany) controls Swiss (the successor to Swissair the national airline of Switzerland), but in both cases KLM and Swiss have maintained their national identities as condition imposed by the Dutch and Swiss governments. In addition, they must maintain a major hub in each country.

World heritage and issues of multi-level governance

The Convention for the Protection of the World's Cultural and Natural Heritage, to give the World Heritage Convention (WHC) its full name, was adopted by a United Nations Scientific, Education and Cultural Organization (UNESCO) Conference on 16 November 1972. The Convention is designed to enable nations to cooperate in the protection of cultural and natural sites of outstanding value to humanity. The Convention is often regarded as one of the pinnacles of world conservation (Hall 2000). 'The philosophy behind the Convention is straightforward: there are some parts of the world's natural and cultural heritage which are so unique and scientifically important to the world as a whole that their conservation and protection for present and future generations is not only a matter of concern for individual nations but for the international community as a whole' (Slatyer 1983: 138).

The Convention came into force in December 1975, when 20 nations had ratified it. The vast majority of the world's countries have either ratified or accepted the Convention. The signatories commit themselves to assist in the identification, protection, conservation and preservation of World Heritage properties. They undertake to refrain from 'any deliberate measure which might damage directly or indirectly' cultural or natural heritage

(Art. 6(3)), and to 'take appropriate legal, scientific, technical, administrative and financial measures necessary for [its] identification, protection, conservation, presentation and rehabilitation' (Art. 5d).

World Heritage Sites are cultural (monuments, groups of buildings or sites) and natural (natural features, geological and physiographical features and natural sites) items which are selected by the definition of the Convention because they are judged to display universal value. Under the terms of the WHC each cultural property nominated should therefore:

(i) represent a masterpiece of human creative genius; or

(ii) exhibit an important interchange of human values, over a span of time or within a cultural area of the world, on developments in architecture or technology, monumental arts, townplanning or landscape design; or

(iii) bear a unique or at least exceptional testimony to a cultural tradition or to a civilization which is living or which has disappeared; or

(iv) be an outstanding example of a type of building or architectural or technological ensemble or landscape which illustrates a significant stage(s) in human history; or

(v) be an outstanding example of a traditional human settlement or land use which is representative of a culture (or cultures), especially when it has become vulnerable under the impact of irreversible change; or

(vi) be directly or tangibly associated with events or living traditions, with ideas, or with beliefs, with artistic and literary works of outstanding universal significance (the Committee considers that this criterion should justify inclusion in the list only in exceptional circumstances and in conjunction with other criteria cultural or natural) (UNESCO 1999: Sec. 24).

In addition, cultural sites have to meet the test of authenticity in design, material, workmanship or setting and in the case of cultural landscapes their distinctive character and components have adequate legal and/or contractual and/or traditional protection and management mechanisms to ensure the conservation of the nominated cultural properties or cultural landscapes. Natural sites must:

(i) be outstanding examples representing major stages of earth's history, including the record of life, significant ongoing geological processes in the development of land forms, or significant geomorphic or physiographic features; or

(ii) be outstanding examples representing significant ongoing ecological and biological processes in the evolution and development of terrestrial, fresh water, coastal and marine ecosystems and communities of plants and animals; or

(iii) contain superlative natural phenomena or areas of exceptional natural beauty and aesthetic importance; or

(iv) contain the most important and significant natural habitats for in situ conservation of biological diversity, including those containing threatened species of outstanding universal value from the point of view of science or conservation (UNESCO 1999: Sec. 44).

In addition, they should also fulfill a number of conditions regarding their integrity. This includes containing all or most of the key interrelated and interdependent elements in their natural relationships; should have sufficient size and contain the necessary elements to demonstrate the key aspects of processes that are essential for the long-term conservation of the ecosystems and the biological diversity they contain; should be of outstanding aesthetic value and include areas that are essential for maintaining the beauty of the site; should contain habitats for maintaining the most diverse fauna and flora characteristic of the biographic province and ecosystems under consideration; a management plan; adequate long-term legislative, regulatory, institutional or traditional protection; and should be the most important sites for the conservation of biological diversity (UNESCO 1999).

The WHC is widely regarded as one of the most significant and successful international heritage agreements. Unlike many international treaties that deal with environmental issues it is widely ratified. Ratification of the Convention imposes obligations on those that sign it. The WHC is an example of 'hard' international law. Hard international law refers to firm and binding rules of law such as the content of treaties and the provisions of customary international law to which relevant nations are bound as a matter of obligation. However, 'soft' international law is also significant for World Heritage. Soft law refers to regulatory conduct which, because it is not provided for in a treaty, is not as binding as hard law (Hall 2000). Examples of soft law include recommendations or declarations which are made by international conferences, agencies and associations.

The nature of the WHC makes it a very good example of the significance of multilevel governance. In the case of the WHC nominations must be put forward by national governments to the World Heritage Committee where they are then analysed by experts from non-government heritage organizations. If site nominations are accepted then national governments in concert with regional governments and various management agencies then have a responsibility to appropriately manage sites. International law cannot be enforced in the same manner as domestic law, because nations can only rarely be compelled to perform their legal obligations. For example, in a study of World Heritage sites van der Aa (2005) found that while most sites have some degree of local or national legal protection, designation does not necessarily lead to an increase in legal protection under domestic law. Of the 64 sites he studied only 39 per cent (25 sites) received further protection under law although, in certain situations, increased protection may be a precursor to nomination so as to ensure that a site has suitable protected status to enable appropriate management strategies. The complexity of multi-level governance is further evidenced in the case of the WHC as there is no standard legislative or regulatory approach that nations use to ensure that their obligations to the Convention are met, although the vast major of sites are protected under existing national and local legislation and regulation. There is no common approach to developing participatory structures in the nomination and management process. In numerous cases listing is not fully supported by people at the local or regional level who may be directly affected by listing with some stakeholders opposing nominations or the boundaries of nominated sites (e.g. van der Aa et al. 2004) particularly if they believe that it may restrict land use or development options. Instead, there is a vastly different array of regulatory and institutional instruments that parties to the WHC use to manage sites ranging from national park acts and heritage law through to planning ordinances and policy statements (Hall 2006).

In England planning policies were changed in 1994 so as to protect World Heritage (WH) properties from inappropriate development (Rutherford 1994; Wainwright 2000). No additional statutory controls follow from the inclusion of a UK site in the WH list. However, inclusion 'highlights the outstanding international importance of the site as a key material consideration to be taken into account by local planning authorities in determining planning and listed building consent applications, and by the Secretary of State in determining cases on appeal or following call-in' (Office of the Deputy Prime Minister 2005: para. 2.22). This has already occurred with respect to an application to engage in mining activities near Hadrian's Wall (Rutherford 1994). Under the Policy Guidance from the Office of the Deputy Prime Minister each local authority, as well as other interested parties, such as other public authorities, property owners, developers, amenity bodies and all members of the public, has to recognize the implications of WH designation as well as other statutory designation, in the formulation of:

> … specific planning policies for protecting these sites and include these policies in their development plans. Policies should reflect the fact that all these sites have been designated for their outstanding universal value, and they should place great weight on the need to protect them for the benefit of future generations as well as our own. Development proposals affecting these sites or their setting may be compatible with this objective, but should always be carefully scrutinised for their likely effect on the site or its setting in the longer term. Significant development proposals affecting [WHS] will generally require formal environmental assessment,

to ensure that their immediate impact and their implications for the longer term are fully evaluated (Office of the Deputy Prime Minister 2005: para. 2.23).

Such an approach means that in England development projects that affect World Heritage sites, 'should always be carefully scrutinized for their likely effect on the site or its setting in the longer term' (Cookson 2000: 698) before planning approval can be given. Significantly, the English planning guidance with respect to World Heritage specifically refers to the Convention's *Operational Guidelines for the Implementation of the World Heritage Convention* (first produced in 1978 and revised regularly) as a document that local authorities should refer to with respect to the planning and management of World Heritage sites. In addition, local planning authorities are encouraged to work with owners and managers of sites in their areas, and with other agencies, to ensure that comprehensive management plans are developed. According to the planning guidance (Office of the Deputy Prime Minister 2005) these plans should

- appraise the significance and condition of the site;
- ensure the physical conservation of the site to the highest standards;
- protect the site and its setting from damaging development;
- provide clear policies for tourism as it may affect the site.

Key sources

Aa, B.J.M. van der, Groote, P.D. and Huigen, P.P.P. (2004). World heritage as NIMBY: the case of the Dutch part of the Wadden Sea. *Current Issues in Tourism* 7(4–5), 291–302.

Hall, C.M. (2006). World heritage, tourism and implementation: what happens after listing. In A. Fyall and A. Leask (eds) *Managing World Heritage Sites*, pp. 18–32. Oxford: Butterworth Heinemann (The above UK example is abstracted from this chapter.).

Hall, C.M. and Piggin, R. (2002). Tourism business knowledge of world heritage sites: a New Zealand case study. *International Journal of Tourism Research* 4, 401–411.

Rodwell, D. (2002). The world heritage convention and the exemplary management of complex heritage sites. *Journal of Architectural Conservation* 3, 40–60.

References

Hall, C.M. (2000). *Tourism Planning*. Harlow: Prentice-Hall.

Office of the Deputy Prime Minister (2005). *Planning Policy Guidance 15: Planning and the Historic Environment*. London: Office of the Deputy Prime Minister.

Rutherford, L. (1994). Protecting World Heritage sites: Coal Contractors Limited v Secretary of State for the Environment and Northumberland County Council. *Journal of Environmental Law* 6(2), 369–384.

Slatyer, R.O. (1983). The origin and evolution of the world heritage convention. *Ambio* 12(3–4), 138–139.

UNESCO Convention for the Protection of the World Cultural and Natural Heritage [adopted on 16 November 1972], UNESCO Document 17 c/106 of 15 November 1972. United Nations Educational, Scientific and Cultural Organisation (UNESCO).

Wainwright, G.J. (2000). The Stonehenge we deserve. *Antiquity* 74, 334–342.

Discussion questions

1 How might local communities and stakeholders be able to influence decisions taken at the international level with respect to the World Heritage Convention?

2 Given that World Heritage sites are meant to be universally significant to humankind should the heritage interests of the global community have precedence over concerns of the local community or even national governments with respect to heritage management?

3 On what basis might it be possible to compare management strategies and their effectiveness at different World Heritage sites?

The roles of government in tourism

The exact nature of the roles of government in tourism changes from jurisdiction to jurisdiction and through the various scales at which governance occurs. Different countries will have constitutions and legislative frameworks that will give different powers over different topics to different levels of government. Furthermore, to make the picture even more complicated the role of government has changed over time. This has meant that in some countries government responsibility for tourism is clearly defined while in others responsibility is taken up to varying degrees at different levels of government. Nevertheless, in general seven roles of government with respect to tourism can be identified. The forerunner to the UNWTO, the International Union of Tourist Organizations (IUOTO) (1974) in their discussion of the role of the state in tourism identified five areas of public sector involvement in tourism: coordination, planning, legislation and regulation, entrepreneur, and stimulation. To this may be added two other functions, a social tourism role, and a broader role of public interest protection (Hall 2000). These roles are outlined in more detail below.

Coordination

Coordination is necessary both within and between the different levels of government in order to avoid duplication of resources between the various government tourism bodies and the private sector, and to develop effective tourism strategies. Government often takes a major coordination role or facilitation role in bringing various tourism stakeholders together for common goals. The importance of government's coordination role has arguably increased in recent years as a result of the focus on governance.

Planning

Planning is the process of preparing a set of decisions for action in the future, directed at achieving identified goals by preferable means. Government planning for tourism occurs over different scales as well as different forms (economic, social, environmental, regional, urban, rural, land use, promotion and marketing, labour force) and is a major focus of government activity with respect to the development of tourism. However, many of the most significant planning activities that affect tourism often occur outside of tourism specific agencies, which usually only have a very limited legal mandate that concentrates on promotional activity. Therefore, much of the most important tourism planning occurs in agencies such as national parks, environment, culture and heritage or in the context of broader urban and rural planning at the regional level (see Chapter 8).

Regulation

One of the most important aspects of government as a sovereign institution is its legislative capacities. Therefore government's regulatory role with respect to tourism is critical. The regulation of tourism ranges from authorities of who can leave or enter countries, through to environmental, land use and health and safety issues. However, again, the vast majority of laws and regulations that affect tourism are actually not tourism specific. Therefore, policy decisions undertaken in other policy jurisdictions, e.g. economic policy, and conservation policy, may have substantial implications for the effectiveness of policy decisions undertaken in tourism. For example, general regulatory measures such as industry regulation, environmental protection and taxation policy will significantly influence the growth of tourism. The level of government regulation of tourism tends to be a major issue for the various components of the tourism industry. Although industry recognizes that government has a significant role to play, particularly when it comes to the provision of infrastructure, promotion or research from which industry benefits, the predominant argument by industry throughout most of the world is that the tourism industry must be increasingly deregulated so as to reduce compliance costs and therefore increase firm and destination competitiveness. However, from a broader public interest perspective governments simultaneously have to manage demands from industry for deregulation with calls from some interest groups for increased regulation of tourism, for example. In relation to conservation and environmental protection, and, increasingly, human rights and social justice.

Entrepreneur

Government has long had an entrepreneurial role in tourism. Governments not only usually provide basic infrastructure, such as roads and sewage, or manage attractions, such as national parks and museums, but may also own and operate tourist ventures including airlines, hotels and travel companies. However, increasingly the role of government as entrepreneur has broadened to include the provision of event and sport facilities as well as sponsoring urban redevelopment projects. At the national level the role of government ownership of airlines, railways and hotel chains has diminished in recent years as such public assets have been privatized or corporatized. However, the local state has arguably increased its entrepreneurial role, particularly with respect to financially supporting hallmark events or major event and urban development programmes as part of a regional competitiveness strategy.

Stimulation

The stimulation role of government is similar to that of entrepreneurship but is more intangible because of the focus on services. Three major sources of stimulation exist: (1) The provision of financial incentives such as low cost loans, depreciation on capital or even direct subsidies to private investors. (2) Government funding of research, often at low or nil cost, that is then available to the private sector. (3) Financial support or the direct undertaking of marketing and promotion, generally aimed at generating tourism demand, although it can also take the form of promotion aimed at encouraging investment in tourism attractions and facilities. However, such is the size of the role that government plays in promotion that it is usually recognized as a separate function.

Promotion

Marketing and promotion has long been one of the main activities of government in tourism (see also Chapter 9 for a discussion of destination marketing). This is possibly because of the territorial relationships between government and destinations although it is also closely related to arguments that tourism promotion represents a 'public good' given the high degree of fragmentation between the various elements of the tourism industry and the various economic and social benefits that are accrued by wider society. Given the extent of producer fragmentation in tourism and the substantial degree of market failure that exists with respect to generic destination promotion government has therefore supported destination promotion, particularly at the national level. In Australia a number of different means to fund national tourism promotion were examined (Hall 2000) including:

- Forcing businesses to pay a funding levy.
- 'User pays'/cooperative funding systems.
- Levies on foreign exchange earnings.
- Making government funding conditional on industry funding.
- Levies on tourism investment.
- Funding from a passenger movement charge.
- A commercial bed tax.
- Funding out of consolidated revenue.
- Funding out of a goods and services tax (GST) (similar to VAT).

After examining the different potential forms of government intervention, it was concluded that the most appropriate form of national government intervention to fund national tourism promotion was the appropriation of funds from consolidated revenue funds through normal budget processes. Several reasons for this conclusion were put forward:

- The inability to capture the benefits of generic marketing activity is severe given the fragmented nature of the tourism industry.

- Levies, user pays charges and business tax arrangements, including bed taxes, will institutionalize the 'freerider' or 'freeloader' problem whereby firms that do not financially support destination campaigns may benefit as much as those that do.
- The benefits of successful generic promotion as a travel destination are dispersed across the community (Hall 2000).

Social tourism

Social Tourism refers to the provision of tourism opportunities for those that are otherwise economically or otherwise disadvantaged. During the period of welfare state provision in many western countries holidays were often provided by governments or by unions or other non-government organizations, often at holiday camps and with subsidized transport. However, this function has declined dramatically over the last 25 years in Western society although some remnants still remain with respect to the roles of charities that often receive a degree of government funding.

Public interest

The final role of government in tourism is with respect to the traditional role of government in many societies to act as a protector of community or public interests as opposed to just being willing to protect tourism interests. Furthermore, tourism policy needs to be understood in the context of broader economic, social and environmental policies that a government is trying to achieve for its polity in that tourism should ideally be seen as a means to an end rather than an end in its own right. Although it is somewhat debatable as to whether it is a particular subset of the public interest role of government or a separate role in its own right concern over the rights of the environment is an increasingly important public interest role of government. Several national jurisdictions have legislation that gives rights of conservation to rare and endangered species e.g. which means that development projects may not go ahead if they are a threatened species.

Types of regulation

Although identifying the different categories of government's involvement in tourism is a useful exercise in terms of differentiating the roles of government between levels of governance and between jurisdictions it is not very helpful in assessing the nature of tourism public policy. One general model that assists in distinguishing between different policies is that of Anderson (1994) who identified four different policy types: regulatory, self-regulatory, distributive and redistributive. These four policy types can be combined in a matrix with the roles of government in tourism as a means of assessing tourism policy (Table 6.1).

Regulatory policy

Regulatory policy refers to the placement of restrictions and limits on the actions of individual persons or organizations. Regulatory provisions may include restrictions on individual mobility for either political or environmental reasons; restrictions on land use or jurisdiction-wide resource protection laws (Parker 1999).

Self-regulatory policy

Self-regulatory policy is similar to regulatory policy in that it refers to controls on the behaviour of identified groups or individuals but is undertaken by the regulated group or non-government organization. Self-regulation may be utilized as a government policy so as to reduce its own costs of policy implementation or to satisfy the demands and needs of particular producer groups to reduce their compliance costs. However, self-regulation, like regulation, is only as effective as the extent to which compliance with regulation is sought. Unfortunately, the tourism industry are often poor self-regulators, particularly with respect to environmental concerns.

Table 6.1 Policy matrix: roles of government in tourism and policy types

Role of government	Regulatory policy	Self-regulatory policy	Distributive policy	Redistributive policy
Coordination				
Planning				
Entrepreneur				
Stimulation				
Promotion				
Social tourism				
Public interest				

Distributive policies

Distributive policies involve the distribution of benefits to particular groups in society. Parker (1999: 320) argues that distributive policy is 'fundamentally promotional in nature and governments rely heavily upon it to stimulate the tourism and ecotourism industries', although he also gives examples such as the use of investment tax credits, accelerated depreciation, leasing of property, subsidization and market support as exogenous distributive policies that are typically used to attract investment from external interests. Such measures may also be made available to domestic interests as well.

Redistributive policies

Redistributive policies are specific policies that government utilize to shift the distribution of wealth or other resources from one group in society to another. This may be undertaken on the basis of income levels, wealth, class, ethnicity or region. For example, in the 1980s ecotourism was conceived as a means of improving the level of economic well being of otherwise marginal communities in peripheral areas. More recently, the notion of pro-poor tourism has become increasingly significant as it reflects a policy idea that tourism can be used as a targeted means of redistribution of wealth through encouraging consumers to undertake certain tourism activities in specific locations that require increased income and/or job creation.

From politics to partnership?

The recent focus on ideas of governance in contemporary tourism within a multiscaled and multi-dimensional policy environment has focused attention on concepts such as partnership and cooperation as if governance implies the 'steering' of policy then stakeholders will need to be working in the same direction (Hall 2005). Partnerships are perceived as 'a search for efficiency within an organizationally fragmented and fiscally discontinuous landscape' (Lowndes 2001: 1962) as well as presenting new opportunities for uniting additional human and financial resources in order to build the capacity of tourism development. The notion of partnerships reflects the ideas of governance discussed above that no single organization is capable of tackling messy policy problems, such as those which occur in tourism, by itself (Bramwell and Lane 2000). As Deas (2005: 205) states, the policy-making consensus within government managerial thinking increasingly sees 'cross-sector, inclusive partnership working as itself inherently preferable to the narrower, out-moded styles characteristically pursued by local government'. Partnership has therefore become the dominant 'common-sense' of tourism policy in ways that make it a taken-for-granted element of tourism governance either within tourism marketing and development, i.e. between public tourism organization and private tourism firms, or in regional development or promotion programmes that utilize tourism as an element, i.e. urban redevelopment projects in which tourism is inte-grated with retailing, sport, entertainment and property development (Bramwell and Lane 2000).

However, many partnership programmes have been criticized for not bring-ing benefits to the communities they were meant to help (Cochrane 2007). Instead, some potential stakeholders are often left out of partnership arrangements, particu-larly with respect to urban redevelopment schemes. Therefore, as Healey (1997: 70) noted, 'unless all stakeholders are acknowledged in the process, policies and practices will be challenged, undermined and ignored'. Genuine collaboration and partnership therefore operates on a model of power, which is in keeping with the idea of the existence of a shared or public interest. A number of benefits of collab-oration can be identified (Hall 2000):

- Broad comprehensive analysis of the domain improves the quality of solutions.
- Response capacity is more diversified.
- It is useful for reopening deadlocked negotiations.
- The risk of impasse is minimized.
- The process ensures that each stakeholder's interests are considered in any agreement.
- Parties retain ownership of the solution.
- Parties most familiar with the problem, not their agents, invent the solutions.
- Participation enhances acceptance of solution and willingness to implement it.
- The potential to discover novel, innovative solutions is enhanced.
- Relations between the stakeholders improve.
- Cost associated with other methods are avoided.
- Mechanisms for coordinating future actions among the stakeholders can be established.

Yet critical to the collaborative process is the opportunity and capacity to participate. Genuine partnership in tourism development therefore may not mean the end of politics but instead provide a structure by which the full range of opinions and perspectives of those impacted by tourism can be heard and addressed. The inclusiveness of collaborative approaches may therefore help assist in dealing with some of the key problems of implementation in an increasingly complex environment for tourism policy and governance:

- Many tourism policies represent compromises between conflicting values of stakeholders.
- Many tourism policies involve compromises with key stakeholders and interests within the policy development and implementation structure.
- Many tourism policies involve compromises with key stakeholders and interests upon whom implementation will have an impact.
- Many tourism policies are framed without attention being given to the way in which underlying forces (particularly economic ones) and policy decisions outside of tourism will affect them.

Such policy-making difficulties for a field as full of diverse stakeholders as tourism are further complicated by the range of impacts that tourism has on destinations and the range of planning approaches that exist. We go on to examine these issues in the next two chapters.

Chapter overview

This chapter has examined the issues associated with governing the contemporary tourism product. Central to this has been the attention given to the changing role of government (the public sector) in governing tourism and the changing notion of governance itself. The concept of governance has been shown to refer to the capacity of government to steer the amalgam of public, private and third-sector stakeholder organizations in the pursuit of tourism policies. The task of government with respect to tourism and tourism destinations is demonstrated to be more complex than ever with increased potential for conflicts not only between different government roles and different forms of regulation with respect to tourism but also different stakeholders. The nature of governance was also demonstrated to be multiscale in nature whereby policy connections exist between international, national, regional and destination scales of governance. Nevertheless, despite the complexities and difficulties associated with governance of tourism and of destinations the state still continues to have a significant role with respect to both tourism policy and, perhaps more importantly for the nature and direction of tourism development, policies that affect tourism.

Self-review questions

1 What are the seven *roles* of government in tourism identified in this chapter?
2 What justifications may be given for government subsidy of *destination promotion*?
3 Why has the extent of *multi-scaled governance* increased, especially at the *supranational* level?
4 What are the key characteristics of *governance*?
5 What are the differences between the four *policy types*?
6 What are the main benefits of *collaboration*?
7 Why is governance increasingly *complex* in tourism?
8 Does the *nation state* still have a role with respect to tourism?

Recommended reading

1 Rhodes, R.A.W. (1997). *Understanding Governance: Policy Networks, Governance, Reflexivity and Accountability*. Buckingham: Open University Press.
   A seminal work on the notion of governance.
2 Bache, I. and Flinders, M. (eds) (2004). *Multi-level Governance*. Oxford: Oxford University Press.
   An important collection of chapters on issues associated with the complexity of multi-level governance.
3 Hall, C.M. (2000). *Tourism Planning*. Harlow: Prentice-Hall.
   Provides an account of tourism policy at various scales of analysis as well as the importance of cooperative approaches in tourism destinations.
4 Hall, C.M. and Jenkins, J.M. (1995). *Tourism and Public Policy*. London: Thomson.
   A seminal work on theories of tourism public policy that is still in print.
5 Jenkins, J.M. (2001). Editorial: tourism policy making theory and practice. *Current Issues in Tourism* 4(2–4), 69–77.
   A good introduction to policy-making issues in tourism. The entire issue is devoted to tourism policy making.
6 Dredge, D. and Jenkins, J.M. (2003). Federal-state relations and tourism public policy, New South Wales, Australia. *Current Issues in Tourism* 6(5), 415–443.
   A good analysis of multi-level policy issues.

7 Doorne, S. (1998). Power, participation and perception: an insider's perspective on the politics of the Wellington waterfront redevelopment. *Current Issues in Tourism* 1(2), 415–443.
A detailed examination of how some stakeholder groups were excluded from partnerships in relation to tourism development.

8 Bramwell, B. and Sharman, A. (1999). Collaboration in local tourism policymaking. *Annals of Tourism Research* 26(2), 392–415.
Useful example of collaboration in tourism.

9 Bramwell, B. and Lane, B. (eds) (2000). *Tourism Collaboration and Partnerships: Politics, Practice and Sustainability*. Clevedon: Channel View Publications.
One of the best collections of works on collaboration and partnership issues in tourism.

10 Lew, A., Hall, C.M. and Williams, A.M. (eds) (2004). *A Companion to Tourism*. Oxford: Blackwell.
Provides a detailed collection of review chapters on key aspects of tourism policy and governance, including the political economy of tourism.

Recommended web sites

United Nations World Tourism Organization: www.world-tourism.org
UNESCO World Heritage site: http://whc.unesco.org/
Nordic Council of Ministers: http://www.norden.org/
European Union: ec.europa.eu/
UNEP Government and policy support: http://www.uneptie.org/pc/tourism/policy/home.htm
Canadian Tourism Commission: www.corporate.canada.travel/en/ca/

References cited

Aa, B.J.M. van der (2005). *Preserving the Heritage of Humanity? Obtaining World Heritage Status and the Impacts of Listing*. Doctoral Thesis, Faculty of Spatial Sciences, University of Groningen, Groningen.

Aa, B.J.M. van der, Groote, P.D. and Huigen, P.P.P. (2004). World heritage as NIMBY: the case of the Dutch part of the Wadden Sea. *Current Issues in Tourism* 7(4–5), 291–302.

Anderson, J.E. (1994). *Public Policymaking: An Introduction*. Dallas: Houghton Mifflin.

Berg, P., Linde-Laursen, A. and Lofgren, O. (2000). *Invoking a Transnational Metropolis: The Making of the Øresund Region*. Lund: Studentlitteratur AB.

Bramwell, B. and Lane, B. (eds) (2000). *Tourism Collaboration and Partnerships: Politics, Practice and Sustainability*. Clevedon: Channel View Publications.

Cochrane, A. (2007). *Understanding Urban Policy: A Critical Approach*. Oxford: Blackwell Publishing.

Cookson, N. (2000). *Archeological Heritage Law*. Chichester: Barry Rose Law Publishers.

Deas, I. (2005). Synchronization, salesmanship and service delivery: governance and urban competitiveness. In N. Buck, I. Gordon, A. Harding and I. Thurok (eds), *Changing Cities: Rethinking Urban Competitiveness, Cohesion and Governance*. Basingstoke: Palgrave Macmillan.

Ek, R. (2005). Regional experiencescapes as geo-economic ammunition. In T. O'Dell (ed.), *Experiencescapes: Tourism Culture and Economy*, pp. 69–89. Copenhagen: Copenhagen Business School Press.

Hall, C.M. (2000). *Tourism Planning*. Harlow: Prentice-Hall.

Hall, C.M. (2005). *Tourism: Rethinking the Social Science of Mobility*. Harlow: Prentice-Hall.

Hall, C.M. (2006). World Heritage, tourism and implementation: what happens after listing. In A. Fyall and A. Leask (eds), *Managing World Heritage Sites*, pp. 18–32. Oxford: Butterworth Heinemann.

Hall, C.M. and Piggin, R. (2002). Tourism business knowledge of world heritage sites: a New Zealand case study. *International Journal of Tourism Research* 4, 401–411.

Healey, P. (1997). *Collaborative Planning: Shaping Places in Fragmented Societies*. Basingstoke: Macmillan Press.

Jessop, B. (1997). Capitalism and its future: remarks on regulation, government and governance. *Review of International Political Economy* 4(3), 561–581.

Lowndes, V. (2001). Rescuing Aunt Sally: taking institutional theory seriously in urban politics. *Urban Studies* 38(11), 1953–1971.

Marks, G. and Hooghe, M. (2004). Contrasting visions of multi-level governance. In I. Bache and M. Flinders (eds), *Multi-level Governance*. Oxford: Oxford University Press.

Maskell, P. and Törnqvist, G. (1999). *Building a Cross-border Learning Region: Emergence of the North European Øresund Region*. Copenhagen: Handelshøjskolens Forlag.

Parker, S. (1999). Ecotourism, environmental policy and development. In D.L. Soden and B.S. Steel (eds), *Handbook of Global Environmental Policy and Administration*, pp. 315–345. New York: Marcel Dekker.

Phillips, D. (2005). National pride, missed connections. *International Herald Tribune* 11–12 June, 13, 15.

Pike, A., Rodriguez-Pose, A. and Tomaney, J. (2006). *Local and Regional Development*. London: Routledge.

Rhodes, R. (1996). The new governance: governing without government. *Political Studies* 44, 652–667.

Rhodes, R.A.W. (1997). *Understanding Governance: Policy Networks, Governance, Reflexivity and Accountability*. Buckingham: Open University Press.

Rodwell, D. (2002). The world heritage convention and the exemplary management of complex heritage sites. *Journal of Architectural Conservation* 3, 40–60.

Intergovernmental Committee for the Protection of the World Cultural and Natural Heritage (1999). *Operational Guidelines for the Implementation of the World Heritage Convention*. Paris: UNESCO.

Chapter 7

Consequences of visitation at the contemporary destination

Chapter objectives

After reading this chapter you will

- Be able to appreciate some of the positive and negative perceptions of tourism's effects
- Appreciate that although the contemporary destination is a focal point of attention to the impacts of tourism that effects occur over all stages of the geographical tourism system
- Understand that the consequences of tourism are *contextual* and *situational*
- Understand that the potential significance of change for the consumption and production of tourism
- Be able to identify some of the key factors that affect the assessment of the effects of tourism

Introduction

Being aware of the consequences of visitation is not just important in terms of environmental and social responsibilities but also in terms of good business practice. As has been stressed throughout this book the multiple layers of the tourism product, especially with respect to the destination product, means that consideration needs to be given to the people and environments that are packaged as part of that product as otherwise the various qualities of a place that make it attractive to visit will be eroded. Therefore, an appreciation of the effects of tourism is vital to understanding the contemporary business environment of tourism as well as tourism's relationship to destinations.

One of the most significant debates in contemporary tourism centres on the positive and negative dimensions of tourism development. For many years tourism was generally seen in a favourable light and regarded as having a benign influence on destinations. However, with the advent of a new generation of jet aircraft in the late 1960s and early 1970s, and a consequent massive year on year growth in international travel which continues to the present day, tourism has now come to be seen as possibly having undesirable effects for destinations in addition to its potential economic benefits.

This chapter discusses some of the effects of tourist visitation. These impacts are discussed under various headings but the chapter emphasizes that these are not discrete categories. The chapter first examines some of the positive and negative dimensions of tourism before going on to outline some of the issues that arise in assessing tourism. These issues are important because they represent an important step in being able to accurately assess the consequences of tourism on people and places. The chapter then concludes by outlining different forms of the relationship between tourism and its various environments.

Positive and negative consequences of tourism

One of the significant dimensions in assessing the consequences of tourism is that the interpretation of the effects of tourism is often seen differently by different people. For example, increases in property values as a result of tourism development are often regarded positively by property owners and municipalities who gain income from property taxes but negatively by those who rent properties as they often lead to increased rents as well as making it more difficult to buy into the property market. In addition, differences in perceptions and understandings of the consequences of tourism will also be different between destinations, depending on the different attitudes towards tourism and the changes, it is related to and broader values and goals in society.

Within the tourism literature the impacts of tourism have usually been divided into three main categories: environmental (referring to the physical environment), social and economic (e.g. Matheson and Wall 1982). These categories are not mutually exclusive and have a significant degree of overlap but they serve as reasonable semantic devices by which to discuss tourism's effects (Figure 7.1). The interrelationships and interdependencies between economic, environmental and social dimensions mean that they also act as the main categories around which the notion of sustainable development is considered (see Chapter 8).

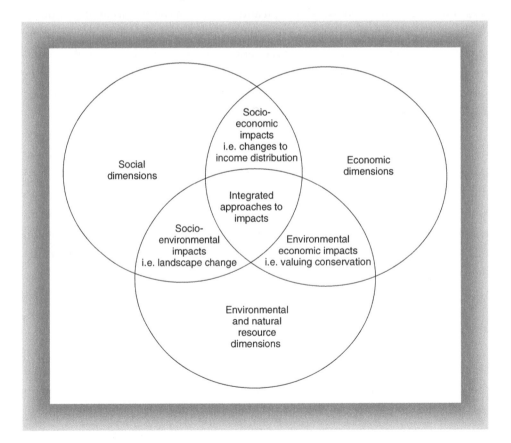

Figure 7.1   Interrelationships between tourism's impacts

For the consequences of tourism to be visible change has to occur. Therefore, change is an integral concept for understanding the impacts of tourism. Where change occurs very slowly and is incremental in nature there is usually relatively little negative attitudes towards tourism. Most circumstances in which negative attitudes towards tourism develop are usually related to rapid rates of change that is seen to be tourism induced. Although change is normal, rapid change makes it difficult for people to adapt to their new economic, social and physical environments. However, in recent years the rapid growth of tourism and tourism-related infrastructure and facilities has meant that the perceived consequences of tourism have been steadily increasing. Tourism is therefore no different than any other form of industrial development in terms of its potential for change. Indeed, some may argue that it may even have greater potential to contribute to change in some areas, such as with respect to culture and social relations, because the co-creation of tourism experiences intrinsically requires social exchange.

An additional issue with respect to assessing the consequences of tourism is that they occur at different scales and at different stages of the tourist trip. For example, with respect to the elements of the geographical tourism system (Figure 7.2) many of the effects of tourism occur outside of the destination. The generation of greenhouse gas emissions from transport primarily occurs along the transit route but has effects on all elements of the system. At the individual level, people living at all stages of the production of the trip will be affected by the co-creation of tourism experience. This will include people working in the tourism industry such as those involved in enabling the tourist getting to and from the destination as well as in the destination themselves as part of the tourism labour force. However, importantly, this will also include the tourists themselves who will be affected by the travel experience. Indeed, one of the most significant insights of understanding that tourism experiences are co-created (Chapter 1) is that this invariably means that there are social exchanges between consumer and producer, as well as, of course, economic and environmental exchanges although the latter is often not so visible. This observation does not mean that such exchanges will be equal in terms of such factors as, e.g. power, roles, income, language or status, but it does mean that such exchanges occur and that both parties will be affected in some way.

People living along transit routes and in the generating region near major transport connections, such as airports, will also be affected by tourism. This is often most visible in terms of their reaction to noise and other pollution as a result of tourism transport but will also include significant economic impacts because of

Relative tangibility of consequences of tourism to external view	Examples of dimensions in which effects of co-creation of tourism are observed	Generating region	Transit region	Destination	Environment external to tourist trip
High	Physical environment				
	Built environment				
	Economic environment				
	Socio-cultural environment				
	Product/ service environment				
	Personal – consumer	Consumer ⇕ Producer	Consumer ⇕ Producer	Consumer ⇕ Producer	
Low	Personal – producer				

Shading indicates relative change as a consequence of the consumption and production of tourism.

Figure 7.2 Change matrix of consequences of tourism

the economic contribution of tourism to employment along transit routes even if people do not stay overnight on their way to their main destination. Although tourism has consequences at all stages of the trip, the greatest concentration of impacts usually occurs at the destination itself (Figure 7.2). Therefore, the next section will discuss some of the key dimensions of destination effects.

Within the tourism literature several key themes emerge (see Lew et al. 2004 for a selection of review chapters that detail some of these themes). The economic dimension is obviously significant as it is the potential income and employment aspects of tourism that drive government and destination policy with respect to tourism marketing and management. In the economic sphere, primary concerns are with the economic contribution of tourism to destination and national growth and economic development and employment generation. Secondary issues focus on the opportunity costs of tourism development, linkages with other sectors and the implications of foreign investment.

With respect to environmental consequences attention has focused on the contribution of tourism to a loss of naturalness, landscape changes, changes to physical environmental systems and habitats and their consequences and issues of biodiversity. Secondary concerns have often focused on specific environments, such as alpine areas or coral reefs, as well as the relationship between tourism and conservation. Perhaps most significantly with respect to the environmental consequences of tourism is the realization that the impacts of tourism occur at more than just the destination and this has therefore led to a substantial reevaluation of the environmental dimensions of contemporary tourism (see Chapter 13 for a fuller discussion of the implications of this).

The social and cultural consequences of tourism are extremely complex as they relate not only to the different scales at which change occurs: cultures, communities and individuals – but also to particular categories of individuals: tourists and the producers of the tourism experience whether they be formally a part of the tourism industry or be part of the broader human resource base of tourism by being a part of the destination to which tourists come to visit. To complicate matters still further the same individual will often fulfil different roles at different times over their life course, at one time being a tourist and at another time being a producer. Indeed, in some situations it is possible that an individual may be both by being a tourist as well as being a part of the tourist experience for someone else (see the Tasmanian case study in Chapter 2 for an example here).

At the destination level, a key theme is the extent to which tourism leads to changes in the sense of place of a community (see also Chapter 5) as well as to cultural change. Such changes are usually seen in a negative light, however, in some instances tourism has been credited with helping to conserve culture by providing a market for cultural activities that had little external value outside of that culture. In one sense this is similar to the value that tourism can bring to the environment by creating a market for national parks and ecotourism products that otherwise may have only limited market value. However, change is individual as well as collective therefore there is also significant interest in how tourism has consequences for personal values and attitudes and how these may change. For tourists many of these consequences will usually be felt back in their home environment after they have had the opportunity to reflect on their experiences in terms of the encounters

Table 7.1 Perceived impacts of tourism on destinations identified in tourism literature

Type of impact	Positive	Negative
Economic	Increased expenditures	Localized inflation and price increases
	Creation of employment	Replacement of local labour by outside labour
	Increase in labour supply	Greater seasonal unemployment
	Increased value of real estate	Real estate speculation
	Increase in standard of living	Increased income gap between wealthy and poor
	Improved investment in infrastructure and services	Opportunity cost of investment in tourism means that other services and sectors do not get support
	Increased free trade	Inadequate consideration of alternative investments
	Increased foreign investment	Inadequate estimation of costs of tourism development
		Increased free trade
		Loss of local ownership
Tourism/ commercial	Increased destination awareness	Acquisition of a poor reputation as a result of inadequate facilities, improper practices or inflated prices
	Increased investor knowledge concerning the potential for investment and commercial activity in the destination	Negative reactions from existing enterprises due to the possibility of new competition for human resources and state assistance
	Development of new infrastructure and facilities, including accommodation and attractions	Inappropriate destination images and brands are used
	Increase in accessibility	
	Improvements in destination image	
Environmental/ physical	Changes in natural processes that enhance environmental values	Changes in natural environmental processes
	Maintenance of biodiversity	Loss of biodiversity
	Architectural conservation	Architectural pollution

(Continued)

Table 7.1   (Continued)

Type of impact	Positive	Negative
	Preservation of natural and built heritage	Destruction of heritage
	Maintenance and recreation of habitat and ecosystems	Destruction of habitat and ecosystems
		Exceeding physical carrying capacity
Social/ cultural	Increased local participation in destination activities and events	Commercialization and commodification of activities, events and objects that may be of a personal nature
	Community renewal	Changes in community structure
	Strengthening of community values and traditions	Weakening or loss of community values and traditions
	Exposure to new ideas through globalization and transnationalism	Increases in criminal activity
	Creation of new community space	Loss of community space
		Social dislocation
		Exceeding social carrying capacity
		Loss of authenticity
Psychological	Increased local pride and community spirit	Tendency towards defensive attitudes concerning host regions
	Tourism as a force for peace	High possibility of misunderstandings leading to varying degrees of host/ visitor hostility
	Increased awareness of non-local values and perceptions	Increased alienation as a result of changes to what was familiar
Political/ administrative	Enhanced international recognition of destination region	Economic exploitation of local population to satisfy ambitions of political elite/growth coalitions
	Greater political openness	Use of tourism to legitimate unpopular decisions or regimes
	Development of new administrative institutions	Tourism used to fund repressive regimes and legitimate their ideologies

Source: Mathieson and Wall (1982), Ritchie (1984), Krippendorf (1987), Hall (1992), Lew et al. (2004) and Hall and Page (2006).

that occurred on the trip but also how such experiences may cast new light on their social relations at home or work and on concepts and understandings of self. For individuals who are part of the tourism product, the service experience may have tasks of performance and emotional labour that also lead to reassessment of notions of self and personal relations. Indeed, the nature of the tourist experience also leads to considerable interest in the values that are exchanged, and their appropriateness, as well as on the very authenticity of the experiences that all parties have, but particularly from the consumer's perspective.

Table 7.1 details some of the main positive and negative effects of tourism that have been detailed in the tourism literature organized by six different categories of primarily collective impact. One of the immediate observations that can be made of the consequences of tourism is that the same consequence can be seen as either positive or negative – even in the same destination – depending on the perspective of the viewer and the situation in which it occurs. A fundamental element of understanding contemporary tourism is that the consequences of tourism are *contextual* and *situational*. This does not mean that they do not occur in an empirical sense nor that they are unimportant. Instead, it highlights the fact that from a services perspective in which we have the co-creation of tourism experiences as the core of our understanding of contemporary tourism phenomenon, then what is critical for managing those consequences is knowing how and why they are identified as consequences over which stakeholder concern is expressed and action may be required. The following case study demonstrates the differing consequences of hosting and bidding for a major sporting event.

CASE STUDY
Impact of the 2006 Football World Cup and bidding for 2018

Football (soccer) is the world's favourite sport. The football World Cup is one of the world's largest sporting hallmark events which has significant impacts on the host nation as well as on participating countries. For example, research by ABN-AMRO (van Leeuwen and Kalshoven 2006) suggested that a World Cup winner enjoys an average economic bonus of 0.7 per cent additional growth, while the losing finalist suffers an average loss of 0.3 per cent compared to the previous year. Hallmark sporting events have long been recognized as being significant for the promotion of sports tourism, urban regeneration strategies and reimaging (Ritchie and Adair 2004; Hall 2005) and being part of a broader political economy of sport (Nauright and Schimmel 2005). According to the UK Treasury, cities and countries bid to host global sporting events for a variety of reasons, other than the pure sporting spectacle:

- The positive economic impact of visitors during the event and potential for new tourism markets.
- As a catalyst for the economic regeneration of a city or region.
- The intangible benefits often associated with sporting events including increases in national pride and strengthened identity.
- The opportunity to showcase an emerging nation or city – this has become especially relevant in recent years with the awarding of the Summer Olympics in 2008 to Beijing and the 2010 Football World Cup to South Africa (HM Treasury 2007a: 5).

A study for Postbank, a German bank that was one of the 2006 World Cup's competition sponsors, reported that the 2006 World Cup in Germany should create 40 000 jobs in the country and that Growth domestic product (GDP) should rise by about €10 billion (approximately US $12 billion) (Milne 2005a), a figure representing 0.5 per cent of the German economy's total domestic productivity. The study also said that World Cup 2006 could help create 10 000–20 000 permanent jobs (Davis 2006). The World Cup was also regarded as important for the morale of German industry given the then downturn of the German economy. According to Herbert Heiner, chief executive of Adidas the world's second largest sporting goods manufacturer and an official World Cup sponsor for which it paid approximately US $56.5 million for exclusive marketing rights (Davis 2006), 'It is a very good chance for us and the whole of Germany to push us out of the agony we have in the country… With a positive World Cup we can bring some optimism to the country and to the economy in general' (in Milne 2005a: 20). In order to maximize returns from the Cup Adidas brought together 100 people to work solely on preparations for the World Cup with the aim of achieving soccer sales of €1 billion in 2006, up from €900 million in 2004. However, actual results were even better with Adidas reporting a 37 per cent rise in sales in first quarter 2006 and reported sales of US $1.5 billion during World Cup 2006, an increase of 30 per cent on the previous Cup (Davis 2006). An example of the impact of a World Cup on Adidas is that Adidas reported sales of 15 million replica footballs. Over double the sales of the 6 million official World Cup soccer balls of the 2002 World Cup (Milne 2005b).

Other companies also believed they would benefit. For example, Jochen Zeitz, head of the world's number three sporting goods manufacturer, Puma, stated that 'it will have a lot of impact on confidence in our industry and in the retail sector' (in Milne 2005a: 20). This was despite the fact that Puma could not be an official sponsor of the World Cup and instead sponsored players, e.g. Freddie Ljungberg of Sweden, and national teams, e.g. Cameroon and Italy. An indication of the commercial importance attached to the World Cup was that Puma even brought forward the launch of its strategic plan by a year so that it coincided with the 2006 competition and ends with the 2010 Cup in South Africa.

The worldwide interest in the World Cup explains its attraction to both government and industry alike. According to FIFA (2007) 'the FIFA World Cup™ represents one of the most effective global marketing platforms which offers sponsors unmatched opportunities for reaching out to the consumer. ... [and] ... reaches an audience of a size and diversity that is unrivalled by any other single-sports body'. The 2006 World Cup in Germany was covered by 500 television broadcasters and generated total coverage of more than 73 000 hours, equivalent to over 8 years of broadcasting. Media interest is also indicated by the 18 850 accredited journalists hosted by the tournament. Of these journalists, 13 400 were television and radio representatives, 4250 print journalists and 1200 were photographers. The official web site FIFAworldcup.com registered 4.2 billion page views in total during the competition (FIFA 2007).

The 64 matches at the 2006 World Cup had a total attendance of 3.36 million people with an average attendance per game of 52 491. This was the second biggest attendance in World Cup history with the largest being the 1994 Cup in the United States which attracted 3.59 million people to games with an average attendance of 68 991 (there were 52 matches in the 1994 event). Nevertheless, in the German tournament many international visitors still travelled to Germany – even though they would never get tickets to see a game live – in order to experience the atmosphere and watch the game on giant screens at 'Fan Fests' which had been organized by the World Cup host cities.

The 2006 World Cup was undoubtedly an opportunity for substantial investment in sport and other infrastructure with investment having substantial legacies with respect to employment, infrastructure and tax benefits (Ahlert 2000). 1510.4 million was invested in stadium development for the World Cup of which 575.9 million was public financed. 124.6 million was invested in new media facilities though the greatest amount of investment was on transport infrastructure. Within the 12 regions in which World Cup matches were staged 3577.1 million was invested in transport infrastructure with total supplementary public investment in transport infrastructure of around 5600 million. The majority of this came from the German federal government and was primarily put into motorways and traffic information and control. Ahlert (2006) forecast that the macroeconomic impact due to the World Cup induced inbound tourism consumption would lead to increases in GDP and consumption in 2006 but that impacts would be almost negligible by 2008. In 2006 under favourable conditions, Ahlert (2006) estimated that the World Cup-induced supplementary inbound tourism consumption (approximately €1 billion) would lead to an increase in the annual German GDP growth rate of up to 0.07 per cent. Ahlert (2006: 10) identified five positive 'sustainable impacts' for Germany of hosting the FIFA World Cup 2006:

- Upgrade of the national transportation system (railway and land transport, traffic steering systems) update of the German football stadium facilities.
- Update of the national tourism information system as a multilingual interactive platform using the Internet.
- New alignment of Germany as a modern and hospitable destination in international tourism with cultural and regional diversity.
- Promotion of the German tourism industry with a relatively low-price level and perfect service and shopping facilities.
- Promotion of Germany as an excellent place for international investors.

The range of benefits of hosting World Cup matches and visitors was also recognized by Karl-Heinz Merfield, head of Cologne Tourism, a city in which five games were played. According to Merfield:

> In the short term, our city's economy will directly benefit from fans and visitors spending money in hotels, shops, restaurants and bars as well as on transport. This will produce an estimated additional income for Cologne's local economy of some 10 million Euro. In the long term, Cologne will benefit from an improved reputation of being an international city of sport and events.
>
> The World Cup represents fantastic public relations opportunity for our city. Tour operators, travel agencies and the whole tourism industry in Cologne and the region will benefit. In addition, the City of Cologne and the German Government are investing millions on public transport, improvement of roads and other areas of infrastructures. Cologne's sports infrastructure is being improved greatly – not only for our guests but also for residents. All of these measures will contribute to the success of the games as well as having long-lasting economic benefit (City Mayors 2006).

However, the long-term benefits of hosting a World Cup at a national level are seen as rather mixed. As Holger Schmieding an economist in the Bank of America stated, 'It is an opportunity… But I don't think on its own it will make a difference, although it could contribute' (in Milne 2005c: 9). An analysis of the soccer World Cups held from 1954 to 1998 indicated that eight of the host countries witnessed increased economic growth after the competition while four had lower growth. While in a study of the 1994 World Cup in the United States the estimated losses of the host cities amounted to US $4 billion as opposed to a predicted gain of US $4 billion (Milne 2005c). For Germany, Otto Schilly, the Interior Minister, stated that he expected GDP to be boosted by 8–10 billion over several years as a result of hosting the event.

The construction industry was clearly a major beneficiary with the World Cup being estimated to be worth 3.5 billion and the creation of 20 000 jobs in the sector. Tourism was also expected to benefit with the German Tourism Office forecasting an extra 5.5 million overnight stays during the month of the competition, an increase of one-sixth above the normal levels for June, leading to approximately a million Euro increase in tourist spending. Nevertheless, overall benefits might not have been as great as expected. Despite double the expected number of tourist visits (approximately 2 million) tourists spending 600 million (approximately US $766 million), German economic growth was approximately 0.25 per cent, half of the expected amount as a result of hosting the Cup (Davis 2006). German Economic Minister Michael Glos wrote in the business daily *Handelsblatt* that 50 000 jobs had been created with only half being temporary, slightly more than planned. However, the best results he believed were that World Cup 2006 '[marked] an enormous gain in Germany's image' (Davis 2006). An observation no doubt encouraged not only by the overall positive media coverage of the management and planning of the event, but also be the perhaps unexpected success of the German team on the football field. Indeed, much of the impact is psychological, a 'feel-good' factor. As van Leeuwen and Kalshoven (2006: 1–2) observed: 'Happier consumers are more inclined to spend more. Leaving aside the fact that the parties in the winning country will last longer (which means higher turnovers at bars and supermarkets) and that there will be a market for souvenirs of the sweet victory (DVDs, shirts and other merchandising), it is undeniable that confident consumers spend more'.

For the 2006 World Cup, the German Football Association has announced that a profit before tax of €135 million had been made from staging the 2006 competition. Net of tax and after repaying the FIFA contribution of €40.8 million, the €56.6 million net profit will be shared between the German Football Association (DFB) and the German Football League (DFL) (HM Treasury 2007a). However, the operating costs and therefore operating profit excludes any major capital infrastructure costs associated with the tournament which, as noted above, were substantial.

Such are the perceived economic benefits of hosting a football World Cup that in February 2007 then Chancellor Gordon Brown released the results of a study into bidding for the 2018 event which concluded that England had an excellent chance of success (HM Treasury 2007a). According to Gordon Brown:

> By 2018, it will be more than 50 years since England first hosted the World Cup, and I believe it is time the tournament returned to the nation which gave football to the world. With the Olympics in London in 2012, hosting the World Cup in 2018 would make the next decade the greatest in Britain's sporting history.
>
> I want every region of the country to share in the benefits of these sporting events, I want every young person to be inspired by them to increase their own participation in sport, and – if The FA decide to launch a bid – I would make it my personal mission over the next few years to persuade countries around the world to support that bid (HM Treasury 2007b).

The feasibility study was launched by Chancellor Brown in November 2005 with the English Football Association working with the Treasury (HM Treasury 2005). Even though any decision on bidding for the World Cup would not be made until 2010, the conduct of the study indicates the long lead time required to bid for major sporting events as well as the relationship of sport to politics. HM Treasury (2007a) concluded that England was well placed because most of the infrastructure is in place and public support for a bid was regarded as strong even given the poor showing of the national team in the 2006 Cup. In addition to FIFA's requirements for government guarantees for hosting a World Cup, six stadia already meet the FIFA requirements and a further five have been identified as possible venues (Table 7.2). The report stressed that unlike the London 2012 Olympics, the bulk of the expense for the event would be borne by football clubs. Indeed, as Kelso (2007) observed, it is a mark of the economic and budgetary concerns raised by the Olympic experience that the study repeatedly warns that the Football Association will have to provide 'robust and realistic assessments of costs' to secure government support. Overall the study (HM Treasury 2007: 3, 21, 24, 27, 36) found a number of positive bases for proceeding with a bid:

- Hosting the World Cup is regarded as being likely to produce a positive economic impact as well as other associated intangible benefits such as pride and a sporting legacy.
- There are at least 11 existing football stadia in England that could potentially host World Cup matches – with Wembley National Stadium providing a centrepiece (others include Old Trafford, Emirates Stadium, St James Park, City of Manchester Stadium, Stadium of Light, Anfield, Villa Park, Stamford Bridge, Goodison Park, Elland Road).

Table 7.2 FIFA requirements for government guarantees and infrastructure technical requirements for a World Cup (abridged)

- Entry and exit permits are to be issued to all officials related to FIFA and national organizations, and to media representatives and visitors.
- Work permits (if required by local law) are to be provided to all officials and staff related to FIFA and finalist teams, and media representatives.
- Customs duty and taxes are not to be raised for the temporary import and subsequent export of goods, supplies, personal belongings, gifts and equipment of players, officials and the media.
- Security shall be provided by the host country, including at airports, city centres, anti-terrorist activities, etc., and a guarantee of safety and personal protection shall also apply to the FIFA delegation, media representatives and spectators during, before and after matches, including when travelling around the country.
- Government shall guarantee unrestricted import and export of all foreign currencies as well as the exchange and re-conversion of these currencies into US dollars or Swiss Francs.
- The government shall guarantee the installation of a telecommunications network.
- The host country shall assist the organizing association in setting up an international broadcast centre and a media centre.
- The national transport network shall provide the transport necessary for the technical organization of a FIFA World Cup.
- A hotel pricing policy is required, that freezes hotel prices for officials related to FIFA and accredited media at the level of the beginning of the year that the World Cup competition will be held.
- The host country shall not exact any kind of taxes, charges, duties or government levies from FIFA or the team delegations.
- Commissions on tickets shall not exceed 10 per cent of the face value of the ticket.
- The host country shall guarantee that all national anthems and flags will be provided at matches.
- The host country shall guarantee the availability of comprehensive medical care including an emergency service for every participant.
- The following stadium infrastructure specifications are likely to be required in a future World Cup bid:
  - eight to twelve stadia are required;
  - prospective stadia must have the following capacity:
    - for group matches, the round of 16 and the quarter finals (excluding media and VIPs) – a minimum of 40 000 people;

(Continued)

Table 7.2 (Continued)

- for the opening match, semi-finals and final (excluding media and VIPs) – a minimum of 60 000 people;
  - prospective stadia must be seated with no perimeter fences;
  - there must be a natural turf pitch measuring at least 105 × 68 metres, with a further 7.5 metres between the pitch and spectators behind each goal and 6 metres around the side touchlines;
  - a minimum of 10 technical and administrative rooms must be available;
  - a choice of training grounds, in good condition, close to competitor's living quarters must be available.

Source: HM Treasury (2007). *Hosting the World Cup: A Feasibility Study*, HMSO: 17, 18, 19 – Crown copyright.

- A solid foundation of public support exists for England pursuing a bid for hosting a World Cup in 2018. This was established through a UK-wide public opinion survey of over 2000 adults aged 16 years or above conducted prior to the Germany 2006 World Cup to inform the study. According to the public opinion survey, over half (56 per cent) of the sample were in favour of England making a bid to host the 2018 World Cup, with almost half of those being very strongly in favour. Only 6 per cent of the sample were against England making a bid, and 34 per cent were neither in favour nor against. Reasons for being in favour of or against the bid are outlined in Table 7.3.
- As a country that already received substantial numbers of overseas visitors the UK is well placed to handle the large influx of visitors that would accompany a World Cup.
- The UK generally has an excellent record of bidding for, and winning, the opportunity to host major sporting events. There are many examples of best practice, such as the London Olympics bid, that The FA could therefore draw upon to increase the chances of success.

However, it was also noted that there were a number of key issues associated with costs of the event that would need to be addressed:

... security costs are likely to represent a substantial element of the operating costs and it is important to accurately assess the costs and financing options to inform

Table 7.3   Reasons for being in favour of or against World Cup bid

Main reasons for being in favour of a bid	% of those in favour of a bid
'Good for the economy'	42
'National pride'	39
'Interest in football'	31
'Better chance that England will win'	9
'Motivating others to play football'	9
'Good for the country'	5
Main reasons for being against a bid	*% of those against of a bid*
'Costs'	49
'Not interested in football'	26
'Football hooliganism/trouble'	19
'Not very good at organizing such things'	5

Source: World Cup Omnibus Survey, April 2006 in HM Treasury (2007). *Hosting the World Cup: A Feasibility Study*, HMSO: 37 – Crown copyright.

any bid. The existing provision and planned improvements to England's transport infrastructure should enable the network to cope with extra demand during a World Cup, but it will be important that the increased operating costs are considered and financing is identified. Responsibility for all costs must be established before any bid is submitted. Emphasis should be put on maximising contributions from across the sporting and private sectors (HM Treasury 2007a: 3).

Key sources

Ahlert, G. (2005). *What Does Germany Expect to Gain from Hosting the 2006 Football World Cup – Macroeconomic and Regional Economic Effects*. GWS Discussion Paper 2005/4. Osnabrück: Gesellschaft für Wirtschaftliche Strukturforschung mbH.

HM Treasury (2007). *Hosting the World Cup: A Feasibility Study*. Norwich: HMSO.

Nauright, J. and Schimmel, K. (eds) (2005). *The Political Economy of Sport*. London: Palgrave Macmillan.

Official web site of the Fédération International de Football Association (FIFA): www.fifa.com

Ritchie, B. and Adair, D. (2004). *Sports Tourism: Interrelationships, Impacts and Issues*. Clevedon: Channel view Publications.

References

Ahlert, G. (2001). The economic effects of the Soccer World Cup 2006 in Germany with regards to different financing. *Economic Systems Research* 13(1), 109–127.

Ahlert, G. (2005). *What Does Germany Expect to Gain from Hosting the 2006 Football World Cup – Macroeconomic and Regional Economic Effects*. GWS Discussion Paper 2005/4. Osnabrück: Gesellschaft für Wirtschaftliche Strukturforschung mbH.

Ahlert, G. (2006). FIFI World Cup Germany 2006™: perspectives for Tourism. Paper presented at *1st ASEM Seminar on Tourism*, Lisbon, Portugal, 8 May.

City Mayors (2006). For one month Cologne will be home from home for Brazilian football fans: an interview with Karl-Heinz Merfield, Head of Cologne Tourism, 15 January: http://www.citymayors.com/tourism/cologne_worldcup.html

Davis, O. (2006). *World Cup 2006 Economics: Winners and Losers Beyond Italy and Zidane*. AC Associated Content Media Company, 26 July.

FIFA (2007) Mass appeal of the FIFA World Cup™. FIFA.com – Marketing and TV, The Official Website of the Fédération Internationale de Football Association: http://www.fifa.com/en/marketing/concept/index/0,1304,22,00.html (accessed 25 January 2007).

Hall, C.M. (2005). Selling places: hallmark events and the reimaging of Sydney and Toronto. In J. Nauright and K. Schimmel (eds), *The Political Economy of Sport*, pp.129–151. London: Palgrave Macmillan.

HM Treasury (2005). *Government Launches Work on England 2018 World Cup Bid*. HM Treasury Press Notices 96/05, 18 November, London.

HM Treasury (2007a). *Hosting the World Cup: A Feasibility Study*. Norwich: HMSO.

HM Treasury (2007b). *Government Publishes England World Cup Study*. HM Treasury Press Notices 19/07, 12 February, London.

Kelso, P. (2007). Henry on call for 2018 as World Cup bid gathers pace. *The Guardian* 13 February.

Milne, R. (2005a). World Cup could bring a German net gain. *Financial Times* 15 June, 20.

Milne, R. (2005b). Operation World Cup: war begins. *Financial Times* 15 June, 9.

Milne, R. (2005c). Germany gets in training to host month of games. *Financial Times* 15 June, 9.

van Leeuwen, R. and Kalshoven, C. (2006). Soccer and the economy. *Soccernomics 2006*. ABN AMRO Economics Department, March.

Discussion questions

1 What are the benefits and costs of hosting a major sporting event such as a football World Cup?

2 Should government be financially supporting the hosting of major sporting events if the income from the event goes to the sporting association?

3 What role might major sporting events have in urban reimaging and regeneration strategies?

Assessing the consequences of tourism

As noted above, the consequences of tourism are both contextual and situational. This means that there are a number of issues that must be clarified in seeking to identify and understand the consequences of visitation (Hall 2008) (Figure 7.3):

1 *Definition*: Given the problems inherent in identifying tourism phenomenon and tourists and distinguishing tourism from other forms of mobility and leisure behaviour (see Chapter 1) it can be difficult in isolating the impacts of tourism from other forms of human mobility.

2 *Differentiation*: Following on from the previous issue, in many social and environmental environments it can be difficult to isolate the impacts of tourism from other industrial and cultural impacts. Nevertheless, tourism has long been 'blamed' for changing places, particularly in destinations in the developing world. For example, one of the first books on tourism planning, by Baud-Bovy and Lawson (1977: 183) commented that tourism: 'degrades irreversibly the very attractions which justified and attracted it, eroding natural resources, breaking up the unity

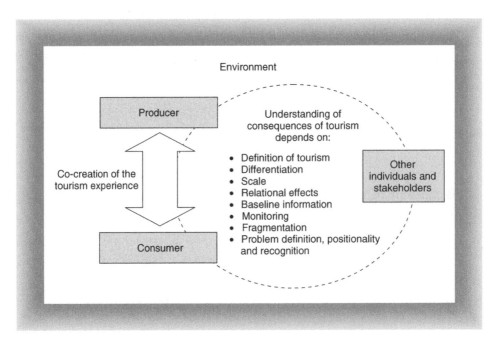

Figure 7.3   Understanding the consequences of tourism

and scale of traditional landscapes and their characteristic buildings, polluting beaches, damaging forests and rendering banal under the inundation of alien facilities of often mediocre uniform design a formerly unique country'. However, any form of development can affect the physical and social environment – for good or for worse. Criticism of tourism has been particularly strong with respect to the effects of tourism on culture yet even though tourism is clearly a part of processes of cultural globalization, its effects may be difficult to separate from those of the media and the Internet or even religion. In such a situation it may be that the very visibility of tourists and tourism facilities may serve to focus attention on tourism as a potential change agent rather than other factors.

3 *Scale*: Tourism has impacts over different scales, from the individual through to communities and destinations and beyond. In addition, tourism has impacts over time. Therefore, in seeking to assess the impacts of tourism it is extremely important to clearly identify the boundaries of analysis and the advantages and disadvantages of the boundaries used. For example, the majority of studies of the effects of tourism are at a site or destination level which may mean that some of the global effects of tourism may be missed (Gössling and Hall 2006; see Chapter 13) and, just as significantly, many tourism studies are one-offs rather than being a part of a longitudinal or time series study. The latter situation therefore potentially affecting our understanding of how tourism affects a place over time.

The issue of scale and the delimitation of boundaries of analysis has a major affect on studying the economic impacts of tourism. There has been a failure in many studies to delimit the implications of the size of the regional economy that is to be studied – the smaller the area to be analysed, the greater will be the number of 'visitors' and hence the greater is the estimate of economic impact. However, this issue of delimitation will also influence what is included and excluded in social and environmental impact assessment.

4 *Relational effects*: Tourism is often discussed as if it had a one-way impact, i.e. tourism affects a destination, without it being highlighted that in reality the impacts, effects or consequences are two-way in that tourism affects a destination and vice versa, the destination affects tourism. This is also an important issue as it stresses that there is an exchange process occurring at all levels with respect to tourism, i.e. from personal exchange between visitors and members of the destination community through to economic and environmental flows. This relational dimension is integral to understanding how tourism systems actually work, but is often not sufficiently stressed in discussions of tourism in many texts (Hall 2000).

5 *Baseline information*: In order to understand the effects of tourism, it is desirable to understand what a location was like before tourism was developed. Unfortunately, in all but a very few circumstances such baseline data do not exist. Therefore, in some cases an approximate estimate may be made. For example, in some locations that have previously had little human impact it may be possible to approximate environmental conditions such as biodiversity and geomorphology.

6 *Monitoring*: There is often little ongoing monitoring of the consequences of tourism. For example, in a review of the environmental impacts of tourism developments in Australia, Warnken and Buckley (2000) noted that only 7.5 per cent of Australian developments were subject to a formal monitoring process. When monitoring did occur there was a greater use of BACIP (before, after, control, impact, paired sampling) environmental impact assessment designs. However, Warnken and Buckley observed that there was often a lack of control sites, and the implementation of monitoring programs was often subject to constraints in time and finance (2000: 459–460):

> One common deficiency is the absence or inadequacy of predevelopment baseline monitoring – the before, after (BA) comparison in the BACIP design. Some human disturbances are unforeseen, and monitoring can take place only after the event. More commonly, however, entrepreneurs are simply reluctant to invest in monitoring until development approvals have been granted, and then want to commence construction immediately after having received approval, without time for predevelopment baseline monitoring.

7 *Fragmentation*: Our knowledge of the consequences of visitation are extremely fragmented. This is partially because of some of the problems outlined above but also because tourism research is often concentrated on some locations or environments and not on others. This has meant that there is arguably a disproportionate amount of research at some places, such as the Great Barrier Reef Marine Park or Yellowstone National Park, or on some types of tourism, such as ecotourism, when compared to mass tourism destinations which is what the bulk of leisure tourists engage in.

8 *Problem definition, positionality and recognition*: Although it may sound somewhat strange one of the most significant issues with respect to understanding what the consequences of tourism are is being able to perceive what constitutes a problem in terms of tourism's effects. Chapter 5 emphasized that tourism resources constitute

a resource because they are recognized as such in terms of a utility value. In exactly the same way many problems are also perceptual in nature. Many of the consequences of tourism may not be recognized or may be recognized by some and not others. Furthermore, one's position in the tourism system may also affect how you perceive the consequences of tourism with those working in the industry often having very different understandings of its effects from those who work outside it. A situation that clearly raises challenges for assessing the consequences of tourism. To rework the insights of Zimmermann (1951) with respect to resources (noted in Chapter 5) in the case of the consequences of tourism: problems are not, they become; they are not static but expand and contract in response to human actions, perceptions and wants. Different people, cultures and nationalities can have different perceptions of the consequences of tourism often as a result of different sets of values or aesthetic judgements. A resort or tourism development may be architectural pollution to one person and deemed as beautiful and aesthetically pleasing to another. Therefore, what is a problem or valuable for one person or in one culture may be 'neutral stuff' to another. Or in other words, what may be a recognized as a consequence of tourism in one culture or location may not be recognized as a problem in another. For example, between May 2000 and 2005 the Tate Gallery in London had received nearly 22 million visits. Between April 2004 and March 2005 it received 4.15 million visits surpassing the 3.6 million visits of the Pompidou Centre in Paris over the same period. In 2004, 60 per cent of Tate Modern's visitors were under 35 and 40 per cent were repeat visitors. As a result it was recognized that the Tate Modern had 'energized' the 'long-neglected' Southwark neighbourhood of London. Art galleries and restaurants have sprung up, buildings are being renovated and new ones are appearing (Riding 2005: 8). Nevertheless, the development created conflicts between the art space and real estate and hence different values of the nature of the resource and how it should be used. 'A development group has acquired a small property barely 30 yards from the ramp leading down to the Turbine Hall, where it plans to build a high-rise that would soar above Tate Modern' (Riding 2005: 8).

9 *Integration*: The majority of studies have examined the impacts of tourism and recreation on a particular environment or component of the environment rather than a range of environments and there has been little attempt to present an integrated approach to the assessment of the impacts of tourism which requires consideration of economic, social and environmental dimensions of tourism as part of

'solving' impact issues (Hall and Härkönen 2006). (This point is taken up further in Chapter 8 in discussing different approaches to tourism planning.) This has meant that problems associated with the consequences of tourism are often treated in a one dimensional often disciplinary fashion rather than seeing issues as being intertwined. For example, environmental problems are usually a result of underlying economic and social issues and physical measures to manage an environmental issue may not work unless the reasons underlying the problem are fully understood in the first place.

Approaches to integrative assessment

In order to address issues of integration, two related approaches are increasingly being utilized. First, the development of new institutional approaches and methods to encourage integrated problem solving. Second, the utilization of post-disciplinary approaches to tourism issues (Coles et al. 2006). The former is especially strong in resource management and connects to the ideas of governance and stakeholder relations outlined in Chapter 6. Collaborative strategies are increasingly used to manage significant environmental and resource problems that have multiple stakeholders and hence multiple perspectives on what actually constitutes both the problem and, potentially, the solution. Collaboration is a process through which 'parties who see different aspects of a problem can constructively explore their differences and search for solutions that go beyond their own limited vision of what is possible' (Gray 1989: 5). It is a process driven by multiple stakeholders that usually involves several components:

1 Agreeing on a common purpose.
2 Ensuring the process is both inclusive and transparent.
3 Allowing participants to design the process.
4 Promoting joint fact finding and creative problem solving.
5 Insisting on accountability.
6 Developing an action plan.
7 Developing collaborative leadership (Margerum 1999; Margerum and Whitall 2004).

In the case of lake tourism, a type of tourism that clearly has implications for a natural resource and its multiple users, Hall and Härkönen (2006) identified four reasons why collaborative and integrated approaches were required in the management of lake systems in which tourism was significant:

1 Increased competition for natural resources, including the recognition of ecological uses, has led to increased conflict in natural resource management with collaborative approaches being seen as an alternative to expensive legal approaches to resolving conflict.
2 As understanding of the complexity of natural and social systems increases, more integrated responses to management must be developed that include a wider range of government and non-government decision-makers and their associated capacities for information and analysis.
3 Many current environmental problems are a result of diffuse actions such as stormwater runoff, land use change and habitat modification, which are not well addressed through traditional regulatory actions therefore a collaborative approach that generates broad scale participation is often better suited to fostering understanding and commitment among a large number of decision-makers.
4 There are many different agencies and organizations with overlapping responsibilities, and it is argued that a collaborative approach offers an opportunity to reduce waste and duplication, reduce conflict and share data and expertize.

Along with changes in governance and institutional approaches, integrated approaches also have a different philosophical base with respect to problem solving. The complexity of many impacts associated with tourism development suggests that more than one disciplinary viewpoint is required to help solve problems. In resource management this has led to calls for interdisciplinary and transdisciplinary approaches in which the problem rather than disciplinary orientation is the key concern (Mitchell 1989). In tourism there have been calls for such approaches as well as post-disciplinary perspectives (Coles et al. 2006). For example, Coles et al. (2006: 18) observed that the emergence of new forms of tourism and mobility as well as the increasing mobility of some segments of society necessitates multiple approaches with contributions from fields outside of the immediate realm of tourism studies. They argued that the unprecedented levels of human mobility and its consequences were such that the complexity of tourism relationships to global environmental change exceeded the capabilities of an individual disciplinary approach (see also Chapter 13). They endorsed the perspective of Visnovsky and Bianchi (2005), the editors of *Human Affairs: A Postdisciplinary*

Journal for Humanities and Social Sciences, who argued: 'Postdisciplinarity in our understanding does not mean that the traditional disciplines have disappeared or indeed should disappear, but rather that they are changing and should change in order to solve complex issues of human affairs. It is not sufficient to approach such complex issues from any single discipline'.

In a seminal paper that sought to describe the connections between tourism and conservation, Budowski (1976) identified three different relationships between tourism and the environment that can usefully be employed to describe the relationships between tourism and all dimensions of the destination environment. Including the social and economic: *conflict, coexistence* and *symbiosis*:

1 Tourism and the environment are in *conflict* when tourism is regarded as having a detrimental impact on the environment by those at the destination.
2 Tourism and the environment are in a state of *coexistence* when tourism does not have negative affects on the environment but neither does it positively contribute to the environment. This situation rarely remains static however as it implies a state of very slow change.
3 Finally, there is a *symbiotic* relationship in which tourism positively contributes to the environment and vice versa. This is a classic win-win situation in which tourists benefit and the overall quality of life of destinations improves as the social, economic and physical environments are all enhanced by tourism.

This last state is obviously regarded as the ideal when it comes to assessing the consequences of tourism and it is the one that requires not only integrated assessments of tourism's effects, but also an integrated planning strategy. And it is to this issue that the next chapter will turn.

Chapter overview

This chapter has provided a review of some of the consequences of visitation to destinations and the effects of tourism overall. As part of a services approach to contemporary tourism, the chapter highlighted the fact that the co-creation of tourism experiences means that consequences are situational and contextual, but as was stressed this does not mean that such effects are any less real. Rather it depends on a number of factors including the perspective and values of the viewer and their location within the tourism system as to whether they are (a) observed as occurring and (b) regarding as positive, negative or neutral. This means that the same consequence of tourism in the same location can be regarded simultaneously as positive by one person and negative by another. Indeed, as the chapter also noted it is even possible that over time an impact may also be perceived differently. Therefore, in understanding the impacts of tourism it was stressed that it was not just the impact that is significant but more importantly how it is perceived and understood. The tourist experience is co-created but the results of that co-creation are perceived differently by the parties involved.

Self-review questions

1 Why has *concern* over the consequences of tourism appeared to have become more significant since the 1970s?
2 Why are the *same* consequences of tourism seen *differently* by different people?
3 What did Budowski (1976) describe as the three different *relationships* between tourism and the environment?
4 What are the two main dimensions of *integrative assessment?*
5 What are the seven main components of *collaboration?*
6 What are the nine key issues that must be clarified with respect to the *assessment* of the consequences of tourism?
7 What is the relationship between our understanding of *resources* (Chapter 5) and understanding the consequences of tourism?
8 What does it mean to say that the consequences of tourism are *contextual* and *situational?*

Recommended reading

1 Margerum, R.D. (1999). Integrated environmental management: the elements critical to success. *Environmental Management* 65(2), 151–166.
   Although not tourism specific, this paper provides a good overview of an integrated approach to environmental problems.
2 Warnken, J. and Buckley, R. (2000). Monitoring diffuse impacts: Australian tourism developments. *Environmental Management* 25(4), 453–461.
   This article represents a good review of environmental assessment of tourism developments in Australia, a country which has often positioned itself as a leader in environmental aspects of tourism.

3 Coles, T., Hall, C.M. and Duval, D. (2006). Tourism and post disciplinary enquiry. *Current Issues in Tourism* 9(4–5), 293–319.
Details the nature of a post-disciplinary approach to examining issues within tourism and some of the implications this would have for the study of tourism.

4 Lew, A., Hall, C.M. and Williams, A.M. (eds) (2004). *A Companion to Tourism*. Oxford: Blackwell.
Many of the chapters in the book deal with the consequences of tourism at a destination level with respect to a range of different impacts.

5 Hall, C.M. and Page, S. (2006). *The Geography of Tourism and Recreation: Space, Place and Environment*, 3rd edn. London: Routledge.
Details consequences of tourism from a geographical perspective over a range of different environments.

6 Newsome, D., Moore, S.A. and Dowling, R.K. (2002). *Natural Area Tourism: Ecology, Impacts and Management*. Clevedon: Channelview Press.
One of the best accounts of the effects of tourism in natural areas.

7 Page, S. and Hall, C.M. (2005). *Managing Urban Tourism*. Harlow: Pearson.
Provides an overview of the consequences of tourism in an urban context.

8 Ryan, C. (2003). *Recreational Tourism: Demand and Impacts*. Clevedon: Channelview Press.
Provides a good general overview of the effects of tourism including on the individual.

9 Butcher, J. (2003). *The Moralisation of Tourism*. London: Routledge.
A thought provoking book that discusses how the consequences of tourism are often stereotyped.

10 Gössling, S. and Hall, C.M. (2006). *Tourism and Global Environmental Change*. London: Routledge.
Provides a sobering account of the impacts of tourism over all the elements of the tourism system and beyond.

Recommended web sites

Millenium Ecosystem Assessment: http://www.millenniumassessment.org/
Tourism Concern: www.tourismconcern.org.uk/
UN Millennium Development Goals: http://www.un.org/millenniumgoals/index.html
UNEP tourism: http://www.uneptie.org/pc/tourism/home.htm
United Nations (1992) Agenda 21: Earth Summit – The United Nations Plan of Action
World Travel and Tourism Council: www.wttc.org

References cited

Baud-Bovy, M. and Lawson, F. (1977). *Tourism and Recreational Development*. London: The Architectural Press.

Budowski, G. (1976). Tourism and conservation: conflict, coexistence or symbiosis. *Environmental Conservation* 3(1), 27–31.

Coles, T., Hall, C.M. and Duval, D. (2006). Tourism and post disciplinary enquiry. *Current Issues in Tourism* 9(4–5), 293–319.

Gray, B. (1989). *Collaborating: Finding Common Ground for Multiparty Problems*. San Francisco, CA: Jossey-Bass.

Hall, C.M. (1992). *Hallmark Tourist Events: Impacts, Management and Planning*. London: Belhaven.

Hall, C.M. (2008). *Tourism Planning*, 2nd edn. Harlow: Prentice-Hall.

Hall, C.M. and Härkönen, T. (2006). Lake tourism: an introduction to lacustrine tourism systems. In C.M. Hall and T. Härkönen (eds), *Lake Tourism: An Integrated Approach to Lacustrine Tourism Systems*, pp. 3–26. Clevedon: Channel View Publications.

Hall, C.M. and Page, S. (2006). *The Geography of Tourism and Recreation: Space, Place and Environment*. 3rd edn. London: Routledge.

Krippendorf, J. (1987). *The Holiday Makers: Understanding the Impact of Leisure and Travel*. Oxford: Heinemann Professional Publishing.

Lew, A., Hall, C.M. and Williams, A.M. (eds) (2004). *A Companion to Tourism*. Oxford: Blackwell.

Margerum, R.D. (1999). Integrated environmental management: the elements critical to success. *Environmental Management* 65(2), 151–166.

Margerum, R.D. and Whitall, D. (2004). The challenges and implications of collaborative management on a river basin scale. *Journal of Environmental Planning and Management* 47(3), 407–427.

Mathieson, A. and Wall, G. (1982). *Tourism: Economic, Physical and Social Impacts*. London: Longman.

Mitchell, B. (1989). *Geography and Resource Analysis*. London: Longman.

Nauright, J. and Schimmel, K. (eds) (2005). *The Political Economy of Sport*. London: Palgrave Macmillan.

Riding, A. (2005). Tate Modern savors sweet taste of success. *International Herald Tribune* June 11–12, 8.

Ritchie, B. and Adair, D. (2004). *Sports Tourism: Interrelationships, Impacts and Issues*. Clevedon: Channel view Publications.

Ritchie, J.R.B. (1984). Assessing the impact of hallmark events: conceptual and research issues. *Journal of Travel Research* 23(1), 2–11.

Visnovsky, E. and Bianchi, G. (2005). Editorial. *Human Affairs* 15/2005: http://www.humanaffairs.sk/editorial.htm (accessed 15 April 2006).

Warnken, J. and Buckley, R. (2000). Monitoring diffuse impacts: Australian tourism developments. *Environmental Management* 25(4), 453–461.

Chapter **8**
Planning and managing the contemporary destination

Chapter objectives

After reading this chapter you will

- Understand the key questions facing tourism planning as a field of planning
- Recognize the five different traditions of tourism planning and their key features
- Appreciate the difficulties of developing a sustainable approach to contemporary tourism
- Recognize how changes in planning approaches may be related to changes in the intellectual and physical environment
- Understand the differences between low- and high-road approaches to regional competitiveness and development

Introduction

Given the inherent characteristics of destination products in terms of their being an amalgam of separate firm and public products, and public and privately owned tourism resources, it may seem unusual to some readers to be able to discuss destination management and planning. However, as the previous chapter indicated, it is the very nature of the contemporary destination that actually makes planning processes so important. Although the desirability for tourism planning is generally accepted in most jurisdictions, the form and method of the most effective method of planning is a highly contested concept (Hall 2000; Dredge and Jenkins 2007). One of the seminal works on tourism planning by Gunn (1979) identified a number of foundation points for the development of an overall approach to tourism destination planning that still remain significant to contemporary tourism:

1 Only planning can avert negative impacts, although for planning to be effective, all 'actors' must be involved – not just professional planners.
2 Tourism is symbiotic with conservation and recreation, not a conflicting use with irreconcilably incompatible objectives or effects.
3 Planning today should be pluralistic, involving social, economic and physical dimensions.
4 Planning is political, and as such there is a vital need to take into account societal objectives and to balance these with other (often conflicting) aspirations.
5 Tourism planning must be strategic and integrative.
6 Tourism planning must have a regional planning perspective – because many problems arise at the interface with smaller areas, a broader planning horizon is essential.

Tourism planning occurs at various scales from individual firms, to regions, nations and even planning on an international basis. Although such planning activities are interrelated, the focus of this chapter is on planning at the destination level. The chapter first examines different traditions of destination planning and their relationship to other forms of planning. It then goes on to discuss the importance of sustainability as a part of the planning agenda. Finally the chapter examines some of the planning strategies that assist in the achievement of planning objectives.

The development of contemporary destination planning

Destination planning is a relatively recent concept that has emerged only since the late 1960s (Gunn 1994; Davidson and Maitland 1997). Prior to that time, planning for tourism was primarily seen within the context of broader urban and regional planning activities (Hall 2000). However, the rise of international tourism with the advent of a new generation of jet aircraft and the consequent recognition of the real economic importance of tourism to places in terms of development and employment saw the development of the first comprehensive attempts to plan for tourism. Nevertheless, destination planning remains very much connected to some of the broader issues and questions that occur within planning in its wider sense. Campbell and Fainstein (2003) identified five questions with respect to planning theory, all of which should also be of concern in tourism planning.

What are the historical roots of planning?

This first question is one of identity and therefore history. Reflecting on the history of a field not only helps answers of how did we get to where we are now in terms of applications and intellectual developments, but also to their implications for planning practice, including being able to learn from previous planning mistakes (Hall 2000). Arguably, in the case of tourism planning one of the biggest issues is that most planning texts fail to acknowledge that tourism planning is grounded within contemporary capitalist society and that there are winners and losers in various types of developments. Furthermore, as Campbell and Fainstein (2003: 6) observed, 'an effective planning history helps the contemporary planner shape his or her complex professional identity'.

What is the justification for planning?

The issue of justification raises the key question of why and when should the state intervene in order to change or modify an existing course of events? Planning, in the sense used in this chapter with respect to destinations, is primarily a public (state) activity that may be done in concert with private and other bodies but for which the original rationale lies within the broader issue of the role of the state.

From the late 1920s on planning in terms of intervention was often seen as a means to counter the effects of the market. This notion of a dualism between planning and the market continued through to the 1980s when, in light of the failure of much centralized planning to achieve desired societal goals, the market came to be championed as a resource allocation mechanism to replace planning activities. This perspective had substantial impact on government in many developed nations as many government assets and authorities were privatized or corporatized in order to meet political demands for 'smaller' government. Tourism was not immune to such changes. In countries such as Australia, Canada and New Zealand, government's development function in tourism came to be replaced with a far stronger marketing role along with the development of new cooperative structures with the private sector (Hall 2000; Dredge and Jenkins 2007).

More recent developments with respect to notions of governance (see Chapter 6) has also led to a rethink of the planning – market dualism. Instead, the necessity of steering hybrid public–private relationships as well as the growth of non-government non-profit 'third-sector' organizations means a significant reinterpretation of the relationship between planning and the market is required. Because tourism is a significant area of public–private relationships with respect to urban regeneration projects or infrastructure, such as airports, destination planning is strongly influenced by debates over what should the nature of government intervention be in destinations with respect to tourism.

What are the 'rules of the game' for planning with respect to ethics and values?

The breakdown of the dualism between planning and the market and the development of extensive public–private relationships raises substantial questions with respect to values of planning. When planning could be clearly interpreted as acting in the public interest such dilemmas were not so significant. However, the reinterpretation of government's role in the economy and in society as well as the creation of new government corporate bodies has meant that the idea of public interest is often interpreted in terms of economic interest or sectional interests. In the case of tourism, this can mean e.g. debates over the extent to which destination planning is about serving the needs of the tourist as opposed to the needs of the local community. Furthermore, ethical issues are also raised with respect to the role of expert knowledge in the planning process and the extent to which expert technical knowledge, and the values that underlie it, can be accommodated by other value positions that exist in destinations.

How can planning be effective in a mixed economy?

Planning intervention raises questions of the authority and power of those who seek to intervene (Dredge and Jenkins 2007). The authority of the planner is constrained by economic and political power of various stakeholders and interests as well as the vagaries of democracy. In such a situation the goals of planners, e.g. with respect to sustainability and the physical and social environment, may have only a low position within the political issue-agenda where immediate economic and employment concerns may be given far greater priority in decision-making. Arguably within tourism planning, economic goals have typically been given priority over social goals despite planning traditions that go back to the early 1980s with respect to the importance of the community in tourism (Murphy 1985; Murphy and Murphy 2004).

What do planners do?

As Campbell and Fainstein (2003: 9) noted, comprehensiveness of approach has often been a main justification for undertaking planning. Yet the comprehensive approaches have suffered serious criticism on several counts. First, the extent to which planners have the necessary capacities of analysis, coordination and knowledge to effectively develop comprehensive approaches to complex situations. Second, ideas of comprehensiveness often assume an ideal common public interest whereas in reality, planning may only give voice to more powerful political and economic interests if other interests or stakeholders are unable or unwilling to participate (Pforr 2001; Timothy and Tosun 2003; Treuren and Lane 2003).

Within tourism planning, the issue of comprehensiveness is extremely significant because tourism planning is often justified on the basis of integrating economic, social and environmental goals (Getz 1986; Gunn 1994; Murphy and Murphy 2004; Ruhanen 2004). However, the capabilities of actually being able to achieve this level of integration in tourism planning are extremely problematic. Indeed, the criticism of Campbell and Fainstein (2003) with respect to comprehensive planning in general could easily be applied specifically to tourism planning:

> Planners often argued about the proper role of planning based simply on the merits of the concepts themselves (e.g. large- versus small-scale; top-down versus bottom-up), while ignoring the vaster political and economic forces that shaped and constrained planning. The articulation and eventual challenge to comprehensive planning was thus part of a broader expansion of planning theory beyond land-use planning into social and economic policy (Campbell and Fainstein 2003: 9).

The latter point is extremely important as tourism destination planning has also expanded substantially from land-use-based approaches to ones that seek to enhance economic and social policies, e.g. with respect to the growth of interest in pro-poor tourism in developing countries and the interest in developing competitive cities and destinations in the developed world. The expansion of approaches to destination planning is therefore the subject of the next section.

Changing approaches to destination planning

Approaches to destination planning change over time as a result of:

- Changes in ideas with respect to planning, e.g. 'new' theoretical insights and developments that transform planning thinking such as sustainability or creative cities, or conceptual developments such as that associated with the concept of governance.
- Changes in the destination's external environment, e.g. new issues and challenges to destinations that emerge as a result of developments outside of the destination such as in terms of competition from other destinations as well other forms of social, economic and environmental change.
- Changes in the destination itself, e.g. environmental or land-use change or political change that may affect the resource base of the destination or its relative accessibility.

Importantly, the different types of change are typically interrelated and rarely occur in isolation. A good example of this in the context of tourism planning is with respect to the environment.

Changing understanding of the environment in tourism

Our understanding of environmental change and its importance as a factor in destination planning has developed not just as a result of change to the physical environment per se, because such changes have often been occurring for much longer than a place has been a tourism destination, but also because our understanding of the importance of the physical environment has also changed with the development of a stronger environmental ethic in tourism studies (Gössling and Hall 2006).

In the 1950s, when tourism started to grow rapidly in the post-World War II period following greater personal car access and personal disposable income, it was mainly seen as an economic sector with great potential for national and regional economies, and providing increased leisure opportunities to large parts of the working population in the industrialized countries. It was not until the rise of a significant environmental conservation movement in the 1960s and 1970s that the negative environmental impacts of industrial development and urbanization began to receive publicity. Although even here tourism was seen as a relatively benign form of economic development as compared with the more obvious pollution and impacts of heavy industries. In addition, at this time the impacts of tourism were perceived as being 'local' in character, i.e. focusing on erosion problems or beach crowding, rather than the more 'global' perspective of present-day analyses of tourism which highlight impacts such as climate change, marine pollution and biodiversity loss.

Gössling and Hall (2006) argue that it was not before the publication of the Swiss tourism academic and environmentalist Krippendorf's (1975) *Die Landschaftsfresser* ('The landscape devourers') that the environmental impacts of tourism began to be perceived by a broader public in mainland Europe. Although there was earlier English language debate on the impacts of tourism in specific environments 'there has not been a publication, similar to that of Krippendorf, that has encouraged a wider public debate on tourism's environmental impacts. Instead, tourism often remains something that impacts negatively 'somewhere else' (Gössling and Hall 2006: 13).

In the late 1970s and 1980s new methodological tools for analysing environmental change came to be developed as tourism brought increasing human pressure to bear on local natural environmental resources, particularly national parks and reserves. For example, concepts such as carrying capacity became increasingly important as did the use of environmental impact assessment or limits of acceptable change assessment (O'Reilly 1986; Hall and Page 2006). Significantly, the 1980s also saw the development of new tourism concepts such as sustainable tourism and ecotourism. The term sustainable development became widely used in relation to tourism (e.g. Butler 1991, 2000; Hall and Lew 1998) following the publication of the 'Brundtland report' in 1987 (WCED 1987), although it had first been used in relation to tourism and the World Conservation Strategy prior to the WCED. Nevertheless, the concept of 'sustainable tourism' became a significant new approach to tourism planning particularly as it emphasized the interrelationships between environmental change and social, economic and political factors that affect change (Hall 2000). But just as importantly it provided a new way to 'see' the nature of environmental problems, as such problems were not just an issue of the physical environment but were instead embedded in social and economic factors. Arguably, the 'international' issue of sustainability also raised questions about the scale at which the impacts of tourism needed to be understood (see Chapter 8) so rather than merely understanding environmental issues as being something that was just a concern to tourism at the destination level, it highlighted how tourism both contributed to and was affected by environmental change at a global scale (Gössling 2002).

Our understanding of the role of the environment in tourism has therefore changed over time simultaneously as the empirical impact of tourism has changed and new management techniques have been developed. This is important as it has also meant that the planning 'problem' in terms of what planning is trying to 'solve' has also shifted over time. However, while change has undoubtedly been significant in our understanding of destination planning issues there has also been continuity as well, with perhaps the most important ongoing concern being how to find a balance between economic development and public welfare concerns (including the quality of the physical environment). Nevertheless, while some concerns have remained constant for public planners perspectives on the best means to accomplish planning goals, particularly with respect to what the relative role of the public and private sectors should be, have changed in light of broader shifts in understanding of the capacities of government (see Chapter 6).

Five traditions of tourism planning

Five approaches or traditions of tourism planning at the destination level can be recognized (Getz 1986; Hall 2000):

  (i) 'Boosterism'
  (ii) An economic, industry-oriented approach
  (iii) A physical/spatial approach
  (iv) A community-oriented approach
  (v) A sustainable tourism approach

The traditions are broadly sequential although they are not mutually exclusive and also occur simultaneously (Table 8.1). This section will briefly outline each of these approaches and their implications for destination planning.

Boosterism

Boosterism is in one sense a form of non-planning. Boosterism refers to the simplistic attitude that tourism development is inherently good and will be of automatic benefit to the destination. Boosterism is characterized as being part of an attitude to development that 'growth is good' and that any negative externalities of tourism development will be outweighed by positive benefits. From a boosterist perspective the primary planning problem is one of how to attract as many people as possible to a given location.

Economic approach

The economic tradition in tourism planning constructs the tourism planning problem around economic questions in terms of tourism's role in regional and national economic growth and development. The economic approach has been dominant in destination planning since places first consciously sought to attract visitors and develop a tourist industry. However, while the role of economic analysis as the main arbiter in destination planning has continued there have been changes in the scale of analysis.

Table 8.1 Timelines for traditions of tourism planning

Dates	Boosterism	Economic	Physical/spatial	Community	Sustainable tourism
1850s	Established by the 1850s with the advent of industrialized mass tourism				
1890s		Established by the late 1890s with respect to discussions to development alternatives of natural area destinations	Antecedents emerge with respect to the conservation of natural areas although secondary to economic approaches		Debates over 'sustained yield' forestry antecedent for sustainable development
1930s		State's role in managing the economy becomes extremely important	Land-use zoning becomes established in urban and regional planning	Idea of planner as expert well established in urban and regional planning	
1960s		Economic analysis of development decisions becomes more commonplace	Emergence of modern conservation movement with environmental agencies established for the first time	Idea of planner as expert comes to be challenged in the late 1960s and early 1970s	UN Habitat and Man and Biosphere programmes begin to be developed in the late 1960s

(Continued)

Table 8.1 (Continued)

Dates	Boosterism	Economic	Physical/spatial	Community	Sustainable tourism
1980s	Neoconservative political approaches with respect to role of the state give boosters a stronger role in destination growth coalitions	Economic analysis dominant in public planning and decision-making	Spatial approaches are weakened as public-private approaches become a popular planning strategy	Increased application of community approaches to tourism through public participation exercises	Sustainable development key concept in World Conservation Strategy and the Brundtland report
2000	Continued role of growth coalitions reinforced by rise of concept of place wars and destination competition	Economic analysis remains dominant. Tourism satellite accounts become important evaluation tool while idea of competitiveness influences destination planning	Spatial planning tools remain important, especially as a result of new geographic information technologies; spatial planning approached at multiple scales	Participation standard in much destination planning although extent to which it affects planning outcomes problematic	Sustainable tourism a significant planning concept although application is contested; increased concern over global environmental change

Source: After Hall (2000, 2008).

Within the economic approach the planning emphasis is on the economic impacts of tourism and the most efficient and effective use of tourism to create income and employment benefits for regions, communities or countries as a whole. Particular attention has been given to the means by which the economic impacts of tourism can be measured. In recent years, this has meant the development of a series of tourism satellite accounts at national and regional levels. In addition, there has been a focus on the competitiveness of destinations and the development of approaches that support competitiveness such as clustering and networks (Michael 2007). However, the role that tourism actually plays in regional development is regarded as somewhat problematic as it is possible that a focus on tourism development may not be the most appropriate strategy in terms of regional competitiveness (Malecki 2004).

Despite the development of new techniques for the economic analysis of tourism, many studies of tourism at the destination level focus on the gross impacts of tourism rather than a more sophisticated approach that evaluates the benefits and costs of tourism development and the opportunity costs of tourism. In addition, economic approaches are often criticized for failing to adequately account for environmental and social values that, from the perspective of some stakeholders, may not be easily assessed within an economic paradigm.

Physical/spatial tradition

The physical/spatial approach has its origins in the work of urban and regional land-use planners, geographers and environmental scientists who advocate an approach to the planning of tourism destinations based on consideration of the renewability of natural resources; spatial interactions, spatial organization and regional planning and development. Although economic considerations are important, economic development is regarded as being dependent on the 'wise-use' or stewardship of natural resources. Therefore, environmental considerations may be given priority over immediate economic ones in order to keep longer-term management options open. Key planning approaches from this perspective include: carrying capacity; hazard and risk assessment; understanding stakeholder attitudes, behaviour and perceptions; resource and landscape evaluation; resource appraisal and allocation; decision-making and evaluation and the development of appropriate institutional arrangements. However, many of the planning techniques within the physical/spatial tradition have tended to be applied more in natural areas, such as national parks, and in peripheral areas. Whereas the economic traditions of planning have tended to have substantial sway in urban destinations and in broader policy decisions of national and regional governments.

Community-oriented tourism planning

The community-based tourism approach emerged in the 1970s and was influenced by two main factors. First, an increased recognition that tourism development was not benign and had negative socio-cultural, economic and environmental impacts on some members of destination communities. Second, a realization in urban and regional planning that community stakeholders often needed to be involved in decision-making if planning interventions were to be successful. Although community-oriented tourism planning was actually being undertaken by practitioners prior to its recognition in the tourism research literature, one of the most influential statements of the community approach to tourism development was found in Murphy's (1985) book *Tourism: A Community Approach*. Murphy advocated the adoption of an 'ecological' approach to tourism planning that emphasized the need for local control over the development process. A key component of the approach was the notion that in satisfying local needs it is possible to satisfy the needs of tourists. Despite the undoubted attraction of a 'win-win' concept to many destinations, the approach was not adopted as widely as it might have been. This was because:

(a) The approach was seen as being more time consuming and expensive than other approaches.
(b) It blurred where control lay in decision-making processes.
(c) The outcomes of the consultation processes and the consequent plans often did not meet the more economically oriented agendas of the tourism industry and government.

Nevertheless, the approach has still had influence on destination planning (Timothy and Tosun 2003) through encouraging at least some degree of consultation and public participation in destination planning even if this is sometimes perceived as tokenism where consultation occurs just with industry stakeholders rather than the wider community; in some jurisdictions encouraging the conduct of social impact assessments on large tourism developments; and, more recently, highlighting the significance of empowerment and equity issues as factors in tourism development which has been particularly important to the concept of pro-poor tourism. This latter dimension is an area in which there has been overlap between the community and economic approaches. Interrelationships between the community and the spatial approaches is best seen with respect to regional and local planning initiatives as well as in consultation exercises in the case of use of natural areas or heritage management (Singh et al. 2003).

Sustainable tourism

The fifth approach to destination planning is the sustainable approach. Although having historical antecedents that go back to the 1870s the sustainable tourism approach is seen as entering its current interpretation from the 1980s following the emergence of the sustainable development paradigm (Hall and Lew 1998). According to Brake and Newton (1995: 117) 'the transitive verb "to sustain" is derived from the Latin *sustineo* meaning to hold up and is variously interpreted as also meaning to bear or support, to relieve or to prolong.' Sustainability has come to incorporate all of these meanings. The primary objective of sustainable development is the provision of lasting and secure livelihoods that minimize resource depletion, environmental degradation, cultural disruption and social instability. The report of the World Commission of Environment and Development (WCED) (Brundtland Commission 1987) extended the basic objective of sustainable development that had previously been expressed in the World Conservation Strategy to include concerns of equity; the needs of economically marginal populations; and the idea of technological and social limitations on the ability of the environment to meet present and future needs.

Ideas of sustainable development have been hugely influential in destination planning discourse as well as affecting planning legislation. However, the transformation of the principles of sustainable development into successful planning interventions has been extremely difficult. Key issues include:

- The time scale in which sustainable approaches operate is greater than usual planning and policy timelines.

- The spatial scale is also greater as sustainable approaches highlight the internationalization of many factors that affect sustainability, such as climate change and economic globalization, which therefore means that these are issues that are multi-jurisdictional and therefore require international cooperation (see Chapter 6).
- Sustainability is an integrative approach that brings together socio-cultural, environmental and economic planning methods. This situation requires careful management and new sets of planning skills that allow for multi-disciplinary or post-disciplinary problem setting as well as new sets of institutional arrangements.
- Sustainable development for a location is different than sustainable tourism development. While tourism may be sustainable it is quite possible that in some destinations it may not be a contributor to the overall sustainability of the location or may even contribute to a non-sustainable situation in other locations. For example, as Chapter 1 indicated, the greenhouse gas emissions from tourism transport affects climate change throughout the world not just at the destination of tourists. This situation therefore provides a significant challenge to the tourism industry.

Several planning strategies have been put forward as integral to a sustainable tourism approach:

(i) *Cooperative and integrated control systems*: Integrated planning seeks to coordinate planning processes at different scales in a more cooperative manner. In part the notion of 'steering' within contemporary governance is an important part of such processes (see Chapter 6).

(ii) *Development of industry coordination mechanisms*: Tourism has historically been a fragmented industry. The development of improved coordination mechanisms is regarded as a mechanism to improve firm and destination collaboration towards common goals as well as being a means by which the concerns of industry stakeholders can be better articulated to decision-makers.

(iii) *Raising consumer awareness*: The nature of tourist consumption obviously affects the resource base of destinations therefore alterations in consumptive patterns may lead to better economic, social and environmental outcomes. In recent years there has been a growth in 'conscious consumption' in which consumers have thought about their purchases with respect to such factors as organic foods, environment conservation and human rights. Such conscious consumerism has influenced tourism with respect to the growth of ethical tourism considerations, codes of tourism conduct, types of tourism such as volunteer tourism as well as destination boycotts.

(iv) *Raising producer awareness*: Making tourism production more sustainable can be undertaken through a combination of regulatory and voluntary approaches. Educating producers to make their products more sustainable is one way of seeking to ensure that destinations benefit however in some cases having more sustainable product may also increase the product appeal in certain markets. Many producer groups have developed codes of conduct and good practice in an effort to make their businesses more environmentally friendly.

(v) *Strategic planning*: Strategic planning requires a process that is integrative in terms of bringing stakeholders together and is also well structured in terms of effective analysis, the development of clear goals and measurable objectives, evaluation and monitoring, and a clear implementation strategy. One of the most important factors in strategic planning for sustainability is the identification of relevant indicators for sustainability which are measurable, meet objectives, and on which stakeholders agree as to their relevance and as to how results should be interpreted. When this is done acceptance of intervention and change management by stakeholders is far greater than with a non-strategic approach.

(vi) *Increased regulation*: Where voluntary procedures to promote sustainability have failed then increased regulation may be the only option available. A range of potential regulatory measures exist but some of the more popular approaches include increased charging, new taxation regimes, licences and permits. However, governments are often fearful of industry and consumer backlash with respect to increased regulation particularly if it also increases the cost of travel or products.

Responsibility for contemporary destination planning

As the above discussion illustrates, contemporary tourism is characterized by there being no single agreed approach to destination planning as there is often no fixed agreement as to what the best methods are or the role of the public sector should be. Instead, there are a number of different approaches that are utilized by different agencies that have different jurisdictions and agenda. Indeed, it is often the case that different organizations involved with destination planning fit within particular traditions, making decision-making potentially problematic. For example, economic development agencies will usually embrace the economic approach, environmental agencies a physical/spatial approach, public interest groups a community-based approach; with sustainable approaches often being part of the mandate and culture of regional planning agencies.

Few destinations have a single body that is specifically responsible for destination planning from a tourism perspective. Most destination management organizations or regional tourism organizations have a marketing function with planning being a secondary and often only advisory role. Instead, destination planning tends to be undertaken by a combination of urban and regional planning bodies and economic development organizations for which tourism is only a part of their overall planning brief. This situation therefore means that destination planning occurs in a complex set of institutional arrangements that include many different organizations. At one level such a perspective might be seen as a positive as it might encourage greater cooperation between different public, private and non-government organizations, although it may also mean that planning for tourism 'falls between the gaps' as no one is clearly responsible. Indeed, even in those organizations that have a clear designated responsibility for planning tourism activities, such as national park and conservation bodies, it may only be a part of their mandate, as illustrated in the following case study.

CASE STUDY
Planning for tourism in Finland's national parks

As well as being important for domestic tourism, nature is an extremely important part of Finland's international tourism promotion and positioning as a destination (Tuohino and Patkinen 2004). 'Finland's national parks are today important tourist destinations for hiking and nature watching' (Lappalainen 2000: 17). As of 2005 there were 35 parks in Finland and in 2002 the total number of visits in Finnish national parks was almost 1.1 million. However, the average number of visits in Finnish National Parks has almost doubled since the 1990s and in peripheral economic areas such as Northern Finland the national park associated tourism development has been even stronger (Saarinen 2003).

Such has been the recognized tourism significance of national parks, that regional and local stakeholders and policy actors usually support the plans for opening parks for the national park status as they believe it increases the attractiveness of the area and promotes nature-based tourism. Consequently, national parks have become a significant tool for regional development and positive image building in numerous peripheral areas that otherwise have limited means of economic development (Saarinen 2003; Hall and Boyd 2005). As a result several municipalities and organizations have proposed that at least a further six national parks should be designated in Finland (Cajander 2003 in Sorsa 2004).

However, while tourism is obviously important for national parks in Finland it is not the sole rationale for their establishment with biodiversity and landscape conservation obviously being important factors. As in other national park jurisdictions, the original Finnish legislation included provision for both conservation and visitation, a balance that has become increasingly difficult given the growth in tourism numbers in recent decades. The original 1923 *Nature Conservation Act* had an aim to preserve untouched nature though it also stated that national parks were meant for pleasure and enjoyment for all citizens, that they should have value as an attraction and that be easily reached by people (Sorsa 2004). Nevertheless, present-day park planning considerations give a substantial weight to nature conservation. Metsähallitus, the Finnish Forest and Park Service, reports that the role of the Finnish network of protected areas can be defined as:

> Finland's protected areas form a varied network intended to preserve for present and future generations a suitable number of representatives and ecologically viable areas of all the ecosystems and natural habitat types occurring in Finland, taking into account geographical variations and the various stages of natural succession. Protected areas also have a very significant role in achieving and maintaining the favourable conservation status of habitat types and species (Metsähallitus 2000: 6).

Under the guidelines on the aims, function and management of public controlled protected areas the network of Finnish protected areas must primarily preserve (Metsähallitus 2000: 7): 'areas of natural habitat, particularly habitat types characteristic of the Finnish landscape, and habitats, land forms and features which are endangered'. As part of the primary aim, or additionally, the following should be preserved:

- Natural gene pools and ecosystem diversity.
- Species, geological and geomorphological features, especially species and features which are either naturally rare, or threatened or declining as a consequence of human activity.

- Landscapes and habitats shaped by previous generations, including the cultural heritage associated with the Finnish countryside, along with endangered domesticated plant and animal breeds.
- The natural succession of ecosystems and other natural processes at various stages.
- Areas of outstanding natural beauty.
- Wild areas (Metsähallitus 2000: 7).

The guidelines then go on to note that only 'within the limitations set by the requirements of conservation, the network of protected areas should also aim to facilitate' (Metsähallitus 2000: 7):

- Research and monitoring work on the state of the environment.
- Environmental education, promoting understanding and interest towards nature.
- Outdoor recreation.

Significantly, the guidelines state that 'the economic utilization of protected areas for ecotourism, for example, is permissible where it does not endanger the achievement of conservation aims' (Metsähallitus 2000: 7). Indeed, earlier in the guidelines, it is noted that the growth of ecotourism and an increase in the number of visitors to protected areas is indicative of a more favourable opinion towards nature conservation. Yet tourism is regarded as only one out of ten different uses of the Finnish protected area system that require a policy statement (the others being everyman's right, fishing and hunting, photography, local residents, traffic, forestry, mineral prospecting and mining and leasing land). Indeed, ecotourism is not explicitly defined within the guidelines although its economic dimension is noted which therefore suggests that ecotourism is regarded as commercial tourism use of protected areas by firms as opposed to access by independent travellers. A clear policy boundary is also established by Metsähallitus with respect to tourism planning. According to Metsähallitus (2000: 42), the agency does not intend to develop its own activities in the field but instead will 'aim to provide a framework and opportunities for independent enterprises in the field of ecotourism. The aims of sustainable ecotourism must be agreed upon with all interested parties (local residents, the tourism sector and other local organizations) by drawing up a strategy for tourism following the principles of participatory planning'.

Nevertheless other dimensions of tourism are included in other sets of plans. The above set of aims are intended to serve as a guide for the development of management and land-use plans for protected areas which may be laid out in a master plan for a given protected area. Planning is therefore regarded as an integral measure to preserving the natural qualities of protected areas along with specific management strategies such as restrictions on access, supervision of visitors, influencing human behaviour, and research and monitoring. However, planning in this context is interpreted both as the process of developing a plan as well as the production and implementation of a plan that sets out 'land use and the location and organization of activities, through the provision of services and facilities. For example, according to the principles of land-use zoning and distribution' (Metsähallitus 2000: 16). With respect to participatory planning processes for the development of tourism in protected areas Metsähallitus (2000: 42–43) identified three main requirements:

1 Survey the problems and opportunities presented in the protected area being planned from a tourism perspective and set economic, social and ecological aims for ecotourism, i.e. encouraging certain activities, identifying preferred routes and minimizing littering and disturbance. In addition, special consideration is meant to be given to local communities and employment generation. Special ecotourism plans can be drafted for areas used intensively for tourism purposes.

2 The tourism sector should seek to develop products that meet client expectations and interests. This should be supported by the undertaking of marketing research on new consumer markets and their level of satisfaction. Infrastructure and facilities built as part of tourism product development should aim to support the preservation of biodiversity.

3 Tourism operators should promote conservation aims. 'The attractiveness of an area should not be prejudiced through its use for tourism, and the overall environmental impact of tourist activities should otherwise be minimised' (Metsähallitus 2000: 43).

To a great extent the Finnish experience mirrors the approaches of the Nordic countries and other national park agencies in the developed world with respect to the relationship between tourism and national park sand protected area planning (Gössling and Hultman 2006). The difficult task of balancing conservation aims while still encouraging visitation is one that is almost universal at destinations that are either national parks or have a significant area set aside as protected area. The Finnish approach of land-use zoning with particular zones providing for specific activities and visitor experiences is an extremely common strategy. However, the recognition of participatory planning approaches that seek to include the local community, tourism industry and other planning agencies as well as an understanding of the market reflect both a greater public–private approach to destination planning as well as the increased complexity of the planning process.

Key sources

Gössling, S. and Hultman, J. (eds) (2006). *Ecotourism in Scandinavia*. Wallingford: CAB International.

Lappalainen, M. (2000). *Finland's National Parks: Seas of Blue, Seas of Green*. Vantaa: Metsähallitus, National Heritage Service.

Metsähallitus (Forest and Park Service) (2000). *The Principles of Protected Area Management in Finland: Guidelines on the Aims, Function and Management of State-owned Protected Areas*. Metsähallituksen luonnonsuojelulkaisuja Sarja B No.54. Vantaa: Metsähallitus – Forest and Park Service, Natural Heritage Services.

Saarinen, J. (2003). The regional economics of tourism in northern Finland: the socio-economic implications of recent tourism development and the possibilities for regional development. *Scandinavian Journal of Hospitality and Tourism* 3(2), 91–113.

Saarinen J. and Hall, C.M. (eds) (2004). *Nature-Based Tourism Research in Finland: Local Contexts, Global Issues*. Finnish Forest Research Institute, Research Papers 916. Rovaniemi: Rovaniemi Research Station, Finnish Forest Research Institute.

References

Cajander, V.-R. (2003). Suomalaiset rakastavat suojelualueitaan! *Ympäristö* 3, 20–24.

Campbell, S. and Fainstein, S. (2003). Introduction: the structure and debates of planning theory. In S. Campbell and S. Fainstein (eds), *Readings in Planning Theory*, pp. 1–16. Oxford: Blackwell.

Sorsa, R. (2004). The role of tourism in Finnish nature conservation from the nineteenth century to the present. In J. Saarinen and C.M. Hall (eds), *Nature-Based Tourism Research in Finland: Local Contexts, Global Issues*, pp. 33–46. Finnish Forest Research Institute, Research Papers 916. Rovaniemi: Rovaniemi Research Station, Finnish Forest Research Institute.

Tuohino, A. and Patkinen, K. (2004). The role of tourism in Finnish nature conservation from the nineteenth century to the present. In J. Saarinen and C.M. Hall (eds), *Nature-Based Tourism Research in Finland: Local Contexts, Global Issues*, pp. 129–150. Finnish Forest Research Institute, Research Papers 916. Rovaniemi: Rovaniemi Research Station, Finnish Forest Research Institute.

Discussion questions

1 To what extent might planning be able to reconcile the twin objectives of national parks to conserve natural heritage and to provide a source of enjoyment for visitors?

2 With reference to national park destinations in your own country: (a) To what extent are master plans developed for parks? (b) How often are they updated and what might be the implications of planning timetables? (c) What are the commonalities and differences in planning priorities for different parks?

3 In terms of stakeholders: (a) How do national park planning processes in your country seek to be inclusive of stakeholders in the planning process? (b) Should all stakeholders have an equal say in park planning or should some stakeholders, e.g. the local community or park users, have a greater say than other stakeholders? (c) Are non-users a stakeholder in national park planning?

Planning sustainable destinations and sustainable regions

At the destination level, a sustainable approach to tourism is concerned with tourism being the most appropriate form of development of the economic, social and physical resources of a region in a manner which conserves the social and physical environment and which promotes the long-term goals of the community. Such a perspective highlights that there is a difference between focusing on tourism development for its own sake, which is how sustainable tourism may be interpreted, versus looking at sustainability within the totality of a regional jurisdiction. While a concern with the sustainability of tourism is obviously important, the adoption of an integrative planning perspective means that tourism's contribution to regional sustainable development needs to be understood within a 'whole of government' or 'whole of region' approach that assesses what can be achieved for a place as a whole rather than just in terms of tourism.

Within studies of regional planning, the contribution of tourism to sustainable place development is often questioned. Tourism is primarily seen as part of an imitative 'low-road' policy in contrast to 'high-road' knowledge-based policies (Table 8.2) (Malecki 2004; Hall 2008). Low-road strategies are focused on 'traditional' location factors such as land, labour, capital, infrastructure and locational advantage with respect to markets or key elements of production as well as direct state subsidies to retain firms: more intangible factors, such as intellectual capital and institutional capacity are secondary (see Chapter 6 and the discussion of government's role on tourism development). Low-road strategies are tied into property-oriented growth strategies linked to urban and regional reimaging strategies (Judd 2003; Hall 2005). However, low-road strategies tend to lead to the serial replication of urban tourism infrastructure such as the waterfront marketplace, heritage precinct, art gallery, museum, casino, marina and retail centre because of the belief of some destination planners that this is what required for tourism-induced economic development. Such factors were described by Harvey (1989: 12) as being a part of 'urban entrepreneurialism' whereby, 'many of the innovations and investments designed to make particular locations more attractive as cultural and consumer centers have quickly been imitated elsewhere, thus rendering an competitive advantage within a system of cities ephemeral.' Yet the sustainability of such serial place competitive strategies is increasingly questionable. The requirements of constantly having to constantly develop and upgrade visitor facilities and

Table 8.2 Low-, middle- and high-road regional competitiveness strategies

Low road *Zero sum*	Middle road *Growth enhancing*	High road *Network enhancing*
Place promotion	Training	Internal networks
Capturing mobile investment,	Fostering entrepreneurship	External (non-local) networks
Firms and capital	Helping and mentoring new firms and entrepreneurs	Benchmarking assessments
Focus on visitors on the basis of numbers	Coordination	Investing in superstructure
Subsidized investment and means of production, e.g. sites and premises	Business advice	Transport links, especially airline and airfreight links
	Reducing uncertainty	Scanning globally for new knowledge
	Investment in infrastructure	Information and communications links

Long-term contribution to sustainable regional development

Marginal	Moderate	High

Source: After Cheshire and Gordon (1998), Malecki (2002, 2004) and Hall (2008).

infrastructure has meant that places 'face the possibility of being caught in a vicious cycle of have to provide larger subsidies to finance projects that deliver even fewer public benefits' (Leitner and Garner 1993: 72).

In contrast to the low-road approach, Malecki (2004) argues that a high-road approach of regional innovation and entrepreneurship is possible although it is a much more difficult path to follow as it requires more of a focus on 'soft infrastructure' (also described as superstructure) and the development of regional innovation and knowledge economies that utilize agglomeration economies, institutional learning, associative governance, proximity capital and interactive innovation (Cooke 2002). Therefore, a high-road approach stresses that regional infrastructure both hard (communications, transport, finance) and soft (knowledge, intellectual capital, trustful labour relations, mentoring, worker-welfare orientation) is required in order to encourage innovation rather than adaptation (Malecki 2004). As Malecki (2004: 1109) observes, in smaller urban centres that cannot really afford the highly visible development projects of larger 'global' cities, even though they may try, it is the 'soft' cultural and social variables that 'matter most for regional development: institutions, leadership, culture and community.' Such elements have been strongly emphasized within the community and sustainable traditions of tourism planning and development. Nevertheless, it is important to recognize that many such high-road strategies are not as immediately tangible and visible to stakeholders as compared with, for example, the construction of a new stadium, museum or convention centre.

Tourism does have a part to play in high-road strategies for sustainable regional development. High-road strategies emphasize connectivity, through transport and aviation as well as communication linkages, and high levels of amenity that may attract visitors as well as being important for residents. In addition, high-road approaches tend to place value on cultural diversity and on the co-creation of services. This means that within the high-road context tourism is clearly seen as a subset of a broader understanding of human mobility, networks, planning and regional development, and services rather than a more simplistic notion of how many visitors have been attracted. At a broader planning level debate now focuses on the fundamental questioning of economic growth as an end in itself or as an inevitable means to achieve higher standards of living (Pike et al. 2006). Indeed, new planning metrics for local and regional development reflect a broader notion of 'development' that include metrics of well-being and quality of life (Morgan 2004). Therefore, as Pike et al. (2006: 114) highlight, 'Recent approaches to sustainable local and regional development seek to integrate economic, environmental and social outcomes together rather than compromise through trade-offs and balances'.

Chapter overview

Contemporary tourism planning is strongly oriented towards the notion of sustainable tourism development. The chapter has noted that the ideal planning style is integrative – in that it seeks to combine, social, environmental and economic planning goals and also seeks to satisfy a range of stakeholder aspirations. However, integrative planning is extremely difficult to achieve and often different organizations and individuals work within particular tourism planning traditions within the same destination. Understanding the different traditions is regarded as important because each approach defines the central planning problem in different ways. Nevertheless, changes in approach have occurred overtime.

This chapter concluded by stressing how from a regional planning perspective, tourism needs to be seen within the context of sustainable regional development rather than just sustainable tourism – as significant as that might be from an industry perspective. In many cases tourism has unfortunately been regarded as contributory to low-road regional development rather than a high-road path that emphasizes the role of soft infrastructure. Nevertheless, tourism does have a significant role in high-road strategies, especially with respect to access, amenity and services.

Self-review questions

1 What are the five *traditions* of tourism planning identified in this chapter?
2 Why is *boosterism* sometimes described as a form of non-planning?
3 What are the key elements of a *sustainable* approach to tourism planning?
4 What are the five questions with respect to planning theory that are of concern in tourism planning?
5 Why do approaches to destination planning *change* over time?
6 What is the *justification* for planning?
7 What are the differences between *low-road* and *high-road* approaches towards regional competitiveness and development?
8 How do *low-road* approaches to regional development fit in with our understandings of *sustainable development*?
9 What *metrics* would you chose in helping to determine an understanding of sustainable tourism development?

Recommended reading

1 Michael, E.J. (2007). *Micro-clusters and Networks: The Growth of Tourism*, Oxford: Elsevier.
One of the best accounts of the role of state with respect to the promotion of tourism clusters and networks.
2 Murphy, P.E. and Murphy, A.E. (2004). *Strategic Management for Tourism Communities*. Clevedon: Channel View Publications.
Updates some of Murphy's earlier work on community tourism within a more contemporary strategic planning perspective.

3 Hall, C.M. (2000). *Tourism Planning*, 2nd edn, 2008. Harlow: Prentice-Hall.
   Provides an account of tourism planning at different scales and the influence of the different traditions of tourism planning.

4 Ruhanen, L. (2004). Strategic planning for local tourism destinations: an analysis of tourism plans. *Tourism and Hospitality: Planning and Development* 1(3), 239–253.
   A useful comparative analysis of the contents of different regional tourism plans.

5 Gössling, S. and Hall, C.M. (eds) (2006). *Tourism and Global Environmental Change*. London: Routledge.
   Provides an account of the development of tourism planning issues that are global in scope.

6 Selman, P. (2004). Community participation in the planning and management of cultural landscapes. *Journal of Environmental Planning and Management* 47(3), 365–392.
   Examines some of the difficulties associated with community-based planning approaches.

7 Dredge, D. (2001). Local government tourism planning and policy-making in New South Wales: institutional development and historical legacies. *Current Issues in Tourism* 4(2–4), 355–380.
   Case study that identifies some of the factors that influence tourism planning processes.

8 Hudson, R. (2001). *Producing Places*. New York: Guilford.
   An excellent general overview of the issues involved in place planning and regional development.

9 Harvey, D. (2000). *Spaces of Hope*. Edinburgh: Edinburgh University Press.
   Discusses issues of political renewal of local and regional development particularly within the context of contemporary globalization.

10 Sharpley, R. and Telfer, D.J. (eds) (2002). *Tourism and Development, Concepts and Issues*. Clevedon: Channelview.
   Provides a good account of the different approaches to development that underlie tourism planning.

Recommended web sites

Australian Department of the Environment and Water: http://www.environment.gov.au/index.html
New Zealand Ministry of Tourism Planning toolkit: http://www.tourism.govt.nz/tourism-toolkit/index.html
UNESCO World Heritage site: http://whc.unesco.org/
United Nations World Tourism Organization: www.world-tourism.org
Utah Office of Tourism planning toolkit: http://travel.utah.gov/research_and_planning/tourism_planning/index.html
World Commission on Environment and Development (WCED 1987): http://daccessdds.un.org/doc/UNDOC/GEN/N87/184/67/IMG/N8718467.pdf?OpenElement

References cited

Brake, M. and Newton, M. (1995). Promoting sustainable tourism in an urban context: recent developments in Malaga city, Andalusia. *Journal of Sustainable Tourism* 3(3), 115–134.

Bramwell, B. and Lane, B. (eds) (2000). A collection of cases and studies of tourism planning issues within the context of collaboration and planning practice. *Tourism Collaboration and Partnerships: Politics, Practice and Sustainability.* Clevedon: Channel View Publications.

Butler, R.W. (1991). Tourism, environment, and sustainable development. *Environmental Conservation* 18(3), 201–209.

Butler, R.W. (2000). Tourism and the environment: a geographical perspective. *Tourism Geographies* 2(3), 337–358.

Cheshire, P.C. and Gordon, I.R. (1998). Territorial competition: some lessons for policy. *Annals of Regional Science* 32, 321–346.

Cooke, P. (2002). *Knowledge Economies: Clusters, Learning and Cooperative Advantage*. London: Routledge.

Davidson, R. and Maitland, R. (1997). *Tourism Destinations*. London: Hodder and Stroughton.

Dredge, D. and Jenkins, J. (2007). *Tourism Planning and Policy*. Brisbane: Wiley.

Getz, D. (1986). Models in tourism planning towards integration of theory and practice. *Tourism Management* 7(1), 21–32.

Gössling, S. (2002). Global environmental consequences of tourism. *Global Environmental Change* 12, 283–302.

Gössling, S. and Hall, C.M. (eds) (2006). *Tourism and Global Environmental Change*. London: Routledge.

Gössling, S. and Hultman, J. (eds) (2006). *Ecotourism in Scandinavia*. Wallingford: CAB International.

Gunn, C.A. (1979). *Tourism Planning*. New York: Crane Russak.

Gunn, C.A. (1994). *Tourism Planning*, 3rd edn. London: Taylor and Francis.

Hall, C.M. (2000). *Tourism Planning*. Harlow: Prentice-Hall.

Hall, C.M. (2005) *Tourism: Rethinking the Social Science of Mobility*. Harlow: Prentice-Hall.

Hall, C.M. (2008). *Tourism Planning*, 2nd edn. Harlow: Prentice-Hall.

Hall, C.M. and Boyd, S. (eds) (2005). *Tourism and Nature-Based Tourism in Peripheral Areas: Development or Disaster*, Clevedon: Channel View Publications.

Hall, C.M. and Lew, A.A. (eds) (1998). *Sustainable Tourism Development: A Geographical Perspective*. London: Addison Wesley Longman.

Hall, C.M. and Page, S. (2006). *The Geography of Tourism and Recreation: Place, Space and Environment*, 3rd edn. London: Routledge.

Harvey, D. (1989). From managerialism to entrepreneurialism: the transformation in urban governance in late capitalism. *Geografiska Annaler* 71B, 3–17.

Judd, D.R. (2003). Building the tourist city: editor's introduction. In D.R. Judd (ed.), *The Infrastructure of Play: Building the Tourist City*, pp. 3–16. Armonk: M.E. Sharpe.

Krippendorf, J. (1975). *Die Landschaftsfresser: Tourismus und Erholungslandschaft, Verderben oder Segen?* Schönbühl, Switzerland: Hallwag.

Leitner, H. and Garner, M. (1993). The limits of local initiatives: a reassessment of urban entrepreneurialism for urban development. *Urban Geography* 14, 57–77.

Malecki, E.J. (2002). Hard and soft networks for urban competitiveness. *Urban Studies* 39, 929–945.

Malecki, E.J. (2004). Jockeying for position: what it means and why it matters to regional development policy when places compete. *Regional Studies* 38(9), 1101–1120.

Metsähallitus (Forest and Park Service) (2000). *The Principles of Protected Area Management in Finland: Guidelines on the Aims, Function and Management of State-Owned Protected Areas*. Metsähallituksen luonnonsuojelulkaisuja Sarja B No.54. Vantaa: Metsähallitus – Forest and Park Service, Natural Heritage Service.

Michael, E.J. (2007). *Micro-clusters and Networks: The Growth of Tourism*. Oxford: Elsevier.

Morgan, K. (2004). Sustainable regions: governance, innovation and scale. *European Planning Studies* 12(6), 871–889.

Murphy, P.E. (1985). *Tourism: A Community Approach*. New York: Methuen.

Murphy, P.E. and Murphy, A.E. (2004). *Strategic Management for Tourism Communities*. Clevedon: Channel View Publications.

O'Reilly, A.M. (1986). Tourism carrying capacity: concept and issues. *Tourism Management* 7, 254–258.

Pforr, C. (2001). Tourism policy in Australia's Northern Territory: a policy process analysis of its tourism development masterplan. *Current Issues in Tourism* 4(2–4), 275–307.

Pike, A., Rodríguez-Pose, A. and Tomaney, J. (2006). *Local and Regional Development*. London: Routledge.

Ruhanen, L. (2004). Strategic planning for local tourism destinations: an analysis of tourism plans. *Tourism and Hospitality: Planning and Development* 1(3), 239–253.

Singh, S., Timothy, D. and R.K. Dowling, R.K. (eds) (2003). *Tourism in Destination Communities*. Wallingford: CAB International.

Timothy, D. and Tosun, C. (2003). Appropriate planning for tourism in destination communities: participation, incremental growth and collaboration. In S. Singh, D. Timothy and R.K. Dowling (eds), *Tourism in Destination Communities*, pp. 181–204. Wallingford: CAB International.

Treuren, G. and Lane, D. (2003). The tourism planning process in the context of organised interests, industry structures, state capacity, accumulation and sustainability. *Current Issues in Tourism* 6(1), 1–22.

World Commission on Environment and Development (WCED) (1987). *Our Common Future*. New York: Oxford University Press.

Chapter 9

Marketing and branding the contemporary destination

Chapter objectives

After reading this chapter you will

- Understand the process and outcomes of contemporary destination marketing
- Appreciate the importance of engaging with all stakeholders in contemporary destination marketing
- Understand the formation and characteristics of the destination image
- Be aware of strategic approaches to contemporary destination marketing
- Understand the formation and characteristics of destination brands
- Recognize the role that technology, particularly the Internet, can play in contemporary destination marketing
- Appreciate the structure and roles of destination marketing organizations
- Recognize that destination marketing is surrounded by a range of issues and questions relating to the ability of a destination to be marketed as the equivalent of a product or brand

Introduction

This chapter provides an overview of the marketing and branding of contemporary destinations. The chapter demonstrates that one of the major issues for destination marketers is the destination image, yet this is something that is very difficult to influence and to change. The significance of the destination image shows that destination marketing is as much a strategic process as it is a tactical one. Indeed, destination branding has to be viewed as a strategic activity as it is closely linked to the destination image and demands the close involvement of destination stakeholders in the design and acceptance of the brand. Of course, this process is now facilitated by technology with the Internet providing a cheap and effective marketing medium for destinations, as well as the opportunity to develop destination portals which provide a sense of ownership for stakeholders. Destination marketing organizations (DMOs) spearhead the technological developments for destinations and the marketing process generally. They act as umbrella-marketing agencies and consolidate the role of destination partners. The chapter closes by identifying a range of key issues relating to destination marketing, including the role of the public sector, involvement of destination stakeholders, the very nature of the destination as a product and the question as to whether the theory of marketing can – or should – be extended to places and destinations.

Contemporary destination marketing and branding

Contemporary destination marketing and branding is both a process and an outcome. The process of destination marketing involves dealing with the complexities of destinations and their myriad stakeholders, whilst the outcome is a brand or the image of the destination. In other words, a good destination marketer will focus upon two key operations. Firstly, managing the destination's many stakeholders and networks; and secondly, formulating and managing the destination brand. Definitions of destination marketing clearly distinguish between the process of destination marketing and the outcome as shown in Table 9.1.

Ward (1998) observes that place marketing dates back to the selling of the frontier to the American people in the mid-nineteenth century. Destination marketing came later in the late nineteenth century when destinations sought to attract visitors in an increasingly competitive market. However, the actual term 'destination marketing'

Table 9.1 Definitions of the process and the outcome of destination marketing

The process

'Destination branding is (the) process used to develop a unique identity and personality that is different from all competing destinations' (Morrison and Anderson 2002: 17)

'Place branding is an extremely complex and highly political activity that can enhance a nation's economy, national self-image and identity' (Morgan et al. 2004: 14)

Place marketing is 'the conscious use of publicity and marketing to communicate selective images of specific geographic localities or areas to a target audience' (Gold and Ward 1994: 2)

Destination marketing can be defined as the promotion of appealing images to attract visitors to a defined destination area (Middleton 2000: 378)

Selecting a consistent element mix to identify and distinguish it [a destination] through positive image building (Cai 2002: 722)

The result

'A destination brand is a name symbol, logo, word mark or other graphic that both identifies and differentiates the destination; furthermore, it conveys the promise of a memorable travel experience that is uniquely associated with the destination; it also serves to consolidate and reinforce the recollection of pleasurable memories of the destination experience' (Ritchie and Ritchie 1998: 17)

A country image is 'the sum of beliefs and impressions people hold about places images represent a simplification of a large number of associations and pieces of information connected with a place' (Kotler et al. 1993).

and the formal process of engaging in a disciplined marketing approach are more recent. They can be traced back to the 1970s when the advent of mass international tourism enhanced competition between destinations and prompted the beginnings of destination marketing as a practice. The concept continues to evolve and increasingly there is a view that it is 'branding' that is the glue that holds the marketing of the destination together. Indeed, some now use the term 'destination branding' in place of 'destination marketing'. Tourism agencies are not alone in their practice of destination marketing – it is also practiced by urban planners who tend to take a broader, more holistic view and include economic and social objectives.

Contemporary destination marketing operates at a variety of scales from the international to the very local. It is central to the activities of tourism organizations, delivering destination competitiveness and a range of benefits to the destination. These benefits focus around the issue of differentiation and competitiveness and include:

- Securing the emotional link to, and loyalty of, visitors.
- Coordination of the private sector and other stakeholders through cooperative marketing.
- Acting as a base for promotion of other products such as investment, economic development, film and TV.
- Facilitating and encouraging the use of local products and design.
- Facilitating seamless market communication of the destination.

However, to be successful, contemporary destination marketing must engage with the complexities of the destination itself, not only in terms of the necessity to be inclusive in the development of the brand, but also to get to grips with the nature of the destination product and the consumption process. Morgan et al. (2004) for example state that destinations are lifestyle indicators for inspirational visitors, communicating identity, lifestyle and status. Their consumption is a highly involving experience that is extensively planned and remembered, in contrast to the purchase and consumption of fast moving consumer goods (FMCGs). A destination is therefore more than a product – it is the physical space in which tourism takes place, where communities live and work and is imbued with symbols and images of culture and history. It is also the space within which tourists and suppliers interact to deliver the tourist experience. This context makes destination marketing so different from marketing FMCGs and is illustrated by the following case study focusing on a DMO that takes a 'whole of destination' approach to its operation.

CASE STUDY
Place-making: the blackstone valley tourism council

Introduction

The Blackstone Valley Tourism Council is an award winning DMO, having won the first ever Ulysses prize for innovation in destination management awarded by the UNWTO in 2006. This case study outlines key features of the Council's award winning approach. Firstly, the Council's commitment to the local community and its development; and secondly, the Council's innovative approach to strategic destination marketing and product formulation.

The destination

Blackstone Valley is in Rhode Island, USA. It is the birthplace of the American industrial revolution, dating from 1790. By the nineteenth century it was dominated by up to 1000 textile mills. Poor economic decisions in the early twentieth century exposed the Valley's over-dependence on textiles and the region became depressed with a 14 per cent unemployment rate in 1982, and the river, the most polluted in America.

The Blackstone Valley Tourism Council is using tourism to spearhead the economic regeneration of the Valley. In addition, the Blackstone River Valley National Heritage Corridor was created in 1986 to preserve and interpret 46 miles of significant historic and cultural lands, waterways and structures in the Valley, and to boost the economy. The Corridor is managed by the National Park Service, which coordinates federal, state and local agencies. Congress established the 'Corridor Commission' to act as the umbrella agency to develop the vision of the Corridor through innovative partnerships. The goal of the Corridor is to create a park system linking parks, historic sites and recreational facilities for locals and visitors along the Valley.

In the early years of the twenty-first century, the Valley had a population of half a million people living in 24 cities, and attracted around 3 million visitors each year. They visit the Valley's attractions, which include:

- historic sites and museums;
- river tours;
- vineyards, farms and orchards;
- events and the arts;
- education and the river classroom.

The organization

The Blackstone Valley Tourism Council was founded in 1985 as a not for profit educational organization, professionally staffed and governed by a board of directors representing tourism interests in the Valley. It is the state-designated tourism development agency for the National Heritage Corridor.

The Council has a portion of public funding (a state hotel tax) and donations, but operates a large proportion of its US $950 000 budget (2005/2006) through running events and private funding. The Blackstone Valley Tourism Council won its awards by demonstrating leadership, innovation, commitment to its mission and the application of sustainable tourism principles in all its actions.

The Council's main functions are as follows:

- Administration – running and coordinating tourism.
- Visitor information services – face-to-face, mail and telephone enquires from the four Blackstone Valley Visitor Centres.
- Special events and programmes – working with partners.
- PR and communication – dealing with the media on behalf of the Valley and working with partners.
- Group travel – working with tour operators and easing packages.
- River programmes – using Council owned heritage boats for accommodation and interpretation.
- Educational programmes – an educational coordinator managing programmes across the Valley.

Strategic destination marketing

The Council works to develop the Valley as a prime visitor and cultural destination. The mission of the Council is *Blackstone* and its purpose is:

> To create positive change, with regard to community values, by developing coordinated responsible and sustainable tourism in Rhode Island's Blackstone Valley.

The marketing of the Blackstone Valley is focused on the river Corridor and demands collaboration across a range of stakeholders at international, national and regional level as well as those in the Valley itself. In the Valley, the two key agencies are as follows:

1 Blackstone Valley Chamber of Commerce, which is focused on the economic development of the Valley.
2 The Corridor Commission, which is focused on managing relationships in the National Heritage Corridor.

The Council's key objectives are framed around a strategic plan that focuses on the marketing of the Valley to create a unified vision. This plan aims to boost visitation and economic yield from tourism by:

- improving the tourism product;
- coordinating attractions and their operation across the Valley;
- encouraging more support services for tourism;

- better promoting the Valley;
- coordinating marketing actions.

This is being achieved through:

- Designation of tourism development zones with high potential to deliver a critical mass of attractions and support services.
- Attraction of entrepreneurs through a tourism development programme with incentives.

In implementing the strategy, the Council has developed two key innovative concepts:

1 *The Blackstone Valley product*: The Council has formulated the Valley's tourism product through the concept of 'geotourism' to sustain and enhance the authentic character of the Valley. Geotourism is defined as 'tourism that sustains or enhances the geographical character of a destination through its environment, culture, aesthetics, heritage and the well being of its residents'. The principles of geotourism are to attract those market segments most appropriate to the destination and to develop an authentic destination with a sense of place involving and benefiting the local community. Sustainability and interactive interpretation are central to the concept. The challenge faced by the Council in this vision is to balance economic regeneration with the socio-cultural authenticity of its local communities and the environmental and preservation needs of the region.

2 *The Blackstone Valley market*: In addition, the Council engages overtly in relationship marketing by building strong relationships with visitors through its activities, communications and web sites. This relationship is then used to encourage 'visitor payback' whereby visitors can pay back the destination for their experience there. This is done though a donation scheme developed by the Council through the Blackstone Valley Legacy Trust. In addition, visitors are encouraged to come back to the Valley as volunteers or employees.

By the early years of the twenty-first century The Blackstone Valley Tourism Council had seen a valley-wide regeneration with a drop in unemployment across the region, an improved quality of life for local communities and return of pride of place in the destination. The Council demonstrates the fact that tourism is but one element of complex functioning communities and destinations. Testament to the commitment to sustainable tourism is the Council's newly developed sustainable tourism planning and development laboratory which brings other communities to Blackstone and shares the Blackstone know-how of sustainable tourism planning in structured workshops.

Key sources

Blackstone River Valley National Heritage Corridor: http://www.nps.gov/blac
Blackstone Valley Chamber of Commerce: http://www.blackstonevalley.org
Blackstone Valley Tourism Council: http://www.tourblackstone.com
Yaeger Communications (2001). *Blackstone Valley Tourism Strategic Plan*. Swampscott, MA: Yaeger Communications.

Discussion questions

1 Visit the Council's web site and map the stakeholders involved in the Blackstone Valley Tourism sector – how could they be grouped?
2 What strategies should the Council consider to balance the needs of tourism development to regenerate the Blackstone Valley, with the imperative to preserve a unique historic industrial landscape?
3 What might be the drawbacks with the Council's concept of 'geotourism'?

Destination image

Understanding the formation and characteristics of the destination image is central to contemporary destination marketing. Destination image can be defined as:

> The attitude, perception, beliefs and ideas one holds about a particular geographic area formed by the cognitive image of a particular destination (Gartner 2000: 295).

Effectively, the destination image is a simplified version of reality, a way of making sense of the many destination stimuli received and processed by the visitor or potential visitor. In other words, the image of a destination is critical to marketing as it affects both an individual's perception of a destination and their choice of destination. The generation of the image is different for destinations to many other products – such as say FMCG. This is because it is the tourists themselves who generate a destination image by selecting different sources of information. As a result, destination marketeers have much less influence on images, despite their critical importance to destination choice. The image is particularly critical for tourist destinations as follows:

1 The intangible nature of the destination product means the image is the only evidence that a visitor has of the destination before they visit. For the tourist, the destination promise is inherently uncertain and decisions depend on the tourist's mental construct, which effectively acts as a surrogate for evaluating the product. The challenge for marketing lies in understanding the complex link between consumer decision-making and the destination image.

2 The inseparable nature of the production and consumption process of tourism means that once they visit, the tourist's image of the destination is immediately changed by the experience.

Whilst image formation is not the same as branding, it is closely related. This is because the choice of branding and brand attributes of a destination reinforce the destination image.

Components of the destination image

The theories of destination image are divided into two camps. The first suggests that the destination image can be disaggregated into many attributes and elements that can be measured. The second, gestalt approach, effectively says that the image is a whole, or holistic concept and cannot be disaggregated.

Gartner (1993) provides an attractive framework for understanding destination image and its link to destination branding. He argues that a destination image comprises three distinct, but hierarchical related elements – components, formation and characteristics:

1 *Components*: There are three components of the image – cognitive, effective and conative:
   ● *The cognitive component* comprises the beliefs and attitudes towards the destination and leads to the internal evaluation of the destination's attributes. This is based on fact, or what are believed to be the facts, acquired over time from many sources. From the tourist's point of view the perceived image is reality.

- *The effective component* represents the value of the destination in terms of what the tourist is looking for from the destination based on personal feelings or motives. It is this comparison of the image with the tourist's needs that determines value.
- *The conative component* is the action component. This is the decision to visit and is based upon evaluation and the value of the first two components.

2 *Formation*: Formation of the destination image is based upon information acquired by the tourist from three sources:
- *Induced agents* are generally controlled by sources external to the individual, such as advertisements.
- *Organic agents* are sources acquired through personal experience. These are normally the most trusted sources of information.
- *Autonomous agents* are media sources or popular culture (such as films or documentaries). They are powerful because they can quickly alter a tourist's image of a destination.

3 *Characteristics*: Destination images are characterized by certain features:
- Distance blurs the image of a place such that distant destinations have a fuzzier image than closer destinations.
- Images change continuously but slowly.
- The smaller the destination image, the more likely its image will be based on its larger political parent.
- The larger the image the more slowly it changes.

The role of images in destination marketing

Destination images are pervasive and powerful, and clearly they play an important role in contemporary destination marketing and branding. As noted already, destination image has a profound effect on visitor behaviour and decision-making with respect to destinations. Destination marketing therefore focuses on the deceptively simple approach of developing a positive image through promotion. In this process, images are used to achieve the following:

- Communicate messages about destinations.
- Redefine and reposition destinations.
- Counter negative, and enhance positive, perceptions about destinations.
- Target key market areas.

Table 9.2 Destination image and marketing actions

Destination image	Marketing action
Positive	Focus on amplifying and delivering image to target groups
Weak	Places that are small lack attractions or do not promote
Negative	Requires fundamental change prior to image development
Mixed	Emphasize selected elements and rectify others
Contradictory	Different groups with opposing images – stress positive points to groups with negative images
Overly attractive	Withdraw publicity

Source: UNWTO (2006).

Marketing then, attempts to manage the image through researching perceptions of the destination, segmenting and targeting image audiences, and positioning destination benefits to support the image. In Table 9.2, the UNWTO shows how images can be classified and appropriate marketing action taken to reinforce or change the image.

Contemporary destination marketing strategy

Destination marketing is a strategic activity, linked not only to tourism but also to sustainability, economic development, investment and residential lifestyle. It is the goal of destination strategy is to convert current conditions at the destination into desired situations using strategic marketing and planning. Pike (2004) breaks this down further by identifying four thematic goals of DMOs:

1 Enhancing destination image.
2 Increasing industry profitability.
3 Reducing seasonality.
4 Ensuring long-term funding.

Whilst this can be done by applying standard strategic marketing approaches to the destination – such as the Boston Consulting Matrix or Porter's Strategic Forces – these approaches do not translate well to the complexity of destinations. This is partly because destination marketing agencies do not control the product that they are dealing with.

Two approaches merit consideration here. Firstly, Gilbert (1990) takes the approach of classifying destinations along a continuum from commodity to status area. The destination's position on the continuum assists in developing an appropriate marketing strategy and can be used to strategically reposition a destination, as was done by Spain in the 1990s. The strategic process is as follows:

1 Assess current position.
2 Select desired position.
3 Strategy to achieve desired position.
4 Implement strategy.

However, Gilbert's approach suffers from the fact that most destinations lie between the two extremes and it omits the evolution of destinations. Instead, the approach devised by Jain (1985) works well and has been adapted for destinations by Cooper (1995). He classifies the strategic options for destinations according to a two-dimensional matrix that takes into account the competitive position of the destination and the stage on the destination life cycle (Table 9.3). This is useful in locating the strategic response of destinations to the wider competitive environment. Jain's framework is linked to a comprehensive research and environmental scanning process, which is essential for destinations to understand not only the competitive environment and the consumer, but also the positive and negative associations of the destination brand.

Positioning

A key component of destination strategy is the positioning of the destination against the competition. This ensures that the destination delivers a unique position in relation to its competitors and occupies a particular place in the minds of potential tourists. Positioning of destinations is based on differentiation, cost and developing a unique focus. Positioning must be consistent with cost and value for money, market trends and consumer preferences, convenience of purchase, technology and demographic trends. Finally, positioning must take into account the capability and resources of the destination to deliver the promise.

Table 9.3 Jain's matrix of strategic action

Competitive position	Stage on life cycle			
	Embryonic	**Growth**	**Mature**	**Ageing**
Dominant	Fast grow Start up	Fast grow Cost leadership Renew Defend position	Defend position Cost leadership Renew Fast grow	Defend position Focus Renew Grow with industry
Strong	Start up Differentiate Fast grow	Fast grow Catch up Cost leadership Differentiate	Cost leadership Renew, focus Differentiate Grow with industry	Find niche Hold niche Hang in Grow with industry Harvest
Favourable	Start up Differentiate Focus Fast grow	Differentiate, focus Catch up Grow with industry	Harvest-hang in Find nice, hold niche Renew, turnaround Differentiate, focus Grow with industry	Retrench Turnaround
Tenable	Start up Grow with industry Focus	Harvest, catch up Hold niche Find niche Turnaround Focus Grow with industry	Harvest Turnaround Find niche Retrench	Divest Retrench
Weak	Find niche Catch up Grow with industry	Turnaround Retrench	Withdraw Divest	Withdraw

Source: Cooper (1995), based on Jain (1985).

Destination branding

Destination branding is central to the contemporary destination marketing process – to quote Kotler (2003) 'branding is the art and cornerstone of marketing' (p. 418). A brand can be defined as:

> A name, term, sign, symbol or design or combination of them, intended to identify the goods or services of one seller or group of sellers and to differentiate them from those of competitors (Kotler 2000: 404).

Brands can be approached from two viewpoints. Firstly, the *product plus approach* views the brand as an addition to the product (along with say, price) and concerned with communication and differentiation. Secondly, the *holistic approach* views the brand as greater than the sum of its parts such that brands reside in the minds of consumers. It is this second approach, which is most common in destination marketing.

Brands signify identity and originated as a means of ownership and identification by farmers or craftsmen. Brands became important as mass markets developed for products in the twentieth century. This was for two reasons: firstly, consumers became more sophisticated and were faced with greater product choice; and secondly branding was developed for FMCG as they are characterized by low involvement products with the need for branding to build loyalty and communicate benefits over competitors. Nonetheless, whilst it may appear that brands are fabricated, they are real entities, based on products, resistant to change and dependent on occupying defensible niches within product categories. Developing and managing destination brands is therefore as much a strategic operation as it is tactical.

According to Hankinson (2004) destination brands:

- Communicate identity and are therefore of strategic importance.
- Are perceptual entities in themselves and so the issue of destination image is central to destination branding.
- Enhance value.
- Can be used to build a relationship with the visitor or supplier.

The link between destination brand and destination image is clear. Like images, brands are created by consumers, but at the same time, brands fast track the information processing of consumers by acting as a means of differentiation and a guarantee of quality. Therefore, to be successful a destination brand should:

- be credible,
- be deliverable,
- be differentiated,
- convey powerful ideas,
- enthuse destination partners,
- resonate with the visitor.

Formulating the destination brand is more complex for destinations than for say, FMCG. This is because the destination comprises many stakeholders, including local residents, and the branding process must be inclusive of these groups, as discussed later in this chapter. Destination branding therefore serves two masters:

1 *The local community* where resident receptiveness is a major element of destination branding.
2 *The tourist* who in turn receives information and market stories about the destination from a variety of sources, including blogs. When they visit they interact with destination products and services and evaluate the brand.

This raises the question of whether destination marketing organizations can in fact control the brand to the same degree that marketers act as the custodian of FMCG brands. In other words, can all the actions that affect visitor perceptions at a destination be managed and coordinated when many dimensions of destination brands are beyond the control of the marketer? This has been clearly demonstrated in the period since 11 September 2001 with the many terrorist attacks on destinations.

Designing the destination brand

The destination brand enhances the favourability, strength and uniqueness of the destination, and so must demonstrate consistency and clarity of design. Designing the destination brand delivers the blueprint for the branding, development and marketing of the destination. This includes:

- Positioning.
- Product formulation and composition (such as seaside, city or heritage destinations).
- The nesting of the brand in terms of identifying a supra-brand (such as Australia) and sub-brands based on geography and products (Queensland, Gold Coast).

- The communication strategy reflected in destination logos, insignia and marketing collateral advertising concepts.

This can be seen as a four-step approach:

1 *Brand assessment*: This begins with an assessment of the current situation of the destination brand including a review of the marketplace, visitors, stakeholders, influencers, competitors and industry conditions as well as the demographic and social setting of the destination. It will be based on facts and research on visitor perceptions, influencers and stakeholders. The stages will include:
   - A review of all previous research.
   - A review of all brand communications and marketing plans.
   - Analysis of data on competitors and visitor research.
2 *Brand promise*: The brand promise is the essence of the commitment to visitors and the benefits (emotional and functional) that visitors can expect throughout the destination experience. The entire destination must commit to the brand if the promise is to be delivered, hence the need for the branding process to be inclusive of all stakeholders, including local residents. The promise is normally expressed in a few sentences to communicate brand attributes:
   - Something will be done.
   - An expressed assurance.
   - A perception of future excellence and achievement.

   All destination brand communication is then consistent with the promise. However, it must be recognized that the destination brand promise will often reflect a compromise between the aspirations of the destination brand and the reality of what the brand can deliver to visitors.
3 *Brand architecture*: The architecture of the brand outlines the various messages to communicate the promise and the essence of the destination brand. This process attempts to signal the destination's values and positioning and increasingly tends to stress more emotional than functional benefits. The process also signals what the destination can deliver using a five-stage approach:
   - Choice of a destination brand name that resonates with the visitor and sets the tone of the destination.
   - Graphics such as logos or visual symbols.
   - A by-line that describes what the destination brand is all about.
   - A tag line that is a phrase to clarify the destination's emotional and functional benefits.

- The brand story, which is used to inspire visitors and explains how the brand came about.

In other words, brand architecture provides a framework within which to communicate the destination brand. It often utilizes events or theming (linking to TV, seasons, history, film or literature).

4 *Internalizing the brand*: This is the road map for how the destination organization delivers the brand promise on the ground at the destination through influencing and training employees, partners, stakeholders and residents. This enables and empowers the delivery of the brand promise at the destination. This is critical as the products delivered at the destination are often the strongest manifestation of brand identity. Brand internalization comprises four stages:

- Creation of brand principles.
- Establishment of brand equity goals.
- Outlining and communicating the brand plan to all stakeholders.
- Completing a culturalization plan for all stakeholders.

The destination branding process therefore delivers a carefully crafted and conceptualized branding strategy that encompasses the entire destination experience reflecting visitor needs and being inclusive of destination stakeholders. Destinations are places where visitors have experiences, therefore brands have to capture visitor imagination and resonate with the market, whilst also being sensitive to, and inclusive of, the local community and destination stakeholders.

Technology

The Internet has revolutionized destination marketing, branding and image formation. At a stroke it has given small destinations with tiny budgets the same market reach as the largest destinations in the world. It brings other advantages too. Internet technology is ideally suited to products such as tourism where the product is intangible and cannot be pre-tested. Indeed, the decision to visit is increasingly influenced by the quality of a destination web site and the degree that it allows interaction and flexibility. DMOs can use the technology to:

- save on print and distribution costs;
- directly target and manage customers through email;
- provide content of great depth and visual quality.

Yet, whilst the Internet has been available for destination marketing since the mid-1990s, many destinations have been slow to take advantage of the cost savings and potential that it provides, and it is a common criticism that content provision by destinations lags behind the technology available to deliver it.

Destination web sites

Nonetheless, DMOs now use the Internet as a central part of their marketing strategy. Here, the key is to have a strategic e-marketing plan to direct traffic to a destination web site and to then capture the visitor. Such web sites service visitors, local industry, media and professionals. The structure of a destination web site will depend on two sets of factors:

1 *Destination factors*: Destination size, the variety of destination products, the number of web updates required, and the role of e-commerce on the site.
2 *Technical factors*: The importance of position on search engines, whether the site is on a hosted or a purchased server, and the screen resolution required.

The WTO (2001) identified the following key features of web site functionality for destinations:

- Accessibility and readability – does the site reach all potential users.
- Identity and trust – trust on the Internet is fragile, especially if e-commerce is involved through online booking. Strong branding, use of logos and a clear statement of purpose all help here.
- Degree of customization and interactivity.
- Ease of navigation.
- Findability and search engine optimization.
- Technical performance – lack of functionality is frustrating for users.
- The quality of the services offered via the web site:
  - Promotion
  - Information
  - Transactions.

Increasingly, destination web sites are being used for more than the straightforward delivery and presentation of destination information. Many sites now include the ability to customize the site and for tourists to interact with the information. As destination web sites have evolved, their levels of flexibility and interactivity have improved and grown. This has been captured by Doolin et al. (2002) in their 'Extended Model of Internet Commerce Adoption' (eMICA).

The eMICA model demonstrates a staged approach to the evolution of destination web sites and provides a destination with a road map of its web site development. The model shows how web sites add layers of complexity and functionality as they develop (Table 9.4).

Good web site design encourages the building of relationships between the destination and the tourist. At the time of writing, contemporary destinations are increasingly achieving this by the development of a web-based interface, or destination portal, which can deliver tangible benefits to both the supplier and the tourist. Effectively, destination portals become the digital version of the destination, unifying web access to the destination, integrating all aspects of the value chain and allowing communication amongst stakeholders.

On the supply side, destination portals allow the integration of destination management systems to draw together all elements of supply at the destination. They allow the identification of high-quality content providers at the destination and can manage them by grouping, categorizing, and providing simplified navigation and straightforward accessibility. Portals also have the advantage of acting to encourage virtual destination communities and cooperation amongst stakeholders.

Table 9.4 The eMICA model

eMICA	Examples of functionality
Stage 1: Promotion	
Layer 1: Basic information	Company name, address and contact details
Layer 2: Rich information	Annual report, and email contact
Stage 2: Provision	
Layer 1: Low interactivity	Basic product catalogue, hyperlinks, and online enquiry form
Layer 2: Medium interactivity	Higher-level product catalogues, customer support (FAQs),
Layer 3: High interactivity	Chat room, newsletters and email updates
Stage 3: Processing	Secure online transactions, order status and tracking

Source: Doolin et al. (2002).

On the demand side, portals act as an interface with the consumer and have the ability to include e-commerce functions through integrated computerized information reservation management systems. These functions are achieved by the presence of both a customer database and a product database with an interface between the two.

DMOs must evaluate their web sites given their levels of investment in web site development and their critical dependence on web sites in destination marketing strategies. There is a variety of approaches to web site evaluation. These include:

- Best practice-based evaluations and measurements that use experts based on a set of quality criteria.
- Online surveys that evaluate the needs, satisfaction and opinions of users.
- Web analytics which track and trace user behaviour.
- Online experiments and laboratory testing of behaviour where visitors to sites are analysed and their behaviour in say, searching is used to devise online market segmentation approaches.

These approaches evaluate web sites in terms of:

- design, content and simplicity;
- search engine compliance;
- navigation and speed;
- customer relationship management and links;
- e-commerce, advertising and response;
- performance tracking and management.

The role of the DMO

Given the investment needed for a destination to develop a fully fledged e-marketing strategy, this is often led by the destination management organization. There are two forces at work here:

1 DMOs face the threat of disintermediation as their role becomes redundant in the face of Internet bookings and tourist information delivered by the Internet.

DMOs typically provide information for the early stages of destination decision-making, but other web-based companies are now moving in to occupy that role (e.g. Expedia, Travelocity).

2 Coordination and leadership is needed at the destination level, and it is this strategic role that can be taken by the DMO. DMOs are often public sector funded agencies and therefore have the mandate to develop IT systems and leverage funding from destination partners.

Destination marketing organizations

Destination marketing is normally spearheaded and implemented by a destination marketing organization (DMO) or a visitor and convention bureau (CVB). Funding tends to be secured by the public sector with additional funds from private sector partners, often on a membership basis. DMO structures vary considerably and continue to evolve; traditionally they were departments or agencies funded by government to market the destination but increasingly they involve the private sector in a partnership arrangement. The International Association of Convention and Visitor Bureaus (IACVB) characterizes DMOs as not for profit organizations representing a specific destination, offering a full range of unbiased information for both the trade and consumer and promoting the long-term marketing and development of the destination. In other words, DMOs have both a strategic aim and a range of tactical activities. Their strategic aim is to act as an umbrella marketing agency by promoting the long-term development and marketing of the destination, and consolidating the role of destination partners in this process. This strategic aim is achieved through a variety of tactical activities, which include:

- Creating the destination brand to deliver awareness of the destination.
- Coordinating destination stakeholders.
- Acting as an unbiased information clearing house for both the public and the travel trade.
- Commissioning research.
- Developing the destination marketing plan.
- Developing funding resources to support the operation of the DMO.
- Developing the destination product and packaging.
- Monitoring service and quality standards.

The IACVB profiled 222 American CVBs in 2005 and summarized their characteristics as follows:

- On average each destination has two visitor centres.
- The average visitor centre utilizes both paid staff (76 per cent) and volunteers.
- Almost half of all visitor centres have a shop.
- Almost two-thirds of CVBs are independent, not for profit organizations whilst 18 per cent are government agencies.
- CVBs source their funding from a mix of government support and membership dues.
- Half of all CVBs are membership organizations.
- Average staffing of a CVB is 12–13 full-time equivalent staff.

The survey also found that the average age of a CVB is 39 years, with the first being established in Chicago in 1896. In 2006, 100 years later some key trends can be identified in the way that DMOs are operating. These include an observable trend towards destination management and away from simply focusing on marketing. This reflects the fact that the DMO is seen to have to manage the product and to generate strategies that resonate with visitors. It is also linked to a trend for professionalism amongst DMOs as administrative structures flatten and the DMO is held accountable to the community. This is changing the way that DMOs report and measure their performance, with statistics of enquiry conversions more important than simply the number of enquiries. Finally, all DMOs are recognizing that innovation and partnerships are a key aspect of their work. The following case study illustrates the role of a particular partnership programme between a DMO and the tourism industry, focused on innovative new product development.

CASE STUDY
Product clubs: building Canadian tourism through partnerships

Introduction

Canada has recognized the imperative of creating and delivering unique destination experiences to its visitors. In this way, Canada is positioned as a leader of vacation destinations.

However, it also has to be recognized that tourism is traditionally a conservative industry and that small businesses in particular are reluctant to cooperate. In response to these potential setbacks to innovation, the Canadian Tourism Commission (CTC) has pioneered partnerships with the private sector to encourage innovation in product development. This case study demonstrates the twin imperatives of destination marketing – innovation and partnerships and the way that they have come together in the concept of the 'product club'.

Product clubs

Canada's tourism strategy prioritizes innovation in product development through partnership with the private sector. The CTC has developed a programme of 'tourism innovation partnerships' that are defined as:

> A partnership established and led by tourism industry stakeholders who pool their resources to achieve the programme's objectives in partnership with the CTC (Canadian Tourism Commission).

Product clubs are one of the most successful of these partnership schemes. They are built around the notion of developing or enhancing tourism products using the resources and know-how of the CTC, combined with the energy and entrepreneurship of the private sector. Product clubs are focused on particular product clusters that have been identified as a priority by the CTC based on research and market intelligence (Figure 9.1). The clubs then develop and package products that will appeal to a global market.

A product club is:

> A partnership built with industry participants who share a common vision for the development of a common vision for the development of a specific tourism product or niche (Canadian Tourism Commission).

Product clubs were developed under the auspices of the CTC's Industry and Product Development Committee in 1996. The CTC acts as a partner to all product clubs working with Small and Medium Sized Enterprises (SMEs) from all sectors of tourism – attractions, accommodation, tourism associations or retailers. Since 1996, 43 product clubs have been formed with 250 partner organizations and over 5000 members and businesses.

The aim of the product club programme was to boost the competitiveness of Canada and to facilitate innovation in tourism products. This is achieved by developing a diversity of market-ready tourism products and encouraging collaboration and partnerships in the

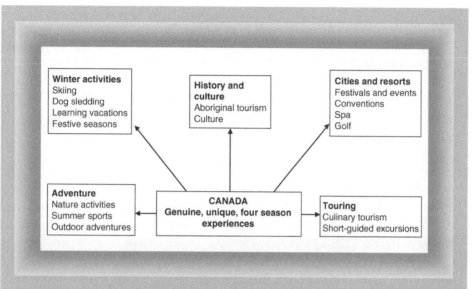

Figure 9.1 Canadian product clusters: the basis for product clubs

(*Source*: Adapted from www.canadatourism.com/productclubs)

tourism sector. In this way, product clubs also encourage the sharing of knowledge and best practice across the tourism sector.

The anatomy of product clubs

Product clubs have a range of drivers that stimulate their formation:

- *Community drivers* – championed by an individual or destination community to develop a local tourism product.
- *Market drivers* – responding to a market opportunity based on market research and intelligence. These have proved to be the most successful.
- *Extension drivers* – where the partners come together to extend an existing association activity, such as indigenous tourism.

Product clubs can be:

- New tour packages.
- New tourism circuits.
- Ways of enhancing service and product quality.
- Ways of adding diversity and innovation to the Canadian experience.
- Ways of delivering year-round tourism.

Product clubs develop the product using three key phases:

1 *Product development* – uses existing market research and intelligence to create or enhance a product that will respond to specific market segments.
2 *Testing* – tests the product to ensure that it responds to the identified demand.
3 *Marketing transition* – positions the product for launch.

Product club partnerships come in a number of forms:

- *Vertical linkages* – with suppliers.
- *Industry sector linkages* – such as wine tourism product clubs.
- *In-market links* – through travel trade distribution channels.
- *Regional linkages* – at a particular destination, such as the Saskatchewan River basin product club.
- *Thematic linkages* – based on particular product themes, such as the travellers with physical disabilities product club.
- *Non-traditional linkages* – e.g. products developed by a particular community, such as the Aboriginal waterways product club.

Product club success factors include:

- Clear focus and vision.
- A partnership with a strong leader or champion.
- Clear lines of responsibility and roles identified for partners, and expectations and outcomes workshopped.
- Recognizing and responding to a market opportunity.
- Proactive partnerships that go the extra mile.
- Long-term commitments with a 5-year time horizon.
- Committed partners with a financial commitment.

Product clubs deliver a range of advantages to destinations. These include:

- Identification of a shared purpose, belonging to a group that presents a united front to the market.
- Clubs allow the local sector to develop critical mass to address a local issue or opportunity.
- Clubs create an advocacy platform for tourism locally.
- Clubs act as a vehicle for local tourism PR and communications.

- Clubs encourage creativity at the local scale and synergy across the tourism sector.
- Successful clubs boost the local economy by attracting visitors.
- Clubs encourage local tourism groups to gain industry credibility.
- Clubs are a smart way to overcome impediments of tourism small businesses and to expose SMEs to good practice and knowledge sharing.

Key sources

The Canadian Tourism Commission (2001). *Best Practices in Canada's Tourism Industry*: *Partnerships*. Ottawa, Onto.: CTC.

The Canadian Tourism Commission: http://www.canadatourism.com

Volpe, C. and Burton, P.E. (2000). *Tourism – New Realities*: *A Canadian Perspective*. Toronto: Prentice Hall.

Discussion questions

1 Identify a potential product in your local area that would suit the product club approach.
2 Discuss the marketing issues faced by SMEs at the tourism destination and how the product club approach can overcome these.
3 Map the three phases of product development used by product clubs, for a tourism product of your choice.

Contemporary destination marketing issues

This chapter has provided a synoptic view of destination marketing and branding. This is a controversial and relatively new area of academic focus and one that generates a range of significant questions and issues. This final section identifies and discusses three key issues relating to contemporary destination marketing and branding.

The role of the public sector

Gold and Ward (1994) identify a contradiction at the heart of place marketing; namely that the public sector tends to treat the process as one involving a policy dimension that also treats the destination as a public good – this of course, contrasts with the marketing approach where destinations overtly compete. This raises the significant issue as to whether government is the appropriate agency to deliver destination marketing and branding. In addition to the basic conflict of philosophies noted above, the public sector may not be the right agency for destination marketing because it:

- controls neither destination product quality nor the private sector;
- cannot address deficiencies in the product such as the accommodation mix;
- has to be even-handed in its dealings with stakeholders and cannot be seen to 'back winners';
- tends not to be entrepreneurial;
- often lacks marketing expertise and is more focused on economic development and investment;
- can only facilitate bookings and often cannot close a sale;
- often has budgets that are inadequate for significant promotion and market research and the typical 12 monthly budgeting cycle is problematic;
- views the destination as bounded by political boundaries which makes a cooperative or regional approach to marketing difficult.

The role of destination stakeholders

A second key issue for destination marketing is to ensure involvement and commitment by all stakeholders in the strategy and branding process. Stakeholders play a critical role in the branding of a tourism destination. Yet, destination politics are notoriously destructive of the marketing process and it is therefore vital to be inclusive from the outset. Here, Gnoth (2002) extends the concept of the destination brand to that of supply driven destination brand communities. These provide a platform for connectivity, trust building and decision-making at the destination to develop and maintain a sustainable brand strategy amongst all stakeholders.

The key here is to manage the relationship between collaboration and power and to recognize that the views of the local community must be included in destination marketing as destinations are places where people live, work and play. Collaboration can be seen to encompass four further issues:

1 *Creation of a shared brand*: It ensures that the destination brand image is built on shared destination attributes. In other words, there is a need to 'internalize

the destination brand' and to ensure that its authenticity is shared and believed in by all stakeholders. This allows citizens to be brand champions (but also enemies if they do not subscribe to the brand). DMOs often use leadership figures to communicate and advocate the brand within the destination.

2 *Collaboration and inclusiveness*: It is essential that the destination brand is the positive outcome of the achievement of unity and collaboration amongst stakeholders; indeed it could be argued that effective destination marketing hinges on relationship building with stakeholders. Yet, collaboration across destination stakeholders is a complex and politicized process. Destinations are often crucibles of conflict and stakeholders do not always agree. The danger for branding is that larger stakeholders will take their own brands and brand attributes to market, which damages the smaller players and the overall destination brand. In other words, support offered by stakeholders makes or breaks the destination marketing process.

3 *Destinations as loosely articulated networks*: Collaboration recognizes that destination stakeholders are critically dependent on each other. This involves joint decision-making with individuals and interest groups operating at different levels of the destination. In seeking agreement amongst groups, destination marketing can recognize that destinations are effectively informal flexible networks based on trust and common interest. This can be encouraged through the use of destination portals as noted above, combined with training and innovative destination business models to connect and coordinate stakeholders.

4 *Relationship versus transactional marketing*: Of course, this begs the question as to whether DMOs should engage strongly in 'relationship' marketing with the destination community, rather than focusing on the more traditional 'transactional' marketing approach. Fyall et al. (2003) note that in theory, relationship marketing transforms a satisfied customer into a loyal customer and could be extended to the concept of destination loyalty by marketing to all destination stakeholders, ensuring quality and targeting and retaining key markets. Relationship marketing is ideally suited to situations where the customer controls supplier selection, there is little loyalty, brand switching is common and word of mouth is a powerful form of communication. It works less well for markets characterized by infrequent purchases and environments where cooperation is difficult. As a result, relationship marketing is difficult to apply at the destination level. This is because of the difficulty of achieving a clear vision, mission and cooperative organizational culture at destinations, which provide the environment of trust, direction and

long-term stability necessary to implement relationship marketing. This means that the contemporary destination still engages in 'transactional' rather than 'relationship' marketing. However, as this chapter has shown, it is vital that destination marketing takes into account not just the 'transaction', but also the 'framework' or 'context' within which the transaction takes place.

The nature of the tourist destination

The two key questions that this chapter poses are as follows:

1 Should the places where people live, work and play be transformed into brands and products?
2 Does the very nature of the tourist destination run counter to the ability to transform it into a brand?

Taking the first of these questions, the development of destination brands may conflict with the community's perception and feelings for the place where they live, work and play. This can be exacerbated by the delivery of the brand on the ground through the use of signage, street furniture and landscaping. Destinations are contested spaces and the various users of this space each hold their own images, identities and interests. They also have their own experiences and perceptions of the history and antecedents of the destination. It is extremely difficult to factor this into the destination marketing process.

Secondly, the theory and growing literature on branding is built largely upon the experience of FMCGs and tangible products. It could be argued that this theory cannot be simply transferred to the marketing of destinations. The nature of the destination as a fragmented and complex amalgam of attractions and support facilities, delivered by many different providers means that the definition and formulation of the destination product is problematic. If it is to succeed, destination marketing must recognize that it is a more collective activity than is normally found in marketing. It can be argued that the branding theory embraced by tourism researchers have been extended beyond its original intent. Quite simply it is a challenge to build and manage destination images and brands, and when this has been done, they are in danger of failing due to the fact that the tourism sector will not take direction and politicians do not recognize the link of tourism and the economy. Hankinson (2004) adds to this view by arguing that the dominance of the perceptual aspect of destination branding – particularly the focus on destination image – has held back the further development of destination marketing in terms of management structures, stakeholder relationships and marketing control.

Chapter overview

Growing competition in the tourism sector has demanded that destinations differentiate themselves through developing strong, unique and competitive destination brands. This is the key to destination marketing and, as has been demonstrated in this chapter, the process is one of branding that takes into account the formation and nature of the destination image. Yet, destination marketing is about more than just increasing visitation; it also has a regional development and investment role and is therefore strategic in nature, as demonstrated by the Blackstone Valley case. It also has an imperative to engage closely with destination stakeholders to deliver a brand that has been derived at with a consensus and which has the support of the whole community as shown by the case study on product clubs. Of course, this is much more difficult than it sounds, destinations are typically crucibles of conflict and the marketing process is therefore inherently political. Nonetheless, destination marketing now has a long history, in its current form dating back to the mid-1970s. DMOs tend to be the implementing agencies and increasingly they are reliant upon technology to reach the consumer, deliver tourist information and, through destination portals, to provide a complete digital representation of the destination. Finally, as this chapter has shown, destination marketing is not without controversy with many significant questions – is the public sector the appropriate agency to lead the marketing process; just how does the process engage all destination stakeholders and perhaps most fundamental, are we confident that marketing theory and approaches can be extended to destinations and the places where people live, work and play.

Self-review questions

1 Distinguish between the *process* and the *outcomes* of destination marketing.
2 What are the *benefits* of destination marketing?

3 Identify the major categories of *destination stakeholder*. For each, what might be their role in the destination marketing process?

4 Why is the *destination image* largely out of the control of the destination marketer?

5 What are the characteristics of a *successful brand*?

6 How might the *brand architecture* of a particular destination be communicated?

7 Identify a destination web site of your choice. How does it perform on the UNWTO's features of *web site functionality*?

8 Recall the key *marketing roles* of a DMO.

9 Is *the public sector* the appropriate agency for destination marketing?

10 Is marketing theory overstretched when applied to destinations?

Recommended reading

1 Buhalis, D. (2000). Marketing the competitive destination of the future. *Tourism Management* 21, 97–116.
A comprehensive overview of the factors relating to destination marketing.

2 Cai, L. (2002). Cooperative branding for rural destinations. *Annals of Tourism Research* 29(3), 720–742.
An excellent review of the nature of cooperation at the destination.

3 Hankinson, G. (2004). Relational network brands: towards a conceptual model of place brands. *Journal of Vacation Marketing* 10(2), 109–121.
Thought provoking paper challenging the translation of branding theory to places.

4 Harrill, R. (ed.) (2005). *Fundamentals of Destination Management and Marketing*. Michigan: Educational Institute of the American Hotel and Motel Association.
Solid introduction to destination marketing in accessible form.

5 Heath, E. and Wall, G. (1992). *Marketing Tourism Destinations*. Chichester: Wiley.
A well-structured book outlining an approach to destination marketing and planning.

6 Kolb, B.M. (2006). Tourism *Marketing for Cities and Towns*. Oxford: Elsevier Butterworth Heinemann.
A useful blend of marketing theory and practical advice applied to the marketing of urban places and given a tourism flavour.

7 http://www.iacvb.org (accessed August 2006).
Comprehensive web site with rich sources of information on the structure and operation of destination marketing organizations.

8 Morgan, N., Pritchard, A. and Pride, R. (2004). *Destination Branding Creating the Unique Destination Proposition*, 2nd edn. Oxford: Elsevier.
Thorough advanced overview of destination branding.

9 Pike, S. (2004). *Destination Marketing Organizations*. Amsterdam: Elsevier.
Excellent overview of destination marketing organizations.

10 WTO (2001). *E-Business for Tourism. Practical Guidelines for Destinations and Businesses*. Madrid: WTO.
A comprehensive guide to e-marketing for destinations.

Recommended web sites

Alberta Travel: www.albertatravel.ca/

Department of Tourism and Commerce Marketing, Government of Dubai: dubaitourism.co.ae/

Destination Marketing Association International: http://www.iacvb.org/

Tourism British Columbia: www.hellobc.com/

Visit Scotland: http://www.visitscotland.com/

References cited

Cai, L. (2002). Cooperative branding for rural destinations. *Annals of Tourism Research* 29(3), 720–742.

Cooper, C. (1995). Strategic planning for sustainable tourism: the case of offshore islands in the UK. *The Journal of Sustainable Tourism* 3(4), 191–209.

Doolin, B., Burgess, L. and Cooper, J. (2002). Evaluating the use of the web for tourism marketing: a case study from New Zealand. *Tourism Management* 23, 557–561.

Fyall, A., Callod, C. and Edwards, B. (2003). Relationship marketing. The challenge for destinations. *Annals of Tourism Research* 30(3), 644–659.

Gartner, W.C. (1993). Image formation process. In D.R. Fessenmaier and M. Uysal (eds), *Communication and Channel Systems in Tourism Marketing*, pp. 191–215. New York: Horwath Press.

Gartner, W.C. (2000) Image. In J. Jafari (ed.), *Encyclopedia of Tourism*, pp. 295–296. London: Routledge.

Gilbert, D. (1990). Strategic marketing planning for national tourism. *The Tourist Review* 45(1), 18–27.

Gnoth, J. (2002). Leveraging export brands through a tourism destination brand. *Brand Management* 9(4–5), 262–280.

Gold, J.R. and Ward, S.V. (1994). *Place Promotion. The Use of Publicity and Marketing to Sell Towns and Regions*. Chichester: John Wiley.

Hankinson, G. (2004). Relational network brands: towards a conceptual model of place brands. *Journal of Vacation Marketing* 10(2), 109–121.

http://www.iacvb.org (accessed August 2006). Refers to International Association of Convention and Visitor Bureaux.

Jain, S.C. (1985). *Marketing, Planning and Strategy*. Cincinnati, OH: Southwestern.

Kotler, P. (2000). *Marketing Management. The Millennium Edition*. Upper Saddle River, NJ: Prentice Hall.

Kotler, P. (2003). *Principles of Marketing*, 2nd edn. Frenchs Forest, New South Wales: Prentice Hall.

Kotler, P., Haider, D.H. and Rein, I. (1993). *Marketing Places*. New York: Free Press.

Middleton, V.T.C. (2000). Marketing, destination. In J. Jafari (ed.), *Encyclopedia of Tourism*, pp. 378–379. London: Routledge.

Morgan, N., Pritchard, A. and Pride, R. (2004). *Destination Branding Creating the Unique Destination Proposition*, 2nd edn. Oxford: Elsevier.

Morrison, A.M. and Anderson, D.J. (2002). Destination branding. *Missouri Association of Convention and Visitor Bureaus Annual Meeting*, Missouri.

Ritchie, J.R.B. and Ritchie J.R.R. (1998). The branding of tourist destinations. *AIEST Conference*, Morocco.

UNWTO (2006). *Destination Positioning, Branding and Image Management*. Addis Ababa: UNWTO.

Ward, S.V. (1998). *Selling Places. The Marketing and Promotion of Towns and Cities 1850–2000*. London: E and F N Spon.

WTO (2001). *E-Business for Tourism. Practical Guidelines for Destinations and Businesses*. Madrid: WTO.

Section 4
The Contemporary Tourism Industry

Chapter **10**

The scope of the contemporary tourism sector

Chapter objectives

After reading this chapter you will

- Be aware of the scale and scope of the contemporary tourism industry
- Understand the difficulties of defining the contemporary tourism industry
- Be aware of the various approaches to defining tourism from a supply side perspective
- Recognize that tourism is a partially industrialized system
- Recognize the issues involved in measuring the contemporary tourism industry
- Understand the status of tourism in standard industrial classifications (SICs)
- Appreciate the tourism satellite account (TSA) approach and its benefits
- Be familiar with the challenges of measuring the scale of tourism employment

Introduction

Tourism is often described as one of the world's largest industries with huge figures quoted for the value of the tourism industry and the numbers it employs. This chapter provides a reality check for this 'boosterism' by demonstrating that we are far from reaching agreement as to just how to define the tourism industry. The chapter outlines the approaches to date in trying to define and measure tourism as an industry and outlines the problems faced in doing so, not least the fact that many industries are involved in delivering the tourism product. It demonstrates that tourism is in fact only partially an industry as governments, communities and others are involved in delivering the tourism product. The chapter goes on to show how tourism is not recognized as an industry in SICs and national statistical systems. It then outlines the recent breakthrough in defining and measuring the tourism industry in the form of the TSA. The TSA has now been accepted by the United Nations as the industry standard in defining and measuring the tourism industry. It can be used to compare tourism with other economic sectors and to provide policy makers and planners with useful information. The chapter closes by considering how tourism employment is measured and some of the problems involved.

The size and scope of the contemporary tourism industry

The World Travel and Tourism Council (WTTC) is an industry lobby group comprising the major tourism corporations in the world. As part of their work they have estimated the size and scope of the tourism industry using sophisticated economic techniques. They state that travel and tourism is:

> one of the largest and most dynamic industries of today's global economy, travel and tourism ... is set to account for 10.3 per cent of global [gross domestic product] GDP and more than 234 million jobs (2006a: 2).

They go on to say that the travel and tourism industry represents one of the most important sectors of the global economy – a US$6 trillion business that employs over 230 million people and a significant portion of the world's workforce

(WTTC 2006b: 1). The WTTC's economic research (WTTC 2006c) estimates the scale and scope of the industry in 2006 at:

- *Demand*: US$6.477 billion in economic activity.
- *GDP*: The travel and tourism economic sector is worth 10.3 per cent of global GDP.
- *Growth*: The travel and tourism economy is expected to grow by 4.2 per cent per annum in real terms 2007–2016.
- *Visitor exports*: Travel and tourism generates 11.8 per cent of total world exports.
- *Capital investment*: Travel and tourism represents 9.3 per cent of total capital investment in the world.

The question posed by these numbers is just how did the WTTC come up with these estimates, and what do they include as being a part of the travel and tourism industry? This is a key issue that is occupying the minds of academics and politicians alike, as well as industry lobbyists such as the WTTC. The problem is simple – how to measure the scale and scope of tourism, because tourism is an industry that challenges conventional paradigms. Yet it is important to do so as tourism is a complex industrial system, a major employer and generator of revenues. Debbage and Ioannides (1998) speak of the commodification of tourism that has created this machinery of production:

> Although changes in consumer demand and the evolution of increasingly more sophisticated consumer preferences can play substantive roles in shaping the tourism product, it is the actual 'machinery of production' that helps to manipulate and facilitate origin–destination tourist flows across the world (p. 287).

Ioannides and Debbage (1998) vent their frustration at the fact that we have not yet satisfactorily got to grips with analysing the supply side of tourism. They point to a lack of quality analysis of tourism as a supply side phenomenon despite the fact that tourism is bought and sold as a commodity and the industry is organized along capitalist lines, albeit with some unique characteristics. These include:

- The tourism industry is highly diverse – from size of establishment (Small and Medium Sized Enterprises (SMEs) to corporations); business type (IT to service provision); sector (air transport to accommodation); organization (public and private sector) and process. It is therefore more a collection of industries than a single industry.

- The fact that tourism is not a single product but a diverse range of products and services that interact.
- It comprises tangible and non-tangible elements.
- It is produced where it is consumed.

To exacerbate this, the tourism industry is both misunderstood and under-explored (Debbage and Daniels 1998). This is because it is amorphous and complex shrouded in conceptual fuzziness and imprecise terminology (Is it tourism or travel?). This chapter aims to dispel some of this mystique and provide as clear description of how we approach examining the scope and scale of the contemporary tourism industry.

A tourism system

Leiper (1979) has clearly located the tourism industry within the wider tourism system as we showed in Chapter 1. His well-known tourism system comprises three key elements: the generating region, the transit zone and the destination region. Cutting across these three elements are the resources and industries required to deliver the tourism product. However, Leiper (1979) agrees that there are problems delineating these resources due to:

1 the difficulty of identifying the tourism element of an industry;
2 the difficulty of separating industry and non-industry elements;
3 the difficulties in specifying the number of industries inherently connected with tourism.

Leiper goes on to define the tourism industry element of the system as:

all those firms, organizations and facilities which are intended to serve the specific needs and wants of tourists (1979: 400).

He further splits the industry into six sectors, each linked and specializing in a particular function:

1 Tourism marketing
2 Tourist carriers

3 Tourist accommodation

4 Tourist attractions

5 Miscellaneous tourism services (e.g. taxis)

6 Tourism regulation (including government and education)

Definitions of the contemporary tourism industry

Smith (1988) is concerned that the continued lack of agreement over definitions of the tourism industry is both frustrating and embarrassing for the credibility of the sector. The debate continues partly because economists refuse to accept that tourism is in fact an industry. Indeed, as recently as 2006 the Australian Productivity Commission, for example, decided that the whole definition needed to be revisited and came up with a range of new definitions. So why do we need definitions of the contemporary tourism industry?

1 For measurement and producing statistics of supply – this includes the size of the tourism industry, the number of jobs it generates and what is included for the range of data collection and legitimate comparison with other economic sectors (Davidson 1994).

2 For legislation purposes – to ensure that laws and policy applying to the tourism sector do actually apply to that sector.

3 For credibility – to define and understand the sector for credibility in government and other economic sectors, as well as a sense of self-identity.

Generic definitions of an industry are based on the manufacturing paradigm. Here, the notion of an industry is a group of independent firms all turning out the same product, and competing over these substitutable products. Another way to approach the definition is to think of an industry as a group of sellers of close substitutes to a common group of buyers. In other words, definitions of an industry focus around the people and activities involved in one type of business, or a distinct group of productive or profit-making enterprises. This clearly is problematic for tourism as follows:

1 The definitions are dominantly rooted in the economics of manufacturing.

2 The growth of tourism, and services more generally, has not been taken into account in such definitions.

3 Tourism statistical data are poor and do not support the sophisticated measurement of the industry.

As a result, supply side definitions of tourism have proven more difficult to resolve and it is only since 2000 that real agreement has been reached. The key issue with supply side definitions is to decide which businesses and organizations should be included in the definition of the contemporary tourism industry. But it is more than simply coming up with a list; there are complex technical issues to be tackled here. Smith (1996) illustrates this with the very practical example of a hotel – initially you may think that the hotel is wholly a tourism business. However, most hotels have a significant proportion of local business in the restaurants and function rooms. How should we apportion the tourists' consumption and the locals' consumption of the hotel's products in order to gauge the size of tourism's contribution to the hotel's income and jobs?

Smith (1988) shows that early definitions of the tourism industry focused on the supply of commodities:

> The tourist sector or tourism industry can be broadly conceived as representing the sum of those industrial and commercial activities producing goods and services wholly consumed by foreign visitors or domestic tourists (UNCTAD 1971).

Smith's revises this with his own definition:

> Tourism is the aggregate of all businesses that directly provide goods and services to facilitate business, pleasure and leisure activities away from the home environment (1988: 183).

Smith's position here is that tourism is an industry that can be approached and measured as any other. However, the issue of apportioning tourism and non-tourism consumption is an important one, as few businesses serve only tourists. Smith (1996) argues that some businesses are almost pure tourism whilst others have a significant element of demand for their commodities from local residents. He quotes the Canadian way around this issue by classifying enterprises as:

1 *Tier 1 firms*, which would not exist in the absence of travel. They include hotels, tour operators and airlines.

2 *Tier 2 firms*, which would still exist in the absence of travel but in a diminished form. They include taxis, car hire firms and restaurants.

This approach is consistent with the way that other industries are defined from a supply side perspective and also allows relatively easy measurement. This, however, depends on the scale of analysis, and as noted above in the hotel example, the best approach is to take the analysis down to the smallest operating unit.

Leiper (1990) however disagrees with this approach and views the tourism sector as comprising a range of industries, rather than a single industry. He sees the tourism industry as a short-hand notation for activities involving tourism, which can be better described as a set of interactions between a set of related markets, characterized by different types of competitive structures. He notes that industry definitions often involve the idea of competition. In other words, when businesses compete they begin to become an industry. Some industries have competition between companies, brands, and products and compete on a national and international level. Whilst there is clearly competition in tourism, it is more unusual to find it at the international level.

A partially industrialized system

There is no doubt that lobbyists for tourism would prefer to define it as a single industry as this allows them to grow the scale and value of industry. However, Leiper disagrees with this approach. It is clear that the tourism industry is now part of a complex tourism system designed to deliver the tourism experience (Britton 1991). This is a huge system drawing statements suggesting it approaches the largest industry in the world as already noted. But there is a debate as to whether tourism is a totally industrialized system or only partially industrialized.

As noted above, Leiper (1979) states clearly that a range of resources and industries are required to deliver the tourism product within his tourism system. Some of these resources will lie outside the private sector and will include the community and government (through say destination marketing organizations, DMOs). Equally, there will be a range of industries involved in delivering the tourism product. He therefore views the tourism system as only 'partial industrialized'. Indeed, he suggests that the degree of industrialization varies over time, and we would suggest, by type of tourism, as the involvement of the community and government will differ. This has major implications for how tourism is viewed from a policy point of view, and also how tourism presents itself to government. Indeed, many industries that supply the tourism product do not in fact see themselves as in the tourism industry at all.

In summary, we can think of a complex tourism system, partially industrialized delivering the tourism product to the consumer. Bull (1995) summarizes this with the following supply side definition:

> The tourism industry, or industries, consists of any organizations supplying goods and services to those people now defined as tourists or excursionists, as part of their tourist requirements (p. 3).

Measuring the scale and scope of the contemporary tourism industry

Given the difficulties of defining tourism from the supply side, it is remarkable that the WTTC is able to estimate the size and scope of the industry as quoted at the beginning of this chapter. Measuring the size and scope of the contemporary tourism industry faces two major challenges: firstly, to develop a coherent and shared view of just what comprises the supply side of tourism; and secondly, to credibly measure it. Until 2000, tourism was dependent on the standard industrial classification (SIC) of enterprises to define the industry. However, since then there have been significant breakthroughs in meeting the challenges of measurement. These have come from major advances led by UNWTO, WTTC and the Canadian Government in the development and implementation of TSAs.

The standard industrial classification approach

Before turning to TSAs, it is important to understand how tourism maps onto SIC systems and as a result, why a new approach was required. Tourism is not a recognized industry in the SIC and as a result the accommodation, restaurant and catering industry is often used as a proxy for tourism (Riley et al. 2002). This is a problem as it means that many parts of the tourism industry are missed from a statistical point of view in terms of employment and turnover.

The idea of an SIC is to classify establishments by their economic activity, where establishments are economic units that produce goods or services. This helps to understand the structure of the economy, the impact of policy changes, and the impact of competition and international events (Roehl 1998). There are a number of types of SICs but all use a similar basis for classification. The idea is to create categories that are externally heterogeneous (e.g. transport and accommodation) but internally homogeneous. The challenge is in the level of aggregation used as there is no sense in every establishment being in a separate category. As a result, accommodation would normally include camping as well as hotels, but exclude restaurants. The international standard industrial classification (ISIC) has been developed by the UN to encourage consistency of SIC codes internationally.

When grappling with the complexities of determining what comprises the tourism industry, an obvious approach is to allocate tourism consumption to different categories in the SIC (such as accommodation or restaurants). But again we have the problem that many enterprises earn a considerable income from tourism (such as shopping malls) but are not categorized as part of the tourism industry. In an attempt to get around this problem, the WTO began a tourism version of the ISIC in 1990 – the 'standard industrial classification of tourism activity' (SICTA) whereby enterprises with substantial tourism revenues were assigned to particular codes. The following classification was used:

- Tourism characteristic products – all tourism services.
- Tourism characteristic activities – activities whose principal output is characteristic of tourism.
- Tourism characteristic industries – a group of establishments whose principal activity is tourism characteristic activity.

Over the years, a number of attempts have been made to assign tourism consumption to establishments using variants of the SIC codes. The following case study shows that whilst there is a level of agreement in this, there are still differences according to different countries.

CASE STUDY
Mapping the contemporary tourism industry onto the SIC system

The SIC does not treat tourism as an industry. However, one approach to defining tourism using the SIC codes is to apportion tourism enterprises to SIC codes. In other words, a number of SIC codes are viewed as containing significant elements of tourism consumption and so tourism can be mapped onto the SIC system. However, getting agreement on just which SIC codes are significant from a tourism point of view is difficult. Table 10.1 (see the following pages) in this case study shows a number of international approaches to mapping SIC codes to tourism, and three country approaches. Table 10.1 demonstrates that whilst there is some general agreement as to what comprises the tourism industry, there is also variation around the edges, particularly in relation to transport, cultural attractions and sport. There is also variation by country, dependent on the particular types of tourism that are important in the particular country.

Key sources

British Tourist Authority/English Tourist Board (1997). *Employment in Tourist Related Industries in Great Britain*. London: BTA/ETB.

Israel Central Bureau of Statistics with Ministry of Tourism (Quarterly). *Tourism and Hotel Services Statistics Quarterly*. Jerusalem: ICBS.

Statistics Canada (2006). *Human Resource Module of the Tourism Satellite Account 1997–2002*. Ottawa, Ont.: Statistics Canada.

UNSTAT (1990). *International Standard Classification of all Economic Activities*. New York: UNSTAT.

WTO (1995). *Concepts, Definitions and Classifications of Tourism Statistics*. Madrid: WTO.

Discussion questions

1 Are you convinced that these classification systems have captured the totality of the tourism industry?
2 Devise your own classification of the enterprises that you would include in tourism, using variants of Table 10.1 and your own ideas.
3 Why do you think it is taking so long to get agreement of the sectors to be included as comprising the tourism industry?

Tourism satellite accounts

Partly as a result of the frustration about the failure to satisfactorily measure the tourism industry from a supply side point of view, and recognizing that national

Table 10.1 Mapping tourism enterprises onto various SIC and country approaches

Sectors	TSAs	ISIC	SICTA	UK	Canada	Israel
Hotels, campsites and other short stay accommodation	Hotels, campsites and other short stay accommodation	Hotels, campsites and other short stay accommodation	Hotels, camping sites and other commercial accommodations	Hotels and other tourist accommodation	Traveller accommodation	Hotels, youth hostels, Christian hospices, field schools and rural tourism
Restaurants and bars	Restaurants, bars and canteens	Restaurants, bars and canteens	Restaurants, bars and canteens	Restaurants, cafes and snack bars	Full service restaurants, limited service eating places drinking places	Restaurants (listed for tourists)
Travel agents and intermediaries	Travel agents and packagers	Included in transport	Travel agents, tour operators and guides	Travel agents and tour operators	Travel arrangement and reservation services	Travels agencies, tour offices and tour guides
Cultural attractions and entertainment	Cultural attractions and entertainment	Entertainment (museums, etc., sporting and other recreational activities)	Operation of recreational fairs and shows	Libraries, museums and other cultural attractions	Recreation and entertainment, including spectator sports	

(Continued)

Table 10.1 (Continued)

Sectors	TSAs	ISIC	SICTA	UK	Canada	Israel
Passenger transport	Passenger transport	Land transport, water transport, air transport, activities of travel agencies and tour operators	Transport, storage and communications		Air transport all other transportation industries	
Sports facilities	Sports facility operators	Included in cultural attractions		Sports and other recreational activities	Included in cultural attractions	
Other			Exchange of currencies, real estate agencies, education, visitor and convention bureaus, gambling and betting operations, and casinos	Public houses, bars and night clubs/licensed clubs	Recreational vehicle parks and camp grounds	

statistical systems did not treat tourism as a single sector, the TSA approach was developed from the mid-1990s.

As noted above, to be defined as an industry, tourism would need to have a single production process, a homogenous product and a locationally confined market. In other words, by conventional definitions, tourism is not an industry. Tourism products are however functionally linked to deliver a single product in the eye of the consumer. This led to the idea of a satellite account which is effectively a subset of a nation's accounts that involves expenditures by individuals defined as a tourists by the UNWTO. A satellite account is a term developed by the United Nations to measure the size of economic sectors that are not defined as industries in national accounts. As such the TSA is a statistical instrument – a satellite revolving around concepts, definitions and aggregates of national accounts.

TSAs represent a real breakthrough in defining tourism from the supply side. Indeed, tourism is the first activity to use worldwide satellite account standards to measure its impact on national economies. The United Nations Statistical Commission approved the methodology in March 2000.

The TSA, surprisingly, is more of a demand side measure than a supply side one as it measures the expenditure made for tourism commodities and non-tourism commodities. Visitors buy goods and services both tourism and non-tourism alike. The key from a measurement standpoint is associating their purchases to the total supply of these goods and services within a country.

The commodities are defined as follows:

1 *Tourism commodities*: goods or services for which a considerable portion of demand comes from tourists – airlines for example.
2 *Non-tourism commodities*: commodities that experience no or little demand from tourists.

In practice, the TSA is an information system that combines, orders and manipulates statistics describing all significant and measurable aspects of tourism within a framework that organizes tourism data according to the real-world relationships from which they originate (Smith 1998). It is based on the financial flows of data.

The TSA allows for valid comparisons of tourism with other industries allows comparison from country to country and between groups of countries.

Such measures are also comparable with other internationally recognized economic statistics. The TSA measures:

- Tourism's contribution to GDP.
- Tourism's ranking compared to other economic sectors.
- The number of jobs created by tourism in an economy.
- The amount of tourism investment and tax revenues generated by tourism industries.
- Tourism consumption.
- Tourism's impact on a nation's balance of payments.
- Characteristics of tourism human resources.

The TSA can be used to:

- Provide credible data on the impact of tourism and the associated employment.
- Develop a standard framework for organizing statistical data on tourism.
- Set a new international standard endorsed by the UN Statistical Commission.
- Design economic policies related to tourism development.
- Provide data on tourism's impact on a nation's balance of payments.
- Provide information on tourism human resource characteristics.

More generally, the TSA can also be used to:

- Increase and improve knowledge of tourism's importance relative to overall economic activity in a given country.
- Provide an instrument for designing more efficient policies relating to tourism and its employment aspects.
- Create awareness among the various stakeholders directly and indirectly involved with tourism of the economic importance of this activity and by extension, its role in all the industries involved in the production of goods and services demanded by visitors.
- Develop predictive tourism indicators, industry outlooks and risk scenarios.

CASE STUDY
The way forward for tourism satellite accounts

In October 2005, 430 delegates attended a conference in Iguazu on the borders of Argentina, Brazil and Paraguay, to assess the actual level of development, analysis and application of the TSA worldwide. The conference focused on ways of unlocking the potential of TSAs and how to best enhance the relevance for policy, trade, market intelligence, employment, the meetings industry and its development at a regional level. Effectively, this conference set the agenda for the development of TSAs for the future. The conference was titled *The Tourism Satellite Account (TSA): Understanding Tourism and Designing Strategies*.

The conference had a number of key themes, reflecting the development of TSAs in the decade from 1995 to 2005. The key themes were as follows:

1 *The TSA's relevance for policy makers*: The role of TSAs in supporting knowledge-led policy.
2 *TSA implications for trade policies*: The role of the TSA in developing credible statistics on tourism to ensure the integration of tourism development and trade – within the national system of developing countries in particular.
3 *Adapting the TSA conceptual framework*: The regional perspective – developing a regional-level model of the TSA using the same framework and language as the national TSA.
4 *Sharing experiences in TSA implementation*: The sharing of good practice and joint solutions to conceptual and measurement issues.
5 *Monitoring labour markets in the tourism sector*: To better inform tourism manpower planning and disentangle the problems surrounding tourism employment statistics.
6 *Measuring the meetings industry*: To better measure a 'hidden' sector of tourism.
7 *Market intelligence for action and forecasting*: The TSA contribution – better using the TSA to develop tourism indicators, risk scenarios and forecasts.
8 *Using the TSA framework to design tourism strategies*: Basic areas of application – the way forward for integrating TSAs into tourism strategy formulation.
9 *Linking environmental accounting and the TSA*: To date little effort has gone into linking environmental accounting systems with the TSA to judge the performance of tourism in terms of sustainability.

The conference developed a range of conclusions and recommendations for the future direction of TSAs. These are as follows:

● Ensuring the legitimacy and credibility of a TSA exercise. This recommendation relates to the danger of over-promising the value of a TSA and the need to manage expectations. This is particularly a problem if a national tourism administration (NTA) is given unreasonable expectations as to the value of tourism, which are then disproved by the TSA.

- Protecting the TSA brand. Here, the conference felt that there was increasing misuse of the terms of the TSA and that to prevent this it should be formally integrated into the United Nations statistical system.
- Guaranteeing its continuity. This conclusion relates to the importance of communicating the importance of the TSA concept to other agencies both nationally and internationally, so creating the so-called 'inter-institutional platform' including tourism statistical and banking agencies.
- The TSA as a work in progress. The experience of the countries at the conference firmly supported the need for flexibility in the continued development of the TSA and its gradual introduction into a country's framework of statistics. Again, this is linked to the ideas of an inter-institutional platform.
- Promoting a strategic alliance between tourism and statistical agencies. TSAs involve close cooperation between national tourism and statistical agencies; cooperation which is beneficial in the long term, as the statistical agency will gain a greater understanding of tourism.
- Bringing economic analysis to the forefront. The TSA is a powerful tool of economic analysis and it is necessary to increase the understanding of the TSA amongst politicians and the business community through the use of correct concepts and language.
- Fostering the use of TSAs to support policy and strategy. TSAs can be used to deliver knowledge-based public policy and business strategy for tourism.
- A new leadership for NTAs. TSAs will allow NTAs to take ownership and leadership in terms of the economic contribution played by tourism and its role in development and employment and to more closely evaluation of marketing activity.
- Sharing knowledge and experience. A huge amount has been learned as to how to develop and implement TSAs. This can now be shared internationally through a UNWTO and UN funded far-reaching programme of technical assistance.

Key sources

UNWTO (2005a). *The Iguazu Conference 'The Tourism Satellite Account (TSA): Understanding Tourism and Designing Strategies'*, Argentina/Brazil/Paraguay: Technical Note, UNWTO, Madrid.
UNWTO (2005b). *The Iguazu Conference: UNWTO Findings and Evaluation*, UNWTO, Madrid.

Discussion questions

1 What type of indicators do you think the TSA could provide to aid policy makers in tourism to be more effective?

> 2 The International Labour Organization (ILO) is keen to measure the quality of jobs in TSAs as well as just the numbers of jobs. What do you think a TSA could measure to help the ILO?
>
> 3 TSAs are now being developed at the regional level. What types of TSA indicators would help destination marketers to be more effective?

There is no doubt that TSAs have become the industry standard for defining and measuring tourism from the supply side. By 2005, 67 countries have or are developing a TSA. The next stage of the TSA development is now underway. A particularly useful adaptation is to implement the TSA methodology for regions and destinations. However, due to the technical complexities involved, only a small number of countries have experimented with the development of these sub-national TSAs. Statistics Canada has been a lead agency here, developing satellite accounts for its provinces and territories. These regional tourism satellite accounts (RTSAs) are designed to meet a growing demand for regional data, particularly as many tourism administrations decentralize their operations. RTSAs are used to provide an economic portrait of tourism at the regional level in Canada and can be used as a policy relevant tool to strengthen regional and local tourism organizations.

Whilst there are clear benefits form the development and implementation of TSAs, there remain a number of challenges to their use (Smith 1998). These include:

1 The fact that they really are a demand side measure.
2 They are expensive to produce as they often need further data collection.
3 They are only updated infrequently and can be anything up to 8 years old.
4 They are shaped by a nation's SIC system and so can be imprecise or a poor fit with the structure of the industry.
5 They demand powerful education of the industry to interpret them.
6 They are dependent on the availability, quality and quantity of data.

Tourism employment

It is important to consider the issues related to the measurement and scope of tourism employment when considering the contemporary tourism industry.

Basically, tourism employment can only be measured once decisions about what comprises the industry have been made and jobs can then be apportioned to the different industry sectors in the TSA. This is normally done using the notion of 'full-time equivalent (FTE) jobs' where part-time or non-standard work is then converted to a FTE on the basis of hours worked. The TSA allows estimates to be made of total tourism employment as well as by sector, such as accommodation, and by demographics and job type, seasonality and productivity.

However, as Riley et al. (2002) note, the statistical reporting of tourism employment is not as mature as other tourism reporting. A better system is needed to understand the functioning of the labour market, immigration, education and training. Specific problems of tourism employment statistics include the fact that:

1 Tourism not seen as an industry for statistical purposes.
2 Tourism has strong linkages with other economic sectors making it difficult to discern pure tourism jobs.
3 Tourism is highly diverse (as noted in the first case study in this chapter).
4 It remains difficult to separate the contribution of tourism jobs serving tourists and those serving locals.
5 It is difficult to factor in the informal economy and family jobs, which are not counted.

Finally, whilst the TSA methodology is relatively good at estimating the number of jobs generated by tourism, it is less effective in discerning the type of work or the quality of the job. The ILO is now working on statistical indicators for their 'decent work agenda;' in other words, the measurement of the quality of the job as well as its simple statistical unit. This is done under the ILO's development of a tourism labour accounting system (TLAS) to coordinate labour statistics. This issue of tourism human resources and the quality of work will be covered in the next chapter.

Chapter overview

This chapter has provided a comprehensive review of the approaches and technical issues involved in defining the scale and scope of the contemporary tourism industry. It began with a range of quotes from the WTTC as to the magnitude of the industry, often claimed as one of the largest in the world. The chapter then considered in detail the various supply side definitions of tourism and the range of complexities involved in defining an industry made up of multiple sectors, some of which are community and public sector based. The chapter has outlined the issues involved in measuring the scale and scope of the contemporary tourism industry, a process handicapped by the fact that tourism is not recognized as an industry in SICs, which themselves are rooted in a manufacturing approach. A case study demonstrated just how difficult it is to map the tourism industry onto these SICs. The TSA approach was described in detail as it is now the industry standard for defining and measuring the contemporary tourism industry. The TSA was examined not only in terms of its development and approach, but also its uses to aid planners and policy makers and its future development, as outlined in a second case study. Finally, the chapter considered the measurement of tourism employment and the challenges faced in developing a contemporary reporting system that is not only quantitative, but can also tease out indicators of the quality of tourism jobs.

Self-review questions

1 Discuss Leiper's view that tourism is a group of businesses in search of an industry.

2 List the key characteristics of tourism that have created problems in coming up with a supply side definition.

3 This chapter has provided a number of supply side definitions of tourism – which do you think captures the nature of the contemporary tourism industry and why?

4 Map the tourism industry onto Leiper's tourism system (generating region, transit zone and destination region). How might you expect this mapping to vary for different types of tourism: e.g. nature-based tourism and business tourism?

5 Do you agree with Leiper's view that tourism is a partially industrialized system?

6 Find the TSA report for your own country. Which of the indicators provided will be of use to those marketing your country on the international stage?

7 Critics of the TSA say that it measures tourism demand, not tourism supply. Do you agree with this statement?

8 Which indicators developed in the TSA will be of most use to tourism planners?

9 The majority of tourism jobs are in the hospitality sector. How true is this statement?

10 Examine the ILO's 'decent work' agenda. As a lobbyist for the tourism industry, how would you present a case that tourism jobs are 'decent jobs'?

Recommended reading

1 Bull, A. (1995). *The Economics of Travel and Tourism*. Melbourne: Longman Australia.
Good coverage of the supply side debate and measurement issues.
2 Ioannides, D. and Debbage, K.G. (eds) (1998). *The Economic Geography of the Tourist Industry. A Supply Side Analysis*. London: Routledge.
Excellent and comprehensive edited volume on the supply side of tourism.
3 Leiper, N. (1979). The framework of tourism. Toward a definition of tourism, tourist and the tourism industry. *Annals of Tourism Research* 6, 390–407.
Classic paper covering all elements of the tourism system.
4 Leiper, N. (1990). Partial industrialisation of tourism systems. *Annals of Tourism Research* 7, 600–605.
Excellent paper outlining Leiper's partial industrialization approach.
5 Riley, M., Ladkin, A. and Szivas, E. (2002). *Tourism Employment. Analysis and Planning*. Clevedon: Channelview.
Comprehensive and readable volume on tourism employment issues and measurement.
6 Smith, S.L.J. (1988). Defining tourism: a supply-side view. *Annals of Tourism Research* 15, 179–190.
A classic paper contrasting with Leiper's views.
7 Smith, S.L.J. (1996). *Tourism Analysis. A Handbook*. Harlow: Longman.
Thorough text on supply side definitions and measurement.
8 UNWTO. *The Tourism Satellite Account*. Madrid: UNWTO.
Excellent summary of the development, concept and use of the TSA.
9 WTTC (2006c). *World Travel and Tourism. Climbing to New Heights. The 2006 Travel and Tourism Economic Research*. London: WTTC.
Comprehensive review of the supply side scale and scope of the tourism industry.

Recommended web sites

Aboriginal Tourism Canada: www.aboriginaltourism.ca/
Tourism Industry Association of Canada: www.tiac-aitc.ca/
Tourism Industry Association of New Zealand: www.tianz.org.nz/
Visit Britain UK Industry web site: www.tourismtrade.org.uk/
World Travel and Tourism Council: www.wttc.org

References cited

British Tourist Authority/English Tourist Board (1997). *Employment in Tourist Related Industries in Great Britain*. London: BTA/ETB.
Bull, A. (1995). *The Economics of Travel and Tourism*. Melbourne: Longman Australia.
Davidson, T.L. (1994). What are travel and tourism: Are they really an industry? In W. Theobald (ed.), *Global Tourism. The Next Decade*, pp. 20–26. Oxford: Butterworth Heinemann.
Debbage, K.G. and Daniels, P. (1998). The tourist industry and economic geography. Missed opportunities? In D. Ioannides and K.G. Debbage (eds), *The Economic Geography of the Tourist Industry. A Supply Side Analysis*, pp. 17–30. London: Routledge.

Debbage, K.G. and Ioannides, D. (1998). Conclusion. The commodification of tourism. In D. Ioannides and K.G. Debbage (eds), *The Economic Geography of the Tourist Industry. A Supply Side Analysis*, pp. 287–292. London: Routledge.

Ioannides, D. and Debbage, K.G. (eds) (1998). *The Economic Geography of the Tourist Industry. A Supply Side Analysis*. London: Routledge.

Israel Central Bureau of Statistics with Ministry of Tourism (Quarterly). *Tourism and Hotel Services Statistics Quarterly*. Jerusalem: ICBS.

Leiper, N. (1979). The framework of tourism. Toward a definition of tourism, tourist and the tourism industry. *Annals of Tourism Research* 6, 390–407.

Leiper, N. (1990). Partial industrialisation of tourism systems. *Annals of Tourism Research* 7, 600–605.

Riley, M., Ladkin, A. and Szivas, E. (2002). *Tourism Employment. Analysis and Planning*. Clevedon: Channelview.

Roehl, W. (1998). The tourism production system. The logic of standard industrial classification. In D. Ioannides and K.G. Debbage (eds), *The Economic Geography of the Tourist Industry. A Supply Side Analysis*. London: Routledge.

Smith, S.L.J. (1988). Defining tourism: a supply-side view. *Annals of Tourism Research* 15, 179–190.

Smith, S.L.J. (1996). *Tourism Analysis. A Handbook*. Harlow: Longman.

Smith, S.L.J. (1998). Tourism as an industry. Debates and concepts. In D. Ioannides and K.G. Debbage (eds), *The Economic Geography of the Tourist Industry. A Supply Side Analysis*, pp. 31–52. London: Routledge.

Statistics Canada (2006). *Human Resource Module of the Tourism Satellite Account 1997–2002*. Ottawa, Ont.: Statistics Canada.

UNCTAD (1971). *A Note on the 'Tourist Sector' in Guidelines for Tourism Statistics 30*. New York: UNCTAD.

UNSTAT (1990). *International Standard Classification of All Economic Activities*. New York: UNSTAT.

UNWTO (2005a). *The Iguazu Conference 'The Tourism Satellite Account (TSA): Understanding Tourism and Designing Strategies'. Argentina/Brazil/Paraguay: Technical Note*, UNWTO, Madrid.

UNWTO (2005b). *The Iguazu Conference: UNWTO Findings and Evaluation*, Madrid, UNWTO.

WTO (1995). *Concepts, Definitions and Classifications of Tourism Statistics*. Madrid: WTO.

WTTC (2006a). *Viewpoint, Fourth Quarter*. London: WTTC.

WTTC (2006b). *Open Mind, Open World. Summit Highlights*. London: WTTC.

WTTC (2006c). *World Travel and Tourism. Climbing to New Heights. The 2006 Travel and Tourism Economic Research*. London: WTTC.

Chapter 11
The tourism industry: contemporary issues

Chapter objectives

After reading this chapter you will

- Understand that tourism businesses have a range of objectives
- Be familiar with the causes of globalization
- Recognize the responses of tourism businesses to globalization
- Appreciate the benefits of knowledge management for tourism businesses
- Realize the explanatory power of network analysis for understanding the tourism industry
- Be aware of the importance of embedding within networks for tourism businesses
- Recognize the distinction between small businesses and entrepreneurs
- Understand the characteristics of tourism small businesses
- Appreciate the critical importance of human resources to tourism businesses
- Be aware of the challenges facing tourism human resources

Introduction

In this chapter we turn to the contemporary tourism industry and identify and expand upon five key issues facing the industry. We begin the chapter with the challenges posed to the contemporary tourism industry by globalization. This section identifies the key drivers of globalization, particularly the lowered cost of travel and technology. Tourism businesses are responding to globalization by internationalizing and building alliances and partnerships, whilst the public sector is concerned to protect small businesses threatened by the shifting competitive landscape that globalization delivers. The chapter then considers the fact that the tourism industry has been slow to embrace the benefits of the knowledge economy, particularly in terms of adopting knowledge management practices and boosting competitiveness through utilizing knowledge for innovation and new product development. Both globalization and the knowledge economy demand that tourism businesses are well networked. Only in this way they can ensure that they benefit from both global trends and the flexible specialization that characterizes the industry. Network analysis can be used to examine networks of destination and tourism business and to diagnose problems and weak links. Embeddedness within networks is identified as a key strategy for survival of the contemporary tourism business. The chapter then turns to small businesses, the lifeblood of tourism destinations, and makes the distinction between small businesses and entrepreneurs. A particular feature of the tourism industry, the lifestyle entrepreneur, is then examined. Finally, the chapter examines the crisis facing human resources (HR) in tourism, a crisis partly due to demographics and partly to the nature of tourism jobs and their working conditions.

Tourism businesses

The contemporary tourism industry comprises a range of businesses each with different objectives. Bull (1995) summarizes these objectives as:

- *Profit maximization*, requiring a long-term view of revenue and cost, a perspective often absent in tourism.
- *Sales maximization*, which is often the default option for service businesses and tourism due to capacity constraints.

- *Empire building or prestige*, here as businesses grow there may be a separation of ownership and control and non-monetary objectives emerge.
- *Output maximization*, which is more relevant for product-oriented businesses where volume is more important and yield.
- *Satisificing*, where the goal is to set satisfactory level of revenue or profit.
- *A quiet life (profit minimization)*, where the business is small, often family owned and may be run for lifestyle reasons.

Together these businesses form the contemporary tourism industry, an industry difficult to define as noted in the previous chapter. Debbage and Ioannides (1998) state that this machinery of tourism production manipulates and permits the tourist experience to happen, and in recent years has been restructured in response to technology, changing consumer demand, increasing concentration in the industry (albeit off a low base) and the demands of flexible specialization creating networks of supply and destinations with vertical, horizontal and diagonal integration.

In this chapter, rather than examining the industry sector by sector we have adopted a thematic approach, drawing out and analysing five key issues which characterize the contemporary tourism industry. These issues are:

1 Globalization
2 The knowledge economy
3 Networks
4 Small businesses
5 Human resources

The globalizing contemporary tourism industry

Globalization is a fundamental consideration for all tourism businesses. Globalization can be thought of as *boundarylessness* and the various organizational responses to it (Parker 1998): responses that are characterized by speed, flexibility integration and innovation (Wahab and Cooper 2001). In other words, globalization not only reduces borders and barriers for trade between nations, but it also renders these boundaries permeable both within and between organizations. Globalization therefore demands both a different perspective and position to be taken on the management and a operation of tourism businesses. Of course, whilst tourism businesses themselves are affected by globalization, so too they themselves enhance and sustain the process of globalization.

Contemporary drivers of globalization

There are a number of drivers of globalization that impact upon the tourism industry, although these are often outside the control of individual businesses. We can identify six interrelated drivers of globalization:

1 *Technological drivers.* Globalization has been facilitated by two technologies:
   (a) Transport technology has reduced both the monetary and the time-related costs of travel and acted as a 'space shrinking' technology, in turn breaking down geographical boundaries and constraints.
   (b) Communication technology with the synergy between the processing power of computers and the transmission capabilities of digital media has boosted both the speed and capacity of communication. Here, tourism has certainly been influenced by the revolution in global communications, allowing international communication, the development of global distribution systems and increasing the reach of small businesses.
2 *Economic drivers.* Economic drivers of globalization include the shifting patterns of production and consumption across the world which are challenging traditional economic assumptions of world trade and markets.
3 *Political drivers.* Political events have fuelled globalization, creating a new world order. As the traditional core-periphery pattern no longer explains the location and success of businesses and nations, Dicken (1992) argues for a multi-polar economy with three economic regions dominant: North America, the European Union and the economies of South East Asia. The resultant trade tensions in the global marketplace between these 'mega-markets' has prompted a response by the World Trade Organization to draw up the General Agreement on Trade in Services (GATS). The GATS has a range of impacts upon tourism businesses including:
   (a) Promoting free movement of labour globally.
   (b) Enabling the international development of, and access to, computer reservation systems.
   (c) Removing barriers to overseas investment.

4 *Cultural drivers.* The rise of global culture impacts significantly upon tourism. Many resorts are criticized for their uniform landscape of fast food restaurants, international hotels and chain stores. This *coca-cola-isation* or *McDonalds-ization* of destinations is a consequence of the globalization process, converging business practices and communication of both ideas and brands through the media.

5 *Environmental drivers.* The natural environment is a global resource for tourism and non-sustainable practices in one destination impact upon others. Whilst globalization does have positive consequences for the environment, there are also a number of problematic issues:

(a) The reduced effectiveness of governments acting unilaterally weakens those who regulate and prevent pollution.

(b) In an increasingly market-based economy, externalities will not be addressed.

(c) Environmental problems do not respect traditional political boundaries, and there will be a blurring between economic and environmental boundaries.

(d) Rapid tourism growth in South East Asia means that governments are grappling with the impacts upon both environments and cultures.

6 *Business drivers.* Creation of a global society means that tourism businesses have the ability to operate globally and many have opted for a competitive strategy of internationalization. Global businesses view the world as their operating environment and establish both global strategies and global market presence. Changing business practices in response to the drivers of globalization in turn, sustain, extend and facilitate the process of globalization, and reshape the very boundaries that previously constrained them. In tourism, these boundary-breaking processes include:

(a) Creating global brands, products and personalities.

(b) International tourism education and training transmitting global concepts and approaches.

(c) Reduced transport costs through innovations such as the low cost carrier business model.

(d) International communication mechanisms such as global distribution systems.

Tourism and the service sector

Many of the forces and consequences of globalization are creating new forms of service company, not only the large trans-national companies such as Disney, but also the small niche specialist that can take advantage of the Internet, international communications, and market positioning and targeting. Whilst much of the writing on globalization is focused on manufacturing, the service sector's response to the challenges of globalization is quite different. Dicken (1992) argues that services internationalize through overseas market presence whilst also demanding the *right conditions* within which to deliver the service – in terms of labour, technology and government regulation. Campbell and Verbeke (1994) argue that there needs to be a clear recognition of the distinctive characteristics of services as they drive the strategy adopted for internationalization. For example:

- Service businesses can use economies of scale in the marketing area, and in particular train personnel to market the product whilst it is being experienced.
- It is more difficult to separate the businesses delivery of the service from marketing as the service is 'produced where it is consumed'. This enhances the role of responsiveness at the national and local level, whilst ensuring strict quality control through head office marketing and quality management procedures.
- The intangibility of the service product underscores the importance of a business' reputation and thus creates a real pressure to choose credible and legitimate partners in any alliance. Also, the enhanced scope for the delivery of all elements of the service product through alliances is heightened. Here networking flexibility is a typical service sector strategy, allowing the business to develop networks of relationships at different levels, as noted later in this chapter.

Campbell and Verbeke (1994) suggest that an international strategy for service sector businesses may be done in two stages:

1 Development of a strategic capability to allow national responsiveness or centralized innovation.
2 Development of an administrative structure to allow networking flexibility.

Poon (1993) terms this approach the new 'post-Fordist' tourism characterized by a more flexible delivery system of loosely linked worldwide-acting businesses and purchased by the 'new' tourist who is experienced and discerning, seeking value-for-money, customized quality-controlled products, but not necessarily low prices. Here, delivery of the product is 'just in time', flexibly produced, customer-designed and uses technology to extend the 'value chain'. By this stage, the labour force is functionally flexible and technically skilled. This post-Fordist 'new' tourism is characterized by a number of key features in direct response to the forces of globalization. These include alliances and partnerships and internationalization strategies:

Alliances and partnerships

One of the consequences of tourism in a boundaryless world is the opportunity to give competitive advantage by working with other organizations to pool resources. Dyer and Singh (1998) list four approaches to inter-organizational competitiveness:

1 Matching relation-specific assets – matching specific assets between organizations to gain competitive advantage.
2 Knowledge-sharing routines and inter-organization communication such as those promoted by international agencies (e.g. The Pacific Asia Travel Association).
3 Integrating complementary resources and capabilities – a critical area in tourism where the product is an amalgam of resources created by differing organizations (including the public sector). The integration strategies of tourism businesses are clearly evident here in the structuring of global conglomerates of tourism businesses such as airlines. Equally, we see a synergy between tourism and the knowledge-based industries utilizing know how, entertainment and information.
4 Developing effective governance – a final critical area in terms of the management of the relationship and the value chain, and one where tourism is lagging behind other sectors.

Internationalization strategy

Globalization is both a consequence of, and an influence upon the internationalization strategy of businesses. Internationalization models are based on businesses slowly acquiring and using knowledge about overseas markets and competitors and increasingly committing to operating internationally. Dicken (1992) argues that the clearest view of internationalization strategy is seen in trans-national corporations where strategies have three key components:

1 *Cost leadership*: lowest cost producer.
2 *Differentiation*: differentiation from competitors.
3 *Focus*: applying these two components to a market.

This section has shown that for tourism, the competitive landscape is changing and driving businesses to rethink their strategies and organizational structures to allow them to operate successfully in a boundaryless world. Globalization therefore raises a number of key questions for tourism businesses:

- How do businesses transfer their corporate practice, culture and operations internationally and maintain their quality standards, particularly given that the tourism product is delivered locally?
- What should be the balance between local or national practices and the international approach?
- How can the public sector develop policies to protect tourism SMEs and workers threatened by global competition, given that businesses can operate across national boundaries and so evade responsibility?

Globalization also demands that tourism creates the ability to balance a global vision (including international standards) with local demands and needs, and can meet the material needs of a global community without increasing inequalities and without destroying the environment. In part, this will require a knowledge-based approach to managing businesses, an approach that we now turn to.

Managing knowledge in the contemporary tourism industry

The generation and use of new tourism knowledge for innovation and product development is critical for the competitiveness of tourism businesses. In fact, researchers, consultants, the industry and government are constantly generating new tourism knowledge. Yet the tourism industry has been slow to harness that knowledge and in particular, the effective *transfer* of knowledge to tourism businesses has been slow to develop. As a result, unlike many other economic sectors, tourism has not been subject to a knowledge management approach and businesses are less globally competitive as a result.

Knowledge management is a relatively new approach that addresses the critical issue of organizational adaptation, survival and competitiveness in the face of increasingly discontinuous environmental change. For tourism, this environmental change is evident not only in the turbulence of the supply environment but also through the changing nature of tourism consumer behaviour. This pace of change underscores the fact that knowledge-based innovation is a core competency needed by all tourism businesses if they are to be competitive in a changing world.

The knowledge-based economy

In the late 1990s, the *knowledge-based economy* emerged from the previous *information age*. There was recognition that not only was knowledge more than information but also that it was a resource to be valued and managed. The knowledge economy can therefore be thought of as an economy directly based upon the production, distribution and use of knowledge. As the next stage of the post-industrial economy, the knowledge economy sees intellectual assets replace goods and services as the basis for growth and power. The knowledge-based economy has a number of important features that demand a rethinking of our approach to tourism business, for example:

1 Structural economic change is driven by the development of new products and innovations that are brought about by technology. Technology, particularly the Internet, breaks down barriers to knowledge sharing. The knowledge-based economy is characterized by the development of interactive knowledge management systems that were only really possible once the Internet was available as a major facilitator.
2 The employment and development of highly skilled labour is seen as a means of competitive advantage and long-run economic growth. This is an important issue for tourism where many of the sector's HR practices militate against employment and retention of highly skilled employees, as outlined later in this chapter.
3 The fact that the knowledge economy is characterized not by the scarcity of a resource, but by the abundance of information and knowledge.
4 The creation of a new paradigm of *knowledge commerce* (k-commerce) where traditional competitive measures, such as location, are less important.

Types of knowledge

Knowledge can be thought of as the use of skills and experience to add intelligence to information in order to make decisions or provide reliable grounds for action. Knowledge management classifies knowledge according to its ability to be *codified* and therefore communicated. For tourism this distinction is fundamental and goes a long way to explaining the failure of businesses to adequately capitalize on and manage knowledge. Polanyi (1966) provides possibly the most useful classification, distinguishing between two types of knowledge:

1 *Tacit knowledge*: Tacit knowledge is difficult to codify, difficult to communicate to others as information and it is difficult to digitize. A good example of tacit knowledge would be the knowledge that is passed from master to apprentice, or from sports coach to player. The majority of knowledge in the tourism sector is tacit (e.g. in tourism organizations and the entrepreneurial community) yet is often ignored. Indeed, estimates suggest that over 90 per cent of any organization's knowledge assets are tacit.
2 *Explicit knowledge*: In contrast to tacit knowledge, explicit knowledge is transferable and easy to codify and communicate. It is therefore usually the focus of an organization's interest and is found in the form of documents, databases, files, customer directories, etc. and other media. Explicit knowledge can be relatively easily formulated by means of symbols and can be digitized. It can therefore be transferred and communicated to those that need it in the organization.

The conversion of tacit to explicit knowledge is critical for tourism, as there is so much tacit knowledge in the sector that could benefit other businesses – and destinations and governments. It is here that the knowledge management approach provides a significant benefit for tourism as it focuses upon the management of tacit and explicit knowledge to create organizational learning, innovation and sustainable competitive advantage.

Rethinking knowledge management for tourism businesses: the question of scale

If knowledge management is to be utilized by tourism businesses to cooperate at the destination level, then the micro-level focus on the organization, which dominates knowledge management thinking, needs to be expanded to embrace knowledge stocks and flows within networks of organizations at the destination. Here, Hislop et al. (1997) provide a solution by arguing that knowledge *articulation* occurs in networks of organizations attempting to innovate and build upon knowledge.

They identify two types of network.

1 Firstly, micro-level networks within organizations where knowledge is created and is dominantly tacit and 'in-house'. This can be thought of as *demand-side* knowledge creation satisfying the organizational needs of new knowledge.
2 A second macro-level, inter-organizational network where knowledge is transferred around a network of organizations – at say the destination – and tends therefore to be explicit in nature. This can be viewed as a *supply-side* response to the need to distribute and transfer knowledge.

Hislop et al.'s (1997) notion of knowledge 'articulation' involves the gradual conversion of tacit knowledge at the individual organization level into explicit knowledge, which is transmitted through the wider network of organizations (i.e. the destination). In this way useful knowledge is widely dispersed across a network to boost competitiveness and the analogy with tourism destinations is clear.

In tourism, knowledge management embraces both levels of aggregation (i.e. both the individual business as well as networks of businesses). At the destination level, the networks of businesses can be either destination or sector specific and the knowledge management process will be facilitated by either:

1 *Traded interactions* where knowledge sharing is facilitated by members of the supply chain or by trade organizations for industry sectors.
2 *Untraded interactions* where knowledge sharing is facilitated by destination management organizations to boost the competitiveness of businesses at the destination.

In both the cases, knowledge sharing demands high degrees of trust and the often competitive environment of small businesses at destinations can work against this.

The benefits of knowledge management for contemporary tourism businesses

A knowledge management approach delivers a range of significant benefits to tourism businesses:

• Managed access to knowledge reduces search time and shortens learning curves, facilitating new product development and innovation.

- Within the organization, a knowledge management approach encourages and facilitates enhanced and smarter problem-solving techniques.
- Managed access to knowledge provides an organization with the ability to respond rapidly to customers, technology and markets.
- Across the organization, knowledge management systems contribute to more efficient business processes.
- Within the organization, knowledge management enhances staff performance by encouraging knowledge sharing, mutual trust and so reducing staff turnover.
- A knowledge management system allows an organization to leverage and use its intellectual assets; indeed there are exponential benefits from knowledge as more people use it within the organization.
- Knowledge management encourages partnering and the sharing of core competencies with suppliers, vendors, customers and other external stakeholders.

Clearly then tourism businesses have to recognize that they are part of the knowledge economy as well as part of a globalizing economy. Both globalization and the knowledge economy demand that businesses are networked and can not only communicate with both their markets and their competitors, but also leverage from the flexible specialization inherent in tourism. We now turn to the central issue of networking and how it can be approached in the contemporary tourism industry.

Contemporary tourism industry networks

We argued above that we are now living in a global knowledge economy, whilst others suggest that the future lies in a network society. In fact, both statements are true as the key resource traded in networks is knowledge, facilitated by technology. The contemporary tourism industry is characterized by flatter structures, globalization driving alliances and partnerships, instant communication, flexible specialization and the imperative to collaborate and share resources such as knowledge. This equates to loosely articulated networks of organizations either configured as destinations, or as economic structures such as value chains.

One way to analyse this new configuration of businesses is through network analysis. In business and economics, network analysis draws upon the 'competencies-based theory' of business, where relationships create competitive advantage through shaping and enhancing organizational performance (Tremblay 1997). This theory argues that organizations evolve according to their internal capabilities and how they can leverage these in the external environment. Applied to tourism, business performance is not only dependent upon the resources of that business itself, but also upon that of other businesses and the nature of their relationships. This system of businesses can then be viewed as a network comprising an architecture of nodes and interconnected relationships. This means that increasingly tourism businesses are competing with networks of businesses rather than with individual businesses. In other words, competitiveness depends upon how well an organization is 'networked' and strategically 'embedded' within its networks. It is this notion of 'embeddedness' that is the fundamental difference in the network approach, contrasting it with economic theories of organization.

Whilst, network analysis has a long pedigree in the social sciences and business disciplines, it has seldom been used in tourism despite the fact that tourism is ideally suited to the approach. Tourism lends itself to network analysis for a number of reasons:

- Firstly, tourism more than most economic sectors, through flexible specialization, involves the development of formal and informal collaboration, partnerships and networks. In other words, the tourism industry and destinations can be viewed as loosely articulated groups of independent suppliers who link together to deliver the overall product. Here, network analysis can provide useful insights on the structure and behaviour of the industry and destinations and can be used to recommend strengthening of links and coordination between destination organizations.
- Secondly, network analysis delivers a flexible tool with which to analyse the dynamics of businesses and destinations as they operate within a turbulent and shifting system. Businesses and destinations represent networks of cooperative and competitive linkages and are fashioned by both their internal capabilities and those of the external environment (Tremblay 1997).
- Thirdly, network analysis provides insights into the behaviour of businesses at destinations. Networks themselves have loose governance systems, which, at the destination level, act as an alterative to the public sector. The behaviour of destination networks acts to encourage cooperative ventures and to avoid cutthroat competition, allowing businesses to find a balance between competition and innovation. For tourism destinations, an important notion is that of networks having their own embedded macro-culture, with the behaviour of suppliers

reflecting the branding, symbols and images of the destination environment (Pavlovich 2001).

- Fourthly, network analysis provides insights as to how a network can be made more efficient in terms of linkage and coordination. For business and destination networks, policy can be effective in increasing the efficiency of the overall network through strengthening links, reducing barriers and encouraging members to share information.

Tourism networks

There are three basic units of analysis in a tourism network:

1 *Actors* perform activities in relationship with other actors and control network resources. These actors can be of different sizes and are very diverse.
2 *Relationships* may be considered as transactions between actors. These relationships are the building blocks of network analysis.
3 *Resources* that are exchanged among actors represent the third element of a network. These resources may include knowledge or money.

Tremblay (1997) identifies three types of tourism network:

1 An innovative network where businesses share complementary assets, such as airline alliances and hotel consortia.
2 Networks of businesses sharing in the marketing knowledge of specific customer segments. Here tourism examples include the vertical and horizontal integration strategies of larger companies.
3 Networks coordinating complementary assets at the destination level. This includes destination marketing alliances and promotion (a common approach in the past) and the more recent approach of jointly shaping new products and innovation. Tourism businesses then strategically position themselves within the network to leverage from innovation and future organizational configurations.

The nodes of any tourism network can be thought of as businesses and other organizations, of varying size, cooperating to compete, as a direct response to an externally turbulent environment. Here the strategy is for a business to 'embed' within a network to gain security as other members develop and maintain effective relation-ships with each other. A member's position within a destination network depends upon the number of its relationships and its role in the network. Members gain power from their position within a network, and, the more centrally located they are, the stronger the power and influence of that organization within the destination. In turn, weaker organizations can develop ties with central ones to leverage benefits.

For tourism businesses membership of a network delivers a range of benefits including:

- Scale and scope economies (such as alliances).
- Coordination of complementary assets (such as marketing synergies).
- Higher strategic benefits where the members of the network share a common vision (such as destination branding).

CASE STUDY
Tourism destination and business networks in Australia

Introduction

This case study shows the clear benefit of using network analysis to graphically show the structure of business networks. This can then be used to remedy any failures in commu-nication and coordination across the network. A study of destination and business net-works in Australia clearly shows how this can be used as an analytical tool to diagnose problems. In each of the examples below we present destination networks made up of nodes, which are the key stakeholders (businesses and the public sector) and the con-tacts they make with each other for business, information, etc. are shown as the links. The networks were constructed from data collected in 2005.

Victoria

The first examples are drawn from the southern Australian state of Victoria. Examining Figure 11.1 we see an integrated network created from the Geelong-Otway regional tourism organization (RTO). This is effectively the Great Ocean Road region of the state, a stunning ocean scenic drive linking three local authority areas. Here the network struc-ture shows the implementation of a strong regional tourism marketing and management

Figure 11.1 The tourism network structure of the Great Ocean Road region

region, due to innovative organization across three separate local authority areas. This has developed from a regional initiative to market the region using the Great Ocean Road as the central coordinating feature.

This network contrasts with that for an inland valley based upon two local authority areas (Figure 11.2). Here the interaction between tourism stakeholders in the Bright and Wangaratta Shires demonstrates a more decentralized structure in which more than one organization assumes the role of coordination. These two local authority areas are geographically and politically dissimilar and there is little incentive for them to link together through the RTO. The network structure suggests that the more centralized network in the Great Ocean Road Region is associated with a more developed RTO structure and highlights the enhanced formal coordination provided in this region. From these Victorian examples it is clear that there are significant differences between local authorities in the organization of tourism.

Townsville, Queensland

The Townsville network demonstrates two distinct clusters of organizations. These two clusters are linked by Townsville Business (the RTO) and to a lesser extent Tourism Queensland (the state tourism organization) (Figure 11.3). The first cluster comprises

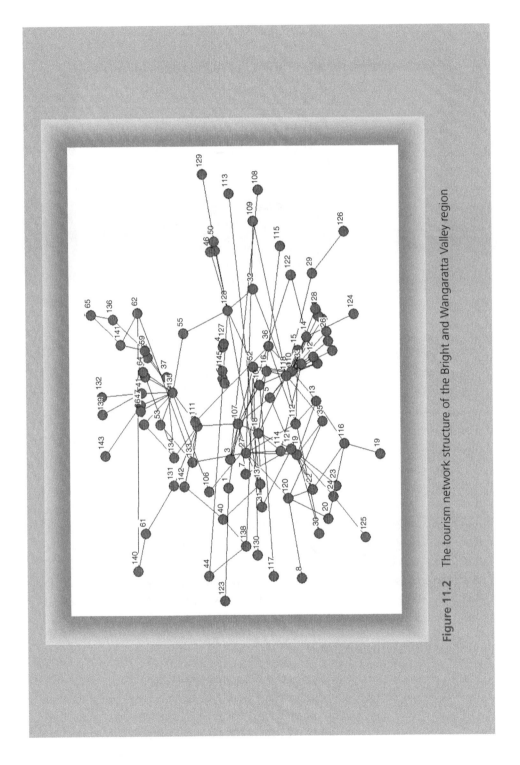

Figure 11.2   The tourism network structure of the Bright and Wangaratta Valley region

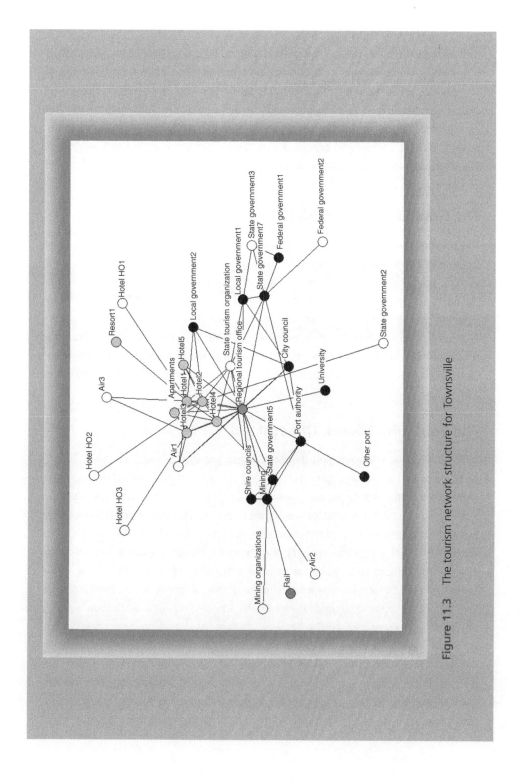

Figure 11.3   The tourism network structure for Townsville

commercial tourism operators in a tightly knit grouping due to their many relationships with each other based upon mutual interest in terms of the value chain and marketing. These nodes are all major hotels or accommodation providers in the region. The second cluster lies below the RTO and is comprised primarily of public sector organizations. This cluster is more diffuse and is made up of organizations primarily involved in planning and projects, or organizations that provide access to other sectoral clusters (such as mining). The Townsville network shows the interconnections of the separate public and private sector networks.

The Gold Coast, Queensland

The network structure for the Gold Coast exposes a structural divide between the Gold Coast itself and its hinterland (Figure 11.4). This appears to relate to geography as well as to the main markets for these two sub-regions. The hinterland cluster is linked both to the nearby largest city RTO (Brisbane) as well as to the Gold Coast RTO as might be expected from the dual source markets for this area. Tourism Queensland, the state organization, is central to the whole Gold Coast cluster. Such structural divides are common in tourism due to political boundaries, geographical features or organizational conflict. The position of the Gold Coast Tourism Bureau in the network indicates that it is addressing this structural divide by performing a linking function.

The Southern Downs, Queensland

In the rural Southern Downs region, the network demonstrates clear sectoral clusters (Figure 11.5). These are firstly, a wine tourism cluster; and secondly a bed and breakfast cluster. It is interesting that the wine cluster overlaps more with the bed and breakfast cluster than the wider tourism sector. This is most likely explained by the need to forge alliances between the two types of complementary tourism businesses in order to deliver the wine tourism product. Instead the wine cluster is represented in the tourism cluster through a number of key industry organizations. Such representative organizations have a gatekeeper function, facilitating the flow of information between different clusters. As gatekeepers, these organizations acquire the ability to influence the issues and activities within the destination.

There is also a structural divide between organizations based on the political boundary of the two local authority areas of Stanthorpe and Warwick. This appears to relate to differences in the economies of these areas. The bed and breakfast and wine clusters are focused on the Stanthorpe area. This area is further from capital city markets and operates as a weekend break destination. In contrast, Warwick Shire is more focused on agricultural production. The RTO links these two areas through its planning and management role.

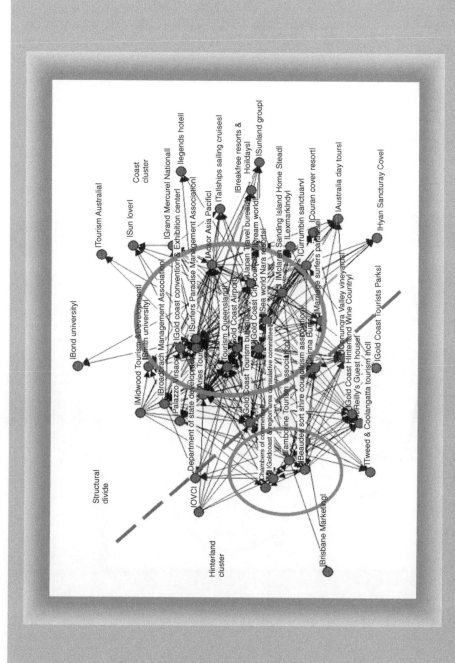

Figure 11.4   The tourism network structure for the Gold Coast

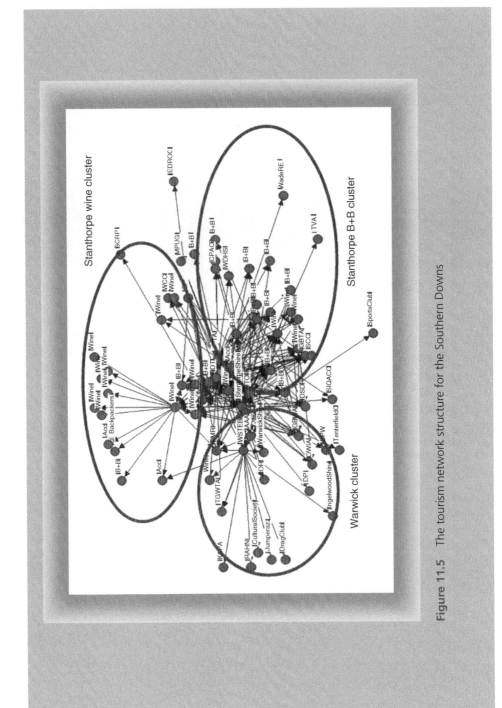

Figure 11.5   The tourism network structure for the Southern Downs

By using these four examples this case study demonstrates how network analysis can provide insights into the structure and functioning of destination and business networks and can be used to both gain insights into their structure and to diagnose and remedy problems.

Acknowledgements:

This case is derived from research funded by Tourism Queensland and The Sustainable Tourism Cooperative Research Centre, an Australian Government initiative. I am grateful to Dr Noel Scott for his work on this case study.

Discussion questions

1 Examining the five network diagrams, discuss the relative influence of the geographical situation of the destination upon the network structure.
2 What types of problems faced by tourism businesses can be diagnosed by network analysis?
3 Examining Figures 11.3, 11.4 and 11.5, tease out value chains and explain their structure.

Networked tourism businesses

There is no doubt that reconceptualizing the tourism industry using a network approach is very beneficial for tourism. Networked organizations are ideally suited to thrive in Poon's post-Fordist era of 'new' tourism, characterized by flexible specialization, rapid communication and globalization. Achrol and Kotler (1999) agree and state that the business of the future will be a networked organization characterized as:

> an interdependent coalition of task- or skill-specialized economic entities (independent firms or autonomous organizational units) that operates without hierarchical control but is embedded, by dense lateral connections, mutuality, and reciprocity, in a shared value system that defines 'membership', roles and responsibilities (p. 148).

They distinguish four categories of network organizations for the future, based upon theoretical and practical grounds:

1 Internal networks that are designed to reduce hierarchy and open businesses to their environments – in other words to enhance customer responsiveness and awareness of the external environment.

2 Vertical networks that maximize the productivity of serially dependent functions by creating partnerships among independent, skill-specialized businesses – essential in the delivery of the tourism product and inherent in flexible specialization.

3 Inter-market networks that seek to leverage horizontal synergies across industries – the rise of the technology companies in tourism distribution channels is a good example.

4 Opportunity networks that are organized around customer needs and market opportunities and designed to search for the best solutions to them – clusters of businesses serving particular specialist tourism products such as adventure tourism are examples here.

Finally, network analysis links neatly with knowledge management to facilitate the flow of knowledge around business and destination systems, whilst it is also perfectly suited to the demands of globalization, driven by technological networks and networked alliances of business. Of course, SMEs also benefit from this approach allowing them to embed securely within business and destination networks for enhanced competitiveness. We turn to SMEs and entrepreneurs in the next section of this chapter.

Small businesses and entrepreneurship in the contemporary tourism industry

Tourism Small Businesses

The contemporary tourism industry is dominated by small businesses (SMEs) and particularly micro-businesses. In France for example it is estimated that over 90 per cent of all tourism businesses employ less than 10 people. Yet, there is no agreed definition of what comprises a small business. Thomas (1998) characterizes them as those businesses which have a small market share, are managed in a personalized way, are independent of external control and do not influence market prices. Goffee and Scase (1983) classify small businesses according to their source of capital and organizational structure. Their classification ranges from marginal self-employed companies to the owner director company (Table 11.1).

Tourism SMEs have become a focus for governments and development agencies. On the one hand they have seen the development of policy to protect them from

Table 11.1 Organizational structures and entrepreneurial characteristics

Category	Entrepreneurial characteristics
Self-employed	Use of family labour, little market stability, low levels of capital investment, weakly developed management skills
Small employer	Use of family and non-family labour, less economically marginalized but shares other characteristics of the self-employed group
Owner controller	Use of non-family labour, higher levels of capital investment, often a formal level of management control, but no separation of ownership and control
Owner director	Segmentation of ownership and management functions, higher levels of capital investment

Source: Goffee and Scase (1983) and Shaw and Williams (1990).

the forces of globalization and the dominance of large multinational companies with increasing concentration in the sector. On the other hand they are seen as a force for good in the economic development of remoter areas or regions that are converting to a market economy (such as the former countries of Eastern European communist bloc). More specifically, SMEs bring a number of advantages to a destination:

- They rapidly diffuse income into the economy through strong backward linkages into the economy of a destination.
- Similarly, they contribute to employment.
- They provide a localized welcome and character by acting as a point of direct contact between the host community and the visitor.
- In a market that increasingly demands tailored experiences, SMEs play an important role in responding to tourists' demand and so facilitating 'flexible specialization' (Ateljevic and Doorne 2001).

However, SMEs also contribute to the 'under-management' of the tourism industry as they are often run and owned by those who are inexperienced in business skills and strategy. Indeed, many micro-tourism businesses are owned and run by one family. As most SMEs are family owned and run, there tends to be an emotional attachment to the business and rational business thinking is not applied. Nor is there a desire for business expansion. Non-economic motives therefore are common in tourism small business. This also means that small tourism businesses may not think strategically in terms of developing their business nor engage in training their staff (Buhalis and Cooper 1998). In addition, most tourism entrepreneurs have little or no tourism training or experience themselves; Stallibrass (1980) for example in her study of the UK resort of Scarborough found only one-third of small hotel owners had previous experience in tourism.

Entrepreneurs

Yet, this tends to go against the views of small businesses as enterprising and entrepreneurial and begs the question, are all small businesses run by entrepreneurs? The distinction here is important: a small business is the organizing unit of production, but it is the individual who is (or is not) the entrepreneur. In tourism it seems the answer to the question posed is that many small businesses are run in an entrepreneurial fashion, but many are not – and there are specific tourism-related reasons for this.

The notion of an entrepreneurial society is a romantic one, a group of businesses and individuals which are nimble, flexible, eager to spot an opportunity in the marketplace and to add value. Entrepreneurial businesses are adaptive, flexible and tend to integrate their operations around customers. They underpin creativity and innovation and take risks. Their flexibility is essential as at each stage of the business life cycle, from launch to maturity, they face particular opportunities and challenges and require a certain level of resourcing. Indeed, small hospitality and tourism businesses tend to be at the forefront of economic cycles and their fortunes can be used as a barometer of economic change.

Entrepreneurship therefore plays a key role in economic development, but in tourism there is a specific type of entrepreneur that seems to break all the rules – the lifestyle entrepreneur. Lifestyle entrepreneurs are common in tourism given the attraction of tourism to special locations. They tend to blur the distinction between production and consumption as they are living in and enjoying the amenity values and products of the destination. Shaw and Williams (1990) identify three characteristics of entrepreneurs in tourism in their study of Cornwall:

1 *Level of experience and expertise*: Many entrepreneurs have little experience in tourism having come to the sector through employment elsewhere in the economy with no obvious access to capital or expertise. In other words tourism, particularly

the accommodation sector, has low barriers to entry – which in turn explains their poverty of resources and expertise, and the ease of entry as a lifestyle entrepreneur.

2 *Business motivation*: Non-economic motives are important reasons for becoming an entrepreneur in tourism, particularly in terms of lifestyle and environment.

3 *Source of capital*: Informal sources of capital are common in tourism SMEs, often using personal or family savings. This is symptomatic of a group who have little idea of the importance of business plans and targets.

Morrison et al. (1999) are clear that there is no entrepreneurial blueprint for success; rather it is the particular fit of an entrepreneurial approach that takes into account the particular dynamic components present in a particular destination or market. Indeed, because of their closeness to the destination and its products, entrepreneurial behaviour in tourism is strongly influenced by locale. Nonetheless there is a growing number of guides, menus and literature available to prospective entrepreneurs as our knowledge increases. These guides are often put out by economic development units and tourism agencies to assist potential entrepreneurs who may be relocating and investing in a region.

The development of strong networks and information sharing is the key to the survival of both entrepreneurs and SMEs in tourism. Morrison et al. (1999) state that small business operates within a context of formal and informal networks:

- Family – support and labour.
- Financial institutes – source of capital.
- Public sector in terms of legislation and policy to foster an environment to success.
- A destination network.

As with all tourism businesses, it is the successful leveraging from these networks that distinguishes a successful SME in tourism.

Contemporary tourism HR

In the final section of this chapter we turn to one of the most important resources of the contemporary tourism industry, that of HR. Tourism is a labour intensive industry, supporting a wide range of jobs in many different sectors. Of course, this is due to the importance of personal service in tourism and, whilst there are question marks over the quality of some of these jobs, there is no doubt that the tourism industry provides job opportunities for the young, women and the less advantaged groups in society. The World Travel and Tourism Council estimates that the travel and tourism sector supports up to 230 million jobs worldwide, representing 3 per cent of the world's employment in directly generated jobs and 9 per cent if indirectly generated jobs are taken into account (WTTC 2006). As we would expect, these figures are higher for countries which have a large tourism industry such as Spain or Mauritius.

HR are an essential pre-requisite to delivering the contemporary tourism product. Yet, they remain the Cinderella of the tourism industry; the industry knows that they are important, but they are not taken seriously. As a result, in the first decade of the twenty-first century the tourism industry worldwide is facing a HR crisis. This final section of the chapter analyses the underlying reasons for this crisis and outlines some possible solutions. The reasons for the HR crisis in tourism are complex and interlinked. They are rooted in the type of work that tourism involves, the working conditions in the industry, the dominance of small businesses (SMEs) and the shifting demographics and social attitudes of the twenty-first century.

Demographics and attitudes

In much of the developing world birthrates are falling. Add to this the fact that many countries have ageing populations who have the income and time to travel and it is clear that whilst this travel is generating tourism jobs, the work force is not being sustained to deliver those jobs. This 'demographic squeeze' is exacerbated by the fact that the new generations of workers, such as generation Y, have very different attitudes to work and careers as we saw in the case study in Chapter 4. This partly explains why there is not only a labour shortage in tourism but also a skills shortage where catering for example is not seen as a desirable profession. Indeed, in some regions of the world, such as much of the Middle East, service positions are frowned upon and seen only as jobs of last resort.

Tourism jobs and working conditions

Tourism jobs have a range of interesting and contradictory features which, when combined with many aspects of their associated working conditions go some way to explaining the crisis (see e.g. Riley et al. 2002). Tourism jobs can be characterized as follows:

- The bulk of service jobs tend to be temporary, held by people with no career aspirations in tourism and no commitment to the industry.
- They are dominated by younger people – the average age of hospitality workers in the Netherlands for example is 23 years.
- Females are in the majority in many tourism jobs.
- They are perceived as glamorous and attractive, often involving work in exotic settings and with opportunity for customer contact. Their attraction is also seen in the opportunities to be creatively engaged in say nature-based tourism or marketing.
- They provide great flexibility in terms of hours and working arrangements. This suits specific groups in society such as working mothers.
- They are accessible with few or no barriers to entry in many jobs; indeed tourism is a highly 'under-qualified' industry.
- They are highly diverse, ranging from hospitality-related jobs, which tend to make up the bulk of employment in tourism but are also the lowest paid and the most seasonal, to the smaller number of jobs in air transport, but also the highest paid.
- They are characterized by a rigid occupational structure with strong job traditions.

Of course, these characteristics are self-reinforcing – young people take temporary tourism jobs to tide them over student life because these are no barriers to entry and the jobs are flexible. This is made worse by the lack of a strong union presence in tourism in many (but not all) countries. As a result, working conditions in tourism are often problematic and can be summarized as:

1 Low paid – in many countries tourism jobs pay up to 20 per cent below the average wage.
2 Demanding anti-social hours – often involving work on holidays, weekends and over meal times. This can impact on the balance between family and work life.
3 Creating emotional pressures, not only in terms of the pressure to deliver good service and always to be smiling – but also in terms of attitudes in working environments such as kitchens. Whilst this may be common to other service sector jobs, it may be that the pressures in the tourism environment are particularly acute and demand coping strategies by employees.

4 Having health and safety issues – for example there are many accidents in kitchens, and workers face safety issues on the way to home after late shifts.

Managing contemporary tourism HR

As noted earlier, we must recognize that the majority of tourism jobs are supported by tourism SMEs. Estimates suggest that worldwide, SMEs (with less than 10 employees) employ at least half of the tourism labour force. This creates a problem of under-management in the sector and under-utilization of the workforce, as many small entrepreneurs do not have a grounding in good HR practice. Add to this the problem of creating career pathways in SMEs, and it becomes clear why there is a crisis in the sector. However, this is not the only reason that there is an HR crisis. The tourism industry is innately conservative and resistant to change. Many companies retain HR management styles from previous decades and have failed to move into the knowledge economy where it is a company's human capital, knowledge and skills which deliver competitiveness, as we saw earlier.

However, it must also be recognized that tourism HR planning is complex. The key is to match the scheduling of employees to the throughput of tourists. This throughput is unpredictable and highly seasonal – on a daily, weekly and monthly basis. As a result, companies find it difficult to plan and manage their HR function and resort to short-term tactics of non-standard employment (such as temporary, seasonal or part-time workers, perhaps keeping a group of employees on call in case of unforecast demand).

Combining all of these factors together and the industry finds itself with a shortage of employees, and high turnover of people in many job functions. Turnover is expensive for the industry and yet it runs at over 100 per cent in many city centre hotels.

Contemporary tourism HR management

Whilst the issues raised above are severe, there are a range of things that can be done. Solutions to the HR crisis in tourism include the following:

1 Greater understanding of the operation of the tourism labour market – how for example do school leavers view the tourism sector against other opportunities (Riley et al. 2002) and what are the views of generation Y to the job market? This

also requires intervention by government and industry to promote jobs in tourism and to polish the image of working in the sector.

2 Recognition that tourism is in the knowledge economy and needs to invest in and develop its workforce rather than exploiting it. This will involve a shift in attitude and operation by the industry, particularly in terms of investing in training and education. However, the industry can also be more innovative in its HR management. For example:

- In seasonal destinations smart companies use the off-peak for training rather than letting staff go.
- Companies can invest in multi-skilling by identifying the core skills needed for job functions.
- The industry needs to develop future leaders.

3 At the destination level, destination marketing organizations (DMOs) can encourage SMEs to work together to create career paths across companies and begin to think beyond *managing people in organizations* and make the jump to *managing people in destinations*.

4 Education and training for tourism is often mired in the final quarter of the twentieth century and for businesses and destinations to be competitive it needs to embrace the new contemporary tourism environment and educate the workforce to deal with change and to be competent in areas demanded by 'post-tourists'. These include specialist fields such as guiding and special interest tourism, as well as providing a thorough grounding in business and people skills, and technology.

5 Finally, there is a need for government and the international agencies to encourage quality jobs in tourism and to move away from simply treating tourism as a means to generate jobs with no eye for quality. The International Labour Organization's 'decent work agenda' is an important initiative here, with the mission of enhancing the quality of jobs and the working environment. Governments will also be increasingly called upon to facilitate international labour movement in tourism to solve the workforce shortage in certain countries. This will demand harmonizing qualifications and educating for the acceptance of foreign workers, an issue we now turn to.

Tourism HR: the impact of globalization

Globalization renders national borders permeable and is encouraging international labour migration and a global market for tourism HR. Indeed, some countries are well known as net exporters of tourism labour – Portugal and the Philippines for example. Globalization is having a major impact upon the way that HR are viewed and managed in tourism (Becherel and Cooper 2002). Whilst, globalization boosts economic growth, it also jeopardizes social equality and threatens vulnerable groups of employees. The impact of globalization on the tourism labour market has three key dimensions:

1 *The informal labour market*: at the tourism destination, the growth of international companies, such as chain hotels creates a demand for labour that is flexible to adjust to fluctuating levels of tourism demand. Managers therefore come to rely upon informal labour markets at the destination, operating through networking, recommendations and word of mouth and so avoid expensive and continual hiring of staff (Baldacchino 1997).

2 *Productivity*: globalization is tending to drive companies towards countries that demonstrate higher productivity. It is also enhancing the role of technology and, in contrast to manufacturing where technology replaces jobs, tourism employees work alongside technology in say hotel reception. Here however, the impact of technology is mixed – it tends to be greater in back-of-house jobs and less evident in face-to-face customer service roles.

3 *Non-standard employment*: non-standard jobs are perfectly suited to tourism as they allow flexibility through part-time, contracting, temping or self-employment. Whilst this is beneficial from the employers' point of view, these types of jobs tend to attract vulnerable classes of workers, such as women, the disabled and in some countries, children.

Different stakeholders are developing responses to the impact of a globalizing tourism workforce. Businesses for example have to decide how to handle an international workforce, from global hiring to language and cultural training and location of the HR function in the company. Governments are developing policies to protect vulnerable workers and SMEs as well as dealing with the impact of international policies such as GATS. Unions are aware that their penetration is very patchy internationally – in Scandinavia for example their influence in tourism is strong, whilst in the UK and Australia it is much weaker. The unions are therefore grappling to come to terms with a labour market that does not respect national boundaries and national union membership.

Chapter overview

This chapter has examined five key issues facing the contemporary tourism industry. A range of factors, including technology and lower travel costs, have driven globalization. Tourism businesses have responded by internationalizing and building alliances and partnerships, whilst we also identified that there are losers in the globalization equation, particularly SMEs who are faced with competition from large companies, and vulnerable workers who can be exploited. Not only are we living in a global society, but also we are part of the knowledge economy. Tourism businesses have been slow to embrace the benefits of the knowledge economy, especially in terms of adopting knowledge management practices and boosting competitiveness through utilizing knowledge for innovation and new product development. Both globalization and the knowledge economy demand that tourism businesses are well networked. Only in this way can they ensure that they benefit from global trends and the flexible specialization inherent in delivering the total tourism product. The chapter identified the benefits of using network analysis to examine networks of destination and tourism businesses and to diagnose problems and weak links. A case study of five different network structures then outlined how networks can illuminate particular structures and issues in tourism. Finally, new networked organizations were recommended as future organizational structures and embeddedness within networks was identified as a key strategy for survival for the contemporary tourism business. There is no doubt that these first three issues – globalization, the knowledge economy and networking – are all linked and combine to create the new paradigm for understanding the contemporary tourism industry in the twenty-first century.

This chapter outlined the characteristics of small businesses, the lifeblood of tourism destinations, and made the distinction between small businesses and entrepreneurs, whilst focusing on a particular feature of the tourism industry – the lifestyle entrepreneur. Finally, the chapter examined the crisis facing HR in tourism, a crisis partly due to demographics and partly due to the nature of tourism jobs and their conditions. A range of recommendations were made as to how this conundrum can be solved. Whilst the chapter has dissected and separated these issues for explanatory purposes, it must be remembered that all five issues are linked and combined to characterize the contemporary tourism industry.

Self-review questions

1 Considering the main drivers of globalization, rank them in order of importance from a tourism point of view and explain your reasoning.

2 Identify possible strategies that tourism SMEs may adopt to survive in the face of globalization.

3 Explain the significance of different types of knowledge from the point of view of tourism businesses.

4 How can tourism businesses take advantage of knowledge management?

5 From a tourism business point of view, what are the benefits of embedding within a network?

6 How does network analysis help understand the functioning of tourism business networks?

7 Is the term 'lifestyle entrepreneur' a contradiction in terms?

8 Construct a definition of an entrepreneur and then test it against the example of Richard Branson.

9 What do you understand by the term *demographic squeeze* in terms of tourism HR?

10 How should tourism businesses respond to the tourism HR crisis?

Recommended reading

1 Becherel, L. and Cooper, C.P. (2002). The impact of globalisation on human resource management in the tourism sector. *Tourism Recreation Research* 27(1), 1–12.
A paper comprehensively analysing the impact of globalisation upon tourism human resources.

2 Cooper, C. (2006). Knowledge management and tourism. *Annals of Tourism Research* 33(1), 47–64.
A review paper covering all aspects of knowledge management and its use in tourism.

3 Dicken, P. (1992). *Global Shift*, 2nd edn. London: Paul Chapman.
An excellent generic review of globalisation.

4 Morrison, A., Rimmington, M. and Williams, C. (1999). *Entrepreneurship in the Hospitality, Tourism and Leisure Industries*. Oxford: Butterworth Heinemann.
A comprehensive review of entrepreneurs in tourism.

5 Pavlovich, K. (2001). The twin landscapes of Waitomo: tourism network and sustainability through the Landcare Group. *Journal of Sustainable Tourism* 9(6), 491–504.
An excellent paper reviewing governance issues in tourism networks.

6 Riley, M., Ladkin, A. and Szivas, E. (2002). *Tourism Employment. Analysis and Planning*. Clevedon: Channelview.
Thorough coverage of tourism jobs and HR planning and management.

7 Shaw, G. and Williams, A. (1990). Tourism, economic development and the role of entrepreneurial activity. In C.P. Cooper (ed.), *Progress in Tourism, Recreation and Hospitality Management*, Vol. 2, pp. 67–81. London: Belhaven.
A very useful case study of tourism entrepreneurs.

8 Thomas, R. (1998). *The Management of Small Tourism and Hospitality Businesses*. London: Cassell.
Excellent volume covering all aspects of tourism small businesses.

9 Tremblay, P. (1997). The economic organization of tourism. *Annals of Tourism Research* 24(4), 837–859.
Review paper with a good section on networks.

10 Wahab, S. and Cooper, C. (2001). *Tourism in the Age of Globalisation*. London: Routledge.
Edited volume examining the impact of globalisation on tourism and the response of various sectors.

Recommended web sites

Belize Tourism Industry Association: www.btia.org/
Queensland Tourism Industry Council: www.qtic.com.au/
Travel Industry Association of America: www.tia.org/
Utah Tourism Industry Coalition: www.utahtourism.org/
World Travel and Tourism Council: www.wttc.org

References cited

Achrol, R.S. and Kotler, P. (1999). Marketing in the network economy. *Journal of Marketing* 63 (special issue), 146–163.

Ateljevic, I. and Doorne, S. (2001). Staying within the fence: lifestyle entrepreneurship in tourism. *Journal of Sustainable Tourism* 8(5), 378–392.

Baldacchino, G. (1997). *Global Tourism and Informal Labour Relations*. London: Mansell.

Becherel, L. and Cooper, C.P. (2002). The impact of globalisation on human resource management in the tourism sector. *Tourism Recreation Research* 27(1), 1–12.

Buhalis, D. and Cooper, C. (1998). Competition and cooperation? Small and medium sized tourism businesses at the destination. In E. Laws, B. Faulkner and G. Moscardo (eds), *Embracing and Managing Change in Tourism*, pp. 324–346. London: Routledge.

Bull, A. (1995). *The Economics of Travel and Tourism*. Longman Australia, Melbourne.

Campbell, A.J. and Verbeke, A. (1994). The globalisation of service sector multinationals. *Long Range Planning* 27(2), 95–102.

Debbage, K.G. and Ioannides, D. (1998). Conclusion. The commodification of tourism. In D. Ioannides and K.G. Debbage (eds), *The Economic Geography of the Tourist Industry. A Supply Side Analysis*, pp. 287–292. London: Routledge.

Dicken, P. (1992). *Global Shift*, 2nd edn. London: Paul Chapman.

Dyer, J.H. and Singh, H. (1998). The relational view: co-operative strategy and sources of inter-organisational competitive advantage. *Academy of Management Review* 23(4), 660–679.

Goffee, R. and Scase, R. (1983). Class entrepreneurship and the service sector: towards a conceptual clarification. *Service Industries Journal* 3, 146–160.

Hislop, D., Newell, S., Scarborough, H. and Swan, J. (1997). Innovation and networks: linking diffusion and implementation. *International Journal of Innovation Management* 1(4), 427–448.

Morrison, A., Rimmington, M. and Williams, C. (1999). *Entrepreneurship in the Hospitality, Tourism and Leisure Industries*. Oxford: Butterworth Heinemann.

Parker, B. (1998). *Globalisation and Business Practice. Managing Across Boundaries*. London: Sage.

Pavlovich, K. (2001). The twin landscapes of Waitomo: tourism network and sustainability through the Landcare Group. *Journal of Sustainable Tourism* 9(6), 491–504.

Polanyi, M. (1966). *The Tacit Dimension*. New York: Doubleday.

Poon, A. (1993). *Tourism, Technology and Competitive Strategies*. Wallingford: CAB.

Riley, M., Ladkin, A. and Szivas, E. (2002). *Tourism Employment. Analysis and Planning*. Clevedon: Channelview.

Shaw, G. and Williams, A. (1990). Tourism, economic development and the role of entrepreneurial activity. In C.P. Cooper (ed.), *Progress in Tourism, Recreation and hospitality Management*, Vol. 2, pp. 67–81. London: Belhaven.

Stallibrass, C. (1980). Seaside resorts and the hotel accommodation industry. *Progress in Planning* 13, 103–174.

Thomas, R. (1998). *The Management of Small Tourism and Hospitality Businesses*. London: Cassell.

Tremblay, P. (1997). The economic organization of tourism. *Annals of Tourism Research* 24(4), 837–859.

Wahab, S. and Cooper, C. (2001). *Tourism in the Age of Globalisation*. London: Routledge.

WTTC (2006). *World Travel and Tourism. Climbing to New Heights. The 2006 Travel and Tourism Economic Research*. London: WTTC.

Chapter **12**

Supporting the contemporary tourism product: service management

David Solnet

Chapter objectives

After reading this chapter, you will

- Further appreciate the linkages and relationships between the various elements that combine to make up the contemporary destination product and experience
- Understand the 'service management' perspective
- Recognize the difference between a 'product' and 'customer' orientation
- Be aware of contemporary issues related to visitor/customer/tourist satisfaction, and whether satisfaction is an ambitious enough aim
- Be familiar with the concept of, and challenges with, managing and measuring service quality
- Understand the conceptual frameworks which link employees, customers and organizational performance
- View human resource management (HRM) as a strategic function
- Understand innovative practices designed to measure and therefore manage service industry performance

Introduction

Tourism is a complex system – an assemblage or interrelated combination of things or elements forming a unitary whole. Chapter 1 explained that this system includes various forms of individual products including the trip product, the destination product, the tourism business product and the service product. Underlying this tourism system is a need to understand how to best manage the experience in order to reach satisfying outcomes for tourists, individual organizations and destinations. The total tourist experience encompasses many aspects, but the primary aim of tourism businesses – customer or tourist 'satisfaction' – is ultimately determined as an emotional evaluation by the tourist. This is done as part of a tourist's overall appraisal of the destination experience through the co-creation of experience between tourist and producers. As a result, the management of each component of the tourism system by tourism businesses either individually or as part of organizational networks is particularly important. This chapter provides the foundation for understanding the key issues related to managing tourism service organizations in contemporary tourism.

The chapter first explains the importance of individual business performance within the context of a contemporary tourism system, and then outlines the ways in which a service-oriented strategy facilitates heightened tourist satisfaction. An overview of the evolution of thought from a manufacturing to a services paradigm is then explained, before a series of service management principles are defined and discussed. Understanding the links between tourism business interorganizational practices, organizational performance and enhanced destination perceptions are outlined in a tourism context, as is the importance of a strategic approach to human resources management. The creation of a service-oriented culture and climate is then discussed. The final section of the chapter overviews an innovative approach to measuring organizational performance in service organizations, linking business strategy to performance measures and the remuneration of staff and management.

Note: This chapter draws extensively from the service management literature, and therefore makes frequent mention of the term 'customers'. It is important, in the context of tourism, to view 'tourists' or 'visitors' in the exact same context as 'customers'. Therefore these terms are used interchangeably.

Context

How do tourists evaluate their tourism experiences? The answer is rather complicated! The following are some examples:

- Think about a tourist's first encounter with a tourism destination. It might be an advertisement for that destination on television or in a newspaper. Or it could be on a website (see e.g. www.Australia.com or www.France.com). Destination web sites often contain many links to travel packages, accommodation choices, car rental business, places to visit and things to do within that destination. Nested within these destination-marketing activities is a reliance on the individual performance of each organization promoted through such a marketing offer.
- Do you think that your impressions of Singapore as a satisfying tourism destination can be influenced by your trip to Singapore on Singapore Airlines? Or a first visit to Australia on Qantas? (Even experiences on non-'national' airlines, such as United in the USA or British Airways in the UK can influence satisfaction perceptions.)
- What if the person you speak to on the phone regarding destination services on a toll-free number is less than friendly or enthusiastic?
- How would a tourist react upon stopping at a Visitor Information Centre and finding that the employees (often volunteers) are indifferent or apathetic about the region's tourism activities?
- What if the reservation in the hotel, where you plan on spending your first night at the destination, has no sign of your reservation – and they have no rooms available?

As you can see, the experience of the tourist is dependent on many component parts, many of which exist before someone ever becomes a tourist at a destination, and destination marketers hope that none of these links will lead to dissatisfaction with the overall tourist experience.

Given the challenges and importance of ensuring that the links in the tourism system are strong, it is important to understand some of the factors which define individual organizational management and performance. The study of management has traditionally been viewed from a manufacturing or industrial perspective.

However, in tourism, a different perspective is necessary, since tourism is about managing not only products and assets, but also, and most importantly, about managing service, experience and customer expectations (as we outlined in Chapter 1).

Evolution towards a 'service' mindset

Contemporary tourism systems are comprised of many individual businesses, organizations and servicescapes (see also Chapter 5), all interrelated and in many cases reliant on each other (think of a ferry service when staying on an island resort, or restaurants which might accompany a cottage rental). Most of these businesses provide aspects of the tourist experience, from flight reservations, rental car arrangements, accommodation, tours, dining and the like. The predominance of these tourist 'purchases' are in fact services, rather than goods or products. This is an important consideration because of the distinct differences in managing goods versus managing services (Bowen and Ford 2002).

There has been a gradual shift in management thinking away from the predominant manufacturing paradigm, towards recognition of the role played by services in the economy (see Figure 12.1) (Fisk et al. 1993). Yet, despite the extraordinary growth, and recognition of the importance that services play in modern economies, many tourism firms still rely predominantly on the management paradigm drawn from managing in the context of manufacturing. This approach has been challenged with ongoing acknowledgment that there are many differences involved in managing service businesses, such as the relative intangibility of services and the heavy reliance on person-to-person interactions. In fact, it is the service aspect of an offering that often itself provides the means of gaining competitive advantage.

It is essential to understand that providing customers with additional services (and service!) over and above the core product in order to add value for the consumer is a clear strategy towards outperforming competitors. It is in fact rare today to find long-term competitive advantage from a core product offering alone (e.g. a room at a hotel), unless the firm has a sustainable competitive advantage based on some core technology or cost structure which allows for continually lower costs for customers (e.g. a favourable lease agreement which negates or significantly reduces

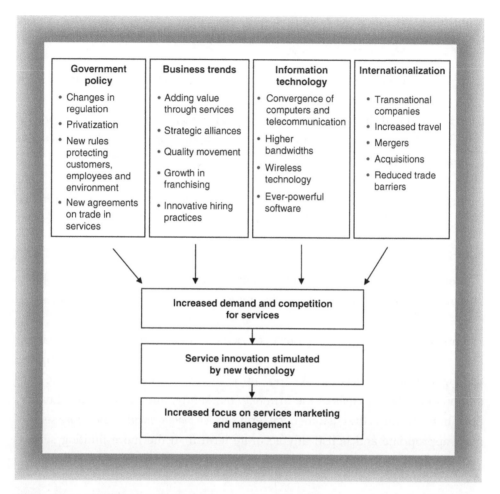

Figure 12.1 Contributing factors to the transformation of the service economy (adapted from Lovelock and Wirtz 2004: p. 7)

fixed overhead costs). However, neither technology nor price can ever be seen as permanently sustainable advantages, because before long somebody will have copied the technology or found ways to reduce prices (even if only temporarily).

Every tourism firm, therefore, has the option of taking a *service* perspective, which enables management to see service from a *strategic* perspective. The driving force behind taking a service perspective is that a core product/offering is a prerequisite for success, but the creation of an entire service offering, with an unending focus on customer needs, satisfaction and loyalty, enhances long-term sustainable competitive advantage. The central requirement of managing a tourism business is therefore to

1 appreciate that a service perspective is a strategic approach – managing service versus just doing service;
2 understand that the 'service management' approach is an alternative approach to the old manufacturing management paradigm, and is geared towards customers, service and value.

Service management has been called 'the new paradigm' in hospitality (Kandampully 2002). The central tenet of this new paradigm was defined by Albrecht (1988: 20) as:

> a total organizational approach that makes quality of service, as perceived by the customer, the number one driving force for the operations of the business.

Essentially, all areas of a tourism firm, or elements of a destination, must be managed with a focus squarely on the tourist, with tourist *perceived value* being the driving force for all decisions. Because a true service orientation requires the integration of all the activities of the firm (e.g. marketing, human resources, finance, operations) towards the customer, the term service *management* is therefore seen as more appropriate and holistically accurate term than the more limiting service *marketing*.

Customer and service orientation

At the centre of the service management paradigm is the idea that all decisions made by the firm must be made with the customer (or tourist) as the focal point (Kandampully 2006). This might seem a logical idea, but businesses for many years often made decisions based on internal motivations – such as cost savings, ease of distribution or convenience for employees. Customer (or in this case, tourist) obsession is at the centre of the service management paradigm.

The idea of customer centricity is not a new one. Management guru, the late Peter Drucker, wrote in his 1954 book *The Practice of Management* that it is a customer that ultimately defines what a business is, what it actually produces and whether or not it will prosper (Drucker 1954). Five trends have been identified in today's marketplace which reinforce the need for tourism firms to make a transformation from a product to a customer-centric focus (Sheth et al. 2000). These trends are given below:

(a) Intensifying pressures to improve marketing productivity.
(b) Intensifying competition.
(c) Increasing market diversity.
(d) Demanding and more well-informed consumers.
(e) Advances in technology.

Clearly, tourism operates within an environment where all of these trends exist, and tourism firms have realized that the best means to develop long-term customer relationships, and which is the most difficult to emulate, is one with the customer squarely in the middle of all efforts. However, many companies today across all industries struggle with this as an underlying concept despite its logic and seeming simplicity (for a thorough explanation, see Shah et al. 2006).

Product centric versus customer centric

Table 12.1 summarizes some of the key differences and distinguishing features of product and customer centricity. The product-centric approach is drawn from the early years of marketing, where scholars and industry directed their attention towards the exchange of goods, and where the prime function of marketing was to find ways to bring its products to the market. The ramifications of Table 12.1 are numerous, but at its heart lies the true essence of a customer-centred management paradigm which proposes not *how to sell things* but rather on *how to create value* for the customer and in so doing, enhance the value of the firm or destination. Customer centricity should be at the heart of the strategy of any tourism business, and because of the high customer contact nature of most tourism businesses, must predominate in the culture of a tourism business (service culture is discussed later in this chapter). The following case study provides examples of the customer-centric approach in tourism firms and how they communicate their strategy.

Table 12.1 Comparison of the product-centric and customer-centric approaches (adapted from Shah et al. 2006)

	Product-centric approach	Customer-centric approach
Basic philosophy	Sell things to whoever will buy	All decisions start with the customer and are focused on present and future customer needs
Business orientation	Transaction oriented	Relationship oriented
Product positioning	Highlight features and advantages of product	Highlight benefits and value to customer
Organizational focus	Internally focused on ways to increase sales and development new products; marketing a separate function	Externally focused, based on making profits as the result of customer loyalty; sees employees as strategic resources; marketing orientation integrated into all departments
Performance metrics	Numbers of products; profit per product; market share by brand	Share of customer, customer satisfaction, customer loyalty, customer lifetime value, service climate
Selling philosophy	How many customers can we sell to? How many tourists can we attract?	How can we most appropriately satisfy each customer by providing as many products and services that are required to meet their individual needs?
Customer knowledge	Customer data a control mechanism	Customer knowledge a valuable asset

CASE STUDY
Customer-centric firms

This case study outlines three examples of how customer-centric firms communicate their strategies both internally (to employees) and externally (to the marketplace). The examples below are drawn from three tourism-related businesses: an airline, a restaurant company and a theme park. Each are industry leaders and respected for the ways in which they are able to engender a customer-oriented culture into their businesses. This, despite being large organizations employing thousands of people.

Disney

Disney is so committed to customers that they coined a term – *guestology* – for the science of knowing and understanding customers. Guestology challenges traditional management thinking. Instead of focusing on organizational design, managerial hierarchy and production systems to maximize organizational efficiency, it forces the organization to look systematically at the customer experience from the customer or guest's point of view. This concept reflects the importance placed on understanding precisely how Disney guests behave, what they want, need, value and expect from the Disney experience. Disney places the customer at the centre of what they call the Disney Service Cycle, which consists of four main elements: the service theme, service standards, delivery systems and integration.

Everything Disney does is based on customer wants, needs and behaviours. For example, hotel room doors at Disney have two peepholes – one at the usual height, and one at a child's level. And rubbish bins are placed at 27-foot intervals around the parks, the calculated distance a person would walk before dropping garbage on the ground. Disney also studies behaviour, such as how long a person would be willing to queue before becoming unhappy. The company then intervenes with entertainment designed to keep people occupied in queues. They have also studied how many drops the elevator in the Tower of Terror must have to satisfy customer quality standards. Disney seeks to measure everything that is important to customers and to manage each of these key elements continuously.

Virgin Blue

This Australian-based airline was launched as a low-cost airline in the Australian market in 2001. Virgin Blue uses a familiar formula pioneered by airlines such as Southwest Airlines and Ryanair eliminating costs such as free in-flight meals and beverages in favour of selling food on-board and using internet booking systems as its primary distribution method. The collapse of Ansett Australian Airlines (in September 2001) facilitated the accelerated growth of the company, particularly among the leisure travel market.

In an attempt to portray the airline as something more than just a 'no-frills' carrier, the company recently launched a campaign to attract business travellers and to demonstrate the way it values each and every individual customer (passenger). One of the methods used to convey their customer focus included a television advertisement showing a fictional businessman (named Tom Andrews), boarding a plane and settling in seat 7C. As Tom Andrews walks into the plane, the advertisement shows the cabin from *his* point of view. The audio which accompanies the advertisement broadcasts: 'This is a Virgin Blue flight as seen by passenger Tom Andrews.'

The advertisement then crosses to the same scene, this time from the perspective of the cabin crew member. When the cabin crew member looks down at Tom Andrews, *all she sees is a completely empty plane except for one seat (7C)*. She only sees Tom Andrews! The audio continues – 'This is passenger Tom Andrews as seen by Virgin Blue crew member, Shey Phillips.'

This campaign has been used in conjuction with other shifts in strategy by the airline including the incorporation of a frequent flyer program and departure lounges. This has helped Virgin Blue shift its marketing position and increase penetration of the business market by portraying itself as a *personal service provider* that values every passenger, rather than just a flying form of public transportation.

The Olive Garden Restaurant

The Olive Garden is a casual dining American restaurant chain specializing in Italian food. It bills itself as a traditional family restaurant with 'old world' inspired dishes. Founded in 1982 in Orlando, Florida, there are presently about 600 Olive Garden locations throughout the United States and Canada. In order to engender the importance of customers to their business, managers at The Olive Garden often use stories to illustrate how the company focuses on the needs of customers. One such story is about a customer named Larry, who after dining at an Olive Garden, wrote a letter to the company, praising the food but complaining about the chairs. Larry is a rather large man, and the armchairs did not allow Larry to sit comfortably in his chair. The company then ordered two 'Larry's Chairs' for *every* Olive Garden Restaurant. These chairs are discreetly substituted for more normal chairs when a particularly large person is taken to their table. This story, when explained to new employees, conveys the message of how far the company is willing to go to meet and respond to customers needs (Ford and Heaton 2001).

These three examples of customer-centric firms demonstrate how some companies can gain significant competitive advantage by being particularly customer focused.

Key sources

The Disney Institute (2001). *Be Our Guest: Perfecting the Art of Customer Service*. New York: The Disney Institute – Disney Editions.
Ford, R.C. and Heaton, C.P. (2001). Lessons from hospitality that can serve anyone. *Organizational Dynamics* 30(1), 30–47.

Discussion questions

1 Explain in your own words how each of these three companies use a customer focus as part of their firm strategy.

> 2 In relation to the three examples above, reflect on similar companies with whom you are familiar. Do you believe that they are truly customer centric? What could they do differently to improve their customer focus?
>
> 3 Identify three tourism firms who you believe would benefit from a customer focus, and list some strategies they might use to achieve this.

Important concepts in service management

As discussed above, the service management mindset is a relatively new one. This section identifies key concepts which encompass the service management perspective, and ones that are useful in understanding service-related issues in a tourism context.

Service encounter

A service encounter can be defined as the interaction between a tourist and a tourism firm through its frontline employees. The outcomes of service encounters thus depend on the skills, knowledge, personality, behaviour and performance of these employees. If successful, effective service encounters can lead to many favourable outcomes, including satisfaction, loyalty and positive word-of-mouth recommendation. It is therefore imperative that tourism firms understand how to manage these critical service encounters.

At the heart of service management is the unavoidable fact that a significant proportion of tourism experiences are delivered by people (tourism employees, managers, owners). The unfortunate irony about this fact is that many customer contact employees are the youngest and least trained of employees (more on that later). Although many services have become more reliant on technology (vending machines, airline self (or 'e') check in), person-to-person interactions still predominate in most tourism businesses. The employees who deliver the service obviously have a direct influence on tourists, as of course do owners, managers and other stakeholders who indirectly contribute to the service. Moreover, other people in the service environment at the time of service delivery, including other tourists, also play a part. The personal appearance, attitudes and behaviour of all involved, directly or indirectly, have an influence on a tourist's perception of a service.

From the tourist's perspective, the most immediate evidence of service quality is the service encounter itself. Interactions with service employees are the experiences that tourists remember best, and employees who are uncomfortable in dealing with tourists or who lack the training and expertise to meet expectations can cause tourists to retain unpleasant memories of a service experience. Service employees are thus the primary resource through which service businesses can gain a competitive advantage (Lovelock and Wirtz 2004).

A number of management approaches have been suggested which can help tourism businesses manage or control service encounters. Examples of these include:

1 *Scripts* – where service providers follow pre-determined statements, such as, 'would you like fries with that?'
2 *Role play training* – putting employees into mock service situations to assist them in correctly dealing with a range of circumstances.
3 *Clearly defined service processes* – a more general approach than scripts, but with clear expectations of steps of service.
4 *Engrained service culture* – embedding the importance of customers into the fabric of the organization.
5 *Effective recruitment/HRM* – ensuring that the right people are employed and that individual development continues throughout the term of employment.

Customer contact employees

Customer contact, or front line, employees have been given many labels, including 'boundary spanners', 'gatekeepers' and 'image makers' (Bowen and Schneider 1985). They are a tourism organization's primary interface with customers and, as such, are often perceived by the customer as *the* product. Bowen and Schneider (1985) insist that employees not only create and deliver the service, but also are the entire image of the organization. Within tourism businesses, service is performed for a customer by a service person (e.g. a waiter, front desk receptionist, a tour guide). From the customer's point of view, service is essentially presented by the performance of the staff who serve as the public face of the organization or in some cases, the destination. It should be noted that most services do have a tangible aspect which must also be acceptable to the customer, yet it is this package of tangible and intangible aspects that define a tourist's experience.

Many challenges exist in relation to the multidimensional role of service workers. For example, the same person must attend to operational (serving the customer) and marketing (up-selling) tasks simultaneously. This multiplicity of roles
in such jobs often leads to role conflict and stress. Lovelock (2004) suggests this
conflict is caused by three underlying relationship paradoxes:

1 Person-role conflict (conflict between what the job requires and the person's
   own personality).
2 Organizational-client conflict (the dilemma of whether an employee should act
   to please the client or adhere to company rules).
3 Interclient conflict (conflict between customers such as smoking in a non-smoking
   section, jumping queues or talking during a movie).

There is a problematic paradox in the tourism industry, in that the skills needed to
provide service quality are sometimes not in alignment with the skills often found
in tourism businesses front-line positions. This disconnect presents an array of
challenges for industry as, in many situations such as in restaurants and hotels, the
lesser-skilled, lesser-experienced and lesser-paid employees are the ones who contribute most to the tourist experience!

Bowen and Ford (2002) argue that managing the service employee is different
to managing employees located in positions with little or no customer contact.
There are six basic differences:

1 Service employees must be both task and interactive capable, because customers
   are present in the service 'factory' (producing and engaging simultaneously).
2 Attitudes and behaviours are more critical than technical skills for service
   employees (and skills can be taught more easily than attitude).
3 Formal mechanisms for employee control cannot be used with service employees. Instead, a service culture and climate must be in evidence to fill the gaps
   which form as the result of unexpected or unplanned customer-interactions or
   circumstances.
4 Emotions play a role with service employees, as observable facial and body displays create impressions, and emotional displays by service providers can have
   positive/negative effects on customers. Therefore, service employees, to be
   most effective, must be skilled to understand which emotions are appropriate in
   different circumstances (empathy when something has gone wrong, excited
   when a customer is, etc.).

5 Service employees must be trained to deal with role-related conflict. For example, if a customer is unhappy with a service standard, he might become angry with the service provider, even though the employee was doing their job as expected by the organization.

6 Service employees are expected to be 'part-time marketers'. This implies that service employees are expected to fully understand their firm's offerings and demonstrate enthusiasm for them. This can be enhanced through the concept known as 'internal marketing'. Here, a firm's products and service should first be marketed to its employees so that they are in the best position to 'sell' when interacting with customers.

Customer (tourist) satisfaction

The term *customer satisfaction* is used often as an ideal to which tourism businesses and destinations strive (refer to the note at the beginning of this chapter which explains the interchangeability of the terms customer and tourist). But what *exactly* is meant by the term? How is it measured? And is mere 'satisfaction' sufficient?

Customer satisfaction is difficult to define. Oliver (1997) concluded that everyone knows what customer satisfaction is, until they are asked to define it. Oliver did however define customer satisfaction as:

> a judgement that a product or service feature, or the product or service itself, provided (or is providing) a pleasurable level of consumption-related fulfilment ... (Oliver 1997: 13).

This section seeks not to provide in-depth detailed discussion as to its definition, but rather provides a brief overview of the construct, its importance and its implications (for a good source of information about customer satisfaction definitions, see Giese and Cote 2000).

Figure 12.2 illustrates some of the drivers of tourist satisfaction, highlighting the challenges in:

- determining specific drivers of satisfaction depending on the nature of the destination and the individual tourists;
- incorporating the right systems and training in order to maximize satisfaction levels to the greatest number of tourists possible.

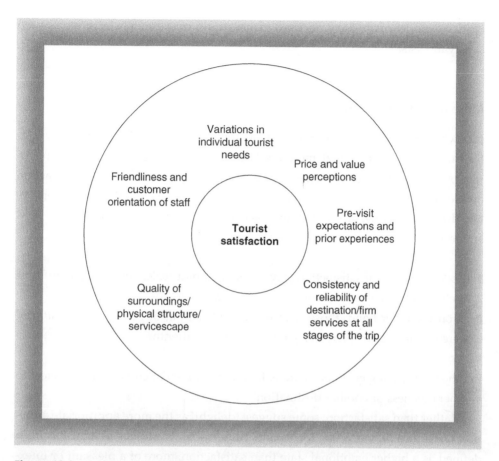

Figure 12.2 Factors which influence tourist satisfaction

Regardless of its definition or conceptualization, there is general agreement that when tourists are satisfied, a range of actions and behaviours follow. Tourists who are satisfied with a destination or tourism business:

1 are likely to become loyal and visit repeatedly,
2 will deepen their relationships with the destination and its individual service providers,
3 are more likely to recommend the destination to others,
4 demonstrate less price sensitivity.

It is therefore important for destination marketers as well as individual organizations within a destination to understand the importance of customer perceptions of their experiences and to work hard to measure and continually improve ways to satisfy tourists.

More than 'satisfaction'

Just when it seems safe to assume that customer 'satisfaction' is the ultimate aim for businesses, we find that merely *satisfied* customers may not be enough! An interesting study suggests a non-linear relationship between customer satisfaction and loyalty (Sasser Jr. and Jones 1995). These authors illustrate that customer loyalty does not increase proportionally as satisfaction levels increase (as logic would suggest it would). Their research concluded:

1 Moderate levels of satisfaction (say a 4 on a 5-point scale) equates to significant likelihood that customers will *defect* to a competitor, but
2 ... on the other hand, those who responded with at or near to *totally satisfied* were *six times* more likely to *repurchase* within 18 months.

In other words, any customer who is less than *fully* satisfied is likely to defect to another business or another destination!

Rather than satisfaction, some suggest 'delight' as the more appropriate ambition (Rust and Oliver 2000; Torres and Kline 2006). Customer delight has been defined as a higher emotional state than satisfaction, more of a pleasant or unexpected surprise. This type of provision, however, does not come without extra effort on the part of the tourism firm. Therefore, some suggest that a policy of customer delight is not sustainable, as the expectations of customers will continue to rise, making it more and more difficult to delight customers on subsequent visits. Nonetheless, the lesson is an interesting one, and one which tourism industry practitioners can learn from: We must do more than aim to merely satisfy our visitors!

Service quality

One of the more prominent themes in service management thinking centres on the idea of service quality. Service quality has been defined as a cognitive evaluation of a performance by a service provider (Parasuraman et al. 1988). There is broad agreement that in terms of conceptualizing and measuring service quality, its dimensions include some degrees (depending on the type of service) of reliability, responsiveness, tangibles, empathy and assurance.

Until the middle 1980s little work had been done to define service quality and identify those elements which determine how service quality could be delivered or measured. Before management can realistically call for improved service quality – it is vital to first:

(a) Clarify the strategic position and objectives of the organization (quality ambitions would be very different for a fast food restaurant versus a five-star hotel).
(b) Identify the relevant dimensions which comprise the delivery of service quality.

There is general agreement in the literature that quality judgments cause satisfaction, or that perceived service quality is an antecedent to satisfaction (Heskett et al. 1997). Both constructs are obviously closely related as each is concerned with how consumers experience a firm's offering and, although the terms are conceptually distinct, in practice they are often used interchangeably (Schneider and White 2004). Perhaps the most important points fundamental to understanding the two constructs are as follows:

(a) Satisfaction tends to be an emotional response ('that was a great experience, and I feel really good as a result').
(b) Quality is more of a descriptive evaluation ('the staff there are very caring and the service excellent').

However, whilst it is clear that the two constructs are highly correlated, researchers disagree on the causal direction of the relationships between them. Regardless of any debate as to distinctiveness or overlap in these two constructs, few doubt the importance of both, yet the ways to measure them remain controversial and unresolved. It is also clear that many aspects of satisfaction can be out of the control of a business (think of a crying baby on an overnight flight, loud customers in a quiet restaurant).

It is clear from this discussion that measuring service quality is particularly difficult, because different people rate individual dimensions of service in different ways and with different weightings of importance. One of the earliest models for service quality identified three dimensions of service quality (Sasser et al. 1978):

1 Materials
2 Facilities
3 Personnel

This early study highlights the importance of people in delivering service as well as highlighting the fact that service quality is not only about an *outcome*, but also about a *process*.

While these approaches differ, most agree that service quality is both elusive and multidimensional. In addition, agreement exists that services are more or less subjectively experienced and perceptions of quality should be as it is *perceived* by the customer, or by the person receiving the service. In his summary of the service quality research, Brady (2001) suggests that scholars have advanced various forms of two distinct models of service quality: SERVQUAL and the Nordic Model.

SERVQUAL

The first of these models is known as SERVQUAL and has five dimensions (Parasuraman et al. 1988: 8):

1 *Reliability* – accurate and dependable service.
2 *Responsiveness* – prompt and helpful service.
3 *Empathy* – caring and personalized attention.
4 *Assurance* – knowledgeable and trustworthy.
5 *Tangibles* – appearance of physical facilities.

These dimensions are used in a pre- and post-evaluation of a service in order to compare the variance between expectation and actual performance.

The SERVQUAL model is known as a 'gaps' model because of its measurement of the variance between expectations and performance. It has been used extensively in the services literature, and to a lesser extent in the tourism literature (see e.g. Kvist and Klefsjo 2006) although it is not without significant criticism (Coulthard 2004). Some of the primary criticisms of SERVQUAL include:

1 Concerns with the disconfirmation paradigm (asking a person to compare a service against their expectations for that service).

2 The lack of evidence as to the validity of the 'gaps' type model.

3 The lack of consistent dimensionality with the five-factor scale.

4 It's failure to work as an effective measure across different type of service industries.

The Nordic model

The second model, developed by Gronroos in the early 1980s, is known as the two-factor Nordic model. This model has two dimensions, a *technical* or *outcome* dimension, which might be referred to as the 'what'; and a *functional* or *process-related* dimension, which might be referred to as the 'how'.

As an example, a hotel guest will be provided with a hotel room, an airline passenger will be provided with transport, or a tourist with a bus tour of a city. All of these 'outcomes' of the service process are part of the perceived quality experience. However, a tourist's overall determination of quality is not based solely on the room, the arrival to the destination or the ride in the tour bus. There will be many interactions, or service encounters, between a service provider and a customer, which will influence the tourist's overall impressions of quality. The friendliness and professionalism of the front desk employee, the airline cabin crew and the tour bus operator, for example, will all influence the tourist's perceptions of quality. In other words, a tourist is influence by the actual service (the 'what') and the way in which the service was performed (the 'how').

The Nordic model also proposes other influences in total perceived service quality. For example, customer expectations can influence their final perceptions of quality, as can company image, which is thought to play a central role in customer perceptions of service quality. It is therefore important for tourism operators to manage their image in the proper manner, as the perceived image might affect quality perceptions. If, for example, a firm has a favourable image, minor mistakes are more likely to be forgiven. Conversely, if the image is negative, the impact of any mistake will often be considerably greater (Gronroos 2000).

Links between tourists, tourism employees and tourism business performance

Although we have been addressing the concept of service from the perspective of how to improve tourist satisfaction within a tourism firm or destination, individual organizations are generally motivated to initiate quality programs which can be directly tied to financial performance. In other words, business owners are most interested in profitability – hence any motivation to improve service must have direct implications for profitability.

Two related conceptual frameworks link internal organizational function to customers and firm performance outcome measures. These are as given below:

1 The service-profit chain.
2 Employee–customer linkage research.

Service-profit chain

The service-profit chain conceptual framework proposes a hypothetical chain of events which link the internal functioning of an organization to employee loyalty and productivity, service value, customer satisfaction and finally to revenue growth and profitability (Figure 12.3) (Heskett et al. 1997).

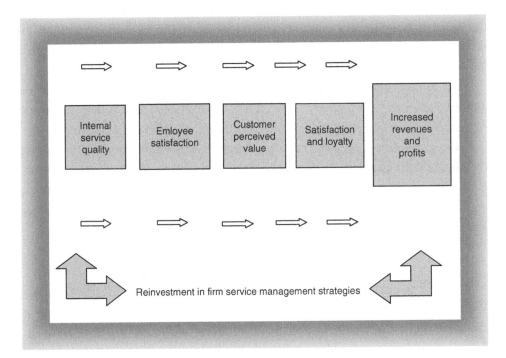

Figure 12.3   The service-profit chain (after Heskett et al. 1997)

Figure 12.3 highlights the fact that tourism firms would benefit from focusing on the left side of the chain, including investment in the various elements that make up the chain, rather than directly focusing on revenues and profits. The internal functioning of the organization is defined as what goes on within an organization in terms of workplace design, and those functions which facilitate employees' ability to service customers. The key aspects of the service-profit chain are as follows:

1 Customer satisfaction drives customer loyalty, which drives revenues and profits.
2 Customer perceived value drives customer satisfaction.
3 Employee satisfaction drives employee productivity which enhances customer value.
4 Solid internal organizational practices drive employee satisfaction.
5 Top-management leadership in the chain underlies the chain's success.

Employee–customer linkage research

The boundaries between employees and customers in most tourism organizations are fairly permeable – a condition termed 'psychological closeness' between employee and customer (Schneider and Bowen 1993). Because of the closeness between employees and customers in services, further interest in better understanding these links has become known as *linkage* research (Pugh et al. 2002). Linkage research is similar to the service-profit chain, in that it suggests a relationship between employees, customers and firm performance. However, linkage research focuses *explicitly* on employee perceptions of various interorganizational practices and the corresponding relationships to customer perceptions. In other words, linkage research is interested in a more detailed picture of the left-hand side of the service-profit chain (Figure 12.4).

The specific dimensions of internal organizational function mirror measures of organizational climate (discussed below). Linkage research finds the specific levers, or drivers, which *link* employee perceptions to customer perceptions. By doing so, management can become acutely aware of these areas which have the greatest influence on customers, and can therefore focus on improving those areas. Figure 12.4 illustrates the fundamental relationships evident in the linkage research stream, drawing assumptions that improved customer satisfaction will lead to corresponding improvements in organizational performance.

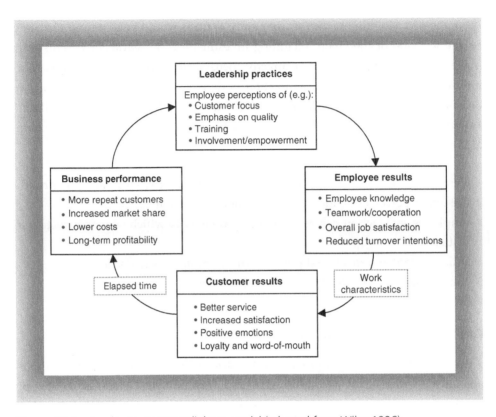

Figure 12.4 Employee–customer linkage model (adopted from Wiley 1996)

The main differences between linkage research and the service-profit chain approaches are as follows:

1 The service-profit chain purports employee satisfaction to be an important part of the chain, whereas linkage research suggests it is more about employee perceptions of service-climate factors which link to customer outcomes.
2 Linkage research focuses on the direct links between employee perceptions and customer perceptions, whereas the service-profit chain conceptualizes links directly to organizational performance criteria.

Given the importance that front-line service workers have in the effective provision of tourism services, it is logical to infer the corresponding importance of HRM practices. The next section examines HRM from a service perspective, suggesting that the task should be seen as a strategic role, central to the success of any service or tourism enterprise.

Strategic human resource management

Today's tourism businesses and destinations must always seek ways to obtain competitive advantage over other destinations and other businesses within a particular destination. There are many means available to try to achieve competitive advantage, including innovation, quality, price and location.

Another strategic approach aimed at competitive advantage involves focusing on the creation of particular strengths inside the firm. According to the resource-based view of a firm (RBV), competitive advantage can be achieved by capabilities that are internal to a firm – including expertise, systems and knowledge (Sheng-Hshiung and Yi-Chun 2004; Voola et al. 2004). Using the RBV approach, it has been found that firm-specific strategic variables explain more than twice as much profit variance as external (or industry-related) effects (Spanos et al. 2004). Apart from the relatively rare scenario of a natural-resource monopoly, the intangible resources of a firm (especially its human resources) are more likely to produce a real competitive advantage – because it is committed people who render the services that are difficult for competitors to emulate.

A gradual shift in the focus of HRM has occurred since the early 1980s, mirrored by the gradually diminishing use of the term *personnel management*. The old human resource function in organizations was often been seen as a passive, administrative function (payroll, benefits, files, etc.). In fact, in a more traditional (non-service) management approach, employees are considered as *costs* rather than as revenue generating resources. However, a *strategic* view (rather than an *administrative* view) places great importance on people as a means to gain competitive advantage, particularly in service businesses with high frequency of employee–customer interaction. Huselid (1995: 636) encapsulated the idea this way:

The belief that individual employee performance has implications for firm-level outcomes has been prevalent among academics and practitioners for many years. Interest in this area has recently intensified, however, as scholars have begun to argue that, collectively, a firm's employees can also provide a unique source of competitive advantage that is difficult for competitors to replicate.

So a strategic human resources management (SHRM) approach is largely about integrating the human resource function into the strategic planning and operations of a business, particularly in circumstances where customers and employee interaction occurs frequently. Wright and McMahan (1992: 298) defined SHRM as 'the pattern of planned human resource deployments and activities intended to enable the firm to achieve its goals' and suggested its application implies four components:

1 A focus on a firm's 'human resources' (i.e. people) as the primary resource to be strategically leveraged as a source of competitive advantage.
2 The concept of 'activities' highlight HR programs, policies and practices as the means to gain competitive advantage.
3 Both 'pattern' and 'plan' describe the goal and the process of strategy; a consistent alignment or design which could also be described as 'fit'. ... vertical fit with the firm's strategy and horizontal fit with all HR activities aligned.
4 All planned HR activities are purposeful and focused on goal achievement.

It is therefore suggested that tourism industry practitioners should provide greater emphasis to the human resource function in their organization in order to enhance tourist experiences and organizational performance. The following case study provides an example of a large international hotel company that made this strategic shift in HR thinking.

CASE STUDY
InterContinental Hotels Group: evolution to a strategic approach to HRM

InterContinental Hotels Group (IHG) is the world's most global hotel company and the largest by number of rooms. The Group has over 3700 owned, leased, managed and franchised hotels and 5 58 000 guest rooms across nearly 100 countries and territories. IHG owns a portfolio of well-recognized and respected brands – including InterContinental Hotels & Resorts, Crowne Plaza Hotels & Resorts and Holiday Inn Hotels & Resorts.

Its current stated corporate strategy emphasizes building brand performance through delivery of a more consistent brand experience for its customers. The company recognizes that people – the ongoing development of vibrant individuals to lead the growth strategy – are of paramount importance to the goal of building brand performance.

Across the company, the HR function has changed over the past 20–25 years along the following general pattern:

1 *1980s* – A 'personnel management' approach, driven by policy creation, procedures, and industry relations, dealing with unions and administrative issues.
2 *1990s* – Evolution to a 'HRM' approach, where training and development and Employee Champion activities were added to the personal and administration issues of the 1980s.
3 *2000s* – A total rethink took place, challenging the ways in which the HR function was integrated into the business. The HR function now works in partnership with operations and strategic planners and partners and has been completely restructured to accommodate the changed focus.

In trying to break free from the old HR model, the company undertook the following steps:

1 A thorough assessment of all HR functions and how and by whom they were being accomplished.
2 A series of meetings took place with senior executives (inside and outside of the company) to find out exactly what senior managers wanted from HR. The message was clear. Senior managers made clear the need for:
   (a) Business-knowledgeable people in HR roles – who understand key performance metrics and important success drivers for the company.
   (b) HR managers to work as integrated partners in the business, providing relevant HR advice, guidance, systems and strategies.
   (c) Mature dialogue between HR and other senior management functions.
   (d) Less focus on administrative/bureaucratic functions and a greater emphasis on change management and strategic partnerships.
3 A new HR structure was formed which included a separation of the recruitment function (currently called 'talent resourcing') and the developmental function (now called 'talent development'). This was coupled with the need to have high calibre specialists delivering improved outcomes in these areas to the business.

4 Specializations became centralized across geographical regions, thus reducing or eliminating duplication in activity and process. For example, one highly trained professional could oversee the 'talent resourcing' function across five to six hotels in one geographical area.

5 Administration functions were localized, and in many cases outsourced or re-allocated to other functional or operating departments who readily accommodate this work. For example, payroll function were distributed to payroll departments and line-level recruitment handed back to departments, thus eliminating the unnecessary delays and bureaucracy of line-level recruitment becoming bogged down in administration.

These strategies created a more strategic and singular long-term future focus, allowing the right type of people to undertake important roles, where traditionally, HR 'generalists' were asked to recruit, train, develop staff and administer which was merely delivering a day-to-day operational focus.

These strategies have created a whole new way of operating, where the HRM function is fully integrated into the hotel operation, where the senior HR managers are part of the senior management group at hotel, regional, national and international levels, and where the right focus is placed on the tasks which HR can help provide in order for the company to most effectively manage the people part of its business.

The journey to ensure that HR creates value, drives performance and delivers measurable results to the business continues in IHG as part of the companies overall strategy to provide the best service and results that it can to its people, customers, owners and shareholders.

Acknowledgements

This case study is derived based on collaborative work undertaken between The University of Queensland and IHG Australia. We are particularly grateful to Chris Bulmer, Regional Director of Human Resources for IHG (Queensland and Northern Territory and PNG) for his assistance in preparing this case study (InterContinental Hotels Group Annual Report and Annual Review, 2005).

Discussion questions

1 What is meant by SHRM? How is it different from traditional HRM?
2 How might the new approach taken by IHG improve the company's service focus?
3 What challenges do you believe face HR managers in today's employment markets?

Service culture and climate

Every organization, whether intended or not, has a culture of some kind. Culture, from an organizational point of view, is often defined as the values and norms embedded into an organization. An organizational culture, particularly in a service business has the ability to fill the gaps between:

1 What the organization can anticipate and train its people do deal with.
2 The opportunities and problems that arise in daily encounters with customers (Ford and Heaton 2001).

Since managers cannot supervise every interaction which takes place between employees and tourists, it is important for tourism service organizations to develop a predominating norm of behaviour which is focused on customers and service quality. Such an approach minimizes the gaps which unforseen circumstances might cause in services and also work to motivate unsupervized employees. One such strategy is to create a *service climate*.

The study of climate is drawn from organizational psychology, a field that seeks to better understand how individuals behave, or are likely to behave, in an organization or business setting. This focus is particularly important when studying tourism service businesses because of the aforementioned 'psychological closeness' between employees and tourists in tourism-related businesses. Knowledge gleaned from the study of individuals in organizational settings can be applied in order to assist organizations function more effectively – a generally accepted precursor to hard performance measures, such as profits.

Organizational climate is defined as employee perceptions of the practices and procedures in the organization (Denison 1996). It differs from culture in that it represents an assessment of how employees perceive various aspects of an organization, whereas culture represents the values and norms, often the aspirations of management. Climate represents how well these aspirations are actually perceived by employees and those who come into contact with an organization. These aspirations are often communicated through artefacts, stories and myths, like the 'Larry's Chair' story mentioned earlier.

Climate is normally obtained by measuring respondent perceptions of what goes on around them, in terms of organizational events, policies, practices, expectations and so on. Tagiuri (1968: 25) defined climate as:

> a relatively enduring quality of the total environment that (a) is experienced by the occupants; (b) influences their behaviour; and (c) can be described in terms of the values of a particular set of characteristics (or attributes) of the environment.

A service climate represents the degree to which all of a firm's activities, policies and practices are focused on service quality and customer satisfaction. Schneider and White (2004: 100) summarize it as follows:

> So, when employees perceive that they are rewarded for delivering quality service *and* when employees perceive that management devotes time, energy, and resources to service quality *and* when employees receive the training they require to effectively deal with diverse customers, *then* a positive service climate is more likely to be the theme or meaning attached to these experiences.

When all of the aggregate conditions are present for excellent service to be provided to customers, a positive climate for service is said to exist.

Climate is usually measured by using a survey methodology. Many best practice tourism organizations employ climate measures as a part of their organizational learning process. With regular measures of an organizational climate, progressive-thinking companies use the results to improve employee perceptions, and then base improvement outcomes as a part of performance measurement (see the final section on Balanced Scorecard for ways in which service climate can be used strategically).

Measuring performance: using a balanced scorecard

Sound management practices align the strategy of tourism firms with operations, human resources and performance measures. Tourism businesses must be tourist-centric, and understand that their employees are paramount to success. Traditionally, however, organizational performance has been based only on a range of financial metrics. Kaplan and Norton (1992) devised a new way to link firm strategy (value drivers) with measuring performance. They named this system the *'Balanced Scorecard'*. Recognizing some of the weaknesses and vagueness of previous management approaches, the Balanced Scorecard approach provides a clear prescription as to what companies should measure in order to 'balance' the financial perspective.

The Balanced Scorecard is a management and measurement system that enables organizations to clarify their vision and strategy and translate them into action. It provides feedback around both the internal business processes and external outcomes in order to continuously improve strategic performance and results. When fully deployed, the Balanced Scorecard transforms strategic planning from an academic exercise into the nerve centre of an enterprise.

The Balanced Scorecard allows managers to look at the business from many different perspectives, based on the strategic objectives of the particular organization. Its application provides answers to four basic questions:

1 How do customers see us?
2 What must we be good at in order to satisfy our customers (internal processes)?
3 How can we continue to improve and grow (learning and training)?
4 How do we look to our owners/shareholders (financial picture)?

When used effectively, the Balanced Scorecard forces managers and employees to focus on key drivers of organizational success. In many ways, the Balanced Scorecard becomes a quantitative yardstick which measures various aspects of the service-profit chain or the linkage research model discussed earlier in the chapter. Whilst there are challenges in its implementation, such as costs, time, expertise and references, the Balanced Scorecard can be an effective conceptual tool or program by which service organizations can be managed and measured.

CASE STUDY
Pier Nine Seafood Restaurant and Oyster Bar, Brisbane, Australia

Pier Nine Seafood Restaurant and Oyster Bar is an Australian icon located in Brisbane, Australia. It is Australia's most awarded seafood restaurant, located on the Eagle Street Pier complex on the river downtown.

Pier Nine's owner, Matthew Hill-Smith insists the success of Pier Nine is based on his vision that 'by giving uncompromising quality of service and seafood, we create a total experience'. This is coupled with Matthew's credo that 'quality only happens when you care enough to do your best' and this creates a culture that thrives. From the back of house to the floor staff and finally the customers, the Pier Nine experience is one that Matthew has created based on quality, innovation and a single-minded determination for excellence.

Always open minded to new ways to improve the business, Matthew attended a seminar in 2004 which highlighted the benefits of implementing a Balanced Scorecard type of system into his restaurant for the purpose of:

(a) Measuring the performance of the business.
(b) Paying staff bonuses based on key metrics *additional to* financial performance.

An assessment was then made of the program's viability in his restaurant. Step one was to clarify the strategic drivers of the business. These were determined to be:

1 Customer satisfaction – based on the entire experience including food, service, value and ambiance.
2 Employee attitudes, opinions and satisfaction.
3 Financial performance – revenue growth and profitability.
4 Human resource practices.
5 Individual performance.

Over the course of the following 12 months, much work was undertaken in consultation with managers and employees to create a diagnostic system which would effectively measure the key strategic drivers listed above. This was designed to help Matthew identify and gauge the long-term performance of the business. This performance system included specific systems which were designed to measure:

1 *Customer satisfaction*: A detailed and complex customized mystery shopper program was created, where about 15 mystery shopper visits were undertaken during every 6-month period. The results are tabulated and scored, with detailed reports which outline opportunities and provide scores for each aspect of each visit. Each report and the corresponding scores are emailed to every employee on the Pier Nine internal email server.

2 *Employee opinions*: A customized organizational climate survey was developed, which integrated service-climate factors coupled with other measures such as staff turnover intentions, internal service quality and perceptions of owner commitment to excellence. The survey is administered every 6 months with scores continually assessed for improvement and opportunities to improve. Managers meet in teams to strategize ways to improve various aspects of the survey results to ensure continuous work is done to improve the way employees perceive their workplace.

3 *Financial performance*: A matrix was created which was modelled on the company budgets for sales and profits. Points were then allocated based on the achievement of the criteria.

4 *Human resource practices/training*: An audit is undertaken twice per year which assesses hiring practices, training, inductions and continuous staff development processes. The results of this audit are scored on a 1–100 scale.

5 *Individual performance*: Each member of staff was given a comprehensive appraisal of their performance by their respective supervisors, and a point score allocated.

The items above are weighted for importance with weightings varying from 1 year to the next, depending on which areas the owner believes need particular focus for that year. All full-time staff and management are given specific goals whereby bonuses are paid provided certain targets where achieved. Table 12.2 provides an example of the way each of the metrics in the Balanced Scorecard are measured and linked to management bonuses.

As a result of this program, major changes have occurred at Pier Nine. Significant bonuses were paid based on the results. Secondly, the entire team at Pier Nine began to rally around the exact performance measures which the owner identified as important drivers for success. By focusing on customers, employees, training and individual performance ('What gets measured gets managed!'), sales and profits naturally flowed. The team has been able to share in small wins, work more closely in teams trying to make their targets and feel as though they could share in the successes of the business.

Rather then driving success through financial measures only, the Balanced Scorecard measurement system has altered the focus to the important drivers of success and have helped take Pier Nine to its best performance in its history.

Acknowledgement

This case study was derived from the author of this chapter in conjunction with Matthew Hill-Smith, proprietor of Pier Nine Seafood Restaurant and Oyster Bar.

Table 12.2 A sample template for a restaurant Balanced Scorecard

	Customers	Employees	Financials		HR related		Totals		
	Mystery shopper average (of 100)	Service-climate scale (of 100)	Profits to budget (of 100)	Revenues to budget (of 100)	HR/training Practices (of 100)	Individual appraisal score (of 100)	Total average (of 100)	Maximum bonus per period	Bonus payout
Employee 1	75	60	65	65	75	80	70	$5000	$3500
Employee 2	75	60	65	65	75	50	65	$3000	$1950
Etc.									

Discussion questions

1 Explain why a Balanced Scorecard would be a particularly useful tool to measure performance in a service-oriented business.
2 Select three different tourism businesses and then create a customized Balanced Scorecard system, justifying each of the aspects chosen and the weightings assigned.
3 What challenges could you foresee in the implementation of a Balanced Scorecard?

Chapter overview

This chapter has introduced 'service' as a vital aspect to understanding contemporary tourism. The context for this chapter is that tourism is an assemblage of inter-related elements, each of which contributes to a tourist's overall experience. By understanding some of the key drivers for managing service, a more holistic understanding for managing tourism destination and organizational performance can occur. The principle of placing tourist perceptions as the predominate and central tenet for all tourism management and planning activities was introduced. This was explained as a contrasting view to conventional management thinking, which places a more industrial or manufacturing paradigm to management, focused on organizational systems, efficiencies, waste minimization, cost controls, distribution (and the like) as the core of management activities. A number of examples were provided by way of a case study which illustrated some specific customer-(tourist) centric strategies currently employed by various tourism businesses.

A number of key concepts were identified as important for understanding service management in tourism. These concepts include the service encounter – and the important role which front-line tourism employees play in tourist experiences; a review of customer satisfaction in the context of tourism; issues of service quality – conceptualization and measurement; and the important links which connect tourists, tourism employees and tourism organizational performance. A more appropriate HRM approach for the tourism industry was introduced, suggesting that HRM should adopt a 'strategic' focus, thus allowing tourism organizations to turn their people into an important resource for competitive advantage. SHRM was further explained by way of a case study of a major international hotel company. Creating a service-oriented culture and climate was introduced, as was a modern approach to linking tourism strategy with performance measurement, called the Balanced Scorecard.

Whilst the chapter has offered a range of concepts and frameworks for understanding why service is such an important aspect of managing tourist destinations, it must be remembered that tourism is complex and that there is no 'off the shelf' approach to tourism management or to managing the service aspect of tourism. However, this introduction is meant to provide a conceptual starting point for better understanding tourism from a service perspective.

Self-review questions

1 Why is it important to understand service management principles in the context of tourism?

2 Why are service encounters such an important concept to understand in tourism?

3 What is meant by the terms 'boundary spanners'? What is the significance of this term to tourism managers?

4 What is meant by the 'problematic paradox' referred to in relation to tourism employees and required skills?

5 Explain the differences between 'tourist satisfaction' and 'service quality'.

6 Why might 'satisfaction' not be an ambitious enough aim for tourism managers?

7 What is SERVQUAL? How might this concept (and the component parts) be useful to understanding the management of tourism organizations and destinations?

8 What is the service-profit chain? How can this principle be used to facilitate improved tourism business performance?

9 How can tourism businesses utilize SHRM as a path towards competitive advantage?

10 What is the Balanced Scorecard? Why is this type of approach sensible in tourism?

Recommended reading

1 Albrecht, K. and Zemke, R. (2002). *Service America in the New Economy*, 2nd edn. New York: McGraw-Hill.
A recent version of one of the first and the most often cited texts on services.

2 Bowen, J. and Ford, R.C. (2002). Managing service organizations: does having a 'thing' make a difference? *Journal of Management* 28(3), 447–469.
Furthering the discussion on differences between managing services versus managing things.

3 Carlzon, J. (1987). *Moments of Truth*. Cambridge: Ballinger Publishing.
Seminal book from a services management practitioner.

4 Gronroos, C. (2000). *Service Management and Marketing: A Customer Relationship Management Approach*, 2nd edn. West Sussex: John Wiley & Sons, Ltd.
A text from one of the top service management academics.

5 Heskett, J.L., Sasser, W.E. and Schlesinger, L.A. (1997). *The Service-Profit Chain*. New York: Free Press.
The book which followed a series of oft-cited journal articles.

6 Lovelock, C. and Wirtz, J. (2004). *Services Marketing: People, Technology, Strategy*, 5th edn. Upper Saddle River, NJ: Pearson/Prentice Hall.
An excellent text.

7 Parasuraman, A., Berry, L. and Zeithaml, V. (1988). SERVQUAL: A multiple-item scale for measuring consumer perceptions of service quality. *Journal of Retailing* 64(1), 12–40.
The seminal article on service quality measures.

8 Pugh, S.D., Dietz, J., Wiley, J.W. and Brooks, S.M. (2002). Driving service effectiveness through employee–customer linkages. *Academy of Management Executive* 16(4), 73–84.
Explains the employee–customer linkage model.

9 Schneider, B. and Bowen, D. (1995). *Winning the Service Game*. Boston: Harvard Business School Press.
An oft-cited book by two of the most renowned services academics.

10 Schneider, B. and White, S. (2004). *Service Quality Research Perspectives*. Thousand Oaks, CA: Sage.
A very good summary outlining the history of service quality research.

11 Lawler, E. and Trotter, C. (2001). *Lessons in Service from Charlie Trotter*. Berkeley, CA: Ten Speed Press.
A very practical book on service from one of the world's most famous chefs.

Recommended web sites

DiscoverHongKong – Quality Tourism Services Scheme: www.discoverhongkong.com/eng/mustknow/qts/index.jhtml; www.tourism.gov.hk/hospitable/hospitality.html
Quality label for Swiss tourism: www.tourism.lt/nsv/engl/ WTO%20seminar/Vilnius_leaflet.pdf
South African Tourism Services Association: http://www.satsa.co.za/pages/
The Virtual Tourist: http://www.virtualtourist.com/

References cited

Albrecht, K. (1988). *At America's Service: How your Company Can Join the Customer Service Revolution*. New York: Warner Books.

Bowen, J. and Ford, R.C. (2002). Managing service organizations: does having a 'thing' make a difference? *Journal of Management* 28(3), 447–469.

Bowen, D.E. and Schneider, B. (1985). Boundary-spanning role employees and the service encounter: some guidelines for management and research. In J. Czepiel, M. Solomon and C. Suprenant (eds), *The Service Encounter*, pp. 127–147. Lexington: Lexington Books.

Brady, M. (2001). Some new thoughts on conceptualizing perceived service quality: a hierarchical approach. *Journal of Marketing* 65(3), 34–49.

Coulthard, L. (2004). Measuring service quality: a review and critique of research using SERVQUAL. *International Journal of Marketing Research* 46(4), 479–497.

Denison, D. (1996). What is the difference between organizational culture and organizational climate? A native's point of view on a decade of paradigm wars. *Academy of Management Review* 21(3), 619–654.

Drucker, P.F. (1954). *The Practice of Management*. New York: HarperCollins.

Fisk, R., Brown, S. and Bitner, M.J. (1993). Tracking the evolution of the services marketing literature. *Journal of Retailing*, 60(1), 61–100.

Ford, R.C. and Heaton, C.P. (2001). Lessons from hospitality that can serve anyone. *Organizational Dynamics* 30(1), 30–47.

Giese, J.L. and Cote, J.A. (2000). Defining customer satisfaction. *Academy of Marketing Science Review* 2000(1), 1–24.

Gronroos, C. (2000). *Service Management and Marketing: A Customer Relationship Management Approach*, 2nd edn. West Sussex: John Wiley & Sons, Ltd.

Heskett, J.L., Sasser, W.E. and Schlesinger, L.A. (1997). *The Service-Profit Chain*. New York: Free Press.

Huselid, M.A. (1995). The impact of human reason management practices on turnover, productivity, and corporate financial program. *Academy of Management Journal* 38, 635–672.

Kandampully, J. (2002). *Services Management: The New Paradigm in Hospitality*. Frenchs Forest, NSW: Pearson Education Australia.

Kandampully, J. (2006). The new customer-centred business model for the hospitality industry. *International Journal of Contemporary Hospitality Management* 18(3), 173–187.

Kaplan, R.S. and Norton, D.P. (1992). The balanced scorecard – measures that drive performance. *Harvard Business Review* 70(1), 71–79.

Kvist, A. and Klefsjo, B. (2006). Which service quality dimensions are important in inbound tourism? *Managing Service Quality* 16(5), 520–537.

Lovelock, C. and Wirtz, J. (2004). *Services Marketing: People, Technology, Strategy*, 5th edn. Upper Saddle River, NJ: Pearson/Prentice Hall.

Oliver, R. (1997). *Satisfaction: A Behavioral Perspective on the Consumer*. New York: McGraw-Hill.

Parasuraman, A., Berry, L. and Zeithaml, V. (1988). SERVQUAL: a multiple-item scale for measuring consumer perceptions of service quality. *Journal of Retailing* 64(1), 12–40.

Pugh, S.D., Dietz, J., Wiley, J.W. and Brooks, S.M. (2002). Driving service effectiveness through employee–customer linkages. *Academy of Management Executive* 16(4), 73–84.

Rust, R. and Oliver, R. (2000). Should we delight the customer? *Journal of Academy of Marketing Science* 28(1), 86–94.

Sasser, Jr. E. and Jones, T.O. (1995). Why satisfied customers defect. *Harvard Business Review* 73(November–December), 88–99.

Sasser, W., Olsen, R. and Wyckoff, D. (1978). *Management of Service Operations: Text and Cases*. Boston: Allyn and Bacon.

Schneider, B. and Bowen, D. (1993). The service organization: human resources management is crucial. *Organizational Dynamics* 21(4), 39–43.

Schneider, B. and White, S. (2004). *Service Quality Research Perspectives*. Thousand Oaks, CA: Sage.

Shah, D., Rust, R., Parasuraman, A., Staelin, R. and Day, G.S. (2006). The path to customer centricity. *Journal of Service Research* 9(2), 113–124.

Sheng-Hshiung, T. and Yi-Chun, L. (2004). Promoting service quality in tourist hotels: the role of HRM practices and service behavior. *Tourism Management* 25, 471–481.

Sheth, J.N., Sisodia, R.S. and Sharma, A. (2000). The antecedents and consequences of customer-centric marketing. *Academy of Marketing Science Journal* 28(1), 55–66.

Spanos, Y., Zaralis, G. and Lioukas, S. (2004). Strategy and industry effects on profitability: evidence from Greece. *Strategic Management Journal* 25, 139–165.

Tagiuri, R. (1968). *The Concept of Organizational Climate*. Boston: Harvard University Press.

Torres, E. and Kline, S. (2006). From satisfaction to delight: a model for the hotel industry. *International Journal of Contemporary Hospitality Management* 18(4), 290–301.

Voola, R., Carlson, J. and West, M. (2004). Emotional intelligence and competitive advantage: examining the relationship from a resource-based view. *Strategic Change* 13(2), 83–93.

Wiley, J.W. (1996). Linking survey data to the bottom line. In A.I. Kraut (ed.), *Organizational Surveys: Tools for Assessment and Change*, pp. 330–359. San Francisco: Jossey-Bass.

Wright, P. and McMahan, G. (1992). Theoretical perspectives for strategic human resource management. *Journal of Management* 18(2), 295–320.

Section 5
Tourism Futures

Chapter **13**

Tourism in the twenty-first century: contemporary tourism in an uncertain world

Chapter objectives

After reading this chapter you will

- Be able to appreciate some of the key factors influencing tourism in this century
- Understand why the condition of the physical environment is directly and indirectly significant for the future of tourism
- Understand the potential significance of climate change for tourism environments and destinations
- Be able to identify some of the difficulties associated with predicting tourist flows and patterns
- Understand the implications for tourism of the end of easily accessible oil supplies
- Be able to appreciate the role that aviation plays with respect to both climate change and energy supply issues in tourism
- Appreciate the value of scenarios as a decision-making tool

Introduction

The future, by definition, is unknown. Trying to predict what the future will bring has become an important element in tourism management because of the need to try and bring a degree of control and certain to business management processes as well as providing desired returns for destinations. Yet such processes are extremely difficult because of the possibilities of 'wildcard' – high impact, low probability – events occurring that affects the consumption and production of tourism. Since 2000, there has been a large number of wildcard events that have affected tourism patterns and flows at a global scale. These include:

- Terrorist attacks such as September 11 or the bombings in Bali.
- Disease outbreaks such as severe acute respiratory syndrome (SARS), foot and mouth disease in the UK or avian flu outbreaks.
- Economic events such as a rapid increase in the price of fuel.
- Political events such as changes in boarding and passport requirements for travellers as a result of increased concerns over security. This also includes sudden changes in terms of what you can take onto aircraft as hand luggage.

To wildcard events there are also a number of other trends that contribute to an increasingly complex business environment for tourism. These include:

- Demographic changes in development countries, such as an aging population and increase in the number of single-parent families.
- Rapid population growth in the developing world.
- Increased urbanization on a global scale.
- Global environmental change (GEC), including climate change and changes in water availability.
- Increasing costs of energy, particularly with respect to the costs of oil.

All of these trends affect the production and consumption of tourism. Production is affected because the resource base of tourism is changed. Consumption is impacted both directly and indirectly. An example of a direct impact is changing costs to get to destinations as a result of increases in the price of fuel. Such an example also highlights that the accessibility of a destination is not just determined by the relative travel distance between a generating area and the destination in terms of kilometres or miles but also in terms of cost. Indirect impacts of the above trends on consumption relate to the overall contribution of these trends to the state of the economy as economic downturns tend to correspond with slowdowns in outbound travel. Ultimately, underlying the health of the economy is the health of the environment, therefore issues of GEC are increasingly influencing consideration of trends in tourism (Figure 13.1).

Trying to anticipate the future of tourism may be a particularly fraught task, especially as there is a very large body of research that suggests that experts in various areas seldom generate better predictions than non-experts who have received some training, and that the predictions of experts are completely outperformed by those made by simple statistical models (Hall 2005b). Furthermore, most experts overestimate their ability to perform accurately in comparison with non-experts, meaning that experts are overconfident in their knowledge and forecasting capacities. In his review of the work of futurists, Sherden (1998) concluded that meteorologists were not always correct, but had by far the best accuracy compared to economists, stock-market analysts, population researchers, management prophets and social-trend spotters. All of this does not mean that trying to predict or anticipate the future is not without value. From a business perspective, examining the future enables firms to anticipate new business conditions and develop new strategies. From a destination perspective, reflections on the future enable consideration of how to maintain or improve the qualities of a destination and work towards desired futures. Importantly, such exercises should always highlight that in terms of wildcards and trends there are opportunities as well as challenges. What may be damaging for one destination or firm may be an opportunity for another (Gössling and Hall 2006a). Similarly, wildcard events in one location will any affect so much of the tourism system and other parts of the system will be unaffected or may even benefit from events elsewhere. Furthermore, as humans make their own futures the future is not set in stone.

Growth in international tourism versus global environmental change?

In examining the future of tourism there appears to be almost a paradoxical situation between different scenarios of what directions tourism may take over the next 20 years. WTO's (1997) *Tourism 2020 Vision* forecast that international arrivals are

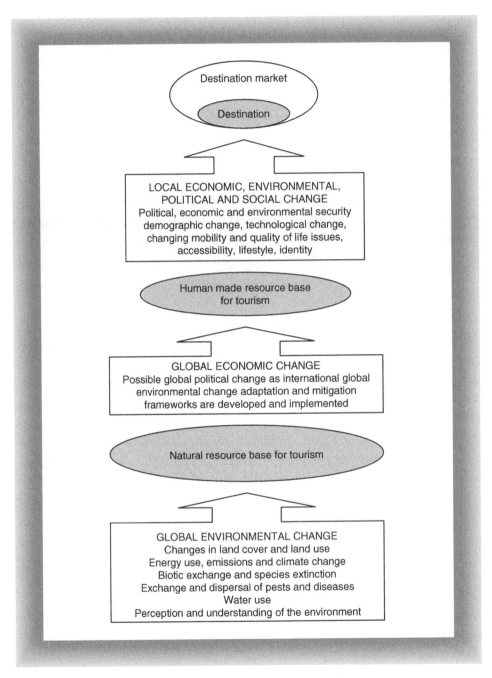

Figure 13.1 Trends and influences affecting contemporary tourism

expected to reach nearly 1.6 billion by the year 2020. Of these worldwide arrivals in 2020, 1.2 billion are forecast to be intraregional and 378 million long-haul travellers. As the growth of international tourism is predicted to increase substantially so to is the amount of air travel with growth in aviation outstripping growth in surface-bound transport. The two major aircraft manufacturers Boeing (2003) and Airbus (2003) predict that air travel will continue to grow rapidly over the next two decades, with average annual growth rates of 5.0–5.2 per cent to 2022/2023. By 2022, the number of aircraft is predicted to increase by 90 per cent to about 20 500, while the number of installed seats will more than double to reach 4.5 million (Airbus 2003). Boeing (2003) also predicts that competition for markets will be strong, as a result of continued economic growth in key markets and continued deregulation of aviation markets leading to more airline entrants, lower fares and improved networks. As a result of growth in the number of aircraft worldwide and demand for travel, the overall distances of flights are predicted to increase, with the average distance flown growing from 1437 kilometres in 2002 to 1516 kilometres in 2022 (Airbus 2003). In addition, it is estimated that a large share of the current fleet of aircraft (60 per cent) will still be in operation 20 years from now (Boeing 2003). The estimated scale of international tourism growth, as well as the enthusiasm of the tourism industry for such expansion is well illustrated in the World Tourism Organization's (WTO) 2020 vision:

> By the year 2020, tourists will have conquered every part of the globe as well as engaging in low orbit space tours, and maybe moon tours. The Tourism 2020 Vision study forecasts that the number of international arrivals worldwide will increase to almost 1.6 billion in 2020. This is 2.5 times the volume recorded in the late 1990s … Although the pace of growth will slow down to a forecast average 4 per cent a year – which signifies a doubling in 18 years, there are no signs at all of an end to the rapid expansion of tourism… Despite the great volumes of tourism forecast for 2020, it is important to recognise that international tourism still has much potential to exploit … the proportion of the world's population engaged in international tourism is calculated at just 3.5 per cent (WTO 2001: 9, 10).

Yet at the same time that there are predictions of massive growth in international tourism as well as positive comments from the UNWTO with respect to tourism's potential to contribute to poverty alleviation, there is simultaneously increased concerns over the impacts of political insecurity, cost and availability of energy, and GEC on tourism (Gössling 2002). Indeed, even though the WTO (2003) has described the interaction of tourism and climate change as a 'two-way relationship' one of the implications of the growth of the global aviation fleet is that there will be longer operation times of aircraft and concomitant high fuel use of the older models that will still be in use (Gössling and Hall 2006b; Peeters et al. 2007). Therefore, it seems almost inevitable that if global tourism can grow at the forecast rate then it will only do so at great cost to the environment. These issues are a concern because with respect to climate change alone global warming is destined to have a far more destructive and earlier impact than previously estimated. The Fourth Assessment Report of the Intergovernmental Panel on Climate Change, indicates that (McKie 2007):

- The frequency of hurricanes and storms will increase dramatically.
- Sea levels will rise over the century by around half a metre.
- Snow will disappear from all but the highest mountains.
- Deserts will spread.
- Oceans will become acidic, leading to the destruction of coral reefs and atolls.
- Deadly heat waves will become more prevalent.

Such changes will undoubtedly have substantial affects on the relative attractiveness of many destinations, an issue which is already being taken seriously by the business community. For example, UK travel insurer Churchill has commissioned two reports on the future of travel. One report (Churchill 2006a) indicated that because of climate change and too many visitors, some certain sites and attractions 'could be in danger of disappearing by 2020'. The destinations that were identified and the reasons why they are regarded as threatened are list below:

- *Puerto de Mazarron* (South-East Spain): Outbreaks of malaria as well as increased threats of flash floods, heat stress and forest fires.
- *Everglades* (Florida, USA): Increasing hurricane danger.
- *Athens* (Greece): Increase in summer temperatures.
- *Crete* (Greece): Increase in high temperatures, increased desertification and water scarcity.
- *Cologne Cathedral* (Germany): Environmental pollution.
- *Dalmatian coast* (Croatia): Increase in visitation.

- *Kathmandu Valley* (Nepal): Increase in visitation.
- *Great Barrier Reef* (Queensland, Australia): Increase in visitation.
- *Amalfi Coast and Tuscany* (Italy): Increase in heat waves.
- Goa (India): Increase in beach erosion and likelihood of greater hurricane danger.
- *Taj Coral Reef* (Maldives): Increased coastal erosion and damage to coral reefs.

Perhaps understandably, not all destinations reacted well to being identified in the Churchill research. For example, the author of the research suggested that there is a conflict between environmental concerns and commercial interests with respect to the conservation of the Great Barrier Reef (Gupta 2006). Given that the reef attracts 1.8 million people a year and generates A $5 billion per annum it is not surprising that the Queensland Tourism Industry Council rejected the suggestion that parts of the Great Barrier Reef should be closed off to tourism. Australian Federal Tourism Minister Fran Bailey said tourism operators were ferocious defenders of the Reef's pristine environment. 'They rely on the health of the Reef and so have become intimately involved in protecting that environment' (in Gupta 2006). Yet the operators themselves realize that there is a problem with their biggest fear being that there will be significant coral bleaching as a result of global warming which may result in (Association of Marine Park Operators (AMPO) 2006):

- coral loss,
- world wide bad publicity,
- development of an algae reef,
- loss of tourists.

In response, marine operators have identified a number of adaption and mitigation strategies that they can undertake themselves but more particularly they have also identified a series of needs (Table 13.1). However, while a marketing and public relations strategy may assist with maintaining visitor numbers or satisfaction, it does not solve the underlying problem of climate change.

Winter tourism

The problems facing reef and coastal destinations with respect to their long-term viability are also to be found at other natural resource-based destinations.

Table 13.1 Operator actions and needs with respect to climate change events on the Great Barrier Reef

What operators are doing	What is needed
Planning to handle bad public relations on coral bleaching through media and marketing campaigns	Research into coral bleaching
Looking at better/stronger vessel and pontoon designs to cope with stronger/cyclonic weather	Development of heat resistant coral
Working with researchers and government to find answers to water quality, COTS and bleaching	An active transplantation/site restoration policy
Hoping that we will still be able to get insurance	Factual information
Lobbying to get bio-diesel and government action	Government recognition of the problem, the costs and the economic and moral need for all Australians to positively contribute to the world's climate If all else fails – a world wide campaign to 'See it now when you can!'

Source: AMPO (2006).

For example, alpine and high latitude destinations are particularly vulnerable (Beniston 2003; Gössling and Hall 2006a). The European Alps are regarded as being particularly sensitive to climate change with recent warming being approximately three times the global average. The years 1994, 2000, 2002 and 2003 were the warmest on record in the Alps in the last 500 years but climate model projections show even greater changes in the coming decades, predicting less snow at low altitudes and receding glaciers and melting permafrost higher up. From 1850 to 1980, glaciers in the region lost 30–40 per cent of their area. Since 1980 a further 20 per cent of the ice has been lost. The summer of 2003 led to the loss of a further 10 per cent. By 2050 about 75 per cent of the glaciers in the Swiss Alps are likely to have disappeared, rising to 100 per cent in 2100 (Agrawala 2007). Such a scenario led Smith (2007) to observe, 'The grandchildren of today's skiers are likely to know the white peaks of Switzerland only from the wrappers of chocolate bars'.

This situation is clearly very serious for the tourism industry as the Alps attract 60–80 million tourists and approximately 160 million skier days in Austria, France, Germany and Switzerland each year (Agrawala 2007).

As of the end of 2006, 91 per cent (609 out of 666) medium to large Alpine ski areas normally have adequate snow cover for at least 100 days per year. The remaining 9 per cent are already operating under marginal conditions. According to Agrawala (2007) future climate change could mean a drop in the number of 'snow-reliable' ski areas with a 1°C increase in temperature dropping the number to 500, to 404 under 2°C, and to 202 under a 4°C warming of climate. Germany is the most at risk, with a 1°C warming scenario leading to a 60 per cent decrease in the number of naturally snow-reliable ski areas from the present-day. Practically, none of the ski areas in Germany will be left with reliable natural snow under a 4°C warming scenario. Switzerland would suffer the least from climate change though even a 1°C increase would reduce natural snow by 10 per cent and 4°C warming would halve the number of snow-reliable slopes (Agrawala 2007).

Winter tourism operators are already adapting to rising snow lines and shorter winter seasons, though most are using technology rather than changing behaviour patterns. Artificial snow-making which is the dominant adaption strategy may be cost effective for ski operators, but increases demand for water and energy and affects the ecology and landscape. The costs of snow-making will increase non-linearly as temperatures warm and making snow will no longer be a viable option if temperatures increase above a certain threshold. Grooming of snow slopes can reduce the mini depth of snow required for skiing by 10–20 centimetres. However, as Agrawala (2007: 2) states, 'no amount of grooming can overcome significant declines or the total absence of snow cover'.

Andermatt, a popular ski resort in central Switzerland has decided to act on the threat to winter sports tourism that climate change represents and has started to experiment with a high-technology protective blanket in order to stop the Gurschen Glacier from melting away (Simonian 2005). Yet the amount of area that can be covered remains limited. Changing the terrain by grading the slopes and rerouting natural streams also carries risks to the natural environment and increases chances of natural hazards such as flash floods and rockfalls. 'Insurance, meanwhile, can reduce the financial losses from occasional instances of snow-deficient winters, but cannot protect against systematic long-term trends towards warmer winters' (Agrawala 2007: 2). Overall Agrawala (2007) concludes that market forces are driving adaptation with more emphasis on preserving the status quo than transitions that might be economically and politically expensive in the short term. Nevertheless, such is the potential for changes in patterns of demand that Churchill Insurance (2006b) claim that the effects of climate change will lead to very different ski travel patterns by British skiers in the future as they seek snow-assured holidays with the ski destinations of 2050 potentially being:

- Valle Nevado, Chile.
- Mt. Xiling, China.
- Mt. Hutt, New Zealand.
- Mt. Hermon, Israel.
- Manali, India.
- Oukaimeden, Morocco.
- Tiffindell, South Africa.

An online survey of 578 UK skiers by Churchill Insurance (2006b) indicated that British skiers currently look to traditional Alpine destinations when they want to ski with nearly half of all skiers (48 per cent) having been to France, followed by Austria (29 per cent), Switzerland (18 per cent) and Italy (18 per cent). Furthermore, 96 per cent of British skiers are unaware of Israel and Morocco as skiing destinations. However, 48 per cent would consider visiting such countries for skiing in the future.

Responding to change

From a global point of view, transport is the most relevant sector in terms of the long-term environmental sustainability of tourism, accounting for an estimated 75–90 per cent of all greenhouse gas (GHG) emissions caused by tourism (Peeters et al. 2007). Within tourism transport, the share of aviation-related GHG emissions corresponds to about 75 per cent of all transport emissions (Gössling and Hall 2006a). However, the contribution of GHG emissions from aviation is obviously not spread evenly across the world and instead is concentrated in the wealthier countries from where the vast majority of tourists actually come from. For example, according to Friends of the Earth (FOE), UK aviation emissions represented 15 per cent of UK domestic emissions in 2000. At present rates of growth in the aviation industry, they are forecast to be 66 per cent of the UK domestic emissions target for 2050. According to Richard Dyer of FOE 'Airlines do not pay for their environmental impact … The industry screams every time there is a chance the government will do something about fuel exemption [Airlines] don't have to pay the taxes the other industries have to pay'. FOE argue that the introduction of a fuel duty which increases the cost of air travel would then have a corresponding impact on demand thereby reducing the number of flights and the amount of emissions. In addition, they argue that many current air routes in Europe could be reached by high-speed rail links (see London's Sustainable Development Commission report). According to FOE, on a typical rail journey from London to Edinburgh, carbon dioxide emissions per passenger are 11.9 kilograms, by contrast carbon dioxide emissions per passenger by air travel rise to 96.4 kilograms. However, industry groups, such as the International Air Transport Association (IATA) argue that it is wrong to single out the aviation industry for its fuel emissions. According to Anthony Concil of IATA:

> Are we saying we are going to try and stop people visiting their grandmothers … We have to look at the economic value that air transport brings to the world. Air transport employs directly 4 m people. It creates \$400bn of direct economic output – and if you add in the indirect employment it takes it to about 4.5 per cent of global gross domestic product.
>
> We are not against paying our fair share. We are taxed in a lot of cases as if we were 'sin' industries like alcohol and tobacco. But at some point we need to bring some sense to this argument and understand we are not a cash cow that can be milked at every opportunity (in Garrahan 2005: 1).

Shortly after the G8 Summit in Scotland in July 2005 a group of travel industry associations jointly declared their opposition to any proposed aviation tax to fund development in poor countries. Airports Council International, the Asia Pacific Travel Retail Association, the Association of Asia Pacific Airlines, the Duty Free World Council, the IATA, the Pacific Asia Travel Association (PATA) and the Tax Free World Association jointly denounced the taxation proposal. Instead, they suggested that any additional tax would decrease airline efficiencies and reduce demand for travel and tourism, which they argued is a major driver of economic development in many poor countries.

The PATA Chairman Nobutaka Ishikure (who is also Japan Airlines Chief industry Affairs Officer) stated: 'We must remind governments that airlines are not under-taxed, but are over-charged. Airlines play a critical role as a catalyst for economic development. Development is a serious issue in need of a serious solution. More tax on air travel is not the way forward' (Travel Press 2005). IATA Director General and CEO Giovanni Bisignani 'slammed the proposal', saying: 'We are not an industry of millionaire customers able to travel at any price. Air transport is an essential part of the fabric of modern life. If governments are truly serious about development, there are glaring opportunities to generate billions for aid simply by removing trade barriers' (Travel Press 2005). Similarly, ACI Director Robert J Aaronson argued that targeted training of a skilled aviation workforce in developing markets was 'far more meaningful than a new tax', claiming, 'Airports are catalysts for economic development by creating jobs, encouraging new business development and building capacity to underpin travel, trade and tourism. Airports have demonstrated their long-term commitment to relevant assistance for developing nations' (Travel Press 2005).

The response of airlines to a pilot project, led by France and Germany, for a 'contribution of air travel tickets to support specific development projects' as part of the G8's funding of extra money for poor African countries as well as contributing to fighting climate change was similarly negative. According to a spokeswoman for British Airways, the notion of a tax was 'illogical ... There is no justification for singling out air passengers for an additional tax to fund development in the Third World'. According to Thornton (2005: 2), 'she said it was hard to see why aid for a small business sin Mozambique should be funded in part by a family traveling from Glasgow to Malaga for a holiday'. Similarly, a spokesman for EasyJet described the proposal as 'confused ... Why only target airline passengers – why not bus passengers? ... If you want to go after a particular industry why not go after the oil industry, where companies such as BP and Shell make record profits'. Nevertheless, there was some support for the proposal. John Stewart, the chairman of Transport 2000, commented, 'Aviation is a great contributor to global warming and it is African countries which will be the greatest sufferers from it ... It seems there is a logic about a tax on aviation, which is a great polluter, to help those will be the top victims. It could be a Live Aid of the air' (in Thornton 2005: 2). Attitudes to GEC are the focus of the case study in this chapter.

CASE STUDY
Tourism entrepreneur attitudes to climate change

This case study presents the results of research undertaken between 2002 to 2005 of 43 rural tourism businesses and entrepreneurs in the Bay of Plenty (North Island) (32) and Otago/Southland (South Island) (11) regions of New Zealand that was a part of a broader study of attitudes and behaviours in relation to GEC. Respondents participated in an annual interview regarding business and environment issues that was conducted either face to face or by phone. Interviews were conducted because of participant preference for interviews over written surveys. All businesses had an accommodation dimension although other tourism activities were also available including hunting, fishing, garden tours, wine and food; all were rural land properties some of which were also diversified commercial farms with others being best described as 'lifestyle' properties. Respondents were selected through a convenience snowball sample developed through personal contact with some respondents who had participated in previous provider research and indicated an interest in being involved in future projects.

In terms of the profile of the businesses the accommodation component tended to be quite seasonal and was managed by respondents usually with the help of other family members. This also meant that there was a relatively low level of employment of non-family staff. There was substantial variation in length of time of family ownership, ranging from 1 to 90 years, with a median of 8 years and a mean of 14 years. Respondents tended to have a low level of formal engagement in the tourism industry, e.g. through association memberships at a regional or national level, although otherwise they did tend to hold a high degree of social capital in their communities through membership of a range of national and local organizations such as chambers of commerce and service clubs. The profile of respondents is consistent with that identified in a previous survey of small accommodation providers in New Zealand (Hall and Rusher 2004).

The majority of interviewees did identify climate change as a potential issue that may affect their business and personal well-being, but importantly climate change ranked well below other more immediate business concerns in terms of changes to business behaviour. Many respondents noted that although they were interested in climate change concerns, it was not an immediate or even main priority as they have more day-to-day concerns with running a business. The five most important issues for respondents being:

1 Costs of operating a business.
2 Regulation by government – in terms of costs and time taken by small businesses to meet regulatory requirements.

3 Competition – in terms of too many operators which may then lead to a loss of market share as well as price-cutting.
4 Quality – concern over the entrance of other operators that provided a poor standard of service which could then be seen as affecting their own business viability.
5 Inappropriate rural development and pollution and its impact on the landscape and personal and visitor amenity.

Climate change was seen by some respondents as a potentially significant business and even personal issue. But in comparison with more immediate issues that were identified as more important in terms of business survival (see above), climate change was recognized as a possible medium to long-term issue (5+ years). Importantly, such comments were consistent over the research period, meaning that climate change was constantly being seen as a problem in the longer term. The comments of one respondent, 'Look, if it doesn't affect my daily business operations then I can't afford to think about it, let alone spend money on it' representing a widespread sentiment among interviewees. The only exception to this attitude being when a storm, flood or other high-impact event had occurred that respondents potentially associated with climate change and which was perceived as potentially damaging to the environment on which the business partly relied and/or on the property of the respondent.

Familiarity with climate change issues was gained through general media, although interestingly other GEC issues (biosecurity, water security) were understood through more technical media such as that available through government agencies at the national and regional level as well as through agricultural field days operated in part through agricultural and farming associations. The extent to which information regarding different dimensions of environmental change was gained through various media appeared to have substantial influence on the extent such information was seen as trustworthy and reliable. A clear hierarchy existed with respect to trustworthiness of information source across all respondents with Ministry of Agriculture and Fisheries information and agricultural field days being regarded as highly trustworthy; Ministry of the Environment, Regional and Local Council sources and other operators and business people were held as moderately trustworthy; and the general media (radio, television and newspapers) and politicians perceived to have a low level of trust with respect to statements regarding climate change and other aspects of GEC.

Innovation and adaption measures were developed by some respondents in relation to environmental change issues with respect to biosecurity and water security concerns but were not necessarily overtly directly to climate change. A number of respondents whose businesses had horticultural or agricultural components in addition to accommodation or other tourism offerings had started to restrict visitor access to parts of their property as a result of biosecurity concerns. However, such restrictions were primarily connected to concerns over visitor health and safety and any breach of law in relation to safety.

Water conservation emerged as a major focus of respondents in terms of making existing use more efficient as well as developing new storage strategies. For many larger properties that also had farm operations, concern over water security was also leading to consideration of new management strategies including irrigation or developing an economic base, i.e. through new crops such as olives or almonds that required less water. Nevertheless, even small accommodation operations were looking at installing dual-flush toilets or other mechanisms to restrict water use. Interestingly, such innovations were often seen as being acceptable to the market as well as having water security and environmental benefits. Several respondents commented that because they had stayed in hotels and motels in the larger New Zealand cities as well as internationally that had dual-flush toilets and statements regarding towel use in bathrooms they felt that they could also adopt such initiatives without affecting the attractiveness of their operation. One respondent stated that they made changes shortly after they commenced their farm accommodation business as a result of feedback from German visitors who told them that they felt that water saving measures would 'fit in' better with the image of such rural tourism operations in a country promoting itself as being environmentally friendly as well as being welcomed by environmentally conscious customers.

Even though many respondents commented that they felt that weather patterns were changing and that these may be related to climate change they generally did not associate climate change with potential new seasonal visitor patterns. Many commented that New Zealand always will have 'Four seasons in one day' and that this was just a part of the visitor experience. Overall, if discussed further, respondents felt that seasonal change was 'usually, something they hadn't thought about' but if prompted respondents suggested that official public holidays and institutionalized periods of holiday-taking, such as school holidays, were the most important determinants of seasonality, although some interviewees did also state that they did not believe that climate change would be so substantial as to, according to one respondent, 'completely change tourist patterns'. Again, these types of statements were consistently held over the research period with many interviewees consistently stating that seasonal change was not an issue for them.

Where changes to operator behaviour were expressed as occurring as a result of climate change it was often associated with perceived immediate weather impacts on business operations, e.g. severe storm and flooding events or extended dry periods in relation to farms which are also used for homestays or other guest accommodation. The greatest expressions of concern over climate change and its potential affects at both a personal and national level were from those respondents who had been directly affected by extreme weather events or has seen the effects of such events. Significantly, those respondents who had directly experienced extreme weather events were also those whose responses to questions of climate change were more likely to have shifted over the study period, although certainly not in all cases.

Despite the recognition of a number of respondents of the potential longer-term effects of climate change and the need for 'government to do something', increased regulation or 'green' taxes on carbon or GHG emissions were opposed if it added to business costs. This reflected the prime focus on respondents on managing day-to-day immediate business risk rather than what was seen as a potential future hazard, even if it was regarded as one that was likely to occur. Responses of businesses whether at the personal (what would they do?) or a national level (what should New Zealand do?) therefore focused on adaption to climate change rather than mitigation. Indeed, concerns were expressed over the potential of 'green' or 'carbon taxes' to increase the cost of aviation or car travel and therefore affect the travel market to the regions in which respondents were located which are away from the main tourist flows in New Zealand as well as any direct cost to the business.

The results of the New Zealand study were reasonably similar to that of a survey of winter tourism entrepreneurs in Finland (Saarinen and Tervo 2007). The Finnish entrepreneurs were aware of the issue of global climate change. However, half of the interviewees did not believe that the phenomenon actually exists and will influence tourism in their destinations in the future. Their main source of information on climate change was the general media. However, more than three-quarters of the Finnish respondents criticized the information provided by the media and it was very common for personal observations of climatic phenomena to be used to not only critically evaluate but also reinforce such information. Half of the interviewees had observed events that had strengthened their image of climate change. These included both events that support changing climate but also events that seem to have run counter to such change. Few entrepreneurs gained information from academic or scientific studies on the subject.

As in New Zealand the issue of climate change was seen only as a minor threat by Finnish tourism operators, if a threat at all, particularly relative to other factors that might have an effect on the industry or their businesses. The Finnish operators were able to rationalize why they had not, or why they were not even considering plans for adaptation strategies and measures to face projected climate change. According to respondents, the most important reason was the slow pace of change. As Saarinen and Tervo (2007) comment, 'A tourism entrepreneur hardly ever plans his future more than five years in advance; in some cases, one year's forethought is sufficient ... Although the tourism business is often based on taking risks, entrepreneurs were not willing to rush into implementing uncertain actions if they do not know if the climate in the future is going to be warmer, colder, or more unstable in their region, and how it will actually affect their operations'. The scepticism towards the climate change may also help explain why there were almost no adaptation strategies. Nevertheless, the lack of adaptation strategies does not necessary imply that the tourism industry could not cope with a changing climate in the future. As many of the Finnish operators argued, they have been working and also struggling with climatic variability and extreme weather events with moderate or good success during the existence of their business career.

Key sources

Hall, C.M. (2007). New Zealand tourism entrepreneur attitudes and behaviours with respect to climate change adaption and mitigation. *International Journal of Innovation and Sustainable Development* 2, 229–37. (This article provides a more detailed account of the New Zealand case study.)

Hall, C.M. and Rusher, K. (2004). Risky lifestyles? Entrepreneurial characteristics of the New Zealand bed and breakfast sector. In R. Thomas (ed.), *Small Firms in Tourism: International Perspectives*, pp. 83–97. Oxford: Elsevier.

Saarinen, J. and Tervo, K. (2006). Perceptions and adaptation strategies of the tourism industry to climate change: the case of Finnish nature-based tourism entrepreneurs. *International Journal of Innovation and Sustainable Development* 2, 214–28.

Discussion questions

1 To what extent might the scepticism of tourism entrepreneurs towards climate change affects on their business be warranted?

2 What sort of communication and information strategies should be developed so as to improve operator knowledge of climate change?

3 Would operator initiatives to lessen their environmental impact improve their attractiveness to consumers?

Predicting change

Despite substantial concerns over the impacts of climate change there are enormous difficulties in predicting the effects of such change as it is extremely unrealistic to assume linearity in tourist behaviour change, i.e. that there will be direct causality in the relationship between changes in temperature and destination choice and behaviour. Such linearity is dangerous because in addition to tempera-ture, the relationship between tourism and climate also includes factors such as 'rain', 'storms', 'humidity', 'hours of sunshine', 'wind strength' and 'air pollution'; and the role of weather information in decision-making (Gössling and Hall 2006b). In addition, destination choice is also predicated on a number of non-climate-related factors such as cost, accessibility, perception and image of destinations, security and other impacting variables, including the travel budget (in time and money) of the consumer.

Even if some climate change does change tourist behaviour this does not neces-sarily mean that the overall number of visitors to a destination will necessarily decline. For example, rather than travel elsewhere tourists may select a different time of travel. In addition, much will depend on the relative elasticity of demand associated with different types of travel. Leisure travel is probably the most flex-ible in terms of destination and time of travel but business travel and visiting friends and relations (VFR) are far more inelastic. Some destinations will also bene-fit from climate change. For example, in the case of the ski industry those resorts that are snow assured will likely increase their market share, while new markets will emerge for other alpine resorts such as year round hiking and mountain biking opportunities. Similarly, even in the case of the predicted dramatic loss of permanent sea ice in the Arctic with the subsequent threats to iconic wildlife such as polar bears it has nevertheless been concluded that there is a likelihood of further expansion of tourism in the Arctic because there will be greater accessibility to the region (Arctic Climate Impact Assessment 2004).

Tourism and oil

As serious as climate change and other aspects of GEC are, one of the most signifi-cant issues facing tourism is the increased costs of energy and issues of availabil-ity. According to the Energy Committee at the Royal Swedish Academy of Sciences (2005: 1) 'It is very likely that the world is now entering a challenging period for energy supply, due to the limited resources and production problems now facing conventional (easily accessible) oil. Nearly 40 per cent of the world's energy is pro-vided by oil, and over 50 per cent of the latter is used in the transport sector'. According to the Committee, mitigation measures must be initiated in the next few years in order to secure a continued adequate supply of liquid fuels, especially for the transport sector. Aviation will be more fuel efficient in the future as a result of technological innovations but possibilities are limited and although energy use per person per kilometre will fall, the overall predicted increase in the number and distance of people flying will mean that overall fuel use and amount of emissions will continue to grow (Peeters et al. 2007). However, over the longer term, completely new energy solutions are required given the decline of cheap oil. Key issues with respect to oil supply are detailed in Table 13.2.

In the immediate term the impacts of increased oil prices on tourism seem relatively small. According to the UNWTO (2006), the impact of rising oil prices on international tourism has so far been limited because the effect of price increases as reflected in constant currency rates has been mainly to catch up with inflation and the direct impact of oil prices in 2005 was within a range of less than 5 per cent which was regarded as insufficient to alter consumer behaviour. Although the WTO did not make any comment with respect to the impact of increased real oil prices they did note that 'uncertainty as to price levels is already affecting behaviour, as tour operators find it increasingly difficult to anticipate short-term

Table 13.2 Key issues associated with oil supply

1 Shortage of oil	The global demand for oil is presently growing by almost 2 per cent per year with consumption at the end of 2005 set at 84 million barrels per day (1 barrel = 159 litres) or 30 billion barrels per year. Finding additional supplies is increasingly problematical since most major oil fields are well matured. Already 54 out of the 65 most important oil-producing countries have declining production and the rate of discoveries of new reserves is less than a third of the rate of consumption as of the end of 2005
2 Reserves of conventional oil	In the last 10–15 years, two-thirds of the increases in reserves of conventional oil have been based on increased estimates of recovery from existing fields and only one-third on discovery of new fields. A conservative estimate of discovered oil reserves and undiscovered recoverable oil resources is about 1200 billion barrels, according to the US Geological Survey; this includes 300 billion barrels in the world's, as yet unexplored, sedimentary basins

(Continued)

Table 13.2 (Continued)

3 The key role of the Middle East	Only in the Middle East and possibly the countries of the former Soviet Union is there potential (proven reserves of 130 billion barrels) to significantly increase production rates to compensate for decreasing rates in other countries. As of the end of 2005 Saudi Arabia provided 9.5 million barrels per day (11 per cent of the current global production rate).
4 Unconventional oil resources	There are very large hydrocarbon resources, so-called unconventional oil, including gas (c. 1000 billion barrels of oil equivalent, much of which could be converted to liquid fuels), heavy oil and tar sands (c. 800 billion barrels), oil shales (c. 2700 billion barrels) and coal. Problems with unconventional resources include long lead times in development, environmental impacts and the availability of water and natural gas for the production process.
5 Immediate action on supplies	Improvements in the search for and recovery of conventional oil as well as the production rate of unconventional oil are required to avoid price spikes, which would lead to instability of the world economy over the next few decades.
6 Liquid fuels and the transport system	Oil supply is a severe liquid fuels problem and less of a general energy supply problem; 57 per cent of the world's oil is consumed in the transport sector. Alternatives need to be developed to oil in the transport sector otherwise not only will there be increased oil prices but also increased competition between transport and other oil users.
7 Economic considerations	In the long run, the price of crude oil will be determined by the price of substitutes. Continued high oil prices are anticipated as long as the pressure from the expanding Asian economies is maintained.
8 Environmental concerns	Unconventional oil will significantly extend the length of the hydrocarbon era and its subsequent contributions to GHG emissions. Constraints similar to those imposed on other fossil fuels (e.g. emission controls and CO_2 sequestration) will be necessary and provide major challenges for industry.

Source: Adapted from Energy Committee at the Royal Swedish Academy of Sciences (2005).

demand. Tourism enterprises unable to make the necessary adjustments in time could therefore find their profitability at risk' (UNWTO 2006: 36). When domestic and international travel markets are combined, the impacts of increased oil prices are more significant. An Australian study by O'Mahony et al. (2006) found that approximately 25–35 per cent of those that had taken a holiday or were planning one did suggest changes to their plans to negotiate the impact of fuel. As may be expected given consideration of the role of budgets in determining travel patterns (Hall 2005a), in the O'Mahony et al. (2006) survey money was the biggest constraint on travel with the price of fuel having most affect on those on the lowest income (under A $50 000), some influence at middle income level (A $50–100 000) and least influence among those on the highest income (A $100 000 plus).

In examining the impacts of climate change or increases in the cost of oil a key finding is that people will continue to travel but that the relative attractiveness and accessibility of some destinations will likely change in relation to other destinations. Such a situation does not mean the end of tourism but instead will provide for new opportunities for destinations and businesses. In such a dynamic environment the provision of positive service and visitor experiences and improved marketing will become even more important. In addition, there will be an even greater onus on destinations and firms to understand key elements of the business environment such as changing consumer lifestyles and the new regulatory frameworks that are implemented by government to manage human mobility at a time of increased concerns over energy and environmental security.

What future for tourism?

People make their own history. They also make their own future. A number of different possible futures for tourism exist that will perhaps be more dependent on factors outside of the industry, such as environmental change, economic conditions and lifestyles, than things within the control of tourism destinations and firms. Therefore, the future of tourism and arguably the study of tourism is embedded as much within concerns over *how* people get there, i.e. issues of human mobility, as it is over more traditional concerns as what they *do* when they get there, i.e. a destination and activity focus.

Much of today's tourism infrastructure is shaped by almost half a century's assumptions that we would have cheap oil and energy, that it was possible to respond to market demand by building more capacity, and that 'predict and provide' assumptions of infrastructure supply would meet transport needs. Not only has infrastructure been shaped by such assumptions but also successive generations of people in development countries who take long-distance mobility as a norm and which lead consumptive lifestyles to which the people of the rapidly emerging economic of Asia seem to aspire too. As the UK Foresight Directorate (2006a) report on Intelligent Infrastructure Systems observed:

> Energy is not cheap, and is most unlikely to be cheaper 50 years hence. Indeed, most people would anticipate significantly higher prices. The idea that the UK could build new roads at the same pace as it did during the past half-century is simply untenable – 'road protests' did not exist 50 years ago. As to market forces, the new presumptions of future circumstances – that we have to anticipate and ameliorate the likely impacts of climate change, and that sustainability now deserves as much attention as economic growth – make it hard to see how the private sector alone can make the difficult choices.

The Foresight Directorate outlined four scenarios set in a post-oil world of personal transport for the future of human mobility, including tourism (2006b). The two main uncertainties which drove the scenarios were:

1 Whether or not we will develop low-environmental impact transport systems.
2 Whether or not people will accept intelligent infrastructure.

Four scenarios were developed which were labelled perpetual motion, urban colonies, tribal trading and good intentions (Table 13.3). Each of the scenarios provides a different picture of people in terms of mobility in the developed world in the year 2055. The role of the scenarios is to allow people to see how certain combinations of events, innovations and social changes could change the future. As the Directorate noted, the real world 50 years from now will likely contain elements of all scenarios. 'The scenarios allow us to see what we might need to prepare for and the opportunities that await us if we set the right path ahead' (Foresight Directorate 2006a: 43).

The different scenarios raise fundamental questions about the future of tourism and the world we will be living in. People are more mobile than ever

Table 13.3 Foresight scenarios

Good intentions	• The need to reduce carbon emissions constrains personal mobility.
	• Traffic volumes have fallen and mass transportation is used more widely.
	• Businesses have adopted energy-efficient practices: they use wireless identification and tracking systems to optimize logistics and distribution.
	• Some rural areas pool community carbon credits for local transport provision, but many are struggling.
	• Airlines continue to exploit loopholes in the carbon enforcement framework.
Perpetual motion	• Society is driven by constant information, consumption and competition. In this world, instant communication and continuing globalization has fuelled growth: demand for travel remains strong.
	• New, cleaner, fuel technologies are increasingly popular. Road use is causing less environmental damage, although the volume and speed of traffic remains high. Aviation still relies on carbon fuels – it remains expensive and is increasingly replaced by 'telepresencing' for business, and rapid trains for travel.
Tribal trading	• The world has been through a sharp and savage energy shock. The global economic system is severely damaged and infrastructure is falling into disrepair.
	• Long-distance travel is a luxury that few can afford and for most people, the world has shrunk to their own community.
	• Cities have declined and local food production and services have increased.
	• There are still some cars, but local transport is typically by bike and by horse.
	• There are local conflicts over resources: lawlessness and mistrust are high.
Urban colonies	• Investment in technology primarily focuses on minimizing environmental impact.
	• Good environmental practice is at the heart of the UK's economic and social policies: sustainable buildings, distributed power generation and new urban planning policies have created compact, dense cities.
	• Transport is permitted only if green and clean – car use is energy-expensive and restricted.
	• Public transport (electric and low energy) is efficient and widely used.

Source: Foresight Directorate (2006: 44).

before, particularly in terms of long-distance travel. Many believe that they have a right to mobility. But at the same time the opportunities for mobility are likely going to become increasingly constrained.

Chapter overview

It is highly probable that tourism itself will have undergone significant change in 50 years time, not only with respect to the products and services that destinations and firms offer but also in terms of how it is conceptualized. To an extent such processes are already taking place as the borders between leisure, tourism and migration become increasingly hazy. These changes will be seen in the working lives of the people who read this text. Yet in all of these the service dimension at the heart of tourism stays a constant.

We cannot understand the consumption of tourism without also understanding its production, and vice versa. In this book, we have sought to emphasize this dimension of co-creation through an examination of the key elements of tourism. People will continue to travel from their permanent home to visit other places, some of which are even so close that they can be visited in a day, and people will continue to provide services that enable such movement and the opportunity to visit elsewhere. Much of the attention to such provision is on the physical infrastructure yet just as significant, if not more so, is the intellectual capital of tourism. A contemporary perspective on tourism understands the complex supply and value chains that affects how services are produced and acknowledges that the consumer and the supplier of tourism are interdependent. And it is this intellectual capital that allows not only for a better understanding of tourism as an area of study but also how the future of tourism may be improved for those who work in the industry, those who are affected by the industry and those tourists who 'make' the industry.

Self-review questions

1 What is a *wildcard* event?
2 How accurate is *expert knowledge* with respect to forecasting?

3 What are the main *values* of undertaking forecasting exercises?

4 What are the forecast key effects of *climate change* and their likely affect on destination environments?

5 Why is it difficult to predict the impacts of climate change on *travel flows and patterns*?

6 What are the key issues for tourism in relation to *oil supply*?

7 What might be the effects of continued high *oil prices* on tourism?

8 What values may *scenarios* have with respect to considering the future of tourism?

9 To what extent do people believe they have *rights of mobility* and how might this affect future transport planning?

10 Should we go see the world's major attractions now before they are destroyed?

Recommended reading

1 Buhalis, D. and Costa, C. (eds) (2005). *Tourism Dynamics: Trends, Management and Tools*. Oxford: Butterworth-Heinemann.
   The book examines trends, issues and potential futures with respect to a large number of tourism topics.

2 Foresight Directorate (2006). *Intelligent Infrastructure Futures: The Scenarios – Towards 2055*. London: Foresight Directorate.
   The four different scenarios provide fascinating accounts of potential trends in human mobility.

3 Hall, C.M. (2005). *Tourism: Rethinking the Social Science of Mobility*. Harlow: Prentice-Hall.
   The last four chapters deal with the future of tourism as well as the future of tourism studies.

4 Gössling, S. and Hall, C.M. (eds) (2006). *Tourism and Global Environmental Change*. London: Routledge.
   The most comprehensive account of the relationships between tourism and global environmental change.

5 Gössling, S. and Hall, C.M. (2006). Uncertainties in predicting tourist flows under scenarios of climate change. *Climatic Change* 79(3–4), 163–173.
   This article outlines some of the key difficulties in determining the influences of climate change and leads a debate on the topic in the same issue of the journal.

6 Hall, C.M. and Higham, J. (eds) (2005). *Tourism, Recreation and Climate Change*. Clevedon: Channelview Publications.
   The first book on tourism and climate change that presents chapters from experts in relation to North America, Europe and the Mediterranean.

7 Agrawala, S. (2007). *Climate Change in the European Alps: Adapting Winter Tourism and Natural Hazard Management*. Paris: OECD.
   An important study on the environmental, economic and social impacts of climate change on winter destinations in Europe that is also significant as it comes from a conservative economic organization.

8 Law, R. (2001). A study of the impact of the Asian financial crisis on the accuracy of tourist arrival forecasts. *Journal of Hospitality and Leisure Marketing* 8(1/2), 5–18.

Examination of the impact of a wildcard event on the accuracy of tourism forecasts.

9 Coles, T., Hall, C.M. and Duval, D. (2006). Tourism and post-disciplinary inquiry. *Current Issues in Tourism* 9(4–5), 293–319.

Argues for a post-disciplinary understanding of tourism that would encourage improved problem solving of 'sticky' issues such as tourism's relationship with global environmental change.

10 Hall, D. and Brown, F. (2006). *Tourism and Welfare: Ethics, Responsibility and Sustained Well-Being*. Wallingford: CABI.

Provides an excellent account of the issues of participation and non-participation in tourism and how this relates to ethical, quality of life and sustainability concerns.

Recommended web sites

An inconvenient truth: http://www.climatecrisis.net/

Hubbert Peak of Oil Production: http://www.hubbertpeak.com/

Intergovernmental Panel on Climate Change: http://www.ipcc.ch/

Stern Review: http://www.hm-treasury.gov.uk/independent_reviews/stern_review_economics_climate_change/sternreview_index.cfm

Millennium Ecosystem Assessment: http://www.millenniumassessment.org/

References cited

Agrawala, S. (2007). *Climate Change in the European Alps: Adapting Winter Tourism and Natural Hazard Management*. Paris: OECD.

Airbus (2003). *Global Market Forecast 2003–2022*. Blagnac, France: Airbus S.A.S.

Association of Marine Park Operators [AMPO] (2006). *A Time of Uncertainty. Presentation at Ecotourism & Climate Change: Challenges for the Future, a Workshop at Ecotourism Australia's 14th International Conference*, 31 October, Townsville.

Arctic Climate Impact Assessment (2004). *Impacts of a Warming Arctic*. Cambridge: Cambridge University Press.

Beniston, M. (2003). Climate change in mountain regions: a review of possible impacts. *Climatic Change* 59, 5–31.

Boeing (2003). *Current Market Outlook 2003*. Seattle: Boeing Commercial Airplanes. Marketing.

Churchill Insurance (2006a). *The Future of Travel: The 'Disappearing Destinations' of 2020*. Press Release 9 September, Churchill Insurance.

Churchill Insurance (2006b). *The Future of Skiing: France and Austria make way for Morocco and Israel*. Press Release 9 September, Churchill Insurance.

Foresight Directorate (2006a). *Intelligent Infrastructure Futures: Project Overview*. London: Foresight Directorate.

Foresight Directorate (2006b). *Intelligent Infrastructure Futures: The Scenarios – Towards 2055*. London: Foresight Directorate.

Energy Committee at the Royal Swedish Academy of Sciences (2005). *Statements on Oil*, 14 October, Stockholm: Energy Committee at the Royal Swedish Academy of Sciences.

Garrahan, M. (2005). Balancing act on fuel emissions. *Financial Times* [Europe], FT Business Travel 13 June, 1.

Gössling, S. (2002). Global environmental consequences of tourism. *Global Environmental Change* 12, 283–302.

Gössling, S. and Hall, C.M. (eds) (2006a). *Tourism and Global Environmental Change*, London: Routledge.

Gössling, S. and Hall, C.M. (2006b). Uncertainties in predicting tourist flows under scenarios of climate change. *Climatic Change* 79(3–4), 163–173.

Gupta, S. (2006). Queensland vehemently quashes concerns pertaining to the Great Barrier Reef. *ETurboNews* 12 October, http://www.travelwirenews.com/cgi-script/csArticles/articles/000097/009786.htm

Hall, C.M. (2005a). *Tourism: Rethinking the Social Science of Mobility*. Harlow: Prentice-Hall.

Hall, C.M. (2005b). The future of tourism research. In P. Burns, C. Palmer and B. Ritchie (eds), *Tourism Research Methods: Integrating Theory with Practice*, pp. 221–229. Wallingford: CABI.

Hall, C.M. (2007). New Zealand tourism entrepreneur attitudes and behaviours with respect to climate change adaption and mitigation. *International Journal of Innovation and Sustainable Development* 2 (in press).

Hall, C.M. and Rusher, K. (2004). Risky lifestyles? Entrepreneurial characteristics of the New Zealand bed and breakfast sector. In R. Thomas (ed.) *Small Firms in Tourism: International Perspectives*, pp. 83–97. Oxford: Elsevier.

McKie, R. (2007). Global warming: the final verdict. *The Observer* 21 January.

O'Mahony, B., Whitelaw, P. and Ritchie, B.W. (2006). The effect of fuel price rises on tourism behaviour: an exploratory Australian study. *Tourism and the End of Oil ATLAS Asia-Pacific Conference*, December. Dunedin: University of Otago.

Peeters, P., Gössling, S. and Becken, S. (2007). Innovation towards tourism sustainability: climate change and aviation. *International Journal of Innovation and Sustainable Development* 2, 184–200.

Saarinen, J. and Tervo, K. (2007). Perceptions and adaptation strategies of the tourism industry to climate change: the case of Finnish nature-based tourism entrepreneurs. *International Journal of Innovation and Sustainable Development* 2, 184–200.

Sherden, W.A. (1998). *The Fortune Sellers: The Big Business of Buying and Selling Predictions*. New York: Wiley.

Simonian, H. (2005). Blanket coverage could save Europe's famed Alps. *Financial Times [Europe]* 14 June, 14.

Smith, A.D. (2007). Melting glaciers will destroy Alpine resorts within 45 years, says report. *The Observer* January 14.

Thornton, P. (2005). G8 wants tax on airline tickets to help world poor. *The Independent* 13 June, 2.

Travel Press (2005). Travel Industry Unites Against Proposed Aviation Tax. Press release Bangkok, Thailand, 15 July, http://www.travelwirenews.com/news/19JUL2005.htm

World Tourism Organization (WTO) (1997). *Tourism 2020 Vision*. Madrid: World Tourism Organization.

World Tourism Organization (WTO) (2001). *Tourism 2020 Vision – Global Forecasts and Profiles of Market Segments*. Madrid: World Tourism Organization.

World Tourism Organization (WTO) (2003). *Climate Change and Tourism. Proceedings of the 1st International Conference on Climate Change and Tourism*, 9–11 April, Djerba, Tunisia. Madrid: World Tourism Organization.

World Tourism Organization (WTO) (2006). *The Impact of Rising Oil Prices on International Tourism, Special Report no.26*. Madrid: World Tourism Organization.

Index

Energy Committee at the Royal Swedish Academy of Sciences (2005). *Statements on Oil*, 14 October, Stockholm: Energy Committee at the Royal Swedish Academy of Sciences.

Garrahan, M. (2005). Balancing act on fuel emissions. *Financial Times* [Europe], FT Business Travel 13 June, 1.

Gössling, S. (2002). Global environmental consequences of tourism. *Global Environmental Change* 12, 283–302.

Gössling, S. and Hall, C.M. (eds) (2006a). *Tourism and Global Environmental Change*, London: Routledge.

Gössling, S. and Hall, C.M. (2006b). Uncertainties in predicting tourist flows under scenarios of climate change. *Climatic Change* 79(3–4), 163–173.

Gupta, S. (2006). Queensland vehemently quashes concerns pertaining to the Great Barrier Reef. *ETurboNews* 12 October, http://www.travelwirenews.com/cgi-script/csArticles/articles/000097/009786.htm

Hall, C.M. (2005a). *Tourism: Rethinking the Social Science of Mobility*. Harlow: Prentice-Hall.

Hall, C.M. (2005b). The future of tourism research. In P. Burns, C. Palmer and B. Ritchie (eds), *Tourism Research Methods: Integrating Theory with Practice*, pp. 221–229. Wallingford: CABI.

Hall, C.M. (2007). New Zealand tourism entrepreneur attitudes and behaviours with respect to climate change adaption and mitigation. *International Journal of Innovation and Sustainable Development* 2 (in press).

Hall, C.M. and Rusher, K. (2004). Risky lifestyles? Entrepreneurial characteristics of the New Zealand bed and breakfast sector. In R. Thomas (ed.) *Small Firms in Tourism: International Perspectives*, pp. 83–97. Oxford: Elsevier.

McKie, R. (2007). Global warming: the final verdict. *The Observer* 21 January.

O'Mahony, B., Whitelaw, P. and Ritchie, B.W. (2006). The effect of fuel price rises on tourism behaviour: an exploratory Australian study. *Tourism and the End of Oil ATLAS Asia-Pacific Conference*, December. Dunedin: University of Otago.

Peeters, P., Gössling, S. and Becken, S. (2007). Innovation towards tourism sustainability: climate change and aviation. *International Journal of Innovation and Sustainable Development* 2, 184–200.

Saarinen, J. and Tervo, K. (2007). Perceptions and adaptation strategies of the tourism industry to climate change: the case of Finnish nature-based tourism entrepreneurs. *International Journal of Innovation and Sustainable Development* 2, 184–200.

Sherden, W.A. (1998). *The Fortune Sellers: The Big Business of Buying and Selling Predictions*. New York: Wiley.

Simonian, H. (2005). Blanket coverage could save Europe's famed Alps. *Financial Times [Europe]* 14 June, 14.

Smith, A.D. (2007). Melting glaciers will destroy Alpine resorts within 45 years, says report. *The Observer* January 14.

Thornton, P. (2005). G8 wants tax on airline tickets to help world poor. *The Independent* 13 June, 2.

Travel Press (2005). Travel Industry Unites Against Proposed Aviation Tax. Press release Bangkok, Thailand, 15 July, http://www.travelwirenews.com/news/19JUL2005.htm

World Tourism Organization (WTO) (1997). *Tourism 2020 Vision*. Madrid: World Tourism Organization.

World Tourism Organization (WTO) (2001). *Tourism 2020 Vision – Global Forecasts and Profiles of Market Segments*. Madrid: World Tourism Organization.

World Tourism Organization (WTO) (2003). *Climate Change and Tourism. Proceedings of the 1st International Conference on Climate Change and Tourism*, 9–11 April, Djerba, Tunisia. Madrid: World Tourism Organization.

World Tourism Organization (WTO) (2006). *The Impact of Rising Oil Prices on International Tourism, Special Report no.26*. Madrid: World Tourism Organization.

Index

CPSIA information can be obtained at www.ICGtesting.com
Printed in the USA
LVOW020726070113

3284LVUK00003B/4/P